PERSPECTIVES IN SOUTH CAROLINA HISTORY
THE FIRST 300 YEARS

PERSPECTIVES IN SOUTH CAROLINA HISTORY

THE FIRST 300 YEARS

edited by
Ernest M. Lander, Jr.
and
Robert K. Ackerman

UNIVERSITY OF SOUTH CAROLINA PRESS
Columbia, South Carolina

LIBRARY OF CONGRESS CATALOGING IN PUBLICATION DATA

F
269
L3

Lander, Ernest McPherson, comp.
  Perspectives in South Carolina history. South Carolina, University
  of South Carolina Press, [1973]
  1. South Carolina—History—Addresses, essays,   431 p.
lectures. I. Ackerman, Robert K., 1933–   comp.
II. Title.
F269.L3   975.7   70-189036
ISBN 0-87249-246-X

CONTENTS

Preface *ix*

Part I: THE PROPRIETARY ERA

1   "Why Carolina Was Granted to the Proprietors"   *3*
    William S. Powell

2   The Fundamental Constitutions   *7*
    M. Eugene Sirmans

3   The Early Settlement   *15*
    Wesley Frank Craven

4   "Victory over the Pirates"   *27*
    Richard P. Sherman

5   "The Surrender of the Charter of Carolina"   *35*
    Charles Christopher Crittenden

Part II: THE ROYAL COLONY AND REVOLUTION

6   "Carolina Golden Rice"   *45*
    Henry Savage, Jr.

7   "The Colony at Mid-Century"   *55*
    M. Eugene Sirmans

v

8 "Christopher Gadsden and the Stamp Act" *63*
Robert Hilliard Woody

Part III: ANTEBELLUM SOUTH CAROLINA

9 Jeffersonian Democracy in South Carolina *75*
John Harold Wolfe

10 The Transition to the Nineteenth-Century Economy *87*
George C. Rogers, Jr.

11 "The Old Order Changes" *95*
Alfred Glaze Smith, Jr.

12 John C. Calhoun and Nullification *105*
Richard N. Current

13 "The Church and Its Auxiliaries" *119*
Rosser Howard Taylor

14 "The Secession Movement Before 1860" *133*
Charles Edward Cauthen

Part IV: CIVIL WAR AND RECONSTRUCTION, 1861–77

15 "Let the Strife Begin" *149*
W. A. Swanberg

16 Robert Barnwell Rhett Denounces Jefferson Davis *161*
Charles Edward Cauthen

17 The Burning of Columbia *175*
John G. Barrett

18 "The Heritage of War" *187*
Francis Butler Simkins and *Robert Hilliard Woody*

19 "Drawing Bureau Rations" *195*
John William De Forest

20 The Constitutional Convention of 1868 *203*
Francis Butler Simkins and *Robert Hilliard Woody*

21 Violence and the Ku Klux Klan *211*
    Joel Williamson

22 Republican Leadership During Reconstruction *219*
    Joel Williamson

Part V: FROM RECONSTRUCTION TO WORLD WAR I, 1877–1914

23 "Hampton's Administration" *235*
    Hampton M. Jarrell

24 "The Background of Tillmanism" *247*
    Francis Butler Simkins

25 "A Cotton Mill Village in the 1880's" *255*
    W. E. Woodward

26 "The Defeat of the Second University, 1885–1890" *269*
    Daniel Walker Hollis

27 "Nullification of the Fifteenth Amendment" *283*
    George Brown Tindall

28 The Revolution in Electric Power *297*
    Henry Savage, Jr.

29 The Sad State of the High Schools in 1910 *305*
    [William H. Hand]

30 Coleman Livingston Blease—Tempestuous Governor *317*
    David Duncan Wallace

Part VI: RECENT SOUTH CAROLINA

31 Yankee Soldiers Invade Spartanburg in 1917 *327*
    Fronde Kennedy

32 South Carolina Views *The Birth of a Nation* *337*
    John Hammond Moore

33 "Palmetto Stump"—'Thirties Style *349*
    [*Anonymous*]

34 Clinging to the "Lost Cause" *355*
    Ben Robertson

35 "Opera in Greenville" *361*
    Rebecca West

36 A Senior Statesman Comes Out of Retirement *371*
    James F. Byrnes

37 "Integration with Dignity" *381*
    George McMillan

38 "The Ring That Isn't" *393*
    W. D. Workman, Jr.

39 South Carolina Looks to the Future *409*
    John C. West

    Index *415*

PREFACE

SOUTH CAROLINA'S UNIQUE HISTORY HAS LONG ATTRACTED THE AT-
tention of a variety of historians from many regions. The fact that
many of these writings are not readily accessible to the public is one
basic reason for this volume. The editors, of course, did not intend
to write a comprehensive history of South Carolina. Instead, they have
attempted to gather a series of chapters, articles, and miscellaneous
excerpts from secondary sources which focus on many of the more
significant events and persons in South Carolina history. These selections were made with three criteria in mind: (1) to include material
concerning each major historical epoch, (2) to select readings which
would be easily understood without extensive introductions, and (3)
to include material representative of some of the best historical literature available. Understandably, the limitation of space prevented the
inclusion of many other desirable selections.

It is hoped that these selections will whet the appetites of the
readers to find and read the entire works from which these morsels
have been borrowed. Furthermore, the editors chose these readings to
ensure that the collection could serve as the basis for discussions by
students of South Carolina history. Needless to say, the volume should
be of some convenience to those teachers of South Carolina history
who have limited access to some of the better secondary sources.

The editors have eliminated footnotes from selections originally
having them; otherwise, they have practiced the most stringent
editorial laissez-faire (as witnessed, for example, by the following
variations in spelling: lowcountry, low-country, Low-country, Low-
Country, and Low Country). The headnotes to selections 1 through

14 were supplied by Robert K. Ackerman and those to 15 through 39 by Ernest M. Lander, Jr.

The editors are much indebted to the Social Studies Division of the South Carolina Department of Education for which they acted as consultants in the publication of *A Guide for the Teaching of South Carolina's History*. It was while engaged in that work that they conceived the idea of a book of readings of broad, general appeal that would benefit both high school and college students and the general public.

Part I:
THE PROPRIETARY ERA

Christopher Columbus, by his discoveries in 1492, directed the attention of Europe to the lands of the New World. The Spanish followed these discoveries by developing a colonial empire in the West Indies and in Central America. In 1513 Ponce de Leon discovered and named Florida. In 1521 Hernando Cortes was master of the Aztec empire of old Mexico. By 1535 Francisco Pizarro had conquered the rich empire of the Incas in Peru. This overseas empire furnished Spain with such quantities of precious metals as to arouse the jealousy of the other European nations. Around 1540 the Spanish DeSoto explored much of the territory east of the Mississippi River and entered the western part of South Carolina. On the basis of these explorations Spain claimed this entire region of America.

In the 1490s King Henry VII sent John Cabot to explore the North American coast. Although the English did not found a permanent settlement until 1607, Cabot's voyages did lay the basis for the English interests in North America. The conflicting interests of Spain, England, and France led to a long and complicated struggle for empire. Nowhere was that struggle more intense than here at the southwestern corner of the English Empire. The Spanish attempted a settlement called San Miguel (possibly at Winyah Bay) in 1526 and a settlement called San Felipe on Parris Island in 1566. The French also attempted a settlement on Parris Island (1562). These settlements failed, and the region to the north of Spanish Florida remained contested. In the seventeenth century the English crown took steps to grant and encourage the settlement of Carolina as a buffer zone against the imperial rivals to the south and west. William S. Powell discusses the actual granting of this province.

1

"WHY CAROLINA WAS GRANTED TO THE PROPRIETORS" *

William S. Powell

In June, 1578, when Queen Elizabeth I made a generous grant of New World territory to Sir Humphrey Gilbert, she included the area which has since become North Carolina. In return for the Queen's bountiful gift, Gilbert was to lead an expedition to America to destroy hostile Spanish fishing fleets, take the West Indies from Spain, seize the gold and silver mines in the Spanish colonies, and make Elizabeth "monarch of the seas." On his first trip to America, Gilbert was rebuffed by the Spanish, and he never returned from his second.

His grant was renewed on March 24, 1584, in the name of his half-brother, Walter Raleigh, who was given authority to establish colonies and to govern them. Raleigh financed several expeditions to the New World including those which explored eastern North Carolina late in the sixteenth century. The famous "Lost Colony" at Roanoke Island was Raleigh's last attempt to plant a settlement in America.

A charter was granted the Virginia Company of London in 1606 permitting settlements to be made along a rather narrow strip of the Atlantic seaboard. Included was a portion of what is now North Carolina. The first permanent English settlement in America developed at Jamestown, less than fifty miles north of the present-day North Carolina-Virginia state line.

The more adventuresome Virginia colonists lost little time in beginning to explore the countryside around them. In 1609 Captain John Smith sent a soldier and two Indian guides to search for the colonists left at Roanoke Island. A little while later two other colonists set out on the same mission but without finding any trace of their missing countrymen. William Strachey, secretary of the colony in 1610 and 1611, recorded that he could learn from the Indians about the territory lying to the south. Not until 1622, however, when John Pory, a later

* Excerpt from *The Proprietors of Carolina* (Raleigh: The Tercentenary Commission, 1963), pp. 1–5. Reprinted by permission of the State of North Carolina Department of Archives and History.

3

secretary, actually visited the region, do we have a Virginian's account of the Albemarle, as the earliest settled part of North Carolina came to be called.

The Virginia Company's charter was revoked in 1624, and the colony became the property of the crown. On October 30, 1629, King Charles I conveyed to his attorney general, Sir Robert Heath, the region immediately south of Virginia. While Heath held title to Carolana, as it was called for the first time, no organized attempts were made to settle it from England. When he finally abandoned any intentions he might have had for colonizing his territory, he assigned his charter to Henry Lord Maltravers who apparently made at least one unsuccessful effort to send over a colony. But where officials in England were failing, private citizens in Virginia were succeeding. About 1648 several Virginians, who had been in Carolana while on an expedition to subdue the Indians, purchased large tracts of land along the Chowan River from the natives.

The first suggestion of a settlement in the Albemarle region is found in a grant made in 1653 to the Rev. Roger Green of Nansemond, Virginia, for ten thousand acres of land for the first hundred persons to settle south of the Chowan River. As a special reward for his own efforts, Green was to have a thousand acres for himself to be located "next to those persons who have had a former grant." This phrase has long been held to mean that a settlement existed here as early as 1653.

A steady stream of colonists appears to have flowed into this new settlement. A number of persons purchased land from the Indians, and the oldest grant still in existence for land in North Carolina is in the records of Perquimans County bearing the date August 4, 1661.

Such a flourishing and promising settlement did not escape the notice of prominent men in England in spite of their having so recently been in exile or otherwise occupied during the Cromwells' Commonwealth. Now they were concerned with the re-establishment of the monarchy. Indeed, these events loomed large in the affairs of Carolina, though the new settler knew little or nothing of them. It was to reward a group of his most faithful followers and supporters that the newly crowned Charles II revoked his father's grant to Sir Robert Heath. After all, Heath had not made good his intentions to settle the country. The King then, in 1663, granted this territory anew to Edward Hyde, Earl of Clarendon, Lord High Chancellor of England; George Monck, Duke of Albemarle, Master of the King's Horse and Captain-General of all his forces; William, Lord Craven, an old friend of his father's who had zealously and ably supported the royal family; John, Lord Berkeley, who had defended the crown in the rebellion which overthrew Charles I and had joined the royal family in exile; Anthony Ashley Cooper, Chancellor of the Exchequer and afterward the Earl of Shaftesbury; Sir George Carteret, Vice-Chamberlain of the King's household; Sir William Berkeley, governor of Virginia who had induced the colony to adhere to Charles II as their sovereign even while he was in exile; and Sir John Colleton, who had supported the royal cause in Barbados.

This grant of 1663 included the area roughly from the present-day Georgia-Florida boundary northward to the middle of Albemarle Sound and from the Atlantic westward to the "South Seas," some vague place in the west not then fully understood. No Englishman had ever gone very far inland from the Atlantic, and American geography was not clear even to the best European mapmaker.

It did not take long for the eight eager Lords Proprietors, as they were designated, to discover that the richest jewel of their new domain of Carolina actually was not within their domain at all. The settlements already made in the Albemarle region lay for the most part just a few miles north of the line marking the northern limit of the territory granted to them. In 1665, therefore, the Proprietors used their influence to secure a still larger territory. A second charter was issued with no important differences from the first, save in extending the boundary northward to the modern North Carolina–Virginia line and southward into Florida almost to Cape Canaveral.

The charters gave the Proprietors power to plant colonies, to create and fill offices, to erect counties and other administrative subdivisions, and numerous other rights and privileges. While very broad authority was given the Proprietors, the rights of the people were also set forth. They had then and they continued to have—or claimed to have right on down to the Revolution—the common rights of Englishmen. Among other things, they were guaranteed the English personal and property rights, liberty of conscience, and all "liberties, franchises, and privileges" enjoyed by the King's subjects actually resident in England.

With the possible exceptions of Berkeley in Virginia and Colleton who had spent sometime in Barbados, the Proprietors surely had slight understanding of the colonial territory over which they held such power. It may be that by sheer numbers—eight Proprietors—the problems were magnified. At any rate, confusion reigned in Carolina more or less continually for as long as the Lords Proprietors remained in charge.

Having received their charter, the major concern of the Lords Proprietors was to attract settlers to their province. Ultimately, regardless of how elaborate the charter was, no colony could succeed without people who were willing to take the risks of moving to the New World wilderness. In order to attract settlers, earlier proprietors and companies had issued concessions or statements of the terms under which people were invited to come and settle in the respective colonies. The typical concessions stated the conditions under which the land would be granted and the political and civil guarantees which the settlers might expect as citizens of the colony.

The Lords Proprietors were not long in producing such a set of concessions. In 1664, in reply to a request from a group of Barbadians who were interested in migrating to Carolina, the Proprietors agreed to a statement known as the "Concessions and Agreements." In this document the Proprietors promised the would-be settlers a system of headright land grants, the apportionment of land according to the number in a settler's family (hence, according to a settler's ability to work the land) and that a representative assembly would be established in Carolina.

In 1669 the Proprietors superseded their first concessions by a far more elaborate document, the Fundamental Constitutions. Largely the work of Anthony Ashley Cooper (later the Earl of Shaftesbury), the Constitutions were easily the most complex and detailed set of concessions produced for any colony. Traditionally, interest in the Constitutions has centered on its feudal elements. Hence, many concluded that this work of Lord Ashley was an anachronism even in the seventeenth century. Historians such as Gen. Edward McCrady concluded that the Constitutions had virtually no effect on the development of South Carolina. Contrarily, it ought to be recognized that the Proprietors expressed in this document their desire that the colony become a society under the leadership of a landed aristocracy, and that colonial South Carolina very nearly became such a society.

More modern scholars have noted that the Constitutions were in some ways progressive for their times. Certainly, the generous land tenure system did not compare unfavorably with that of the mother country. The assurance that the common land holders would assume a proportionate share of the political power compared favorably with England until the Reform Act of 1832. The promise of toleration and civil rights for religious dissenters were indeed liberal measures for that century. Still, the Constitutions were too complex for a frontier society. Their major effect was to encourage the establishment of a landed aristocracy and a colony of large plantations.

M. Eugene Sirmans discusses the significance of these concessions.

2

THE FUNDAMENTAL
CONSTITUTIONS *

M. Eugene Sirmans

At the heart of the Fundamental Constitutions lay Lord Ashley's dream of creating in Carolina his version of the perfect society, one in which power and property preserved "the Balance of Government" between aristocracy and democracy. Ashley set forth his social and political theories in the preamble, proposing to maintain "the interest of the Lords Proprietors with Equality" by avoiding the dangers of "erecting a numerous Democracy"; such a balanced government would be "most agreeable to the Monarchy under which we live." "It is as bad," he wrote later, "as a state of Warr for men that are in want to have the makeing Laws over Men that have Estates." At the same time, Ashley could not tolerate the possibility that the government of Carolina might fall into the hands of an irresponsible upper class, and he tried to devise a system that would force the nobility which exercised political leadership to develop a sense of *noblesse oblige*. He agreed with the political philosopher James Harrington, who believed that "a nobility of gentry overbalancing a popular Government is the utter bane and destruction of it, as a nobility or gentry in a popular Government not overbalancing it, is the very life and soul of it."

Ashley proposed to create an aristocracy that would include both the proprietors in England and a local nobility in Carolina. He would have preferred that the proprietors migrate to America and take their places at the head of the ruling class, but he realized that such a development was unlikely. As a compromise, he undertook to give each proprietor a direct voice in the government of the colony through

* Excerpt from *Colonial South Carolina: A Political History, 1663–1763* (Chapel Hill: University of North Carolina Press, 1966), pp. 10–16; Copyright © 1966 by the University of North Carolina Press. Reprinted without footnotes by permission of the University of North Carolina Press.

7

the agency of a deputy. The oldest proprietor would automatically assume the office of palatine, the chief position among the proprietors, and his deputy would become the governor in America. As for the local aristocracy, the royal charter of 1665 empowered the proprietors to grant titles of nobility and the Fundamental Constitutions provided for the creation of two orders of nobles, the higher rank to be called landgraves and the lower cassiques. In order to force these noblemen to accept their responsibilities in making and enforcing laws, the Constitutions established penalties for those who refused to do so; irresponsible nobles might lose the income from their estates or even forfeit their estates and their titles.

One of the primary responsibilities of the nobility was the administration of the colony, for which Ashley devised an elaborate scheme of eight administrative courts. Seven were to manage specific executive matters, such as finance and defense; each would be composed of a proprietor or his deputy and six councilors, all of whom were required to be noblemen. The highest court was to be the palatine's court, and its members were to be the eight proprietors or their deputies; this court was to supervise the work of the other courts. All members of the eight administrative courts—the palatine, the other proprietors, and the forty-two councilors—would form the Grand Council, which would settle disputes between courts and prepare legislation for the parliament.

The system of land ownership provided for in the Fundamental Constitutions reflected a corollary to Ashley's aristocratic preference. He accepted Harrington's dictum that power follows landed property, and when he formulated a land system for Carolina, he tried to make sure that the nobles would be large landowners. The Constitutions directed that Carolina be divided into counties, each consisting of 480,000 acres. Each county in turn would be divided into forty 12,000 acre tracts. Each of the eight proprietors was to own one 12,000-acre seignory in every county. In each county there was to be a resident aristocracy of one landgrave, who was entitled to four baronies of 12,000 acres, and two cassiques, each of whom was to receive two baronies. Thus, the nobility would own two-fifths of the land in every county, and the remaining three-fifths of the land was reserved for the people. The people's land would consist of twenty-four 12,000-acre tracts called "colonies," and every group of six colonies would be organized as a precinct. All land was to be held in free and common socage and granted by deed. The grantee could bequeath or convey his rights to someone else, but each freeholder had to pay the proprietors a quit rent of 1d. per acre every year. The Constitutions stated further that freeholders must pay their rents in silver and that the first rent payments were due in 1689.

Similarly, the Carolina judicial system represented another phase of Ashley's attempt to establish an aristocratic government. His hope was to keep the judiciary from falling into the hands of lawyers, who might otherwise usurp the prerogatives of the nobility. The Constitutions banned the professional practice of law, deeming it a "base and vile thing." In order to keep the laws relatively simple, the Constitutions declared that all legislation would automatically become void sixty years after enactment; it also prohibited legal commentaries, because "multiplicity of Comments, as well as of laws, have great inconveniences, and Serve only to obscure and perplex." In short, Ashley hoped to establish a legal system simple enough to be administered by aristocrats untrained in the law.

Ashley modified his aristocratic system somewhat when he came to local courts. The Constitutions provided for manorial courts on every barony or seignory for the tenants he expected to settle there, but he also provided for precinct and county courts in the areas occupied by freeholders, with membership open to freemen, provided only that they meet minimum property qualifications. But the county and precinct courts were weakened by provisions stripping them of the traditional administrative duties of local courts in England. The Constitutions entrusted all executive responsibilities to the administrative courts, which were made up only of nobles; Carolina's local courts were to be limited to the trial of civil and criminal cases.

When Lord Ashley was working on the Fundamental Constitutions, he was trying to establish a balanced government, one which not only guaranteed the rights of the aristocracy but which also protected the rights of all men, even from encroachment by the proprietors. Ashley believed that the Constitutions would achieve exactly that kind of balanced government. "By our Frame," he observed a few years later, "noe bodys power noe not of any of the Proprietors themselves were they there, is soe great as to be able to hurt the meanest man in the Country." The Fundamental Constitutions carefully enumerated such judicial rights as trial by jury and freedom from double jeopardy. Despite the proprietors' fear of "a numerous Democracy," they gave freemen a limited share in the legislative process. Freeholders who owned at least fifty acres could vote for representatives to the Carolina parliament, but the delegates were required to own a minimum of 500 acres. The parliament, which would be composed of the eight proprietors or their deputies, one landgrave and two cassiques from each county, and one freeman from each precinct, would sit together as a unicameral assembly. Although each man would have one vote, the distribution of membership tipped the scales toward the nobility rather than the people's representatives. With four precincts in each county, freemen would always outnumber the local nobles, but the proprietors or their deputies and the nobles acting together could command a majority in the parliament until the time when nine or more counties had been created. The Constitutions limited the power of the popular element in parliament in other ways as well, for it could only accept or reject laws proposed by the Grand Council; it could not amend them or initiate legislation itself. Moreover, any legislation enacted by parliament could be disallowed by the palatine's court. Finally, the parliament would have no executive powers, which were entrusted solely to the administrative courts.

Although the Fundamental Constitutions thus limited the political power of the freemen. Ashley opposed absolutely rigid class lines and made it possible for an ambitious man to rise socially. If a freeman accumulated an estate of at least 3,000 acres, he could petition the proprietors to proclaim his estate a manor and grant him manorial rights. Should a vacancy occur in the ranks of the landgraves and cassiques, a lord of a manor would be eligible for elevation to the nobility.

Two classes of inhabitants in Carolina were to enjoy not even the limited rights of freemen. In addition to tenants who were expected to occupy the manorial estates, Ashley assumed that the great feudal domains would be inhabited in part by leetmen bound to the land for life in a status not unlike that of a medieval serf, men whose children would inherit their father's status and whose service would be part of any transfer, by sale or otherwise, of the estate from one manor lord to another. It is not clear why Ashley assumed that there would be candidates for this social station among colonists who were to be recruited chiefly from the West Indian and other American colonies. Perhaps he had doubts himself, for when he revised the Constitutions in 1669 he amended it to make sure that no man became a leetman except by his own consent. At the bottom of the social scale were the slaves, who recently had come to play an important role in the economy of the West Indian colonies and Virginia. Ashley, who had earlier invested in slave-trading ventures, inserted in all drafts of the Fundamental Constitutions a provision which became of crucial importance in shaping the development of Carolina. "Every Freeman of Carolina," it was stipulated, "shall have absolute power and authority over his Negro Slaves, of what opinion or Religion soever."

Finally, a significant feature of the Fundamental Constitutions was the care which Ashley took to identify Carolina with the principle of religious toleration. Colonists in Carolina had only to "acknowledge a God, and that God is publicly and Solemnly to be worshipped." If seven persons agreed to form a church and to state their doctrines publicly, the proprietors would allow them to worship as they pleased. The policy would apply to all religions, even to "heathens, Jews, and other dissenters," but the promise of religious freedom did not end there. Every political office was to be open to members of every religion; registries of births, marriages, and deaths were to be kept by the agencies of the secular government, instead of by the church, as in England; the Constitutions forbade the use of "reproachful, Reviling, or abusive language against the Religion of any Church or Profession"; and the Constitutions permitted men to meet the requirement for an oath of office and testimony in a trial by making an affirmation rather than by swearing an oath, this last a point of particular importance for the rapidly growing sect of Quakers. Unfortunately, not all of the proprietors shared Ashley's religious liberalism, and when they reviewed the Constitutions in 1670 they insisted on adding a clause proclaiming the Church of England to be the "National Religion" of Carolina and empowering the Carolina parliament to levy taxes for its support. Even so, Carolina still offered a greater degree of religious freedom than England or any other American colony, with the single exception of Rhode Island.

The Fundamental Constitutions was a plan for the future, and the proprietors, being practical men, accepted it as such. In 1669 and 1670, while the Constitutions was still under consideration, the proprietors turned to the problem of a temporary government. They set up the palatine's court in London on October 21, 1669, with the Duke of Albemarle as the first palatine and Ashley as chief justice, but they left the rest of the Constitutions for later implementation. Sketching the framework of a temporary government, their instructions to the first governor ordered him to set up a temporary Grand Council which would include the governor, the proprietary deputies, and five freemen to be chosen by parliament from its own membership; twenty freemen were to be elected to form with the council a parliament as soon as the settlers had landed in Carolina. The parliament would have the power only to approve legislation proposed by the Grand Council; all other powers of government were vested in the council, including all judicial powers and, if necessary, the right to issue decrees which would have the force of law.

In no way did the proprietors display their practical knowledge of colonial affairs more than in their provisions for the distribution of land. They understood the attraction land would have for prospective colonists, and they offered liberal terms of settlement by authorizing the governor and council to make headright grants on a sliding scale. Every settler in the first fleet was entitled to 150 acres of land for each adult male he took to Carolina, including himself, and 100 acres for each female and for each male under sixteen. Colonists who arrived during the first year of settlement would receive 100 and 70 acres, respectively, while men arriving after that could claim 70 and

60 acres. As a further inducement, the proprietors promised to accept quit rent payments in commodities, rather that silver. The proprietors also directed the governor and council to force the people to settle in towns, as in New England, rather than allowing them to disperse on isolated farms. Township settlement, according to Lord Ashley, was the "Cheife thing that hath given New England soe much the advantage over Virginia," and he especially wanted Carolina to avoid the "Inconvenience and Barbarisme of scattered Dwellings."

Prof. Wesley Frank Craven's work in *The History of the South* series is a classic contribution to the historiography of the seventeenth century. The following selection gives an interesting insight into the actual establishment of the colony. Contrary to the charges that the Proprietors as the authors of the Fundamental Constitutions were an impractical lot, the planning and founding of their colony showed them to be the most practical of the colonial founders. The planning of this colony gave evidence that the founders had learned from the mistakes of the earlier settlements. The first Carolinians were instructed to bring certain specified tools and supplies. Furthermore, many of the first Carolinians, especially the leaders, were already experienced in the business of colonialism. Many came to this province from the West Indies, especially Barbados. These people had concluded that the West Indian islands were so overpopulated that the opportunities for improvement were limited. Hence, there was an interest in the first westward movement within the New World. The first governor, William Sayle, had already served as governor of Bermuda. The care for the proper supplies and experience aided the first South Carolinians in avoiding a "seasoning time" comparable to that of so many of the earlier settlements. The mortality rates in these times of adjustment had often been shockingly high. This is, of course, not to deny that there was a struggle in founding this colony.

The Proprietors realized from the beginning that the great attraction to settlers was land. Hence, the headright system was implemented quite early. The instructions to Joseph West to operate an experimental farm and to seek the ideal staple crop indicated the desire that Carolina should be a plantation, staple colony. Subsequent developments proved these plans to be most realistic.

3

THE EARLY SETTLEMENT *

Wesley Frank Craven

Three ships purchased at a cost of over £600 were refitted with the evident intent of keeping them in the regular service of the province. Appropriately renamed the *Carolina, Port Royal,* and *Albemarle* and made ready for sailing by August, they carried to America, in addition to passengers, a stock of provisions, seeds, clothing, arms, ammunition, tools, ware, tackle, and trading truck representing an investment of better than £1,500. An additional £270 in goods were forwarded direct to Virginia under a plan to establish a credit in the older colony against which the proprietors' agents at Port Royal could draw for the provision of livestock and other staples. Captain Henry Brayne, who had accompanied Sandford to Port Royal in 1666, sailed now as master of the *Carolina* with orders to call first at Barbados. His instructions for the period following the landing at Port Royal necessarily were elastic, but the general nature of his intended employment is clear. Guided by circumstances, he was to go to Virginia for cattle and other cargo to be picked up as directed by William Burgh of the James River; or back to Barbados, taking on timber and such additional freightage as could be had, to load passengers and cargo for a return voyage to Port Royal; or if the proprietors' Barbadian correspondents thought it best, he was to load products of the island for Virginia and return to England by way of the Chesapeake. It is impossible to offer a full chronicle of the *Carolina*'s later service. Let it be noted, though, that a letter of September, 1670, brought word from the colony of the ship's recent return from Virginia with an eight months' supply of provisions, and stated that it had since gone to Barbados for additional colonists. There, on November 4, Captain Brayne proclaimed a purpose to sail

* Excerpt from *The Southern Colonies in the Seventeenth Century, 1607–1689* (Baton Rouge: Louisiana State University Press, 1949), pp. 335–59; copyright, 1949, by Louisiana State University Press and the Littlefield Fund for Southern History, the University of Texas. Reprinted without footnotes by permission of The Louisiana State University Press.

for Carolina in thirty days and advertised that subscribers to earlier ventures might now claim land dividends to their definite advantage. He offered both passage and supply to such persons as were unable to meet their own charges, in return for an obligation to repay the proprietors within two years in tobacco, cotton, or ginger.

Instructions to Joseph West, who was in command of the fleet prior to its arrival at Barbados, provide equally interesting testimony to the sort of aid the proprietors now undertook to provide. A commission as governor and commander in chief was forwarded in blank by him to Sir John Yeamans, who was to assume the post himself or to assign it to some other fit person. Having thus surrendered the command, West's first duty became that of securing from Thomas Colleton a supply of cottonseed, indigo seed, ginger roots, sugar cane, vines, and olive sets, a supply that was to be supplemented in case the ships called also at Bermuda. On arrival at Port Royal he was to select a site, with an eye to the variety of its soil, for an experimental farm. Thirty servants to be procured on the proprietors' account in Ireland on the way out were assigned to him. With them he was to clear the ground, erect necessary housing, and make experimental plantings in March, April, May, and June on several varieties of soil, not neglecting to try both low and high ground. Except for the time and ground devoted to food crops, his efforts were to be for the moment wholly experimental and according to instructions which read: "you are never to thinke of makeing any Comodity your buisiness further than for experience sake & to have your stock of it for planting encrease till you have sufficiently provided for ye belly by planting store of provisions which must in all contrivances be looked upon by you as ye foundation of your Plantacon." The farm was to be laid out in accordance with the proprietors' headright claims for thirty servants, and having served its experimental purposes it would be divided. One is reminded of a similar function of the public estate in the early days of Virginia and of Bermuda. . . .

The further plans of the proprietors in 1669 offer ample testimony of a continuing purpose to rely chiefly upon experienced men in the actual work of settlement. Whether because of some feeling of a prior commitment to Yeamans or because of a conviction that the planters of Barbados would enlist more readily under the leadership of one of their own number, Sir John was requested either to assume the governor's post himself or to fill in the name of some fit person of his selection. The ships under West's command reached Barbados in October, and from there early in November he wrote Ashley of the hope of providing a total complement of two hundred settlers for Carolina by recruitment among the local planters.

That fall in the Caribbean proved to be one of storms and generally unfavorable weather. A gale which wrecked the *Albemarle* at Barbados delayed the departure for Port Royal, and when the expedition got under way again, the *Albemarle* having been replaced by a Barbadian shallop, additional misfortunes overtook it. Separated from the rest of the fleet, the *Port Royal* in January suffered shipwreck in the Bahamas. The *Carolina* and the Barbadian shallop found their way to Bermuda, where some refitting was required and where, it would seem almost incidentally, the colonists picked up a governor. Yeamans had sailed with them from Barbados, but in Bermuda he seems to have grown impatient with the delay. Desirous of making a prompt return home, he filled in the governor's commission with the name of William Sayle. By Yeamans' own admission, Sayle was "a man of no great sufficiency yet the ablest I could meet with." An old Puritan now approaching the age of eighty, Sayle had known the years of his greatest activity in the mid-century. He had been identified during the English Civil War with the Puritan settlement at Eleuthera in the Bahamas, islands to which the Carolina proprietors in 1670 acquired title, and he had served as governor of Bermuda prior to his resignation in 1662. After little more than a year of service as a pioneer governor in Carolina, he died there in the spring of 1671.

Governor Sayle and his new charges had left Bermuda in February of the preceding year. The weather continued unfavorable but the *Carolina* reached the Port Royal region toward the close of March. Driven south off its course, the Barbadian shallop did not come in until the latter part of May and even then there were missing a few of its passengers who had fallen into the hands of the Spaniards on St. Catherine's Island, northernmost of the Spanish outposts based on Florida. Meanwhile, a decision had been made to abandon the Port Royal area for another site of settlement. Perhaps it was some recollection of Ribaut's early and unsuccessful challenge to Spanish monopoly in that very area which served to remind the colonists that the place lay "in the very chops of the Spaniards." Perhaps of greater influence were the urgent entreaties and invitations of the friendly Kiawahs, who sought an ally against the warlike Westos on the Savannah River, to occupy a part of their own country lying north of Port Royal. It may be well not to overlook the all too familiar inclination of experienced colonists to substitute their own judgment for instructions from England. Whatever the case, Governor Sayle and his advisers, after some preliminary exploration, agreed upon a site which they called Albemarle Point, located some twenty-five miles inland on the western bank of the Kiawah or Ashley River. . . .

For a while progress necessarily was slow. At Albemarle Point the colonists undertook to fortify a position of natural strength and to build a town which, in honor of the King, they named Charles Town. The alarms raised by the Spanish expedition of late summer held the people close to their defenses, "more like souldiers in a garrison than planters," and interfered with the accomplishment of initial objectives which West described for Sir George Carteret in the following spring as "being . . . in the first place to provide for the Belly and to make some Experiment of what the land will best produce." For provisions during the first winter the colony depended chiefly upon an eight months' supply of Indian corn, peas, and meal brought in by the *Carolina* from Virginia near the end of the summer. With this food came also a stock of cattle and hogs, but at a price which led Thomas Colleton to advise Sir Peter that New York offered a more advantageous source of supply. Relieved thus of the fear of want, the colonists bent their energies to clearing and building. As early as September, 1670, Stephen Bull reported to Ashley that a semicircle about the town had been marked out for grants of ten acres per head "for present planting." Such grants were obviously intended chiefly for subsistence farming, but already men were testing a variety of seeds and plants brought for the purpose—oranges, lemons, limes, pomegranates, figs, plantains, wheat, potatoes, tobacco, cotton, flax, and others. It had been planned to try ginger, but the roots intended for that test had been lost with the ill-fated *Port Royal*. The Barbadians, whose experience lent special weight to their opinions, were reported as regarding the soil and climate especially promising for the production of sugar, wine, silk, tobacco, and cotton.

The return of the *Carolina* from Barbados in February with sixty-four new settlers brought substantial proof of a growing interest in the new project among the Barbadian planters. During the same month another forty-two came in on a vessel provided for the voyage largely through the efforts of Thomas Colleton. A report in the following March indicated a total population of about two hundred persons, of whom some forty to fifty were freeholders. The people still lived in a relatively compact community immediately surrounding Albemarle Point, and were still subject to the limitations of life in a garrison. But West reported to Sir George Carteret that in addition to having cleared about thirty acres, which he intended to use immediately for food crops and experimental planting, he had "taken up" three hundred acres of land near the town on the joint account of Carteret, Ashley, and Colleton. Through a letter of William Owen's, we gain a glimpse of the hopes with which others looked about for favorably situated land that year. "If I had 10000 £ per. annum in England," he wrote, "yet would I have an Interest here and if Ginger continues a price no doubt not of more then an ordinarie Liveing."

Unfortunately, the year proved a dry one in Carolina, and comments on experimental plantings began to be marked by certain reservations. There was discouragement over the prospects for sugar cane and cotton, but hopes survived for indigo, ginger, wine, silk, oil, hemp, flax, and tobacco "as good as ever smoked." The records suggest that from an early date men displayed an understandable inclination to seek out and mark for their own particular use favorably situated lands lying beyond the immediate environs of the town. An indication of the main lines of exploration followed in this quest, as well as the advent of another stage in the colony's development, is found in the council's appointment of a special commission in October, 1671, charged with "convenient speed" to view all those places on the Ashley and Wando (Cooper) rivers which might be "most convenient to situate Towns upon soe the same may be wholy reserved for these and the like uses." The council gave anticipated further additions to the population as the chief reason for the action taken. New arrivals from England and New York during that summer and fall contributed to the colony's growth. On January 20, 1671/72, an official report to Ashley declared "that 337 men and women 62 children or persons under 16 years of age is the full number of persons who have arrived *in,* and *since* the first fleet out of England to this day, whereof 43 men 2 women 3 children are dead, and 16 absent so as there now remains 263 men able to bear arms 69 women, 59 children or persons under 16 years of age."

For the accommodation of new settlers the council had taken steps during the preceding September to locate below Charles Town a second town in the neighborhood of Stono Creek, and in December a thirty-acre plot "in a Creeke Southward from Stonoe Creeke" was ordered laid out and given the name of James Town. Oyster Point at the juncture of the Ashley and the Cooper, where the later city of Charleston would rise, had been selected as still another townsite as early as February, 1672. Additional evidence of an attempt to follow the proprietary instructions emphasizing the desirability of settlement in towns is found in the council's decision of the following April to lay out three colonies of 12,000 acres each, one for Charles Town, another for James Town, and a third for Oyster Point. The actual warrant to the surveyor for laying out this third colony has survived. The warrant was dated April 30 and directed him to survey 12,000 acres of the land beginning at Oyster Point and lying between the Ashley and the Wando "in a square as much as Navigable Rivers will permitt." Surviving, too, are subsequently issued warrants for the survey of individual grants which show some care to protect such townsites as had been set aside and a concern for deduction from the total acreage to be surveyed of such town lots as may have been received by the grantee. According to the usual phrasing, the land would be situated for the grantee "in such place as you [i.e., the surveyor] shall be directed by him or his Attorney soe as the same be not within the compass of any lands heretofore layd out or marked to be layd out for any other person or Towne." But somehow the modern student tends to linger over the evidence thus provided of a reasonably free choice of site enjoyed by the grantee, for that kind of freedom runs counter to the procedures of planned settlement.

For evidence of the increasing prevalence of a free choice, which with a growing disregard of the proprietors' orderly plan of settlement followed the natural highways provided by the Ashley and Cooper rivers, one has only to look further into the land warrants. At first glance this fundamental source appears monotonously uninteresting for all save the genealogist, but when conscience prompts a second examination, the men and women whose names are recorded there begin once again to take on life as one follows them in their quest of favorably situated land. The governing consideration in their minds, as it had been with men pursuing a similar quest in Virginia and Maryland, was ready access to those waterways upon which the community chiefly depended for transportation. Each warrant stipulated for the surveyor's instruction that if the grantee's choice of land lay "upon any navigable River or any River capable of being made navigable you are to allow only the fifth part of the depth thereof by the water side." Indeed, it might almost be said that the first settlers divided among themselves not so much the land as they did the land's water frontage.

Of the proprietors' elaborate scheme of settlement one gains an occasional glimpse, as in the warrant for laying out a seigniory of 12,000 acres for Shaftesbury in 1675 and another for Sir Peter Colleton in 1678. Here and there a landgrave or cacique makes his appearance. Expansive grants made in the spirit of the Fundamental Constitutions, for the most part prior to 1700, would carry over into the eighteenth century land titles held chiefly for speculative purposes which contributed to one of the most sordid chapters in the history of

American land speculation. But one gains an impression from the warrants that at least through the first decade of settlement grants were made largely in return for services rendered, albeit in accordance with a purposely liberal land policy.

The main burden of the story told by the warrants is of grants received in payment of headright claims under the several conditions laid down by the proprietors. Thus to Henry Wood on June 29, 1672, goes 200 acres of land "for himselfe and Alice his wife arriveing in the first ffleet"; on May 21 to Henry Jones, "arriveing a servant in the first ffleet," 100 acres; to Thomas Clutterbrooke of Barbados on June 23 a grant of 670 acres "for his disbursements on the discovery of this province by Capt. Hilton" and for two servants, Robert and Mary Thomas, who had arrived in February, 1671. Joseph Dalton in July received 1,150 acres for George Prideaux, Thomas Young, William Chambers, John Dawson, William Rhodes, William Burges, and Jane Lawson, all of them brought in as servants with the first fleet; for the same number of servants arriving in February and June of 1671, Major Thomas Gray received on August 24, 1672, the lesser figure of 700 acres. A warrant in November of that year issued in behalf of the executors of the late Governor William Sayle allowed 1,300 acres for the governor himself, Captain Nathaniel Sayle, Mrs. Mary Gand, Charles Rilley, George Roberts, "John Senr. a Negroe Elizabeth a Negro and John Junr. a Negroe arriveing in September 1670." Record of the early arrival in the colony of other Negroes is provided in the warrant of September 5, 1674, issued in the right of Simon Berringer for 3,000 acres "for himselfe and soe many Servants and Negroes arriveing in the yeare 1671 & 1672." Notice should also be taken of a warrant of the same date which allowed Lady Margaret Yeamans, widow to the late deceased Sir John, a grant of 1,070 acres. Of this grant 880 acres were "for her self and eight of her own proper Negroes namely Hannah, Jone, Jupiter, Rentee, Gilbert, Resom, Jossee & Simon, and one man servant John: Hopkins arriveing in August 1672, and ffebruary 1674." The remaining 190 acres were granted on the understanding that she would transport "soe many persons more to settle the same as shall be sufficient for that Appropriation."

That the proprietors enjoyed some success in their effort to enlist the aid of persons capable of making substantial investments of capital and labor in the development of the province is amply attested by these and other warrants. But not to be overlooked in considering the contributions made to Carolina's growth are such grants as that of 180 acres on October 14, 1682, to William Driver "for himselfe, wife, & two Children arriveing in October 1682," or the laying

out in October, 1680, of a town lot in Charles Town for John Cot-
tingham, "one of the free persons of this province" who in April,
1681, received a grant "of one hundred acres of land not yett layd out
or marked to be layd out for any other Person or use." Nor can we
slight the "seaventy acres of land" brought, among other attractions
no doubt, to Evan Jones by his marriage with "Jone his wife," who,
according to a warrant of June 17, 1676, had reached Carolina "a
servant in March 1672."

In the end there remained of the original plan for a town type of
settlement only Charles Town and its unique position in the life of
the province. The custom among the great planters of the eighteenth
century of keeping a town house in Charles Town in addition to the
fine dwellings on their outlying plantations carried over into the
years of the colony's maturity a faint trace of the founders' intention
that a man's property in Carolina should be divided between a town
lot and the acreage he cultivated outside the town. It is not too much
perhaps to suggest that the earlier plan helped to shape the peculiar
features of South Carolina's social and political life resulting from
that custom. But in the very movement of population which after
1680 so quickly built up Charles Town one finds chiefly an adjustment, with the abandonment of other townsites, to a basic geographi-
cal consideration. The settlers, in their quest of favorably situated
land, had followed the waterways of the Ashley and the Cooper. The
confluence of those two rivers at Oyster Point in a good harbor
readily accessible from the sea lanes leading in from England, the
Antilles, Bermuda, Virginia, New York, and New England made that
site the logical choice for the colony's first city.

The site itself had been chosen for a town as early as 1672. Warrants for town lots there date from the spring of 1677, and by June,
1680, the name "Charles Town" had been transferred across the
Ashley to take the place of "Oyster Point." For a short time yet men
felt an occasional need to specify "New Charles towne," but the old
town already had become "Kaiawah sometimes called Charles towne,"
and soon was "Kaiawah formerlie called Charles towne" or simply
Kiawah. . . .

Through the first years in all colonies men had little occasion to
draw a distinction between provincial and local areas of government.
Control at first was centralized, and only gradually did the need
appear for some parceling out of the right to govern among lesser
and geographically distributed agencies. Thus it had been in Virginia
and in Maryland, and now in Carolina government had its beginning

in the control exercised by a governor and a council which, for all practical purposes, was distinguished only by the presence in the council of specially elected representatives of the freemen. An even fuller recognition of the principle of representation had been provided in the Fundamental Constitutions, and though the clumsy question of the rate at which its elaborate scheme should be effected apparently postponed the calling of an assembly beyond the time considered desirable by some of the planters, a local parliament met as early as July, 1670. There soon developed a contest for the right to initiate legislation by the more representative element of the Assembly, a controversy given certain special turns by James Harrington's notions regarding the function of a Grand Council. Other complications in the early political scene arose from the presence of men who had been designated proprietary deputies, landgraves, and caciques. But their numbers were few and the designations seem to have served principally to mask the normal struggle for place and influence on public policy and occasionally to give an advantage in that struggle. Of greater importance, or so it would seem in a general survey of the sort attempted in this volume, is the fact that the governor in Carolina did not enjoy absolute powers, that like the governor of Virginia he tended as one of the larger landholders to be identified with the interest of the community itself, and that he found his office dependent upon some working alliance with the leading planters.

Adjustments of the machinery of government to a growing dispersal of settlement came as early as 1673. They consisted of provision to eliminate expensive jury proceedings through agreement of the parties to civil actions before the council, and "for ye speedy & more easy administracon of justice" through authorization to any two members of the council, one being a proprietary deputy, to call to their aid two or more freeholders to hear "small misdemeanors." But the legal establishment in 1682 of three counties—Berkeley to include Charles Town, Colleton lying south of it, and Craven to the north—was not followed by development of the usual machinery of county administration. This failure is chiefly significant for the promise it gave of a continued concentration of governmental agencies in Charles Town that would long restrict the normal development of local self-government both in and outside that city.

Of the more recent immigrants into the colony, forty-five Huguenots reaching Charles Town in 1680 on His Majesty's ship *Richmond* are especially interesting. Not only were they forerunners of other French Protestants destined to contribute significantly to the life and the tradition of the province, but they came with a special commission

to introduce the production of silk and wine. The silkworms, unhappily, hatched aboard ship and died before they reached Carolina,
and wine would remain among the perennial hopes of the English
colonizers of America. Though abortive, the project serves again to
remind us of a continuing interest in agricultural experimentation
that was heavily relied upon in current efforts to promote emigration to the colony. Of the many commodities already tried in the
colonists' search for staple crops, the easiest success apparently had
come with tobacco, but "the great Quantities which Virginia, and
other of His Majesties Plantations make, rendring it a Drug over all
Europe" lent little encouragement to its production. Discouragement
with cotton, in later years to shape so much of Carolina's history,
had come early. Optimism regarding indigo, another great staple later
perfected, persisted for a time, but, whether because of difficulty in
extracting its profitable dye or for other reasons, the planters gave
up attempts to grow the plant. Rice rather than cotton or indigo would
be the first great staple of South Carolina's plantations. . . .

Meanwhile, the planters had confronted the necessity of finding
immediate means of subsistence and of making payments called for
especially in Barbados and England. Like others before them, they
experienced trouble in attempts to grow European grains. Finding in
the Indian corn a natural staple of amazing hardiness and reproduc-
tivity, they made a not too difficult adjustment of taste and undoubtedly at an early date some of their number preferred cornbread to
any other, as well they might. The hogs brought down from Virginia
found the rooting good, and who can question that the gravy soon
ran red in Carolina, or that vegetables on the table were not left dependent for flavor on their own juices? Among the vegetables were the
potato brought from Barbados and the English pea, ready to eat in
late April. Game, the ubiquitous American turkey included, and fish
gave variety to the diet, as did also in season wild strawberries,
blackberries, grapes, and peaches, not to mention the hickory nut
and the black walnut; but the Carolinian was already noted, like his
contemporary in Virginia, as a man who had little time for gardens.

That in addition to pork he frequently ate beef is suggested by the
fact that his cattle at an early date provided a chief staple of export.
Samuel Wilson declared in 1682 that some of the planters "have
already seven or eight hundred head," and commenting on the custom
of allowing stock a free range and the absence of need to provide
fodder for "the little Winter they have," he declared "an Ox is raised
at almost as little expence in Carolina, as a Hen is in England." He
forecast that these natural advantages would soon permit a flourishing

trade in supply of meat for the northern provinces, where men were compelled to "spend a great part of their Summers Labour in providing three or four Months Fother for the Cattle in the Winter." On this point he proved to be wrong, but Carolina did and would continue to share with the more northern plantations in the provision of food, especially of salt pork and beef, for the West Indies. Thus the first planters made payment in Barbados, or secured title there to sugar and molasses for payment to London. Wilson wrote as a promoter of the Carolina settlement, but he compressed much of its history into a few words when he described "many Planters that are single, and have never a Servant, that have two or three hundred Hogs, of which they make great profit: Barbados, Jamaica, and New-England, affording a constant good price for their Pork; by which means they get wherewithal to build them more convenient Houses, and to purchase Servants, and Negro-slaves."

Also, payments abroad increasingly were made with peltries acquired through an expanding Indian trade and, unhappily, with Indian slaves, but we will return to that subject later. For the moment, there appears to be some advantage in closing this discussion of the settlement of Carolina by noting other details of advice given by Wilson to prospective settlers in 1682. In behalf of the proprietors he advertised that passage from England to Charles Town might be had at five pounds for a man or woman. For the benefit of those who wished to settle free of quitrents, the land could be bought at fifty pounds for a thousand acres. Men were advised to take with them "An Ax, a Bill, and a Broad Hoe, and grabbing Hoe, for every man, and a cross cut Saw to every four men, a Whip-saw, a set of Wedges and Fraus and Betle-Rings to every family, and some Reaping Hooks and Sythes, as likewise Nails of all sorts, Hooks, Hinges, Bolts and Locks for their Houses." For "the Provision he hath need of," a man should take the "Merchandizes which sell best in Carolina"—"Linnen and Woollen, and all other Stufs to make clothes of, with Thread, Sowing Silk, Buttons, Ribbons, Hats, Stockings, Shoes, etc."

For further advice one of the proprietors or their secretary might be consulted at eleven o'clock every Tuesday at the Carolina coffeehouse in Birching Lane near by the Royal Exchange. There, presumably, a man might secure with his coffee some elaboration of the promise that in Carolina the "Ayr gives a strong Appetite and quick Digestion, nor is it without suitable effects, men finding themselves apparently more lightsome, more prone, and more able to all Youthful Exercises, than in England, the Women are very Fruitful, and the Children have fresh Sanguine Complexions."

South Carolina's role in the suppression of piracy forms one of the most impressive chapters in the history of this colony and state. The real seat of piracy in the New World was in the Caribbean Sea, the focus of intense imperial rivalry between England, Spain, France, and Holland. In time of war each nation licensed ship owners as privateers to prey on the commerce of the enemy. The people who profited as privateers in wartime often carried on in peacetime as pirates, with little regard for whose ships they raided. These privateers and pirates used certain of the West Indian islands and the North Carolina inlets as their bases of operation. Hence, South Carolina was situated between the concentrations of piracy.

In 1713 the War of the Spanish Succession (or Queen Anne's War, as the Americans called it) ended, and many privateers slid over to the practice of piracy. The Charleston trade had now become prosperous enough to tempt these entrepreneurs. The plague of piracy reached something of a climax during the first administration of Gov. Robert Johnson, one of the more capable of the colonial executives. The biographer of Governor Johnson tells the story of the Carolinians' struggle with the pirates.

4

"VICTORY OVER THE PIRATES" *

Richard P. Sherman

Confronted with the Indian menace on its southwestern frontiers, South Carolina had another serious problem on the Atlantic
coast, where it faced the scourge of the sea—piracy. Unsavory characters had from time to time harassed shipping, and immediately
preceding and during Johnson's administration there was an especially heavy concentration of pirates in the area. Trade plummeted
as ships using Charleston harbor faced the probability of capture.
Imports, exports, passengers, and the mail suffered severely, as cap-
tures became a daily occurrence.

One notable example was an experience of one William Guy, missionary for the Society for the Propagation of the Gospel, who was
returning to Charleston from Narragansett. The vessel in which he
was sailing had arrived off Charleston harbor and lay off the bar of
Ashley River, waiting for a pilot to bring it in safely. Hoping to
obtain a pilot sooner, Guy went ashore in a small boat. During his
absence, a pirate suddenly appeared and took the waiting ship, in
which were Guy's wife, children and their possessions. After having
kept them three days, the pirate sent his wife and children ashore,
robbed of everything. Not only was his family destitute of clothing and
household goods, but Guy had lost most of his books, papers, and
other valuables. Upon hearing of his plight, the Society in London
voted Guy a gratuity of £40 sterling beyond his regular allowance.
There were other victims, less fortunate than the Guy family, who

* Chapter 3 from *Robert Johnson: Proprietary and Royal Governor of
South Carolina* (Columbia: University of South Carolina Press, 1966), pp.
31–37; Copyright © 1966 by The University of South Carolina Press. Reprinted without footnotes by permission of the University of South Carolina
Press and the author.

had no place to turn for help or relief. Many even forfeited their lives.

Although the South Carolina government was exerting itself to the utmost, it seemed too weak to withstand the pirates. In a letter to the Board of Trade, Johnson informed the members that the Province was under a continuous alarm, and trade was at the stage of utter ruin. Twice within the preceding nine months, he wrote, pirates had stationed themselves off the bar and had captured all ships entering or leaving the port. Only about two weeks previous to his writing, four pirate vessels had appeared in sight of the town. This force, reported to be under the command of the pirate Edward Teach, or Thatch (best remembered as the notorious "Blackbeard"), consisted of a ship of forty-odd guns, three sloops, and more than 400 men. They took the pilot boat and captured eight or nine other vessels, aboard which were several of the chief inhabitants of the Province. The pirates were quick to realize their advantageous position: they sent a message that unless the Governor dispatched a chest of medicines, which they sorely needed, all the prisoners would be put to death. Left with no alternative, Johnson complied; whereupon the prisoners, already plundered of all they had, were sent ashore almost naked.

To help abolish piracy, the British Government had issued a proclamation offering pardon to those pirates who would surrender and promise to stop their illegal activities. Johnson was given a commission to pardon pirates, but he did not feel that the proclamation had any good effect. He noted that a few had given themselves up and received a certificate of pardon, but several of these had already returned to their old ways. Johnson had received reliable information that on the seas between Carolina and New Providence there were more than twenty sail of pirates. Governor Johnson told the Board that unless ships were sent against them, the trade of this part of America would be entirely ruined. He asked particularly that a frigate or, better still, two frigates be sent to cruise in the vicinity of Charleston harbor. Concerning the assignment of Captain Woodes Rogers, then on his way to New Providence, Johnson wrote that he hoped that he had frigates with him and a good force of soldiers. Otherwise, Johnson said, he would run the risk of being attacked by the pirates, who were at that place in numbers of 600 or 700. Since it was their "Nest & Rendezvous," Johnson felt that they would be unwilling to have the place settled.

At this time—the summer of 1718—South Carolina enjoyed a brief respite from piratical mischief. While the pirates were on the coast that summer, they did not care to bother the few vessels then sailing, as the cargoes were of little value. They preferred to wait for the fall season when the produce of the Province had been readied for shipment abroad; and when September and October came, pirate action reached its zenith.

Johnson again complained bitterly to England about the pirates who were blocking Charleston harbor for periods of eight to ten days, taking and plundering all vessels entering or departing, but soon was forced to use his own initiative. Two vessels commanded by Vane waited off the bar, one day taking a slave ship from Guinea and two other sloops, and the next assaulting four outbound ships. Disgusted with these continuing insults to the Province, and hearing that another pirate vessel careening at Cape Fear was likely to pay its respects to the Charleston port, Governor Johnson decided to attack. Two sloops and a force of 130 men were prepared and placed under command of Colonel William Rhett, who first steered in a southerly direction looking for Vane. Not finding him, and being unable to gain any information as to his whereabouts, Rhett changed course and headed north for Cape Fear. There he found a sloop of eight guns and fifty men, commanded by the notorious pirate Stede Bonnet, together with two of Bonnet's prizes.

Bonnet tried to escape the next day. Rhett followed, and in the chase, both Bonnet's sloop and the two from Carolina ran aground on the shoals. Rhett's vessel was within musket shot of the pirate sloop, and as the tide ebbed, his ship heeled toward the pirates'. Exposed to the fire from the pirate craft, the guns of Rhett's ship were pointing uselessly downward. After taking the pirate fire for six hours, Rhett's ship was freed by the incoming tide, while Bonnet's sloop was still held fast on the shoal. Seeing that Rhett was about to board his vessel, Bonnet sent out a white flag. He threw himself on Rhett's mercy, Rhett promised to intercede, and the pirate surrendered. Carolina casualties included ten men killed in the encounter and nineteen wounded, four of whom later died of their wounds. The captured pirates were taken to Charleston, where they were imprisoned while awaiting trial.

Bonnet, who was described as "a Gentleman of a Plentifull Fortune in Barbadoes, who turned Pyrate," escaped his confinement once but was recaptured, and sentenced to death. Twenty-two of his crew had already been executed.

Governor Johnson was naturally pleased at the turn of events, but he worried over the expense of the expedition, and he also feared that it had antagonized other pirates who infested the coast. Once again he urged the British government to send a frigate to protect Charleston harbor.

His apprehension proved only too well founded, for soon the harbor was blocked by several pirate vessels, a menace compared by the Reverend William Tredwell Bull to the "Pestilential Fever" that had raged in Charleston during the fall. Hoping that the fever had finally passed, the minister remarked that "the greatest Plague to us now is by Piracy on our Coast."

Since Governor Johnson's pleas to England for assistance in fighting the sea rovers had brought no response, he decided to enlarge his fighting force. His plan became especially imperative when it was learned that another pirate, the notorious Christopher Moody, was approaching the port, his ship carrying fifty guns and 200 men. The Province—now in an impoverished state—knew well the danger if the pirate should decide to turn his guns ashore. There was the further possibility that the town would be sacked, in keeping with other pirates' methods. There was no time to be lost. An embargo was placed on shipping; and the Governor sent scout boats to patrol the Charleston harbor entrance to resist any attempted landing. Meanwhile, he began assembling his fleet.

Before preparations were completed, an unidentified ship and sloop were sighted; but they made no hostile movements for three days. By then Johnson had readied four ships, and this time, the Governor sailed in person as the leader of the expedition. His fleet moved out into the harbor disguised as merchant ships. The pirates, completely deceived, prepared to intercept the vessels; the black flag was run up and the ships were called on to surrender. Johnson replied by raising the King's colors, opening the gun ports, and delivering a stinging broadside to the nearest pirate ship. Before the pirates could recover from their surprise, the Governor's fleet attacked them with unrelenting fury.

Through skillful maneuvering, and spurred on by its desperate plight, the pirate ship managed to escape, heading for the open sea. Johnson gave chase after ordering two of his vessels to remain to take care of the pirate sloop left in the harbor. The pirates on board, knowing what fate would be theirs if they were captured, put up a desperate fight to resist capture. After four hours, however, they were subdued by the Carolina forces.

On the seas, Governor Johnson's determined pursuit of the pirate ship caused the crew to throw overboard its boats and cannon in an effort to gain speed, but this was to no avail. Johnson sailed to within gunshot and opened fire. The pirates struck their flag and surrendered unconditionally. When the Governor's men boarded the craft, it was the Carolinians' turn for a surprise. Secluded in the hold was a crowd of women! The ship which the pirates had appropriated was on a routine trip from London bringing 106 convicts and indentured servants to the colonies of Virginia and Maryland. Thirty-six of this group were women. This was not the end of the surprise; the pirate commander slain in the struggle was not Moody, but the notorious and hunted Richard Worley.

Tally for the chase equalled "two vessels taken; twenty-six pirates, including Worley, killed in the struggle, and several others wounded." Nineteen captives were removed to Charleston where they were tried and received death sentences.

The exultation of the Province over the extermination of the Worley gang was tempered by the realization that Moody was still at large and might at any moment swoop down upon the port. To prevent this occurrence, Johnson resolved to keep his ships mobilized until the immediate danger had passed. Some time afterward, the Province was relieved to learn that Moody, apprised of Charleston's preparations, had decided to take advantage of the royal proclamation of pardon. After plundering one last ship, he had set sail for New Providence to take pardon at the hands of the governor there.

So far, the Province had achieved brilliant success against the pirates, but Johnson "was no dreamer." He would not allow past victories to lull him into a false belief that all was secure, because he knew that the Province was still a prime target for other rovers sailing the seas.

Johnson persisted in trying to secure aid from England; but from the Lords Proprietors, he received only a letter of thanks for his judgment and conduct of actions against the pirates. Johnson was not deterred. With the Council, he again plead to the Crown to supply a ship of war to protect the Province, citing to the Board of Trade the importance of South Carolina to Great Britain, especially to the King's navy. He pointed out that in the preceding year, the Province had produced for export to Britain 32,000 barrels of tar, 20,643 barrels of pitch, and 473 barrels of turpentine, "all Stores very useful for his Majesty's Navy."

At last, action was taken in Great Britain on the repeated requests from Carolina. The Board of Trade requested the Lords Commissioners of the Admiralty to send such assistance as the public service would admit, and the Admiralty agreed to send a frigate there as soon as possible.

Even without this assistance, however, the harbor had been reopened to commerce. In the hour of greatest need, the Lords Proprietors and the Crown had turned a deaf ear. The South Carolinians in time of peril had courageously banded together to relieve their beleaguered settlement, under the leadership of the Governor. Just as he had acted against the Indians, Johnson had also taken the offensive against the pirates, refusing to allow insidious individuals, whether pirates or Indians, to overcome his people.

Nor did he tolerate any "neutralist" position, such as the Creeks had attempted in their effort to hold the balance of power between the French, Spanish, and English colonies. The Governor was equally unrelenting in action against the pirates, despite the fact that some prominent persons, including Colonel William Rhett, tried to intercede on behalf of Stede Bonnet. Bonnet paid the price his crimes demanded.

Despite these accomplishments, Johnson recognized the fact that the Province had not reached a satisfactory level of security, because criminals still sailed the ocean, with reports flowing in of their piratical invasions.

There were no further steps that the Governor could take because the treasury was depleted; and still no word had come that the Admiralty intended to send any assistance. No longer did Johnson lend hope that outside help would come, but instead insisted that Carolinians must provide for themselves. The Assembly was induced to pass a bill providing funds for the payment of debts contracted in the fitting out of the two expeditions.

In one of South Carolina's darkest hours, when pirates ravaged the coastline, as Indians attacked the settlements and the Spanish and French invasion loomed as imminent threats, many citizens were ready to flee the Province. Johnson influenced them to stay, convincing them that they could save themselves, showing them how it could be done.

Most of the early colonies had begun under charters granted to private individuals or to companies; but after 1680, with the growing concern to regulate the commerce of the Empire, it became the policy of the royal government to be more reluctant in the granting of authority to proprietors or companies and, when possible, to bring the already-established charter and proprietary colonies under direct royal control. Because of this policy, Massachusetts and Bermuda lost their charters, and the proprietary charters granted for Pennsylvania and Georgia were much more restrictive. For a time the royal officials toyed with the possiblility of taking over all of the charter and proprietary colonies at one blow. On concluding that such a drastic measure was impractical, the crown adopted the policy of beginning legal proceedings against any charter when its possessors appeared to have violated any of their obligations.

Pertinent to South Carolina, beginning in 1706 there were a number of efforts to overthrow the charter by process of law. These attempts having failed, the royal government in the years 1726–29 entered into negotiations with the Lords Proprietors to purchase the province. In 1704 and 1706 the South Carolina legislature established the Anglican church and attempted to deny political rights to the dissenters. Considering that the Proprietors' approval of these laws was a violation of their charter which had promised religious freedom, the crown instructed the attorney general to begin proceedings to have the charter declared void. These proceedings came to nought largely because of the practical inviolability of the Proprietors who were members of the House of Lords.

The following selection by Charles Christopher Crittenden relates the story of the ultimate downfall of the Proprietary regime.

5

"THE SURRENDER OF
THE CHARTER OF CAROLINA" *

Charles Christopher Crittenden

For a number of years following 1708 the proprietors were allowed to enjoy their rights in peace, and it was not until 1715 that a new attack upon the charter was begun. This attack, like the preceding one, had its beginnings in South Carolina, and was made upon the ground that the proprietors were unable to defend their province, and that therefore the South Carolinians had the right to be brought under the immediate protection of the Crown. In May the Yamassee Indians, former allies of the colonists, opened an attack along the southern and western frontiers. The Indians had available between 8,000 and 10,000 warriors, while the Carolinians could muster only 1,200 able-bodied white men, and thus there was grave danger that the whole settlement, including Charleston, would be wiped out. Urgent appeals for aid were sent to the neighboring colonies and to England.

In the summer of 1715 petitions to the proprietors, the King, the Secretary of State, and the Board of Trade began to arrive in the mother-country. Although the proprietors at once voted to give to the province the use of all quitrents and taxes, this was not one-tenth of what was needed, and in July the Board of Trade took the matter up. The agents of Carolina and the proprietors were called before the Board for discussion as to what steps should be taken, whereupon the proprietors declared that they were unable to protect the province. They had tried to borrow money to finance a relief expedition, they said, by mortgaging their property rights under the charter, but had been unsuccessful because some of their members were minors and could not be bound; and so they were forced to petition that men and money be sent. If they did not repay the money spent in their interest the King would have the right to take the province under

* Excerpts from "The Surrender of the Charter of Carolina," *The North Carolina Historical Review,* I (October 1924), 384–400. Reprinted without footnotes by permission of The State of North Carolina Department of Archives and History.

his immediate protection. When they were asked whether they were willing to surrender the government of Carolina they replied that they had, at great expense, built up a settlement which was very valuable to England, and that they did not wish to give up their control of that settlement except for an "equitable consideration."

Wishing to try all available methods, the agents, seconded by a number of merchants trading with Carolina, on August 2 petitioned the House of Commons to succor the "miserable Inhabitants of that distressed Province." Having considered the matter through one of its committees, the House of Commons addressed the King with a recommendation that aid be sent, and soon afterward the Privy Council ordered that a specially chartered ship carry arms to the province. But what the colony needed most, of course, was men and these could not well be spared just at this time because of a Jacobite uprising in Scotland.

From 1715 until 1719 the inhabitants of South Carolina continued to bombard the authorities in England with petitions. Having discovered that the proprietors were utterly unable to protect them, they began to ask not only that aid be sent, but also, in order to prevent the recurrence of such a situation as then existed, that the province be put under the immediate government of the Crown. The Board of Trade, the Secretary of State, and the King all received a number of these addresses. The British government was, of course, entirely ready to assume control of the province; the trouble was that there seemed to be no suitable means whereby this end could be attained. Certainly it could not be said that the inability of the proprietors to provide for the defense of the province constituted a violation of the charter, especially since they had made all the efforts in its behalf that could reasonably be expected of them. The argument of expediency was the strongest which could be advanced by the advocates of the Crown's assumption of the government. The present owners, they said, could not defend the province; therefore, charter or no charter, it was necessary for the Crown to assume control of the province in order that it might be protected from the attacks of the Indians.

However, it is probable that nothing would have been done for some time to come had not events in South Carolina made it imperative that some action be taken. In 1716 the Assembly, in an effort to provide funds for financing the war, had levied a duty of ten per cent upon all goods imported into, and exported out of, the province. For some reason the act was not sent to the proprietors for their approval, but the Board of Trade heard of its passage and ordered the proprietors to disallow it at once. Thereupon the latter wrote to the governor requiring that this act, together with several others recently passed, be repealed by the assembly. This was adding fuel to the flames. The Carolinians, already out of patience with the proprietors, felt that the disallowance of the laws worked a severe injustice upon the province, and in 1719 the governor and council sent Francis Yonge to represent their grievances to the proprietors. Having arrived in England in May, Yonge at once took the matter up, but was kept waiting for three months, and was finally sent back with sealed letters which, when opened, were found to order, as before, that the laws in question be repealed.

Thereupon the inhabitants of the province decided that, if the British government would not help them, they would help themselves. Having formed a revolutionary organization, on November 28 they sent an address to Governor Johnson, declaring that from that time forth South Carolina was to be under the immediate government of the Crown. The letter requested, however, that Johnson, since his administration had been satisfactory, continue to serve as their governor. The latter had been appointed by the proprietors, and so was forced by a sense of duty to try to maintain their government and to resist this revolutionary movement, but, finding himself without adequate support, he was compelled to retire to his home in the country and let events take their course. Thus the proprietary government was overthrown and, on December 21, a convention meeting in Charleston issued a proclamation to the effect that the proprietors had violated their charter; that henceforth South Carolina was to be under the immediate control of the Crown; and that, until instructions could be had from England, James Moore was to be governor of the province.

When the news of this revolution reached England it became evident that something must be done. The Board of Trade sympathized with the inhabitants of the province in their accusations against the proprietors, who, on the other hand, claimed that the revolution was not due to any misgovernment on their part, but rather to the character of the people of South Carolina who were so unmanageable that it would be impossible for any government to control them. And certainly, when the turbulent condition of the province under a provisional royal governor, 1721-1729, is considered, it seems that it did indeed contain people who were very difficult to hold in check. However, regardless of right or wrong, the fact remained that the government of the proprietors had been overthrown; that they were unable to put down the revolt; and that unless the Crown lent them assistance they probably could not again secure control. The question to be settled was: Would the Crown, as a matter of expediency, be justified in recognizing such a revolutionary movement? For twenty years the Board of trade had been seeking, by one method or another, to bring this province under the immediate government of the King. Now, since it was only necessary to sanction what was already an accomplished fact, it seemed that the opportunity had at last come.

During the spring of 1720 several addresses from the revolutionary assembly of South Carolina arrived in England. These attempted to justify the Carolinians in their recent actions, stated various charges against the government which had been overthrown, and asked that henceforth the King control the province. However, the proprietors, as soon as they learned what had happened, petitioned the King that orders be given for the suppression of the revolt. The various petitions were referred to the Board of Trade, and during the spring and summer of 1720 a number of hearings were held. On August 11, pending a final settlement, the Privy Council commanded that, in consideration of the great importance of Carolina and the acute danger of its being lost at such a critical time, the government be provisionally taken into the hands of his Majesty. And thus a few weeks later General Nicholson was commissioned royal governor of South Carolina.

This action of the Privy Council was based upon an opinion of the Attorney-General and Solicitor-General, dated January 7, 1708, which stated that in cases of "extraordinary exigency" the King might appoint civil governors in the proprietary or corporate colonies—and it certainly did not require any very broad interpretation of that opinion to justify the temporary assumption of the government of South Carolina. The proprietors, of course, opposed such a step, but there was nothing they could do to prevent it and until 1726 they made no very marked effort to regain control of the province. . . .

It seems to have been understood on all sides that the assumption of the government of South Carolina by the Crown was merely a temporary expedient designed to tide over affairs until a definite settlement could be reached. That this was the case is proved by the wording of the order of the Privy Council, which commanded that the government be *provisionally* taken into the hands of his Majesty, and by the fact that the South Carolinians continued to petition that they remain under the control of the Crown. The fact that the proprietors had lost control of the government, however, did not mean that they had surrendered their property rights in the province. All land (except what had already been granted away) remained in their possession, and no grant could lawfully be made without their consent.

In 1720, as in 1706, an attempt was made to vacate the charter by process of law. Upon several occasions the Privy Council summoned the proprietors to a hearing, but each time they asked for delay, saying that Lord Carteret, the Palatine, who was absent, had in his possession papers which they were obliged to have in order to make out a case for themselves. After the hearing had been postponed a number of times, finally, on September 27, the Privy Council, impatient of further delay, ordered the Attorney-General to bring *scire facias* against the charter. The prosecution was never begun, however, possibly because the evidence was thought to be insufficient, possibly because privilege of a peer in Parliament interfered. . . .

After 1720 no further attempt was made to overthrow the charter by process of law. The government of South Carolina remained in the hands of the Crown and for a number of years the proprietors did not make any serious attempt to regain control of the province. In 1726, however, Nicholson, the provisional royal governor, returned to England, whereupon they saw a chance to recover what they considered their rights. In a representation to the Privy Council they took the position that the Crown had appointed a governor merely as a temporary expedient during "some commotions in that Province," and that, since the agitation had quieted down and the provisional governor returned, they had a right to resume the government. They had appointed Samuel Horsey governor, they said, and asked that this appointment be confirmed. This petition was followed by others of a similar nature.

For a time it looked as if the request might be granted. The only way the Crown could justify the assumption of the government was by the "extraordinary exigency" opinion of the Attorney-General and Solicitor-General, and there was some question as to whether conditions in the province could now be called extraordinary. It was quite true, as the proprietors said, that the commotions in the province had quieted down, at least to some extent. However, Yonge, agent for the province, was active in his efforts to prevent the granting of the request. In a memorial to the Privy Council he declared that, were the proprietors permitted to choose the governor, the inhabitants would "speedily fall into the same commotions again." This declaration must have had its effect upon the British government, for, according to a statement of the proprietors, it was owing to the effects of

Yonge that the Board of Trade, on May 21, informed them that their request could not be granted.

But the proprietors, anxious to recover control of the province, on June 26 presented a new memorial, praying that certain articles be introduced into the instructions to the governor of the province, namely: that he be commanded to assist the proprietors in obtaining their just dues and rights granted by his Majesty's predecessor; that he be directed to employ such officers as they had power to appoint by their charter; and that he be instructed to eject from their lands those who, after deposing their governor, had committed various excesses, cutting timber, etc. The petitioners asked, furthermore, to be restored to their ancient inheritance.

The agents for South Carolina did everything in their power in behalf of the province. It was evident, wrote John Sharpe, one of the agents, that the granting of the request would result in a return, for all practical purposes, of the government to the proprietors. The Privy Council was prevailed upon to postpone a final decision until the South Carolinians could have time to return a reply to the memorial, and, this delay having been allowed, Nicholson, who was working in the interest of the province, sent a copy of the petition of the proprietors to the assembly of South Carolina with instructions that a reply be carefully drawn up and sent back as soon as possible. The agents also wrote to the assembly, urging that addresses expressing the loyalty of the province be sent to the President of the Privy Council, the Secretary of State, and the law officers of the Crown. These addresses, it was hoped, would influence the decision of the British government by showing the strong sentiment of the province in favor of being governed directly by the King's officials.

There is some doubt as to just what happened next. There is evidence sufficient to show that the South Carolina assembly carried out the instructions of its agent, replying to the memorial of the proprietors, and affirming the loyalty of the province to the Crown, and that in due time the various addresses were received in England. But here the uncertainty begins. It had been thought that, as soon as these letters were received, the Privy Council would again take the matter up, but there is no record to show that any hearing was held or that any action was taken. However, it stands to reason that something was done and it is almost certain that the proprietors were given to understand, in one way or another, that their petition would not be granted, for on May 31, 1727, they completely changed their tactics by petitioning that the King take the supreme sovereignty of the province into his own hands; which meant, it seems, that they were ready to sell their rights. This new step would hardly have been taken had there been any hope that their request of June 26, 1726, would be granted. . . .

Two factors had combined to prevent an earlier sale. Until 1720 the Crown, hoping to be able to overthrow the charter by act of Parliament or by action at law, had been unwilling to pay what would have been demanded in return for a surrender. After 1720 several years were required for the conclusion to be reached that the only way to gain permanent control of Carolina was to purchase the rights of the proprietors. The latter, for their part, had never been anxious to part with their interests, and it was only when they found that under the provisional government quitrents were not being paid, and furthermore that there was no immediate prospect of their being permitted to reassume control of South Carolina, by far the more valuable of the two provinces, that they were ready to sell.

The offer of the proprietors to surrender their rights completely changed the aspect of the problem and made possible the opening of those negotiations which led to the final agreement. The matter was referred by the Privy Council to its committee, and during 1727 various hearings were held. However, progress was slow, and on October 12 the proprietors again petitioned that the King take the government of South Carolina into his own hands, rather than send a provisional governor thither. Their interests suffered under the temporary arrangement and they wished either to recover all their charter privileges, or else to surrender them completely. Again, in December, they represented their desire that their offer be accepted.

Several similar petitions from the proprietors were presented during the winter of 1727–1728, but no definite step could be taken until they stated the exact terms upon which they would be willing to give up their interest. This they finally did on March 5, 1728, when they proposed a complete and entire surrender of the province in return for a payment to each of them for £2,500. It was at first thought, however, that each proprietor intended to keep the title to those grants of land which had been made to him individually and, since the Crown would hardly have been willing to buy from them under such conditions, it seemed that an understanding was as far distant as ever. When the proprietors were questioned in regard to the matter, however, they declared that [it] was their intention, in case a purchase price could be agreed upon, to surrender not only their joint right in the province but also their separate rights by virtue of any grants. They also requested that assistance be rendered them in collecting arrears in quitrents, whereupon the committee asked them to draw up an account of all such arrears as were due. This estimate, drawn up by the proprietors, stated that, although no exact calculation was possible, the amount due was approximately £9,500, while unsettled claims upon them were thought to be only £4,827. 7s. 1d. It was stated that, if the Crown would pay them £ 5,000 additional, they would turn over all these accounts for settlement. On March 25 these terms of surrender were, upon recommendation of the committee, approved by the Privy Council, and the Treasury was ordered to "consider the properest methods" for the consummation of the bargain.

At this point the difficulty of paying the purchase price arose, and it was thought necessary to ask the House of Commons to authorize the expenditure. Little or no trouble was encountered here, however, for on May 24, only ten days after the appeal had been made, that body in an address to the King declared that "this House will make good the Expense his Majesty shall be at on Account of the said Purchase, out of the next aids to be granted by Parliament." And so on July 13 the Privy Council ordered the Lords of the Treasury to prepare the instruments necessary for the transaction.

Apparently the deal was complete except for the drawing up and signing of the necessary papers, but now another obstacle was encountered. The Attorney-General and Solicitor-General, having investigated the titles of the proprietors, reported to the Lords of the Treasury their opinion that a good title could not be made to the King without an act of Parliament. Thus, during the spring of 1729, a bill prepared by the Attorney-General and Solicitor-General with the assistance of the Solicitor of the Treasury was introduced into Parliament, passed both houses without serious opposition, and received the signature of the King. This act provided for the purchase of the seven shares which belonged to Henry Somerset and Charles Noel Somerset, Joseph Blake, Henry Bertie, James Bertie, Sir John Colleton, William, Lord Craven, and John Cotton. For each share £2,500 was to be paid and, in addition, a lump sum of £5,000 was to be given for the right to all arrears in quitrents, with the understanding that the Crown was to settle all unpaid debts which the proprietors had incurred in connection with Carolina.

John, Lord Carteret, believing that his one-eighth interest in Carolina would eventually become very valuable, refused to surrender his share, and he and his heirs continued to hold it until the American Revolution. He was, however, forced to give up all right of participation in the government.

Part II:
THE ROYAL COLONY AND REVOLUTION

The Lords Proprietors intended that Carolina should be a
plantation colony, producing a staple crop for sale to the mother
country. It was for this reason that they had instructed
Joseph West to operate an experimental farm and to try to
discover the crop most adaptable to the colony. In the late 1600s
the Carolinians found their ideal, "Carolina Golden Rice."
Henry Savage, Jr., uses an interesting literary device to relate
the story of rice planting in South Carolina. Although his
interests center on the Santee River, the story does not vary much
from that of South Carolina rice planting in general.

Rice really was at the very heart of early Carolina. No other
crop closely rivaled it for 100 years. In the nineteenth century
cotton became king, and rice had to give ground. The
author's relating of the race problem to the plantation system
is as accurate as it is interesting.

6

"CAROLINA GOLDEN RICE" *

Henry Savage, Jr.

In sight of the maple-hued expanse of the lower Santee, a dozen miles from its mouth, stand the truncated remains of a giant cypress, surrounded by curiously shaped, rootlike growths, called "breathers" or "cypress knees." Sixty feet above the knee-studded ground a few lateral branches, heavily draped with long pendants of gray moss, still carry their delicate fernlike foliage, bearing alone the whole burden of providing sun life to the great mass of their supporting trunk. The old giant owes its survival through the recent timber-hungry centuries to the fact that its heartwood had rotted away and the timber that could be got from its hollow shell was not worth the great task of felling it. And, because most of the time-telling annual rings that once filled the ten feet of its diameter are gone, its age can only be estimated by comparison with cypresses of similar size, whose soundness invited the loggers' saw. No doubt it was sometime during the period when Europe was vegetating under the paralyzing dark blanket of the Middle Ages that the tiny seed from which it grew spun to a likely spot and became the one in several million of the seeds of its long-gone parent which sprouted and survived its first dangerous years.

Through all the centuries during which it grew from seedling to sapling and finally to its ultimate equivalent of a ten-story building had this old riverside dweller had eyes, few humans would it have seen—an occasional canoe, paddled by naked red men, sometimes a group of them passing en route to or from the seacoast for salt, sting ray spines, sharks' teeth and sea shells, now and then being beached in its shadow for an overnight camp on the nearby bluff. Less frequently, men and fire had appeared together, working together to drive and corral the wild creatures of the forest into the natural trap

* Reprinted from *The Santee* (New York: Rinehart and Company, 1956), pp. 111–23; copyright © 1956 by Henry Savage, Jr. Reprinted by permission of the author.

of the boggy swamp in which it stood. That was all for half a millennium.

But, still supposing the old tree had eyes, as the seventeenth century waned it would have seen more and more of those canoes fashioned from its more perfect brethren of the Santee swamps; but now they are manned by men of other colors. To the red are added white and black—the propelling being done by the red or the black. As time went on less and less red and more and more black.

They passed and passed, upstream and downstream. Then, one day there were those who didn't pass. They pulled their craft in close by the old tree, carried their meager belongings to the nearby bluff and stayed. During the years that followed, a four-room house of squared logs and several sheds of logs roofed with palmetto leaves came to occupy the small clearing which had been wrested from the forest canopy of the bluff. Behind, away from the river, year by year, to the accompaniment of the ring of the broad axes through the smoke of the clearing fires appeared evergrowing openings, as the settlers' axes pushed the forest farther and farther back on the dryer second level of rich alluvial swamp. In the stump-studded red fields, which had so long been the forest floor, rows of corn, peas, and melons, and lawns of grain appeared.

Hark back a score of years and back to Charles Town Harbor. A New England brigantine, Captain John Thurber, master, on a voyage from faraway Madagascar, on the other side of the world, had just put in to the port for supplies and repairs. While awaiting his ship's readiness to put to sea again, Captain Thurber made the acquaintance of some of the leading citizenry of the town, among them being the extraordinary Dr. Henry Woodward, the mentor of the infant colony. As the captain described for the doctor the wonders of the distant island, he told of the wonderful rice grown there by the native blacks, some of which he had purchased to round out his cargo. The ever-alert Woodward was greatly interested and expressed a desire to make a trial planting here in Carolina. Grateful for the hospitality which had been accorded him, the Captain obliged with the offer of a small sack of the unhusked grain. Woodward and several of his friends with whom he divided his gift planted these seeds from Madagascar, and from them grew Carolina golden rice. And from these tiny beginnings, the rice fields spread—up the rivers, over to and up the nearby rivers, and, in later years, up into North Carolina and down into Georgia.

So one day, about the year 1705, the master of the log house on the bluff began to give intent attention to the boggy acres which extended quite a way downstream from where the old tree stood and through which a sluggish stream ran its devious course, from its source in a large elliptical savanna back in the pine flats beyond the river swamp to where it ran into the river some distance below. Then in a little while this saturated swamp area was seething with activity. Uncouth black men speaking in strange tongues, and powerful oxen, both doing the bidding of white taskmakers—hacking, hewing and hauling—building an earthen dam from the bluff, downstream to the next bluff below. It was the fortuitous salvation of the old cypress that, by its being left on the river side of the earthwork, the dam would be shortened; and at the same time the necessity of removing it and ditching through the great roots from which sprang the miniature steeples of its obtruding knees would be avoided.

When the dam was completed all the way down, omitting only the spot where the stream entered the river, the work was concentrated there. Piling and thick heart pine and cypress planks were driven into the soft earth, and upon this embedded foundation a stout wooden sluice was constructed. Either end of the sluice or "trunk" was then equipped with a massive hanging door; the one on the river end would be automatically closed by the pressure of the rising water as the flowing tide ran up the river and would open and let out any accumulated water in the dammed-off area as the counter pressure was reduced when the tide ebbed. The inside gate worked in exactly the reverse manner. Either gate could be made inoperative by raising. Gates so constructed could be used to catch automatically and to hold high tides in the dammed-off area or else, by letting only the outside one function, the low level could be maintained inside, allowing the enclosed area to dry out.

When this ingenious structure was completed, the outside gate was commissioned and in a matter of a few ebb tides the dam-enclosed area was free of all standing water. Soon men and animals could find there earth that would sustain their weight. Then came the incredibly arduous undertaking of removing from the enclosure the subtropical jungle it bore: great trees, stumps and all; underbrush; tough, hard-to-kill grapevines; the deep-bedded giant tubers of the smilax; and the wire-tough network of the native bamboo. The amazing feature of such an undertaking is that anyone without the aid of the most modern machine equipment would dare to try it. But the dauntless spirit that had brought the river settlers from far mellower places to this raw region was not cowed by the prospect. Since daring to try was their greatest hurdle, they succeeded. The jungle was felled, dried and burned. The stumps, roots and tubers were painstakingly grubbed out. At last, behind the dam running between the bluffs the old cypress looked down on a flat, dark-chocolate field of some hundred acres, cleft through its middle by the snakelike channel of the stream.

But the objective of all this effort, a producing rice field, was still far from attained. First the meandering stream through the field must, by backbreaking digging with mattocks and shovels, be converted into a straight ample canal. Around the whole field a lesser canal would have to be dug and the excavated earth spread evenly over the fields. Between these there would then have to be a grid of smaller ditches or "quarter divides," located about fifty feet apart, to round out the aqueduct system necessary for a finished rice field to provide drainage, irrigation or flooding as needed.

When the last redolent golden tubes of jessamine are falling and the snowy sepals of the flowering dogwood are being suppressed by the sudden unfurling of its fresh green leaves, it is rice planting time. Painstakingly, in shallow drills a few inches apart the selected seeds are dropped and lightly covered. To stimulate sprouting, kill the challenging weeds and protect the seeds from the birds, the field is flooded for a few days as soon as the planting is completed. Growth is stimulated and the crop protected by hoeing and periodic flooding, through the growing season. Finally as the long, hot summer draws to a close, if by the grace of God the region has escaped that scourge of the rice planter, a tropical hurricane, the old cypress will look down on a waving golden sea of ripened grain, forty bushels of heavy grain to the acre. Singing bands of brightly clad slaves, men and women, swinging shining hooks, cut and stack the harvest. From the field to the threshing shed go the laden carts, carrying in the cut of the previous day. In the shed, through the long hot day, the most powerful of the slaves, with long flails, beat the golden grain from the straw. Through the fall and into the winter in wooden mortars the husks will be pounded from the kernels, the most tedious task of all.

Finally, one winter day, several oversize dugouts will tie up at the little wharf at the rise of the bluff and take aboard their golden cargo —to be poled downstream and through the back waters to Charles Town, fifty miles away. There part will be delivered to the colonial authorities for the quitrents due by the planter to his absentee landlords, the Lords Proprietors, and the rest will be delivered to the warehouse of the planter's factor for shipment to England.

As the years passed, the name Carolina Golden Rice was to prove symbolic indeed of the worth of the crop. The old tree would see rooms added to the planter's house and neat white weatherboarding placed over its hewn log walls. Two long rows of slave quarters facing each other with a "street" between would rise at a respectful distance to the rear. Where another creek entered the river, a substantial mill would be built with a great undershot water wheel supplying its power, whenever the tide was either rising or falling, saving greatly the tedious labor of preparing the grain for market.

Years later a handsome mansion adorned with superbly fashioned woodwork would replace the origional home of the master. Extensive stables would be added to the outbuildings behind the great house. Coaches and carriages would come and go as roads released the plantation from its former riverbound existence. To avoid the deadly fevers which were associated with the proximity of rice fields, to flee the oppressive heat of the humid swamps, and to get a taste of urban society, which the isolation of plantation life did not permit, the rice planters would take their families elsewhere for the summer months. From the Santee plantations, many would go to beach homes on Cedar Island at the mouth of the river, for from there the planter could by boat continue to visit and supervise the plantation.

At other seasons, festive occasions would become frequent, while an increasing number of black men toiled their lives away to support the elegant but extravagant society of these river planters.

There were less spectacular but more significant changes occurring on the tawny waters of the great river itself. Almost a century after the first rice dams were being built, there passed downstream a barge heavy-laden with cotton bales and navigated by a stout slave crew wielding long poles. In the years that followed, the passing of such craft became commonplace until they were diverted by the completion of the Santee Canal. It was those cotton barges that proclaimed that a new king was challenging the long rule of rice, and there could be no joint rule. It was one or the other. As the cotton shipments increased, the river grew ever muddier. Freshets increased in frequency and severity, as the forest and grass cover were stripped from more and more of the watershed upriver to prepare the land for the clean-tilled fields of cotton.

The rice planters raised their dams again and again, but the height of the floodwater level rose even faster. More and more frequently crops were lost to August floods, and there was still, even as always, the threat of the September hurricanes.

Yes, old King Rice was already ailing when the challenge of the

young king came forcibly to bear. The first generation of free Negroes
were far inferior to their forebears as laborers. The wages paid by the
booming logging business was attracting the best of them, leaving
the less energetic on the plantations. More efficient methods of culture could be used in the extensive new rice areas of Louisiana and
so reduce the price that there was little profit left in the crop for the
Carolina planters. Consequently it took but the *coup de grace* of the
growing freshet menace, coupled with a series of severe tropical storms,
to bury the monarch beneath his own rubbish-strewn fields.

As August, 1893, drew to a close, the old cypress surveyed a bountiful crop of yellowing grain waving in the summer breezes that gently
swept the field, whose clearing it had witnessed almost two centuries
before. High in the air, fluffy clouds sailed across the sky at an uncanny pace, considering the gentleness of the breeze which fanned
the tree's delicate foliage. The breeze stiffened and became gusty.
The clouds lowered and thickened until they scudded across the sky
loosing intermittent showers. In spite of the wind, an oppressive
humidity gave a sort of staleness to the air. Through the day the
wind rose to a gusty gale as the intermittent showers changed into
a slashing downpour, blotting all view of the field below. Through
the night and all through the next day, the tempo of the storm
mounted. The night of the second day the tide which backed up the
river almost topped the protecting dam. And when it was due to
ebb, the water level did not drop. The furious east wind driving up
the river was building a powerful, even though vaporous, dam across
the river's mouth. The next wind-assisted flowing tide met the rain-
swollen volume of the river, cluttered with floating logs, uprooted
trees and all manner of rubbish. Higher rose the muddy floodwater—
over the pitifully inadequate dams, ripping great holes here and there
as seething torrents rushed in over the flattened and broken remains
of what, but two days before, had been the hope and subsistence of a
whole community. And with the crops those brown floodwaters sub-
merged the graceful society which for more than a century and a
half had dominated first a colonial province and then a proud state.

As the storm passed and the sun broke through the melting clouds,
it shone mercilessly on a scene of awful devastation on every hand.
Muddy water, miles of it, extended in all directions, over the fields
and under the forests, into the "street" of the now shabby half-
abandoned slave quarters, around the foundations of the great house
on the bluff, into the stables, halfway up the side of the old rice-
mill. Great trees by the thousands lay uprooted or cocked at angles

against stouter sustaining neighbors. Others, whose roots had held, were broken and torn. And for the giant old cypress, it was the end of glory. No longer would it be a river landmark. Midway its height, the hollow bole had proved too weak to stand the ninety-mile-an-hour gust which struck when the storm reached the height of its fury. With a resounding crack the wind had snatched its upper sixty feet, hurling it a full five hundred yards to the middle of the park-like lawn which stretched from the great house to the riverbank.

Even in the Low Country, where the atmosphere of timelessness is its greatest fascination, time inexorably moves on, ever taking its toll as it flows by. Three decades after the storm that gave the final, mortal blow to rice culture in what had been the principal rice-growing area of the Western Hemisphere, discouragement, retrogression and decay were all-pervading across the entire Low Country. When plantation houses burned, they were rarely, if ever, rebuilt. Instead, the owners either moved into the empty overseer's house, which was now more appropriate to their reduced circumstances, or they gave up the struggle against too much water and a forest too ready to take back to itself the rich domain it had formerly held, and moved away to find a new way of life in the cities or on the more easily tilled but less fertile higher country away from the river. Those places which fire, through the years, had spared, were left to the slower but no less relentless action of decay, where the means of maintenance are absent. The elements soon substituted unkempt ghostliness for beautiful splendor. The battered, sagging out-buildings rapidly diminished in number as they consumed each other, the material from the less essential being torn away to repair the more essential.

The house on the bluff by the remains of the old cypress was among those few which were left to the insidious hand of the elements. There it stood amid the great, somber, moss-draped live oaks, which rose from a weed- and brush-cluttered lawn—in spots even now giving the appearance of a lawn thanks to the herd of goats roaming the place unmolested. There it stood, gray and gaunt, with crooked brow and vacant stare, shutters gone, the once imposing portico sagging and windows all but paneless. It was 1925, when most of the country was fairly drunk with prosperity. As the exuberant waves of plenty rolled, bits of their spray fell even on this now nearly forsaken lower Santee. With money guaranteed from the humming East and North came tycoons, still insatiable, now possessed with a contradictory yearning for the glamorized version of the way of life of the rice tycoons of a day long gone.

Because its boards and mortar gave it a continuity with a proud and romantic past—of which many of the tycoons felt the lack—it was inevitable that to this place a backwash of the prosperity would sweep. And so it did. As the leaves on the few remaining limbs of the old tree yellowed with the first frost, at long last there was once more a hum of activity on the bluff. Architects, restorers, artisans, interior decorators, tree surgeons, and others directed their forces. The grounds were searched for every discarded old brick, the cellars for the cast-off remains of household articles of the long gone planters, that they might be carefully restored or duplicated. Finally, to the rice fields came an assortment of machines, purring and belching, rebuilding the broken dams and gates, that the old rice field might be planted and its crops purposely flooded, unharvested, to entice the mallards, the scaups, and the widgeons into the range of the new "planter's" guns. All in a futile attempt to restore an environment which being dead could never be truly revived, for the essential of that environment was not tangible.

The arduous and hazardous way of life of the rice planters was dead and buried—but here and there magnificent snowy monuments to it were being carefully maintained.

By way of epitaph—which will not be found subscribed in words upon these monuments to their vanished glory—it should be recorded that interred here in this rich brown earth is a civilization which had far more significance than simply being the inspiration for a never-ending stream of romantic novels. To perform the gargantuan tasks of wresting the rice fields from their jungle state, to supply the endless labor in those stifling, insect-ridden, miasmic fields, and to provide servants to wait upon the households of the planters to whom the profits of all this labor flowed, an enormous number of Negro slaves were required on the rice plantations. Consequently, in the last analysis, to the rice plantations can be traced a large part of the race problems which have been the heritage of the South even to this day. And with those black slaves came another heritage which was to curse the South for two centuries. From the Gold Coast, the Ivory Coast, Nigeria, and the Cameroons, in their veins came the germs of the malarias which were indigenous to those faraway lands. Here, through the ubiquitous mosquitoes of the Low Country, those germs were transmitted to the susceptible whites, decimating and chronically disabling the best human stock of the region.

Finally, yet another fact might have been added to that epitaph. The vast supply of cheap Negro labor with which the exigencies of rice growing endowed the Low Country has even to this day so discouraged the immigration of other labor into the area, that, except for such as are based on local resources, industry has avoided the whole so-called "Black Belt," to the end that that balance of industry and agriculture essential for economic good health is still lacking there.

In 1729 South Carolina became a royal colony under the governorship of Robert Johnson, who was also the last Proprietary governor. The ten-year interim since the Revolution of 1719 had been unsettling to the colony in many ways. Governor Johnson and his successors were faced with the responsibilities of supervising the colony's adjustment of such problems as the contested land titles, relations with the Indians, relations with the neighboring Spanish and French, the settlement of the interior townships, concern over the large number of Negro slaves present in the colony, and the founding of the colony of Georgia. These adjustments were obviously rather successful, because by 1750 the colony had achieved a very real measure of stability and prosperity.

In politics the most significant development was the growth of the power of the Commons House of Assembly. By mid-century this lower house of the legislature was challenging the traditional power of the governor and of the governor's council, normally representative of the colony's wealthy gentry. The government and society was so remarkably concentrated in Charleston that some have spoken of colonial South Carolina as a city-state. This selection by Eugene Sirmans gives an interesting insight to the colony in the mid-1700s.

7

"THE COLONY AT MID-CENTURY" *

M. Eugene Sirmans

By the middle of the eighteenth century South Carolina had grown up as a colony. The frontier outpost of 1670 or even of 1700 had long since disappeared and been replaced by a more sophisticated and more complex society. Indeed, South Carolina's society and economy had reached an advanced stage of maturity that did not change markedly again until after the American Revolution. The colony had built up a prosperous economy based on a variety of staple products. In turn, economic prosperity had given many white Carolinians the opportunity to improve their social positions and the time to enlarge the scope of their social activities. A few critics grumbled at the ways in which leisure was used, but Charles Town became a social capital as well as a major port.

South Carolina's political institutions had likewise matured, although they continued to change more rapidly than either economic or social customs. The governor was still the central figure in politics, and his office had changed little since the establishment of royal government. Change was more evident in the council and Commons House. Each house had developed its own set of traditions, notably a tradition of freedom from outside interference, and its own methods of procedure, especially the elaborate network of committees in the Commons House. Other parts of the government, such as the court system and local administration, had matured less fully and remained in a rather primitive state. The governor, council, and lower house continued to be the most important elements in the provincial government, and as such they deserve more careful consideration than other political institutions.

The increasing maturity of political institutions in eighteenth-century South Carolina coincided with a remarkable economic expansion which created the most affluent society among the English settlements on the American mainland. Life in South Carolina at mid-century rested upon a bedrock of economic prosperity, and widespread prosperity generally kept economic issues out of politics. The colony reaped profits from a varied economy that drew returns from the Indian trade, livestock, and timber as well as rice, and the introduction of indigo in the 1740's gave the economy even greater variety and stability. Consequently, South Carolina enjoyed a prosperity that could be matched by few other colonies, if any, and the good times lasted without interruption until the Revolution, except for a recession in the middle and late 1740's. Individual Carolinians amassed some of the largest private fortunes in the colonies and the Carolina low country gloried in the highest per capita income in America. The assembly in 1742 calaculated the total value of property in South Carolina at £15,000,000 currency, or about £2,000,000 sterling. With a white population of about 20,000, the assembly's estimate indicates that the average value of the property belonging to white families would have been about £4,500 currency (£600 sterling) per family.

Not every colonist, of course, struck it rich in South Carolina. Men often extended their credit too far, especially in order to buy slaves, and went bankrupt. Creditor's auctions were all too common during the recession of the 1740's, but the bankruptcy of a few men should not obscure the basic prosperity of the colony. The debts of South Carolinians never approached the size of those of Virginia planters, and the health of the South Carolina economy made it possible for a good businessman to amass a fortune quickly. According to some of the colonists, an intelligent planter could often regain his initial investment in land and slaves within three or four years.

A key figure in the provincial economy was the lowcountry planter, who might own as many as a dozen plantations and five hundred slaves. Wealthy planters preferred to buy several small plantations, rather than a single large one, because rice was most profitably grown in comparatively small units. Consequently, the planters of South Carolina, unlike those of Virginia, could not supervise their plantations in person and made a practice of hiring overseers. They usually placed about thirty slaves and a white overseer on each of their plantations. Nor did the consignment system, so familiar in Virginia, develop in South Carolina. After harvesting his crop the rice planter either sold it to a Charles Town merchant or made his own arrangements for shipment. The poorer lowcountry planters could not afford overseers and directed their farms themselves, but even the poorest of them owned two or three slaves. They sold their produce to middlemen called "country factors," who resold it in Charles Town and then brought goods from the city to the outlying plantations. Farmers who lived in the townships led a harder life than any of the lowcountry planters. They owned few slaves or none at all, tilled the land themselves, raised livestock, and grew wheat, corn, and vegetables. The township farmers lived on the edge of poverty for years, but in the 1740's they began to enjoy a modest prosperity by selling foodstuffs to the lowcountry.

The second key figure in the provincial economy was the merchant, the prototype of the individual entrepreneur who sat in a small countinghouse and carried on a world-wide correspondence. Most mercantile offices were in Charles Town, but there was enough trade at Beaufort and George Town to support a few businesses there, too. Whatever his location, the merchant was a jack of all trades. He imported slaves, English goods, rum, wine, and other wares and exported rice, deerskins from the Indian trade, lumber, and, beginning in the 1740's, indigo. He often accepted commissions from London or Bristol merchants, but he was never a factor in the sense of being a permanent representative of a single British firm. If he were one of the wealthier merchants, however, he might have a partner in England, most likely a relative. He owned few ships, if any, and usually rented space for his cargoes from English and northern sea captains. Two of the busiest merchants in the 1730's and 1740's were Joseph Wragg and Gabriel Manigault, and their business typified the trade of Charles Town. During the fiscal year 1735–1736, according to records kept by the public treasurer, Wragg imported 6,230 gallons of rum from Antigua and Barbados, 341 slaves from Africa, and paid duties amounting to £296 currency on sundries imported from Philadelphia and Barbados. He exported 6,095 deerskins to Bristol and London. Manigault eschewed the slave trade, but in the same year he imported 11,333 gallons of rum from Barbados and Antigua and paid £640 in duties on goods from Barbados, New York, Philadelphia, Jamaica, and Madeira. He exported 6,600 pounds of leather to Barbados. Both men also exported rice and imported English goods, but the provincial treasurer did not keep records of these goods because there were no duties on them.

Economic differences divided South Carolina's white population into social classes whose existence was generally recognized although men disagreed on the number and composition of classes. Governor James Glen divided the whites into four groups. He said there were five thousand people "who have plenty of the good things of Life," another five thousand "who have some of the Conveniencys of Life," ten thousand "who have the Necessarys of Life," and five to six thousand "who have a bare subsistance." Other writers simply divided the white population into the rich and the poor; there was no middle class except for a few artisans in Charles Town. When contemporaries referred to the upper class by name, they most often called it the gentry, and because of South Carolina's wealth, an unusually large number of people had the money necessary to claim membership in that class. According to a reliable observer, Dr. George Milligen, "The Men and Women who have a Right to the Class of Gentry . . . are more numerous here than in any other Colony in *North-America*." Differences between classes were well understood. For example, Lieutenant Governor William Bull, Sr., often invited the congregation of Prince William's Parish to Sheldon plantation after Sunday services. He received the gentry himself inside his house, while the rest of the parishioners remained outside and were entertained by his overseer. Although class distinctions were recognized, class lines were not rigid, because economic prosperity enabled many men to accumulate fortunes and to rise into the gentry in the middle of the eighteenth century. Among them were such well-known South Carolinians as Gabriel Manigault, Charles Pinckney, Andrew Rutledge, and Henry Laurens.

Social life in South Carolina was dominated by the gentry, the five thousand or so whites who had "plenty of the good things of Life." Like most colonists who had money the South Carolina gentry tried to reproduce the life of the English gentry. They imitated English fashions and amusements, and they bought English goods whenever possible. There were still traces of a Barbadian influence in South Carolina, as the people retained some West Indian customs and blended them with English imitation. Such blending was most obvious in architecture, for South Carolinians usually added West Indian piazzas to their Georgian houses. Visitors to the colony often found the people to be irresponsible pleasure-seekers; for example, Josiah Quincy, Jr., a native of Massachusetts who visited South Carolina in 1773, said, "State, magnificence and ostentation, the natural attendants of riches, are conspicuous among this people. . . . Cards, dice, the bottle and horses engross prodigious portions of time and attention: the gentlemen (planters and merchants) are mostly men of the turf and gamesters." Wealth and the employment of overseers freed South Carolinians from constant attention to work, and unlike many people in the northern colonies, they lacked a strong puritanical sense of moral duty. Pleasure became the goal of social life, and as Eliza

Lucas complained, "It is become so much the fashion now to say everybody that is greave [grave] is religiously mad." The high style of living and the quest for pleasure shocked native conservatives as well as visitors; Chief Justice Benjamin Whitaker once used his annual address to the grand jury as the occasion to deliver an exhortation to the people of the colony "to return to our former Frugality, Temperance and moderate Enjoyments."

If a South Carolinian was looking for pleasure, Charles Town was the place to find it. An excellent system of roads made it easy for planters to travel to the city, and in the 1750's they began to build town houses there. Every winter the roads were crowded with planters and their families on their way to town for the annual social season, which began in January and lasted into the spring. When they arrived they were soon caught up in a social whirl that was hectic, fast-paced, and exuberant. South Carolinians were the most socially minded people in colonial America. They delighted in the theater and in music. Professional actors appeared more often in Charles Town than anywhere else in the colonies, and the best musicians in America were more likely to perform there than elsewhere. The St. Cecilia Society was the first musical society organized in America. Moreover, Carolinians were not content merely to listen to music. They danced better and more often than any other colonists; too often, perhaps, for Henry Laurens once complained that the Commons House was planning to adjourn early so that its members could attend a ball. It was often said that during the social season a South Carolina gentleman could be found anywhere except at home. He was most likely to be found at his club, or rather, at *one* of his clubs, for another Charles Town superlative was its incredible number of clubs. There was a club devoted to smoking, another to beefsteak, and a third to laughing. Other clubs were known simply as the Monday Night and Friday Night Clubs. If a gentleman could not be found at his club, the next place to look for him was the race track. The sport of kings was popular in Charles Town throughout the middle decades of the eighteenth century. The purse for a race occasionally amounted to £1,000 sterling, horses often sold for £300, and as much as £2,000 might be bet on a single race. Henry Laurens, who could be a kill-joy when he wanted, once lamented the fact that he could not get a ship unloaded because his workmen had gone to the races.

Life on the plantations moved at a more leisurely pace. Planters who lived near the colony's borders suffered from the same kind of isolation that plagued Virginia planters. Most of the lowcountry was more thickly settled, however, and isolation was not a problem for the majority of planters. Eliza Lucas Pinckney has left us a charming picture of the normal pattern of life on a lowcountry plantation. A half-dozen families lived near the Pinckneys, and there was frequent visiting back and forth. When they were alone the Pinckneys enjoyed playing musical instruments, tending their formal garden, and reading from the works of such authors as Virgil, John Milton, John Locke, Joseph Addison, Alexander Pope, and Samuel Richardson.

In a pleasure-seeking society like South Carolina, it is not surprising that the people neglected religion. Josiah Quincy, Jr., said, "The state of religion here is repugnant not only to the ordinances and institutions of Jesus Christ, but to every law of sound policy." Quincy undoubtedly exaggerated, but many clergymen echoed his criticism. One Anglican rector inveighed against the "fashionable principles of Libertinism and infidelity"; a second was upset because the "People are not much given to marriage"; and a third reported that in all the marriages he had performed during the last year only two or three of the brides had not been pregnant.

Symptomatic of South Carolina's religious indifference was the failure of the Great Awakening to have any lasting impact on the colony. Despite three visits from George Whitefield the religious revival affected South Carolina less than any other mainland colony. Whitefield's failure was not due entirely to religious indifference, however, for he also faced two other insuperable obstacles. The first was the opposition of Anglican Commissary Alexander Garden. Whitefield's official position was that of rector to the Anglican church at Savannah, a circumstance which placed him under Garden's jurisdiction. When Whitefield's sermons in Charles Town antagonized Garden, the commissary simply hauled Whitefield before an ecclesiastical court and had him suspended from his office. The second obstacle was ridiculous, but perhaps even more decisive. Whitefield's chief disciple in South Carolina was a planter named Hugh Bryan, a religious mystic who let his evangelical fervor get the better of him. He preached to Negro slaves and predicted that they would revolt against their masters and win their freedom. For this he was forced to appear before the assembly, where he promised to mend his ways. Instead, Bryan convinced himself that he was endowed with supernatural powers. He tried, like Moses, to divide the waters of a river with a wand, and when that failed he tried to walk across the river on top of the water. When news of Bryan's misadventures spread throughout the colony, he became the laughingstock of South Carolina and thereafter few people were able to take evangelism seriously.

The religious indifference of South Carolina was matched by a pervasive intellectual indifference. The colony's active social life left little time for intellectual pursuits, and few Carolinians made the effort necessary to fit such activities into their crowded schedules. There were, however, two groups that stood out as notable exceptions to this generalization. The first were the colony's physicians, who took an active interest in science, especially botany and zoölogy. The doctors often collected specimens of South Carolina's flora and fauna and sent them to scientists in Europe, and one South Carolina physician, Dr. Alexander Garden, won an international reputation for himself as a biologist. The second group consisted of the merchants, artisans, and professional men who belonged to the Charles Town Library Society. Organized in 1748, the society loaned books to the general public and sponsored scientific experiments. Such men were exceptional, however, and it was more typical of South Carolina that the colony neglected education even by the low standards of the eighteenth century. There were free grammar schools in Charles Town and a few of the rural parishes, but the assembly was notoriously unwilling to spend money on schools and repeatedly turned down petitions to establish them. Rich planters and merchants hired tutors and sent their children to England, but the children of the poor could only attend an inadequate grammar school at best. At worst, in most of the rural parishes, they could not even learn to read and write.

Thus the society of South Carolina was characterized by a wholehearted devotion to amusement and the neglect of religion and intellectual pursuits. Economic affluence certainly contributed to the formation of such a society, but an even more basic reason for the development of the Carolina society can be found in the colony's religious tradition. The New England and middle colonies had been founded by Calvinistic or pietistic religious dissenters, who took a stern view of earthly pleasures but at the same time believed in the need for an educated clergy and laity. By contrast, South Carolina at mid-century was predominantly Anglican, and the Church of England made little effort either to regulate the lives of its communicants or to promote intellectual pursuits. Consequently, while colonies like Massachusetts and Pennsylvania had produced socially dull but mentally stimulating societies, South Carolina had developed in just the opposite direction.

In the mid-1700s the relations between the colonies and England were generally happy. Both the Americans and the mother country prospered from the imperial connection. It is true that Parliament had passed the first Navigation Act in 1651, and that later Navigation laws added to the mercantilistic attempt to control the trade of the colonies for the benefit of England. However, the royal government made little effort to enforce these laws, and the colonials enjoyed a state of "salutary neglect."

The Treaty of Paris of 1763, which ended the French and Indian War, doomed this happy relationship. The British now found themselves the possessors of a great empire and of a large war debt. Faced with the expensive task of protecting and governing the widespread colonies, the ministry reasoned that the Americans, who shared in the benefits of the victory over the French and who enjoyed the protection of the royal navy and army, should accordingly bear a portion of the imperial expenses. Beginning with the Sugar Act of 1764, the British began to tax the Americans. Essentially, the difficulty arose from the fact that the colonials also shared in the English political traditions, and one of those traditional rights was that of representative government. The colonials argued that they, as English subjects, could not be taxed by a legislature which did not actually represent the people of the colonies. Hence, the revolutionaries developed the shibboleth, "Taxation without representation is tyranny." The Stamp Act of 1765 required the colonials to purchase revenue stamps for newspapers, playing cards, diplomas, and various legal documents. Opposition to the Stamp Act began the process of unifying the colonies against the mother country. The following study of Christopher Gadsden, one of this colony's most important radicals, relates the South Carolina reaction to the Stamp Act.

8

"CHRISTOPHER GADSDEN AND THE STAMP ACT" *

Robert H. Woody

Grenville's proposed stamp tax on America did not go unchallenged in South Carolina. A letter to Charles Garth, the colonial agent, found among the papers of Christopher Gadsden, made it clear that a committee of the House, of which Gadsden was a member, thought Garth's letter on the subject "so alarming and important that they prayed the special direction of the House," which could not be given before Lieutenant-Governor Bull prorogued the House. The committee, however, proceeded to give "the principal reason" against the measure as "its inconsistency with that inherent right of every British subject, not to be taxed but by his own consent. . . ." Other objections included the difficulty with which the existing provincial taxes were paid, they being greater, "in proportion to the value of our estates . . . than the land tax raised in Great Britain"; the fact that "almost all" the goods exported were on the enumerated list; the danger from Indian attacks; a tender regard for the people of the back country; the sickliness of the climate; the expensive way of living in the province; and the necessity of keeping up the spirits of the people. All alike made it hard to believe that Parliament, "instead of alleviating, parent-like, the many hardships and difficulties . . . will endeavor still to augment them, and that to a degree so as to reduce us almost to despair. . . ."

There can be little doubt that Gadsden was a prime mover among those who urged the assembly to heed the call of Massachusetts for a general congress. Captain Gadsden, for the committee appointed to consider the proposal, recommended that South Carolina appoint a committee to meet with the others in New York in October. At the age of forty-one, Gadsden had had an active and varied career.

* Reprinted from *The Proceedings of the South Carolina Historical Association, 1939* (Columbia: South Carolina Historical Association, 1939), pp. 3–12; copyright, 1939, by The South Carolina Historical Association. Reprinted by permission of The South Carolina Historical Association.

His brief service in the navy and his more active military career demonstrated a martial spirit; his controversy with Grant and Laurens in regard to the Cherokee war bespoke a man of courage; the Boone controversy, in which Gadsden was a central figure, suggested a certain stubbornness and impetuosity. Ramsay, who was well acquainted with him, stated that he had "a strong love for independence," was a "born republican," and "could not brook the encroachments of any man or body of men intrenching on his rights." Many years later Gadsden wrote William Henry Drayton that "No man in America strove more (and more successfully) first to bring about a Congress in 1765, and then to support it afterwards than myself."

On August 8 a committee consisting of Gadsden, Thomas Lynch, and John Rutledge was appointed to attend the Stamp Act Congress, and upon learning of their arrival at New York on September 15 Captain Gadsden's Artillery Company "fired 3 vollies of small arms, upon the joyful news. . . ."

To state "the rights and grievances of the colonists," and to prepare petitions to the King, the Lords, and the Commons, at this critical time, without claiming too little or too much, and in a period of two weeks, required able men. Two of South Carolina's delegates, Lynch and Rutledge, were chosen to head the committees drafting the addresses to the Lords and the Commons. Gadsden was ready to deny the sovereignty of Parliament, as colonial rights were held only from the King, but he was willing to acquiesce in the power of Parliament to regulate trade. Since South Carolina had no charter, Gadsden did not wish to see too much dependence placed on their protective power. "I have ever been of opinion," he said, "that we should all endeavor to stand upon the broad and common ground of those natural and inherent rights that we all feel and know, as men and as descendants of Englishmen," and he had "always thought this bottom amply sufficient for our future importance." The charters, being different in different colonies, were in danger of being "the political trap that will ensnare us at last by drawing different colonies upon that account to act differently in this great and common cause, and whenever that is the case, all will be over with the whole." To Gadsden's mind the union of the colonies was essential, for "That province that endeavors to act separately will certainly gain nothing by it," he wrote to Garth. "There ought to be no New England men, no New Yorker, etc., known on the Continent, but all of us Americans."

Gadsden returned to Charleston on November 13, 1765, to find that the city had been the scene of a degree of excitement and turmoil the like of which had not been seen since the revolution of 1719. Despite the fact of Gadsden's absence, there is reason to think that the Sons of Liberty, who were responsible for most of the disturbance, were under his guidance; at least no one else can be called the prime mover of the enterprise. When the Sons of Liberty were first organized, and by whom, is an unanswered question, but Gadsden's Artillery Company would have been a splendid nucleus for such an organization.

The Stamp Act was to go into effect November 1, and on October 19, the day after the arrival of the stamps, William Bull took the oath to enforce it, as a member of his Council "Observed that . . . there . . . [was] some appearance of disturbance being Committed by giddy minded and evil disposed persons in consequence of the Arrival of the Stamps." That these "giddy minded" persons were not to be taken lightly was soon evident, for the distributor of the stamps was hanged in effigy in the center of town, and in the evening a large procession demanded that the residence of George Saxby, the supposed distributor of the stamps, be opened for a searching party; later the effigies were committed to the flames, and a coffin inscribed "American Liberty" was decently buried. These proceedings brought an ironical comment from Henry Laurens who "saw not the farce" but was convinced by "some sensible men" that "Six Men of Spirit could have in the beginning have crushed the whole shew." But "meeting with no opposition they carried their point . . . & those Sons of Liberty as they stile themselves or as others call them Devil Burners, did not close the play in Defence of Liberty before they had most shamelessly given the Lie to their pretended Patriotism" and had "committed unbounded acts of Licentiousness & at length Burglary & Robbery. . . ."

But it was not sufficient for Laurens to confine his thoughts to private letters, for on the evening of October 23 the mob appeared at his house and demanded the privilege of searching it for stamps. This he was able to prevent, but one of the crowd, taking hold of his shoulders, "said they loved me and everybody would love me if I did not hold way with one Govr. Grant. This provoked me not a little as it exhibited to me the cloven foot of a certain malicious villain acting behind the curtain." The reference to Grant, around whom centered the first Laurens-Gadsden quarrel, left no doubt in Laurens' mind that Gadsden was the man who "could be reached only by suspicion." Laurens' long-standing enmity with Gadsden, linked

with the circumstantial evidence, gives much reason to think that
Laurens was correct in this suspicion. After making Chief Justice
Skinner drink "Damnation to the Stamp Act" the crowd went home;
by the first of the week the stamp inspector, Saxby, and the stamp
distributor, Caleb Lloyd, had given a "voluntary" declaration that
they would suspend the duties of their office.

When the assembly convened on November 26, Gadsden presented
a report of the proceedings of the Congress which were approved
unanimously (with the exception of William Wragg), and the next
day, as Gadsden was pleased to tell Garth, "the House did us the
honor to give us their thanks . . . in the most ample and obliging
manner." On the twenty-ninth Gadsden was named chairman of a
committee "to draw up such particular Resolutions on the present
occasion as were thought necessary" respecting the several acts of
Parliament. The committee, in practically the same terms as the
addresses of Congress, stated "their most essential rights and liberties,"
and they were ordered to be made public.

On December 16 the committee of correspondence, to which Gadsden had been added on the first day of the assembly, addressed a
long letter to Garth in which it particularly desired that he act with
the utmost openness towards the agents of the other colonies, "consulting with them in every Article" in order to guard against the
"most distant suspicions" that there might be the "least wish to make
a separate bargain for ourselves, which the House would look upon
with abhorance." The committee boldly asserted that "in taxing ourselves & making Laws for our own internal government or police we
can by no means allow our Provincial legislatures to be subordinate
to any legislative power on earth." Nothing less than the repeal of
the Act was desired, and "in order to avoid the possibility of a mistake
that may be of the greatest consequences" it was observed that the
words "would otherwise relieve" in the petition had been allowed
to stand as "words of mere form" only. Verging on a threat was the
thought that no one knew how soon another war might come: how
dangerous was it to drive men to despair, and how apt were drown-
ing men to clutch at straws! God forbid that any Prince of Europe
should at this critical time make himself master of any one of the
colonies. There was an equal plainness in the suggestion that Britain
would suffer more than America from any ill consequences of the
Act. Should the Americans be treated kindly, there would develop
a mutual confidence, and if the colonies were applied to in a constitutional manner there were no lengths to which they would not

go to assist the mother country. "It has ever been an observation with regard to the English," Garth was reminded, "that they are a people easily led but with difficulty drove."

There can be little doubt that Gadsden was the chief author of this communication. His previous correspondence with Garth contains many of the same ideas; the language, too, seems in accord with his forthright manner. Yet he was not shouting for independence. In his private letter to Garth of two weeks previous he had hoped that God might "send the desired success" to the petitions "and establish harmony once more. . . ." He wanted liberty, home rule, and self government in all internal matters, but not independence. The following spring he was writing to his friend William S. Johnson, of Connecticut, whom he had met at the Congress: "God grant that our stand may be of service to the cause of liberty in England and effectually awake the starters and big talkers in their sleep there."

While the people of Charleston were perhaps more united in opposition to the Stamp Act than they were on any other issue preceding the Revolution, Gadsden found that, as he wrote Garth, "we have a number of cunning, jacobitical, Butean rascals to encounter, that leave nothing untried to counterwork the firmness and loyalty of the true sons of liberty among us; these are such infernal fiends as none of the sister colonies north of us have to dread, but with all their cunning" he had no doubt but that "the wretched miscreants will find themselves disappointed" and "our just rights and privileges" preserved, "whether they will or no."

Because of the cessation of shipping due to the inability to get stamps, there was a large increase in the number of sailors in the harbor, and there was a fear, as Gadsden explained, "that the number of sailors would force the stamps upon us, as had been done in Georgia. . . ." In fact, Gadsden found "a number of artful Jacobites in town" who left "nothing untried to poison the minds of the people," and who were continually saying: "We don't like the Stamp Act any more than you do, but why don't you get the Port open upon the same terms as they are in many places to the northward?" Then when the port was about to be opened, Gadsden said "these contradictory wretches did everything in their power to prevent it." There is a strong suggestion that the Scotch merchants of Charleston constituted a large proportion of the "Jacobites," for in a letter to James Parsons, Gadsden warns against the Scotch representations.

The ardor of Gadsden received only sneers from Laurens. Writing to John Lewis Gervais at Ninety-six, and commending him for the vigilance of the "Loyal Frontier-Friends-Club" there, Laurens proceeded to give Gervais a well-informed view of the situation in Charleston. In addition to the "two industrious anti-parliamenterians" mentioned by Gervais, there were "my neighbor," Gadsden, and "the Secretary of the Post Office," presumably Peter Timothy, who did "not slacken their opposition to the . . . Stamps, but except a little private cruizing along the Water side at Nights to see if anything is moving among the Shipping they are pretty quiet & I have been assur'd that more than a few of their Brethren declare their repentance of having interfer'd in matters which did not come properly under their cognisance." Sometimes, he said, these vigilant gentlemen were "a little humm'd too, as the phraze is," by certain deceptive notices calling for meetings to be held at "Bacchies" tavern. On one such "artfully made" occasion, "my said neighbor who attended & plumply took the Chair—as if of right it did to him belong—was exceedingly Chagrin'd to find that nobody knew what they were conven'd for; he first attempted to wheedle a confession from some of the Company but none would Father the Child & then he grew very crabbed which it seems made other folks laugh & me too when I heard it."

Gadsden might be the hero of the Liberty Boys and hold sway in Charleston until the Lieutenant-Governor, the Chief Justice, the stamp distributor, and the group represented by Laurens, might, as the better part of valor, bow before the storm. But not so to the settlers of the back country. Without clergy, churches, courts, sheriffs, jails, and schools, the frontiersmen were without the benefits of civilization; and that which they lacked they greatly desired. Were not their grievances greater than any threatened internal tax that would fall upon those who could bear it best? Where were their liberties? Were they not without representation in the assembly, and in all practical respects denied even the vote of a freeman? By 1765 these people were finding a voice in the person of one Charles Woodmason, a clergyman. The Liberty Boys in general and Gadsden, "the Scriblerus of ye Libertines," in particular, aroused Woodmason and his cohorts. Contrasting their condition with that of the Charlestonians, Woodmason could exclaim: "While these provincials were roaring out agst the Stamp Act & Impositions . . . , they were rioting in Luxury and Extravagance—Balls—Concerts—Assemblies—Private Dances—Cards —Dice—Turtle Feasts—Above all—A Playhouse—was supported & carried on." The back settlers could have no sympathy with the "Men who bounce, & make such Noise about Liberty! Liberty! Freedom! Property! Rights! Privileges!" The tyranny the Sons of Liberty pretended to fear, they made others to feel.

What they point in Idea, the People experience in reality And these very Scriblers, & Assembly orators, who raise such an Outcry agst Statesmen & Government, who ride, oppress, distress and keep under the lowest subjection, half of the Inhabitants . . . not caring who may starve so they can eat—who sinks, so they swim,—who labour, & are heavy laden, so they can keep their Equipages. Their Throats bellow one thing—But their Hands would execute ye reverse. . . . These are the Sons of Liberty!

To find the Charleston conservatives and the up country frontiersmen of one mind on the Liberty Boys was remarkable indeed, and it was a hint of a division which was to extend through the Revolution. In point of fact, however, Gadsden was sympathetic with the back country; he it was who reported a bill for establishing courts in Granville and Craven counties and the Congarees in March, 1765.

In the controversy with Chief Justice Skinner, Gadsden, no lawyer, was an interested commentator. When his friend Rawlins Lowndes wrote the majority opinion of the court, holding that the court should be opened because stamps could not be had, Gadsden "differed from him in the principle he went upon, that is, I should have built chiefly on the constitutionalness of the Act and, asserted it so, roundly; he, I know, thinks it as unconstitutional as I do, but imagined it more prudent and advantageious in our present circumstances not to touch upon that string." The Chief Justice Gadsden referred to as one "whose character and abilities (if he has either), you cannot be unacquainted with. . . ." When His Majesty's Council refused to yield to the court on a disputed point, Gadsden described it as "consisting chiefly of Placemen and men of known arbitrary principles and very slender abilities." He likewise expressed this fairly accurate opinion of Bull:

Our Lt. Governor in his private character is a very agreeable polite man and very well beloved, but as a Governor is and always has been the weakest and most unsteady man I ever knew, so very obliging that he never obliged. The regard for him as a private gentleman has had too great weight with many in our house and occasioned great difficulties. In short 'tis a great and common misfortune, that weak and good natured men . . . are often driven . . . into the greatest inconsistencies being as it were tossed perpetually from one particular feeling or compassion to another without any permanent principle to rest upon. . . .

News of the repeal of the Stamp Act reached Charleston early in May, and there was a great and prolonged celebration. "The joy of the people on this occasion," wrote Bull, "was demonstrated by running almost to Excess. . . ." And Gadsden was perhaps the most excited of all. The Speaker of the House, Peter Manigault, wrote to Gadsden's brother Thomas, then in London: ". . . at last the happy news of the repeal of the Stamp Act arrived, and all was jollity and mirth. Your honest brother was so overcome at hearing it that he almost fainted, and the Corner Club having met on the occasion were attacked by some rascals and got several broken heads."

This was a stirring time for Gadsden and his colleagues who attended the Stamp Act Congress; on May 7 a committee of the House requested them to sit for their portraits which were to be hung in the assembly room as a memorial of the high esteem which the House had for them and for the great service they had rendered their country.

On June 4, the King's birthday, there was a further demonstration of the people, and Captain Gadsden's Artillery Company, together with a new company of light infantry, was drawn up in Broad Street and reviewed by the Lieutenant-Governor and other notables; two days later Gadsden was one of a committee to prepare an address thanking the King for his "great goodness" in "graciously relieving" the people of the Stamp Act; and when the new governor, Lord Charles Montagu, arrived on June 11, Gadsden again had his Artillery Company drawn up to greet the reading of the governor's commission with a general discharge of cannon followed by a volley of small arms.

In the midst of this universal rejoicing there was one aspect of the repeal of the Stamp Act that was generally overlooked but in which Gadsden and certain Sons of Liberty saw something ominous. That was the Declaratory Act, passed by Parliament, "for the better securing the dependency of his Majesty's dominions. . . ." Therein were a few carefully chosen phrases fixing the supremacy of King and Parliament to a degree never anticipated before the Stamp Act. Soon the determined Gadsden was meeting with William Johnson, Tunis Tebaut, Johnson's partner in the blacksmith business, Daniel Cannon, carpenter, and the oldest and most influential mechanic in Charleston, Edward Weyman, upholsterer, and some twenty other painters, coachmakers, sadlers, and wheelwrights, under an oak tree in Mr. Mazyck's pasture in Hampstead on Charleston Neck. There can be no doubt that this score of men constituted the nucleus of the Sons of Liberty, and their place of meeting was henceforth known as the Liberty Tree. What Gadsden said there is not known, but he is reported to have "harangued" the group "at considerable length, on the folly of relaxing their opposition and vigilance, or of indulging the fallacious hope that Great Britain would relinquish her designs or pretensions." Another reported that "reviewing all the chances of succeeding in a struggle to break the fetters whenever again imposed on them, he pressed them to prepare their minds for the event. . . ." This "address was received with silent and profound attention; and, with linked hands, the whole party pledged themselves to resist. . . ."

It seems doubtful that Gadsden advocated complete independence of England at this time. One may well believe that he was profoundly disturbed by the Declaratory Act, and that, knowing as he did the many other grievances which the province still labored under, he might anticipate future troubles. But only in case of failure to devise a way to reconcile conflicting interests could revolution come. It seems unlikely that Gadsden, being the forthright man he was, could at the same time report an address of thanks to the King, salute the governor with his company of artillery, and advocate colonial independence. Deeply moved by the passing and threatening events, he was probably fearing revolution rather than advocating independence.

Part III:
ANTEBELLUM SOUTH CAROLINA

Modern historians have generally agreed that the American Revolution was a part of a democratic movement which swept through much of the western world, resulting not only in our revolution, but also in the French and Latin American revolutions and in democratic reforms in many of the western nations. In keeping with this line of thought, we now view the American Revolution as much more than a struggle to break the ties with Great Britain, much more than a political revolution. There was also an internal social conflict, a struggle leading toward social equality not completely unlike that of the French Revolution. The Treaty of Paris of 1783 ended only the political phase of the American Revolution. The United States were in fact independent, but "All men are created equal" was not yet a true statement of American society. This was the continuing revolution, the social revolution.

No man better represents the social revolution than Thomas Jefferson. In fact that phase of our revolution became known as Jeffersonian democracy. The development of the Jeffersonian ideal in South Carolina involved the disputes between the low-country planters and the up-country small farmers, and between the supporters and critics of the French Revolution, as well as the struggle for a more democratic system of representation. The South Carolina Jeffersonians won a striking victory in 1800, but this progress was at least temporarily stymied by the interests of the slave-plantation economy. South Carolina's Jeffersonian nationalism was subsequently perverted into the sectionalism leading toward the Civil War. John Harold Wolfe discusses the development of Jeffersonianism in this state.

9

JEFFERSONIAN DEMOCRACY IN SOUTH CAROLINA *

John Harold Wolfe

The recognition of the independence of the thirteen states by Great Britain in 1783 ended only the political phase of the American Revolution. The social phase continued. Much of this social revolution and many of its leaders became a part of Jeffersonian democracy. Soon its roots took a firm hold in the American culture—so firm a hold that it has never been broken loose.

In the changes which accompanied or followed the Revolution hardly a single institution escaped. This was true even in South Carolina, which historians until recently considered one of the early strongholds of Federalism. The strong tendency toward popular control is shown emphatically in the post-Revolutionary churches. Only the influence of Francis Asbury prevented the Methodists from adopting congregationalism, the Catholics defied one of their bishops, and the self-governing Baptists increased very rapidly. A contemporary thought that the popular doctrines of Jefferson "found nowhere a more genial soil to take root, than in the state of South Carolina. They were cherished here with enthusiasm." According to Jefferson, it was Aedanus Burke who first attacked the aristocratic tendencies of the Society of Cincinnati. Partly to offset and partly to deride exclusive social groups, popular organizations with such curious names as "the Free and Easy" and the "Ugly Club" were formed.

The controversies during the period of the Confederation and the struggle over the ratification of the United States Constitution foreshadowed the later party divisions in South Carolina. Geographically and culturally the state was divided into two general sections known

* Excerpt from "The Roots of Jeffersonian Democracy: With Special Emphasis on South Carolina," *Essays in Southern History Presented to Joseph DeRoulhac Hamilton by His Former Students at the University of North Carolina,* ed. Fletcher Melvin Green (Chapel Hill: University of North Carolina Press, 1949), pp. 3–15; copyright, 1949, by The University of North Carolina Press. Reprinted without footnotes by permission of The University of North Carolina Press.

as the up country and the low country. When political lines became
more clearly drawn Jefferson gained most of his followers from the
former region though he was never without supporters in the latter.
Many of the supporters of Jeffersonian democracy became highly dissatisfied with the aristrocratic state government and its conservative
economic policies during the 1780's. They attacked these forces and
won partial victories. Moderate inflation was forced in 1785; when
this proved insufficient the agitation continued, and sometimes resulted
in extra-legal action. Although Charles Pinckney, who was soon to become one of Jefferson's most ardent leaders, helped frame the Constitution of the United States and led the fight for its ratification, most
future South Carolina Republicans opposed it. Speaking for the opposition, Rawlins Lowndes reached his climax when he declared that
he wished no other epitaph than to have written on his tomb, "Here
lies a man who opposed the constitution, because it was ruinous to
the liberty of America." No attempt was made to prevent the calling
of a convention to decide the question of ratification, but only by
the narrow margin of one vote did the low country friends of the
constitution obtain Charleston as the meeting place. Because the basis
of representation gave the lower part of the state many more delegates than its population warranted, ratification was achieved by the
comfortable vote of one hundred forty-nine to seventy-three. Even then
the delegates appended their interpretations of certain sections and instructed future representatives of the state in Congress to work for
amendments.

Without the rise of national political parties, local differences would
have been sufficient to continue the existence of at least two strong
state factions. Having settled their region first the people of the low
country had established the local government. When the up country
was settled later by people of different background and culture, those
already in power refused to give up control even after they came to be
outnumbered. When the sharing of power could be postponed no
longer, concessions were made; and the subsequent internal history of
South Carolina became a story of struggle and compromise between
its two sections. All forms of sectionalism have never been eliminated,
but the removal of the capital from Charleston to the more central
location of Columbia was a step in that direction. Even this, however, was a compromise for several state officers maintained headquarters in both towns. By 1790 several democratic gains had been made.
Primogeniture and religious qualifications for voting were abolished,
and there were easier property qualifications for the suffrage and for
office holding. Nevertheless the low country still controlled both houses

of the legislature and thereby the election of many officers including the governor. Fearing that its older and more firmly established social and economic institutions might not be safe in the hands of the more vigorous and democratic representatives from the up country, the low country held on tightly to its control of the state legislature. Not until South Carolina's economic interests became unified and the state grew into a kind of low country "writ large" did the more populous up country secure, through a redistribution of representation, the control of one of the houses of the legislature and the establishment of white manhood suffrage. The struggles which culminated in these two victories in 1808 and 1810 were contemporary with and a part of the larger Jeffersonian movement. Clearly the roots of Jeffersonian democracy in South Carolina were deeply embedded in the local culture.

In spite of the fact that the state's constitutional structure was at least potentially aristocratic and undemocratic, a majority of South Carolina's first congressional delegation were supporters of what later became known as the Jeffersonian or Republican policies. Their chief departure was their support of the assumption of state debts, an action which they justified on the ground that South Carolina would not have given up the right to levy impost duties if it had not been understood that the state debt would be assumed. William Loughton Smith, soon to become one of the principal Federalist leaders, was the only South Carolina representative who voted to establish the first Bank of the United States. In the first Congress South Carolina began its long struggle against high tariffs. Arguing that high duties hurt the importing South especially, most of the representatives would support only moderate protection and then only to those industries which actually needed aid. Most of the people in the up country and many in the low country agreed with Burke that the excise tax was "universally odious." Apparently considering secret meetings undemocratic and dangerous the South Carolina legislature called upon the United States Senate to open its sessions to the public.

In the election of 1792 the Republican Thomas Sumter was defeated but the election of Lemuel Benton, also a Republican, by the newly formed Pedee District prevented a Federalist majority in the state's congressional delegation. In the presidential contest George Washington received eight electoral votes, John Adams seven, and Aaron Burr one. Of course party lines were still rather loosely drawn but forces and influences both within and outside of the United States were fast tightening them.

As in the rest of the nation, South Carolina Republicans and Federalists divided on the question of approving or disapproving the

French Revolution. At first, however, both local groups were inclined to be sympathetic. The news of the fall of the Bastille called forth a public celebration in Charleston. While traveling in France and Great Britain during the early stages of the Revolution, John Rutledge, Jr., later one of the most ardent Federalists, praised the French and condemned the British. The newspapers were flooded with pro-French letters. In 1792 a French Patriotic Society, affiliated with the Friends of Liberty and Equality of Bordeaux was formed. The establishment of a French republic and news of military victories occasioned many public gatherings. Under such propitious circumstances Citizen Genêt, minister plenipotentiary of France to the United States, arrived in Charleston. Enthusiastically received by the public and believing that he had the approval of Governor Moultrie, Genêt began arrangements for an attack upon the Spanish possessions. His journey through other South Carolina towns was a triumphal procession. These activities were repudiated and condemned by both Washington and Moultrie, but the fact that an attack on East Florida was barely averted and that the movement continued for nearly a year is proof that many who did not openly support it were at least silent observers.

During 1793 another important development in party politics occurred in South Carolina—the beginning of the activities of the Republican and the Democrat societies. The year 1794 was described by a contemporary as a time

When Sansculottes and their principles had great ascendancy in Charleston —when the tri-colored cockade of France was the great badge of honour, and Ca'ira and the Marseillaise hymn the most popular airs—and "Vive la republique Francaise!" the universal shout.

During this period Jefferson's association with the Washington administration had made it nearly impossible for him to promote actively the work of the Republican party. In fact James Madison was mentioned more frequently at the meetings of the above-named societies than was Jefferson. Learning from Ralph Izard that "a society under the democratic garb has arisen in South Carolina with the name Madisonian," Secretary of State Edmund Randolph reported the occurrence to President Washington in October, 1794. By this time the formation of such organizations had disturbed both Washington and Randolph. In a message to Congress shortly afterward Washington made what Madison called "Perhaps the greatest error" of his political career when he denounced the "self-created" societies. Jefferson considered them no more deserving of presidential attack than the Society of Cincinnati.

Even greater popular agitation developed when the news of the Jay Treaty reached South Carolina. The sending of John Jay to England, where Thomas Pinckney, one of the state's native sons, was already the American minister had been resented. This, together with the nature of the treaty, aroused almost universal opposition. It was felt that the South's interests had been disregarded by Jay. Senator Pierce Butler was commended for voting against ratification while the Federalist supporter, Senator Jacob Read, was hung in effigy. On one occasion William Loughton Smith, John Adams, Timothy Pickering, Jacob Read, and "His Satanic Majesty," all supposedly connected with the Jay Treaty were hung in effigy "the whole day, polluted by every indignity, and, in the evening, were carried off to the Federal green, where they were burnt." The opposition, however, was not confined to the Republicans. John Rutledge's very severe denunciation of the treaty was largely responsible for the refusal of the Senate to confirm him as Chief Justice of the Supreme Court of the United States. A very different response greeted the more satisfactory treaty which Thomas Pinckney in the meantime negotiated with Spain. There were, however, surprisingly few letters published in the South Carolina newspapers concerning it.

Although political lines had not become rigid by 1796, the elections of that year were much better measurements of party strength than any previously held. Hoping to gain votes especially in South Carolina and the South because of the supposed popularity of Thomas Pinckney and his treaty, the Federalists linked his name with that of John Adams in the presidential and vice-presidential contest. There were two electoral tickets supported in the South Carolina legislature —one for Jefferson and Pinckney and one for Adams and Pinckney. The overwhelming choice of the "Jefferson ticket" showed an obvious victory for the Republicans. Charles Pinckney, who had become a Republican leader, was elected for the third time governor of South Carolina. In the congressional elections the voters chose two Republicans, two Federalists, and two who had not committed themselves but who had definite leanings toward the former. Before long, however, each party had secured one of the last group. In the Senate both parties continued to have one each. Thus in this initial nation-wide test of the two political parties, South Carolina had chosen Jefferson electors, a Republican governor, and a congressional delegation evenly divided. Clearly the party of Jefferson was rapidly gaining control of the state.

The excesses of the French Revolution, especially those connected with the "X.Y.Z." affair, caused a set-back for the Republican friends of France between 1796 and 1799. Since the American minister, Charles Cotesworth Pinckney was a very much respected South Carolinian, the people of the state resented his treatment abroad. William Loughton Smith and Robert Goodloe Harper, who had become the two foremost Federalist leaders in the House, were joined by their colleague, John Rutledge, Jr., in the most severe condemnation of the indignity to Pinckney. Even Jefferson wrote Thomas Pinckney, brother of the American minister to France, praising the latter's conduct. In the contemporary issues of the Charleston *City Gazette* and the *South Carolina State Gazette* the friends of France and England carried on a heated controversy. Thomas Sumter made one of his few recorded congressional speeches attacking a preparedness measure which he thought would grant powers to the President unwarranted by the circumstances.

In the meantime members of both parties in South Carolina loyally supported preparedness. The Federalists became confident, even defiant, and formed a military organization known as "the Federalist Club." At one of its meetings, Miss Mary Legare, presenting the club with a standard, spoke of an inevitable war between the United States and France; she denounced France as "a nation of atheists." The high point of co-operation among South Carolinians of both parties was the financing and the building of the sloop-of-war *John Adams,* constructed in the Cooper River shipyard, named after the President and launched on June 5, 1799.

Although the Republican support of preparedness prevented the Federalists from profiting from the "X.Y.Z." affair as much as they had hoped, they did make political gains in the election of 1798. Thomas Sumter was the only Republican representative sent by South Carolina to the next Congress. This was partly offset, however, by the choice of a Republican majority in the state legislature and the election of Charles Pinckney, Jefferson's chief local supporter, to the United States Senate. For governor, the legislature chose Edward Rutledge, who had been a Jefferson elector in 1796 and remained one of his closest friends. Thus it was only in the congressional delegation that the Federalists made notable gains. Soon the Alien and Sedition Acts, the Jonathan Robbins case, and other incidents caused a reaction in favor of the Republicans. The earlier appointment of William Loughton Smith as minister to Portugal and the removal of Harper to Maryland in 1799 meant that the Federalists would be without their most aggressive leaders in the election of 1800.

For the campaign of 1800 the Federalists, as in 1796, chose a South Carolinian as the running mate for John Adams. This time it was

Charles Cotesworth Pinckney, the chief American participant in the "X.Y.Z." affair. The break between Adams and Hamilton and the pamphlet of the latter stating a preference for the election of Pinckney as President, greatly weakened the party's chance for success. In contrast, the Republicans presented a united front both as to the candidates and their relative positions on the ticket. As the campaign unfolded it became as much a contest of personalities as of issues. Unsavory rumors were circulated about Jefferson and his supporters. Newspaper correspondents made insinuating remarks about the public and private life of Charles Pinckney. The hostility between Adams and Hamilton further divided the Federalists as the election approached. At one time Charles Cotesworth Pinckney was almost ready to recommend that Adams be replaced by another candidate. Almost every device known to newspaper correspondents and pamphleteers was used by both sides. They defined their own principles favorably and cleverly attacked those of their opponents. They published many imaginary dialogues with this in mind. Especially did they seek to label their adversaries with catchy, disparaging phrases. Hardly a single issue of the Federalist *South Carolina State Gazette* or the Republican *City Gazette* appeared without several examples of such political tactics.

In no previous election had voters been confronted with such a flood of campaign literature. Not confining his activities to his own state, Charles Pinckney, wrote Jefferson, "We have Literally sprinkled Georgia and North Carolina from the mountains to the Ocean." Perhaps the two ablest pamphlets were the one signed "A Federal Republican," a presentation of the Federalist cause by Henry William DeSaussure, and the one bearing the signature, "A Republican," a statement of the Republican views by Charles Pinckney. According to DeSaussure, the Federalists had saved the country during the trying times which followed the Revolution. Washington and Adams had kept the United States from going to war with either Great Britain or France and had repelled aggressions by both. American commerce had grown and agriculture had been encouraged. Furthermore, he argued, the Federalists had prevented the supporters of Jefferson from carrying the country into war on the side of France and thereby interrupting prosperity, decreasing revenues, and necessitating higher taxes. DeSaussure compared Jefferson and Adams to the advantage of the latter. Jefferson had only "shewy talents" and "theoretic learning," had been an inefficient governor of Virginia, an enemy of the constitution, had cast insinuations against Washington, was an opponent of slavery, and an open friend of France. On the other hand,

DeSaussure considered Adams a tested public servant worthy of South Carolina's support. In an election as close as the one about to take place, the vote of one state might be decisive. In arguing for the election of Jefferson and Burr, Charles Pinckney attacked the commercial interests and appealed for the support of the agricultural group. In spite of all the taxes, Pinckney said, the Federalists had increased the public debt greatly. The direct taxes had injured the planter especially, but the business group had largely escaped. Jefferson, a planter, had to pay heavy direct taxes; but Adams, who probably owned a good deal of stock, did not. Furthermore, Jefferson did not favor the abolition of slavery in the southern states as the Federalists charged. Clearly Pinckney was stating pointedly that the agricultural South should vote for Jefferson because he was a friend of agriculture, and against Adams because he was the candidate of the "monied interest, which is by far the largest in the Northern States and the greatest favorite of the federal party." With the record open before them they could not vote for Adams and Charles Cotesworth Pinckney unless they were "content to be more oppressed and degraded and to bear heavier and more unequal burdens" than he thought they were.

It was commonly believed by both parties that the outcome in South Carolina would determine the national results, so nearly balanced were the Federalists and Republicans elsewhere. With this in mind the Federalists hoped that the state's electoral votes would go to one of their candidates if not to both. Since the narrow coast section chose such a large proportion of the members of the legislature, the Republicans knew that it would require all their energies to elect enough members to insure the choice of their electoral ticket. Against them were the commercial interests, the friends of the Bank of the United States, the unpopularity of France, and the popularity of Charles Cotesworth Pinckney. In addition to Pinckney's candidacy for the vice-presidency—or according to some the presidency—the Federalists added to the strength of their local ticket by running him for the state senate also. So bitter did the campaign become that the two branches of the Pinckney family attacked each other and would not speak when they occasionally met. On election day, according to Charles Pinckney, several hundred Federalists voted who had not paid taxes. The "lame, crippled, diseased and blind were led, lifted or brought in carriages to the Poll." In order for the "Bank & federal officers & English merchants" to be sure that those under their influence voted as directed "the novel and unwarranted measure was used of voting with tickets printed on *Green & blue & red & yellow paper* & men stationed to watch the voters."

It was soon discovered that two Federalist representatives in Congress would be replaced by Republicans, thereby evenly dividing the South Carolina members of the next House. And the defeat of Jacob Read, a little later, meant that both senators would be Republicans. However, the contest which attracted most attention was the choosing of the presidential electors. In order to use his influence with members of the legislature, Charles Pinckney delayed returning to the United States Senate. After several days of vigorous political activity the Republicans won by an average majority of about nineteen.

The election of Jefferson was celebrated throughout the state. At a meeting held in Charleston for that purpose, the following toast was offered: "The State of South Carolina, whose voice secured to the United States their present Chief Magistrate:—his voice should not have been a blank at the city of Washington." In recognition of his leadership during the campaign, Jefferson consulted Charles Pinckney on patronage and appointed him minister to Spain.

Since South Carolina had elected Republicans to high local and federal positions for several years and since no radical changes now occurred, the so-called "Revolution of 1800" was more noticeable in the nation at large than in South Carolina. Christopher Gadsden, the "conservative radical" of the Revolutionary period, thought that social and political changes already had gone too far. Newcomers had been "cajoled and imposed upon by emissaries from without, and egged on by a numerous or rather innumerable tribe of young law-followers amongst ourselves." In a letter of consolation to John Adams, Gadsden expressed disappointment and pessimism.

> Long have I been led to think our planet a mere bedlam, and the uncommonly extravagant ravings of our times, especially for a few years past, and still in the highest rant, have greatly increased and confirmed that opinion. Look around our whirling globe, my friend, where you will, east, west, north or south, where is the spot in which there are not many thousands of these lunatics.

Thus did one of the "old order" view the beginnings of Jeffersonian democracy on a national scale. But even he hoped that the new President would receive "the constitutional assistance and countenance of every citizen of the Union; and that his public actions may be judged with candor and generosity without any captious hole picking." Most of all he hoped for the restoration of harmony.

Throughout the remainder of the Jefferson era South Carolina remained predominantly Republican at least politically and the more populous section of the state was Republican socially. No more Federalist governors or United States senators were chosen, thus indicating a consistently Republican majority in the legislature. With the retirement of John Rutledge, Jr., in 1803, South Carolina ceased to have aggressive Federalist leaders in national politics. In the congressional elections of 1802, Republicans won in six of the state's eight districts. In spite of reverses the Federalists remained active, and the establishment of the *Charleston Courier,* a very vigorous Federalist newspaper, in 1803, frightened the Republicans for a time. By 1804 partisanship had subsided sufficiently for the local Society of the Cincinnati, once extremely anti-Jefferson, to toast the President and declare—"Party Spirit: may it be kept within due bounds—we are all Republicans—all Federalists." In the elections of 1804 the Republicans won in the hitherto Federalist districts. Thus, except for a few seats in the legislature and other local positions in certain areas, the Federalists were completely without offices in South Carolina.

During the second half of the first decade of the nineteenth century, foreign affairs again became an important issue. South Carolina loyally accepted the Jeffersonian policy of economic coercion as a substitute for war, but even some of the Republicans preferred armed conflict. Charging that the administration unduly favored France and discriminated against Great Britain, the Federalists had a reawakening. But in 1806 and again in 1808, despite hot local campaigns, the Republicans won all major state and federal offices. The election of younger and more vigorous Republicans, including John Caldwell Calhoun, William Lowndes, and Langdon Cheves, to Congress in 1810 indicated that a new phase of Jeffersonian democracy was about to begin. Dissatisfied with the policies of Madison, they had a prominent part in forcing him to agree to war in 1812. As chairmen of important committees they were active in the prosecution of the war. In spite of the many military reverses, they unceasingly preached patriotism and justified the beginning of the conflict. At the close of the war, they claimed a glorious victory, continued to preach patriotism, and actively supported the nationalistic trend of the day. To have continued this nationalistic trend, however, would have necessitated the tearing up and replanting of the roots of Jeffersonian democracy in South Carolina. This incipient nationalism had been the product of the war and war-time conditions. With the coming of peace, the people of the state soon questioned whether the interests of an area apparently destined to remain agricultural could be served best by encouraging the development of a centralized government in a nation in which they ultimately would be outnumbered in the Senate as they already were in the House of Representatives. High tariffs and other measures or policies might discriminate against agriculture and the South's "peculiar institution." An emphatic answer was soon given against nationalism, although a few leaders seemed a little slow in discovering it. South Carolina remained Republican or Democratic, as the party later came to be known, in so far as political names were concerned. The Federalist party also continued to live for many years but its members soon realized that they had little in common with the Federalists in other parts of the country.

Thus South Carolina had become an early and, at least in form, an almost unqualified convert to Jeffersonian democracy. During most of the period Republicans made up a majority of the congressional delegation and after 1800 few Federalists were chosen to either house of the federal Congress. In local politics the dominance of the Republicans was decisive but not as complete. In other matters dear to the heart of Jefferson progress was also made. In 1801 the legislature voted to set up in Columbia, the South Carolina College, an institution which later became the University of South Carolina. Several governors recommended public school systems, and in 1811 the legislature established what has been referred to by some as "the free school system." The education act of 1811 accorded with Jeffersonian principles in theory but in practice it fell far short.

By way of a general summary of subsequent developments it can be said, in conclusion, that while the Republican party was evolving into the Democratic party of a later day, less immediate evolution took place in South Carolina than in the nation at large, for her particular economic system had already developed over most of her area and was fast becoming solidified. After the state had gone far toward the erection of what might have served as the political, social and educational framework of a democratic structure, economic forces delayed the work of the builders. In truth, South Carolina was inclined to return to the form, if not the spirit, of early Jeffersonian Republicanism which for the time was more to her liking than the new democratic impulses. The democratic structure in South Carolina has never been completed. But no higher testimonial to the lasting influence of Jeffersonian ideals upon the people of the state can be written than the simple statement that men still struggle for their fulfillment.

By the late 1700s the low-country rice planters and the Charleston merchants had developed an impressively cosmopolitan society. Federalist in their politics, these aristocrats were uneasy at the demands of the up-country Jeffersonian Republicans, demands for a more equitable share of the state's political power. It appeared for a time that the aristocratic values of the low country would not be safe if the more democratic up-country people had their way.

Beginning in the 1790s, Eli Whitney's cotton gin led the South into a veritable revolution in agriculture. As cotton planting spread into the interior, many of the less democratic values of the older region took root throughout the state. The blend of the cotton plantation system with the Jeffersonian traditions eventually resulted in the southern version of states' rights democracy. George C. Rogers, Jr., discusses the decline of South Carolina Federalism.

10

THE TRANSITION TO THE NINETEENTH-CENTURY ECONOMY *

George C. Rogers, Jr.

With the decline of commerce, agriculture emerged supreme. By 1808 the planters in Carolina had become the unchallenged economic masters. The victory was, however, more the victory of cotton than of rice. Rice planters continued to flourish, but their numbers not only did not increase, but for a few years after 1800 actually declined as coastal planters found sea island cotton more profitable than rice.

Indigo, which had supplemented rice as a Carolina staple, declined in importance with the Revolution. The loss of the British bounty had been disastrous; in the 1780's indigo planters were already looking for a new crop and cotton was the answer. A few bags were shipped before 1790, and there was a small annual increase in production until the invention of the cotton gin in 1793. During the following decade, cotton swept the state; production increased eightfold from 1794 to 1804. Cotton actually came of age in 1799, for by that time indigo had almost completely disappeared and rice itself had yielded first place.

The letters of William Murrell, a Stateburg planter, to his Charleston factors in the year 1799 speak of "a considerable number of planters" embarking "in the cultivation of cotton" due to the losses suffered in the past "on the accursed article," indigo. The letters of Barker and Lord, agents for the Browns of Rhode Island, in the same year, chart the rising importance of cotton. On April 16: "Cotton is being bought up as fast as it comes in. We never knew European freights so much in demand as at present—wanted mostly for some port in G.B." On August 13, Barker and Lord observed that there was much more land being planted in cotton in the back-

* Excerpt from *Evolution of a Federalist: William Loughton Smith of Charleston (1758–1812)* (Columbia: University of South Carolina Press, 1962), pp. 369–75; Copyright © 1962 by The University of South Carolina Press. Reprinted without footnotes by permission of the University of South Carolina Press and the author.

country of Georgia and South Carolina than during the past year. With little rice being planted "in proportion to a few years back in the lowcountry owing to their attention to cotton the price of rice would stay up and the price of cotton would be going down."

The political revolution of 1800 reflected this economic revolution of 1799. The Federalist party, when it had represented planters, had represented rice planters. The Jeffersonian party in South Carolina was to be dominated by the cotton planters. To go from rice to cotton was to change from Federalist to Republican. The clean, sharp, hard grain of rice symbolized the realism of the Federalist mind, while the round, soft, fluffy ball of cotton symbolized the vague idealism of the Jeffersonian mind.

Between 1800 and 1808 many of the backcountry farmers became cotton planters. The rapid increase in wealth brought a rapid change in status which brought a rapid change in political outlook. The greatest backcountry success story was that of Wade Hampton. He had come from Virginia to the South Carolina frontier just before the Revolution. At the end of the war Hampton had been a member of the Jacksonborough legislature, where the itch for lands and slaves had prompted great confiscations. He had gotten his share of both and had borrowed money to start his inland empire. When the capital of the state was placed near his lands on the Congaree River, his fortune leaped forward. As a spokesman for the backcountry, he became a Jeffersonian. However, when in 1801 Jefferson offered him a reward for faithful support, the position of postmaster of the United States, Hampton refused, for, as he said, he would be sacrificing too much. By 1809, his income was so vast that he stood to lose a possible $30,000 a year as a result of absence on military duty in the Southwest. In 1811, he was able to buy a great sugar estate on the Mississippi River for $300,000.

The Hampton family was merely the most successful. Other families by 1808 had made the change in status from farmer to planter. The Sumters, the Calhouns, the Winns, the Taylors, the Pickenses, the Andersons, and the Mannings had been Jefferson's yeoman farmers but were now desirous of aping their "betters" on the coast. As these families grew rich, they married their sons and daughters into the lowcountry aristocracy. In this fashion the differences between the "prior immigrants" who had come in from the ocean and the "subsequent immigrants" who had come down from Virginia and Pennsylvania were rubbed out. It had been this difference in origin that Timothy Ford had pointed to in 1794 as the reason why there should be no change in representation at that time. After the marriage of Wade Hampton's son to the daughter of Christopher Fitzsimons, a wealthy Charleston merchant of loyalist background; after the marriage of Langdon Cheves to the daughter of Joseph Dulles, a British merchant with world-wide connections; after the marriage of John C. Calhoun and Floride Bonneau Colhoun, a veritable union of cotton and rice, could there be a need much longer to distinguish the upcountry planter from the lowcountry planter?

South Carolina College, which was established by the state legislature in 1801 and which opened its doors in 1805 was founded for the purpose of educating the backcountry leaders. Among those who sponsored the bill were Henry William DeSaussure and Thomas Rhett Smith in the House and Charles Cotesworth Pinckney in the Senate. DeSaussure, the most important architect of the measure, said: "We of the lower country well knew that the power of the State was thence forward to be in the upper country, and we desired our future rulers to be educated men." Schaper thought the lowcountry wanted to bring "a greater like mindedness through a common system of education before granting [the upcountry] any controlling influence in the legislature." Daniel W. Hollis, the historian of the college, states, "It was the work of the Low Country aristocrats." Petigru later called it "the last will and testament of the expiring" Federalist party. Education would erase the differences in manners and ideas.

As the cotton plantations sprang up in the interior, slavery moved inland. Schaper's figures indicate that during the decade 1800–1810, slavery was spread much more evenly over the state. After the Revolution it was the backcountry that had consistently urged the reopening of the slave trade. The new men won their point in 1803, and the trade flourished for the last time until 1808 marked the end of that business. As the plantation with slave labor became the basic economic unit throughout the state, the lesser white men who had not made the change in status from farmer to planter moved westward. South Carolina became a hive of migration. In the 1790's, the white population of the state had increased forty per cent while in the first decade of the nineteenth century it increased only nine per cent. Many of those who moved had been small shopkeepers and manufacturers of household things. There had been in existence a system of domestic manufacturing which had made the upcountry somewhat self-sufficient, but this system now gave way to the large plantations, specializing in one crop and demanding finished products from outside. Also among those leaving were Quakers who disapproved of slavery. Between 1805 and 1819, twelve hundred Quakers left for the Northwest.

It was during this decade that two extremes in the old society disappeared. On one hand the merchants were declining, the men who had imported not only goods, but ideas, who had acted as ties with the great Atlantic community of Lisbon and London, of Bordeaux and Boston, of Rotterdam and Philadelphia, who had brought a sense of struggle and competition, who represented the thrust of the new middle class. On the other hand, the raw, untutored democrats, the element for which Aedanus Burke had spoken so forcefully, were drifting westward. This exodus of ardent democrats and early antislavery elements skimmed the milk of bitterness. Those who remained were fast forming into a society of almost feudal units, dominated by great planters. What was left was a planting world, drawn partly from tired Federalists and partly from Jeffersonians quite willing to forget their pure republicanism. Ironically, what was left was Shaftesbury's ideal of a neatly balanced agrarian society. And William Loughton Smith surveyed the new scene from Ashley Barony.

In 1794, the lowcountry had told the upcountry that equality of representation would come when upcountrymen could think and act like gentlemen. The year of change came in 1808. In 1794, Timothy Ford had asserted that the rich men of the lowcountry could not possibly influence the poor voters of the upcountry, for a rich man could only influence those he came in contact with. With the whole state carved into plantations and with the leading planter in each county now able to influence his neighbors, it was time for a change. Hampton is a good example of the altered farmer. In 1806, he confessed to Edward Hooker that he had come to agree with leading characters of the northern states, such as Governor Strong, Governor Treadwell, Mr. Tracy, Dr. Dwight, and the clergy in general, who thought "that the turbulent spirit of the people might lead to licentiousness" and that this tendency might "weaken the government." He believed, however, that "there was more of the turbulent, licentious, fractious spirit in the common people of the northern states than of the Southern. . . . He thought there was more civility to strangers, to gentlemen riding in their carriages, more submission to the laws, and respect of authority in the South." If the upcountry Hamptons held these views, what reason could the lowcountry have for denying them equality in representation? On June 28, 1808, the bill to alter representation was carried in the House by a vote of one hundred one to two.

The first solid South Carolina had been formed.

Just as South Carolina took a step backward, the United States and the western world took a step forward. The age of commerce which had begun with Columbus came to an end in 1808, and in the western world it was succeeded by an age of industry, not by an age of agriculture as it was in South Carolina. The age of commerce died amid the Napoleonic struggles; as supply lines were cut, each western power was forced to build up its own industrial system in order to be as independent of England as possible. For the United States, the dividing line between the two ages was quite definitely 1808, a year more significant in American history than either 1776 or 1861.

The embargo provided American manufacturers (the industrialists, who were to become richer and more powerful than the merchants had ever been during the age of commerce) with a golden opportunity. The history of cotton manufacturing proves that many New Englanders perceived the advantages. Samuel Slater had come out to Rhode Island from England and successfully set up the first cotton manufacturing establishment in America before 1800. By 1803, there were still only four mills. By 1808, there were fifteen in operation with 8,000 spindles. By 1809, there were sixty-two with 31,000 spindles, and twenty-five more mills under construction. By 1815, there would be 500,000 spindles in operation in the United States. This was a period when clever New England merchants transferred their fortunes to industry. Continental countries, as well as the United States, found a need to industrialize. A young Essen merchant named Friedrich Krupp began making steel when Napoleon's blockade cut off his supply of high-quality English steel.

New England's factories needed the South's raw materials. The coastal trade was open and the South was grateful for a market. In 1800, New England used only five hundred bales of cotton; by 1815, she needed 90,000 bales. Consequently there began to appear in southern ports northern agents to buy up cotton.

The Brown family of Rhode Island had realized at the time of the *Chesapeake* and *Leopard* affair that "the commercial capital of the country" was "greatly exposed," so they transferred more of their capital from commerce to manufacturing. By January 1809, they were ordering two hundred fifty bales of sea-island cotton from their Charleston agent. "The cotton must be of the very first quality, it is intended to be manufactured by us and it is of importance that the first year, should be approved, to establish the credit of the manufactory." In March 1809, they asked their agent to help Richard Waterman, a son of Rufus Waterman, who had just established a cotton manufacturing company in the vicinity of Providence, buy cotton. Behind the embargo, the non-intercourse acts, and the War of 1812, South Carolina commerce began a slow but fundamental reorientation. It was now to flow north to New York, Newport, and Boston under the direction of northern agents, and eventually the direct trade between Charleston and Europe would be destroyed. This shift in lines of communication was to relegate the state to a backwater.

J. N. Cardozo, who was connected with Charleston's commercial life from 1794 until the Civil War, also considered 1808 as the great dividing line. He wrote that it would be convenient to divide the history of Charleston's commerce "into two epochs":

1. The period before the Berlin and Milan decrees, and British Orders in Council, and

2. The period subsequent to those measures which resulted in the war of 1812.

As a consequence of the neutral position of the United States, a large share of the carrying trade was thrown into the hands of the Americans, soon after the breaking out of the French Revolution, and the Southern ports were made the depots, as we have said, of large quantities of European and West India merchandize—the produce of the latter, their bulky products—sugar, and coffee—requiring a large amount of shipping, being exchanged for the manufactures of Europe. Charleston, from her proximity to the former, became a convenient half-way house for the supplies indispensably necessary on both sides. She enjoyed, consequently, a lucrative commerce from 1792 until about 1807, when the embargo, and non-intercourse acts, followed by the war of 1812, took place. This was the great dividing line before and subsequent to this period.

Cardozo saw on each side of the line two distinct groups of merchants: "the Russells, Crafts, Winthrops, Tunnos, Hasletts, Hazelhursts," who were connected with the direct foreign trade of Charleston to the ports of Europe, disappeared and "were replaced by those who were connected with the indirect trade through Northern ports."

New England took the place of old England. Those who had once railed against British influence would soon rail against Yankee influence. Thomas Shirley, a British merchant, had warned the Carolinians in 1773 that revolution would only mean an exchange of masters. John Rutledge, in securing an exemption for rice in 1774 at the time of the non-exportation agreement, had recognized Carolina's peculiar economic position. In 1787, Charles Pinckney had not been satisfied with the protection for southern economic interests written into the Constitution; Rawlins Lowndes had found this lack the chief reason for opposing ratification. William Loughton Smith had frankly recognized the predominance of Britain in the Carolina trade in the 1790's. As late as 1806, he was explaining how American trade must dovetail with English trade. Yet the *Chesapeake* and *Leopard* affair, the embargo, and the arrival of northern agents—like three swift blows—altered his view. He grasped more clearly than any of his contemporaries the meaning of these events. The South must manufacture or stagnate.

South Carolina had played a prominent role in the American Revolution and in the formation of the new national government. In the War of 1812 no state supported the Union with greater loyalty. The politics of this state were predominantly nationalistic. South Carolinians gave at least a qualified support to protective tariffs and federal aid for internal improvements. In the bonanza years of cotton production, South Carolina occupied a leading position. Then came the economic crash of 1819 and the opening of the new cotton lands of the Southwest (Alabama, Mississippi, and Louisiana). The Palmetto State's cotton culture sank into what seemed to be a permanent depression.

The resulting loss of economic preeminence contributed to South Carolina's departure from the mainstream of the American development. The economic changes, coupled with the growing anti-slavery movement and the rapid industrialization of the North, contributed to the social and intellectual, as well as economic, isolation of South Carolina and the entire South. In defending the outdated institution of slavery and in opposing protective tariffs, this state began the process of turning inward from nationalism to sectionalism. Alfred G. Smith, Jr., discusses the economic changes of 1819 and after.

11

"THE OLD ORDER CHANGES" *

Alfred Glaze Smith, Jr.

In the entire history of the United States perhaps no period has witnessed changes of greater magnitude and significance than those which took place during the 1820's. The shift from a society that was largely argricultural to one partially industrial, the quickening of the pace of westward expansion, the beginnings of the labor union movement, new developments in transportation, the growth of inter-city competition, the decline in the importance of foreign commerce, the rise of the West to political power—all these and other factors made their influence felt during the decade. No part of the country was immune to the rapid changes taking place. For the Old Cotton South the most striking was the spread of cotton culture into the new and more fertile areas of the Southwest—a development with an impact so great that it marked the end of one era and the beginning of another.

Before the spread of cotton production into the interior, South Carolina was virtually divided into two parts, the costal area, or Low-Country, and the Up-Country. The economy of the former was based largely on the rice plantation supplemented at an early date with indigo and after 1785 with Sea-Island cotton, dependent on a foreign market, and served by a well-developed system of commerce which handled exports of staple crops and imports of finished goods. Generally speaking, the plantation type of economy was confined at that time to the coastal area. While this expanded rapidly in the years before the Revolution, afterward the loss of markets and occupation of the available physical area slowed down the rate of expansion con-siderably. The coastal area had always been and in 1795 was still

* Excerpts from chapter 1 of *Economic Readjustment of an Old Cotton State, South Carolina, 1820–1860* (Columbia: University of South Carolina Press, 1958), pp. 1–18; Copyright © 1958 by The University of South Carolina Press, Columbia. Reprinted without footnotes by permission of the University of South Carolina Press and the author.

dependent on foreign markets to which it exported rice, indigo, lumber, naval stores, cotton, and other relatively minor items. Financing, both for working capital and development capital, was largely provided by Great Britain.

The Up-Country was settled to a considerable extent by the process of overland migration which came from the frontiers of Pennsylvania, Virginia, and North Carolina, roughly about the time of the Revolution. Before 1795 this area was largely shut off from the rest of the world by the difficulties of transportation. A thick belt of swamps made connections with the coastal areas extremely difficult, and communication with Philadelphia, though much farther in distance, was no further in time. As a result, self-subsistence was a major characteristic of the economy. The Up-Country raised for sale cereals, particularly wheat, flour, and some tobacco. These were virtually the only products which could bear the expense of transport to the market.

This economic organization was radically changed by the development of short staple cotton production after the invention of the gin. Cotton production spread into the Middle and Upper Districts after 1795 and quickly displaced tobacco. Wheat production was also affected, though more gradually. As a result, the years from 1795 to 1819 in South Carolina were mainly a period of prosperity and rapid expansion. Breaks in price levels, like that brought about by the lessened demand for cotton during the Embargo and the War of 1812, were temporary and largely recognized as such at the time. On the whole, economic progress, as measured by the growth of wealth and population, was satisfactory to the dominant commercial and social groups and took place in a manner at least bearable to others.

While the prosperity of South Carolina before 1820 was based chiefly on Upland, or short staple, cotton, it depended also to some extent on Sea-Island cotton and rice. The last two crops were of less importance simply because the areas in which they could be grown were small in size; and, indeed, Sea-Island cotton and rice limited each other, since they were often in competition for the same resources. The production of Sea-Island cotton steadily increased from the time of its introduction, about 1785. While, during the year ending September 30, 1790, less than 10,000 pounds were exported, eleven years later shipments amounted to more than 8,300,000 pounds. But such expansion could not continue indefinitely as Sea-Island cotton could not spread out of the coastal region and it depleted the soil on which it was grown.

In the last half of the eighteenth century the tidal flooding method of rice cultivation was effected and production of that grain increased rapidly. Exports maintained a steady level, however, probably because greater domestic consumption kept a large part of the crop at home. Competition between Sea-Island cotton and rice for available land and labor undoubtedly served to keep production of the latter crop down, but rice could count on the richness of its alluvial soils and their partial renewability through flooding to bring constant yields. Prices remained good, and rice was an important source of income not only before 1820 but in nearly every succeeding year until 1860.

Of far more importance than rice to the prosperity of South Carolina before 1820 was the spread of short staple cotton into the interior in response to a growing demand for the commodity.

Changes in both production and marketing methods were necessary before there could be any large scale demand for raw cotton. A long series of inventions during the eighteenth century resulted in improvement in the techniques of the English textile industry and made possible the factory system with its resulting expansion of production. As a result, between 1760 and 1800 cotton consumption increased rapidly in England, more than doubling in each decade. Demand continued to mount rapidly thereafter. Cotton manufacturing in continental Europe and the United States, although small at this time, also rose. Owing to the reduction in the cost of manufacture, the prices of yarns and finished goods fell. This in turn caused the price of raw cotton to increase.

The spread of cotton production into the interior of South Carolina took place following the removal of a number of obstructions to its profitable growth. Before the Revolutionary War the interest of the British government was in other crops, particularly wool and silk, which it attempted to encourage in the colonies. Cotton was excluded from consideration. The difficulty of separating the seed from the fiber, the too sparse population of the back country, and the physical difficulty of access to that area as well as the profits to be made from other crops were barriers to cotton growing.

The development of the saw-type gin by Eli Whitney in 1792 was the last step necessary to permit large-scale cultivation. Production had apparently already begun in the Up-Country. Two or three million pounds were produced in 1792, but due to the difficulty of preparing it for market only a small amount had been sold. The invention of the gin therefore constituted the removal of a bottle-neck, in a very real sense.

There is every indication of unparalleled prosperity prior to 1820.

It is true that cotton prices had their ups and downs but on the whole they remained at high levels until they broke suddenly in March, 1819. The annual price ranges in Charleston for the five years prior to 1819 were: for 1814, .23 to .37; for 1815, .20 to .28; for 1816, .23 to .32; for 1817, .25½ to .35; for 1818, .25 to .35.

Other evidences of prosperity and expansion that accompanied the new cotton production are not hard to find. One index of growth was the increase of population. While whites commenced to move out of the State after 1800, their number nevertheless continued to rise. But the slave population especially grew rapidly, indicating that they were being brought into the State in large numbers to provide a labor supply for an expanding agriculture.

This last development also reversed an earlier trend. Between 1775 and 1795 a fairly strong abolition movement had developed. It paralleled the drop in slave prices due in turn to the decline in the profitability of staple crop agriculture. This was reflected by the prohibition by the legislaure in 1792 of the importation of slaves into South Carolina either from abroad or from other states. The ban on imports was continued to the end of 1803, when it was rescinded. Many slaves were then brought from Virginia and Maryland, where their value was not so great. Whereas there had been more whites than slaves in the State in 1790 (140,178 to 107,094) by 1820 there were more slaves than whites (258,475 to 237,440). Between these dates, the budding abolition movement withered. While as late as 1820 many people had strong reservations about both the efficacy and morality of slavery, such opinion was voiced less and less frequently.

Cotton production spread and fixed the plantation-slave economy firmly upon the State. This development reversed a trend which set in after the Revolution. In 1783 the plantation system seemed to have only a limited future. The output of indigo was declining. Sea-Island cotton and rice provided only restricted employment for slaves and slavery appeared to be on the way out. But short staple cotton production revived the slave system and made it an integral part of the economy of the State. . . .

Subsistence farming was by no means displaced by the early introduction of cotton, but it was reduced. Growers concentrated their efforts on cotton, neglecting other crops in its favor, and relying more on the market to secure other goods for themselves. Thus the Fall Line towns of Augusta, Hamburg, Columbia, Camden, and Cheraw, which stood at the head of easy navigation, became important market depots for the surrounding areas. These centers were dependent on Charleston for the provision of marketing facilities connecting with the foreign market, which supplied both an outlet for cotton and a source for manufactured goods, luxuries as well as necessities. . . .

It was the spread of cotton production to newer and more fertile areas outside the State that was the basic cause of South Carolina's troubles and the necessity for its economic readjustment. In 1801 South Carolina produced 20 million pounds of cotton, half of the nation's crop. The same ratio prevailed in 1811, with the crop at 40 million pounds. But by 1821 production had increased only to 50 million pounds, less than two-sevenths of the American total of 177 million pounds in that year. Meanwhile, cotton prices had fallen from their bonanza levels. With this situation, in addition to increasing competition from areas which could produce cotton more cheaply, the South Carolina economy was in trouble.

The drop in cotton prices was related to the drop in the general level of prices in the United States and in the world. Indices of general price levels and of wholesale prices show lower levels for 1819 than for 1818. But the chief significance of the break as far as South Carolina was concerned was the great dependence of the economy on cotton, plus the fact that in the preceding years high cotton prices had provided a boom era. This period of prosperity, which might well be termed the golden age of the plantation in South Carolina, came to an end with the drop in cotton prices accompanying the depression of 1819. The depression was portentous, as it marked the beginning of secular change as well as of cyclical trouble. While a certain amount of recovery and revival took place in 1822 and 1823, cotton prices, the most important index of the State's economic welfare, remained low. It is clear that the depression in South Carolina was due not to temporary conditions but to fundamental changes.

Notwithstanding the lower price, however, cotton production in South Carolina continued to expand. From the fifty million pounds in 1812 it increased to seventy million in 1826. The cause of the continued increase is not difficult to find. Hezekiah Niles, editor of *Niles Register,* writing in 1822 noted that although the price of cotton was dropping its production was increasing. The reason which he gave, "The capital invested must be employed; and cannot be suddenly and generally changed," seems essentially sound, although his basic price of ten cents per pound, at which cotton production would be "unworthy of the attention of a capitalist, if he has the power to turn his capital to almost anything else," might be the subject of argument.

As a result of the end of the boom era there was an acceleration in the outward movement of population. The early emigration had been due in part to the preemption of the best lands by an expanding cotton plantation system and this continued. In addition, there were those who by their own bad judgment and mismanagement had placed themselves in a position in which they saw little alternative to flight. For purposes of expansion or for other reasons they had incurred obligations during flush times with the expectation of being able to repay them out of profits. While bonanza prices prevailed for cotton these parties were able to keep out of trouble. Newspapers of the period 1815 to early 1819 show little in the way of property offered for sale or legal action taken against debtors. But in the latter part of 1819 the same papers reveal a great deal of distress. Land, Negroes, and farm equipment were offered for sale by their owners or, more significantly, by the sheriff. In many instances the same property was offered at several successive sales, indicating that there was no rush to take it up. But primarily emigration was the response of ambitious men to the lure of better lands and greener pastures somewhere to the West. When cotton prices declined this attraction loomed larger. Of those who left, the great majority went to the Southwest in search of cheap land on which to grow cotton while a smaller number moved northwestward in search of better opportunities. After 1820 there was also for the first time a net out-movement of slaves.

Most of the small farmers who did not emigrate retained their independent status. During the pre-1820 bonanza period, especially, the more able began to grow cotton as land and market opportunities opened up, bought slaves with their profits and their credit, and became planters. Others, particularly after 1820, who lacked the ambition or ability either to emigrate or to adapt themselves to changing conditions, fell back or continued to rely on subsistence farming. Many were pushed into the less desirable lands, swelling the ranks of the so-called poor-white class.

Mercantile houses failed also, three closing their doors in Camden alone in the last four months of 1819. Since it was customary for such establishments to grant credit to their customers, their collapse is not surprising in view of the drop in the price of cotton during the spring of that year. Even coroners' juries took cognizance of the times. In a report on a suicide, a Charleston jury held that "the deceased came to his death by destroying himself in a fit of mental derangement by blowing out his brains with a pistol. The cause was losses in trade, occasioned by the pressure of the times."

The most marked aspect of the changing times was the decline in the volume of foreign trade handled by Charleston. Although this was due to some extent to the substitution of domestic areas as markets and sources of supply, the drop was far too great to be accounted for entirely by this shift. Foreign commerce, in fact, showed little tendency to revive throughout the whole of the decade of the 1820's.

This decrease was in reality a reflection of the economic difficulties of South Carolina, and Charleston lost the preeminence which it had long enjoyed among the port cities in the United States. This regression was felt the more keenly because the total value of the business of the city, foreign and domestic combined, had suffered an absolute as well as a relative decline. To some extent the loss was also the result of the development of commercial centers along the Fall Line. But the drop in the price of cotton is alone sufficient to explain the reduction in the value of business, since cotton production formed a large part of the base on which the commerce of the port rested. . . .

By 1822 the cyclical crisis was over and economic conditions had improved. Still, it is apparent that the affairs of the State's citizens were not going too well. A large body of material in the newspapers of the times bears painful testimony to this effect. For example, since slaves were considered to be the best collateral that could be given as security for loans, it would be expected that any distress would be reflected by foreclosure sales primarily concerned with these items. Such was the case. During the summer and fall of 1823 and 1824 the sheriff was busy through the State, and lists of properties offered for sale for non-payment of 1822 and 1823 taxes were long. The lists of attachments *in assumpsit* and notices of sales on account of debt were equally extensive. The following ad was rather typical:

From 30 to 50 negroes for sale. The subscriber will offer for sale at his Plantation, on the Wateree River, in Fairfield District, the above number of Negroes on the last Thursday and Friday of the present month. The Negroes are not sold for any faults in themselves, being a first rate set of hands, but merely to relieve their owner from his pecuniary embarrassments.

The terms of the sale will be twelve months credit, purchasers giving Note and approved security. Wm. A. A. Belton. [. . .]

The economic situation of the State continued to deteriorate. Cotton prices were not satisfactory and markets were unsettled. While non-foreclosure sales were also heavy, the sheriff was still busy in 1825 and 1826, and exceptionally so in 1827. Merchants had their share of troubles, too. In the summer of 1826 the property of one Camden merchant came under the hammer, while another advertised that "The subscriber being aware of the difficulty of obtaining cash, under present emergencies, will sell the above articles at a more moderate profit than he has been in the habit of receiving, especially groceries of which he has lately received more than an ordinary supply." . . .

By 1827 the continuing depression had thoroughly aroused the people of the State. They contemplated drastic action. Fuel was added to the fire by the tariff. Nor did Charleston take kindly to seeing itself outstripped by other cities of the Atlantic seaboard.

The mercantilistic type of economic philosophy which predominated is a factor helping to account for the general concern. For example population growth was considered to be an index of progress. The populations of other areas were increasing more rapidly than that of South Carolina. As a result its citizens felt that the State was losing the position of political preeminence which it had long held in national councils. It was not until 1840 that the State's congressional representation was reduced absolutely, but even in the 1820's its politicians, who had held such a large share of the important positions in the federal government, were losing part of the important role which they had played in the national scene.

The State's leaders were well aware of the fact that the westward spread of cotton production was redounding to the disadvantage of South Carolina. Governor Bennett in his message to the legislature in 1822 made reference to the internal improvements program, and in enumerating the resulting benefits he stated,

The facility thus given to our own citizens will enable them to enter into successful competition with their western brethren in the staple commodity of this state. It will produce an immediate and salutary influence over the morals of the community, give life and facility to industry, develop the resources, add to the political importance, and establish permanently the prosperity of the state.

In a way, this statement could be taken as a keynote. The same idea was expressed many times in subsequent years and was used to justify much of the legislation enacted for internal improvement and other programs. . . .

Changed economic conditions in South Carolina were marked by changed attitudes on the major political issues of slavery, the tariff, and internal improvements. During the 1820's the viewpoint of most of the people of the State underwent radical alteration on these subjects. . . .

It may be said that in South Carolina a long period of preeminence, both economic and political, had come to an end by 1820. The most significant factor in the close of this era was that western competition brought about the decline in the profitability of growing cotton. Closely related factors were soil exhaustion and emigration. The expansion of agriculture in South Carolina before 1820 had involved the cultivation of much fresh land and with acreage relatively plentiful and labor rather scarce, few took the trouble to take care of the soil which they were cultivating. The condition was made worse by the knowledge that there was a plentiful supply of land in the West while the decline in fertility in South Carolina areas furnished an immediate incentive to emigrate.

No man better personified antebellum South Carolina than John C. Calhoun. In a very real sense this highly talented man represents both the state's impressive achievements in political leadership and its tragic withdrawal from the nation's progress. Richard N. Current in the following article traces the life of Calhoun through his early phase of nationalism to his leadership of the state in the Nullification crisis. As his state turned from nationalism, so did Calhoun.

Calhoun served in the Senate until 1843. In 1844 he became the secretary of state under John Tyler. In March 1845 he returned to the Senate. To the close of his life he adamantly insisted that the South could remain in the Union only if the security of slavery were guaranteed.

12

JOHN C. CALHOUN AND NULLIFICATION *

Richard N. Current

"Judged by later times and his meaning for them, Calhoun stands in the first rank of men America has produced," one of his biographers concluded a hundred years after his death. "For as a thinker and prophet he was more important for later times than his own."

A number of present-day Americans share this view of John C. Calhoun. They consider him as somehow more relevant to the twentieth century than any of his political contemporaries, including his great rivals Daniel Webster and Henry Clay. His admirers look upon him as a defender of minority rights and an inventor of democratic techniques.

If the neo-Calhounites are to be believed—if Calhoun speaks for the democratic-minded citizens or for the minorities of today—then he is, indeed, more important for our times than for his. Not only that. He must also have a rather different significance now than a century and more ago.

To understand fully the meaning of his ideas for his own time, if not also for ours, we must review the circumstances in which Calhoun presented them. He wrote and spoke as a politician and advocate, not as a disinterested scholar or philosopher, though there was much of the scholar and the philosopher in him. He put forth his thoughts in the course of a long political career, extending from 1810, when he first ran for Congress, to 1850, when he died. During those forty years he served, at one time or another, as Congressman, Secre-

* Excerpt from *Great American Thinkers: John C. Calhoun* (New York: Washington Square Press, 1963), pp. 3–19; copyright, © 1963, by Washington Square Press, Inc. Reprinted by permission of publishers.

tary of War, Vice-President, Secretary of State, and United States
Senator. And he aspired continually to become President.

For approximately the first third of his career he was a nationalist
who urged the bold use of governmental powers to develop and
strengthen the country as a whole. For the remaining two-thirds, he
was a state-rights man and a sectionalist who strove to limit the powers
of the federal government and thus to protect the interests of the
South, that is, the interests of the slaveowners.

FAMILY BACKGROUND AND EDUCATION . .

Slavery and state rights featured the world that Calhoun first knew,
in the back country of South Carolina, where he was born on March
18, 1782. He was descended from Scotch-Irish pioneers who, in these
Carolina hills, had faced the danger of hostile Indians (one of his
grandmothers had died in a massacre) and then, during the Revolutionary War, had faced the danger of British redcoats and American
Tories. His father, Patrick Calhoun, prospered after the war. By 1790,
when John was eight years old and the first federal census was taken,
his father owned thirty-one slaves, a larger number than most slaveholders owned in his part of the state. Patrick Calhoun also rose to
prominence in local affairs. He opposed the ratification of the United
States Constitution in 1787-88. Already he had fought a war on account
of taxation without representation, and he feared that the new Constitution would revive the very same evil, for it would permit the
representatives of other states to impose taxes upon the people of
South Carolina.

When his father died, John was fourteen and was studying at a
log-cabin academy operated by his brother-in-law, Moses Waddell.
He now left school, worked on the family farm for a few years, and
then decided to resume his studies and go on to college. With the
financial support of his brothers, he went back to Waddell's academy
for a while. At twenty, he left for faraway Connecticut, to enroll as a
junior at Yale.

In those days Yale was the intellectual home of the extreme New
England Federalists who, now that Thomas Jefferson was President,
turned his state-rights arguments against him in opposing almost everything he did or tried to do. The college president, Timothy Dwight,
was fond of denouncing the Jeffersonians as atheists and Jacobin

revolutionaries. After two years in this intellectual atmosphere, during which he won election to Phi Beta Kappa, Calhoun was graduated. For commencement he prepared an address on "the qualifications necessary to constitute a perfect statesman." After leaving Yale, he spent a year in Litchfield, Connecticut, at the law school of Judge Tapping Reeve, another state-rights Federalist.

Upon the completion of his studies, at twenty-four, Calhoun was a tall, wiry, handsome man, with black hair and burning eyes. Like the devout Calvinist he was, he took life seriously and had little time or inclination for fun. He lacked a sense of humor. He also lacked money and social position, but he possessed plenty of self-confidence, ambition, and determination. The wealth and position that he wanted, he was in due time to get by marriage.

While a student in New Haven and in Litchfield, he had occasionally visited and often corresponded with Mrs. Floride Calhoun, a South Carolina low-country aristocrat, his cousin's widow and heir, who summered at Newport, Rhode Island. Mrs. Calhoun had a daughter, also named Floride, who was ten years younger than Calhoun. Through the mother, he began to court the daughter. Eventually he got permission to woo the young Floride directly, by mail. He is said to have composed and sent her a love poem each line of which began with "Whereas" except the last line, which began with "Therefore." In 1811, when he was approaching twenty-nine, the two were married in the bride's home near Charleston.

Before the year's end, without waiting for the birth of his first child, Calhoun left his bride to go to Washington and sit with Congress. From that time on, his career always took precedence over his family life.

THE NATIONALIST

During the session of 1811–12 Congress wrestled with the problem of the proper American response to current British policy. The British impressed seamen from American ships, infringed upon neutral rights, and abetted the Indians who threatened the Northwestern frontier. The new young congressmen from the frontier areas, Jeffersonian Republicans, who followed the lead of Henry Clay, of Kentucky, demanded the use of force. They were dubbed War Hawks, and Calhoun was one of them. Clay put him on the Foreign Affairs Com-

mittee. As acting chairman and then chairman of this key committee, Calhoun took an important part in preparing Congress and the
people for war. He called for patriotism. "The honor of a nation
is its life," he said. "Deliberately to abandon it, is to commit an
act of political suicide." He introduced the resolution for declaring
war on Great Britain.

Throughout the War of 1812 Calhoun contended, against the ob-
structionism of New England state-rights men like Daniel Webster,
of New Hampshire, for measures and men with which to win the
war. He came to be hailed as "the young Hercules who carried the
war on his shoulders."

After the return of peace, Calhoun rose to be majority leader of the
Jeffersonian Republicans in the House. He used his influence to promote what he referred to as an "enlarged policy" and what Clay called
the American System. This was a program of national planning for
prosperity and defense. According to the program, the federal government was to levy tariffs for protecting and encouraging manufactures,
set up a bank for providing a uniform currency and abundant credit,
and spend freely to build a network of highways and waterways. Calhoun was especially enthusiastic about transportation improvements
(then commonly known as "internal improvements"). "We are under
the most imperious obligation to counteract every tendency to disunion," he declared. "Let us, then, bind the republic together with a
perfect system of roads and canals. Let us conquer space."

Clay and Calhoun succeeded in two of the three items in their post-
war legislative program. Congress passed and President James Madison
signed a bill imposing protective duties (the Tariff of 1816) and another establishing a second Bank of the United States. Congress also
passed—but the President vetoed—a bill for devoting to internal improvements the "bonus" and the annual sums which the bank was to
pay for its charter. Though Madison professed to favor the betterment of transportation, he thought he saw in the Constitution serious
impediments to federal expenditure for that purpose.

Calhoun was disgusted by Madison's constitutional reasoning. "I am
no advocate for refined arguments on the Constitution," he said. "The
instrument was not intended as a thesis for the logician to exercise his
ingenuity on. It ought to be construed with plain, good sense; and
what can be more express than the Constitution on this very point?"
Nothing, obviously, could be more explicit than the constitutional

authority for spending on the improvement of transportation, for the Constitution in so many words gave Congress the power to lay taxes and provide for the common defense and the general welfare. So it seemed to Calhoun in 1817—about a decade before he himself began, as a logician, to exercise his ingenuity upon the Constitution.

That same year he received his first appointment to an administrative position, as Secretary of War in the cabinet of James Monroe. Immediately the new secretary undertook to bring vigor and system into the affairs of his department. In his plans for extensive border and coastal fortifications he was frustrated by the parsimony of Congress and the Treasury, but he carried forward the work of removing the Indian tribes to the West, and he provided for regulating the Indian trade through the licensing of private traders and the competition of government trading posts. He also reorganized the army supply services, unified and clarified the command system, reinvigorated the academy at West Point, and cut the cost-per-man of maintaining the armed forces. In his eight years in office he gained, as he deserved, a lasting reputation as one of the ablest of War Secretaries—one to be compared in later generations, with such successors as Jefferson Davis, Elihu Root, and Henry L. Stimson.

While Calhoun was in the War office, there occurred three events that were vitally to affect his future, though at that time he could not be fully aware of their significance. First, in 1817, General Andrew Jackson led his army on a punitive raid into Florida, then Spanish territory, and Secretary Calhoun, as Jackson's superior, sought in vain to have him reprimanded. Second, the Panic of 1819 touched off a business depression that aroused popular discontent and thus heightened political and sectional tensions. Third, the Missouri controversy of 1819-21, when Northern politicians tried to prevent the admission of Missouri as a slave state, awakened Jefferson like "a fire-bell in the night" and increased the sectionalization of politics—which, in turn, destroyed Calhoun's chances of riding into the presidency, at an early date, on a wave of nationalism such as he had been seeking to arouse.

The omens were not immediately clear. In 1821, at thirty-nine, Calhoun thought he saw a presidential opportunity by 1824. Other members of Monroe's cabinet were in the running; why not he? There was John Quincy Adams, of Massachusetts, the Secretary of State, and there was William H. Crawford, of Georgia, the Secretary of the Treasury. There was also Clay, the Speaker of the House. Calhoun felt he was as good a man and had as good a chance as any of the three. No opposition was to be expected from the Federalist party, for it was now defunct as a national organization. All the contenders belonged to the Republican party.

Before long Calhoun's calculations were upset by an outsider: by General Jackson, the hero of New Orleans, who had the backing of astute politicians in his home state of Tennessee and in other states. Calhoun counted upon the votes of Pennsylvania, for the Pennsylvanians were devout protectionists and so was he, as his record in Congress demonstrated. Yet, long before election time, the Pennsylvanians clearly showed their preference for Jackson. Reluctantly but wisely Calhoun withdrew from the presidential campaign and entered the vice-presidential. He doubled his chances of success by running on two tickets, with both Jackson and Adams.

In 1824 no candidate gained a majority of the electoral vote, so the final choice was left to the House of Representatives. Clay threw his support to Adams, and the house chose him as President. Then Adams, once he had been inaugurated, appointed Clay as Secretary of State. It appeared that Adams, in return for Clay's assistance was naming Clay as his successor, for most of the previous Secretaries of State, like Adams himself, had succeeded to the presidency. Raising the cry of "corrupt bargain," the Jacksonians began at once to campaign for vindicating Jackson—the people's choice, they said—at the very next election. Calhoun, while Adams' Vice-President, cooperated with the Jacksonians to bring about Adams' defeat in 1828. That year he ran again for the vice-presidency, but on the Jackson ticket only.

Meanwhile Calhoun and other political leaders throughout the nation had been brought to reconsider their views on national policy in consequence of economic changes that were affecting the various regions in different ways. Earlier, as a congressman, he had been free to urge nationalistic policies because his own constituents in South Carolina, or large numbers of them, had favored such policies. As late as 1816 a majority of the South Carolina representatives in Congress had voted for the protective tariff. At that time it seemed that the state had a promising future in industrialization, for she possessed ample water power which might be used for manufacturing textiles in the same areas where the cotton itself was grown.

After 1816, however, the Carolinians devoted themselves more and more to planting, and few mills appeared. The planters came to look upon the tariff as no help but a hurt to them. It cut down imports and hence exports. By reducing the foreign market for cotton, it lowered the price of what the planters sold; by limiting the competition of foreign with domestic manufactures, it raised the cost of what they had to buy. It produced revenues with which to pay for internal improvements, and these in turn were cited in justification of the tariff. Most of the internal improvements, the Carolinians and other Southerners felt, provided connections between the Northeast and the Northwest and thus encouraged the growth of the North at the expense of the South.

While Southerners were turning against the tariff (and internal improvements as well), New Englanders were coming to its support. Among New Englanders, as among Southerners, ideas changed with changing interests. A majority of New England representatives, including Daniel Webster, had voted against the Tariff of 1816, because the predominant interest of their region then lay in the shipping business, in the import trade. But Jefferson's Embargo and the War of 1812 stimulated the rise of cotton mills along the streams of New England. Merchants and shipowners put more and more of their accumulated profits into manufacturing. By about 1830 New England sentiment was to be, on balance, protectionist. By then Webster, once a free trader, already was a tariff advocate, and he was to devote the rest of his career to refuting his own early arguments.

The middle states, especially Pennsylvania, had been protectionist all along. Their representatives, together with allies from other sections, obtained an increase in duties in 1824. In 1827 the Woolens Bill would have raised still higher the rates on manufactured wool. The bill passed the House but was held up by a tie vote in the Senate. As the Senate's presiding officer, Calhoun could cast the deciding vote. He now made a choice that marked the beginning of the end of his nationalist phase. He voted no.

The defeat of the Woolens Bill aroused protectionists everywhere to renewed efforts, and these culminated, in 1828, in an act imposing the highest general level of duties yet. The Tariff of 1828 resulted from a good deal of logrolling, the motives for which were mixed. John Randolph of Roanoke said the measure was concerned with no manufactures except the manufacture of a President, and there was a bit of truth in his remark. Certainly some of the Congressmen who tacked on amendments did so in the hope of unmaking Adams as President and making Jackson President instead. The scheme was to produce a bill so outrageous that Adams would have to veto it and thus would lose protectionist votes in the fall. Other congressmen, however, sincerely desired protection for this or that commodity— for the cotton products and the wool and woolens of New England, the hemp of Kentucky, the lead of Missouri, even the lemons of Florida. Webster now made *his* great reversal and, though protesting some of the bill's features, cast his vote for the measure as a whole. It passed, and President Adams signed it.

Southerners dubbed the new law the Tariff of Abominations and, particularly in South Carolina, blamed all their economic troubles on it. The troubles of South Carolina were real enough. Plantation profits were declining, abandoned fields were filling with sedge grass, roads and bridges were falling into disrepair, and people were leaving the state in such numbers as to check its population growth. For all this the tariff was blamed. Certainly it did not help, but in fact there were other and more important causes. On the red clay of Carolina, eroded and relatively worn out, cotton growers could not compete with those on the fresher and richer lands of the Black Belt or the farther Southwest.

In South Carolina a faction of radicals demanded immediate and drastic action. They talked of withdrawing their state from the Union that treated them so ill. They would escape the tariff levies through secession. They advocated revolution, no less. And they were rapidly becoming a majority in the state.

Calhoun had to keep the state's support if he was to remain in politics. He needed Jackson's friendship and Northern backing if he was to succeed Jackson as President. He could not do this if he joined the Carolina revolutionaries. He could do still less if he defied them.

THE NULLIFICATIONIST

Thus, in 1828, Calhoun confronted a dilemma. That summer, in the quiet of his Carolina plantation, he tried to work his way out of it. He had to satisfy the Secessionists in his state without antagonizing the Unionists throughout the country. To do so, he had to find a *legal* and *constitutional* alternative to the revolutionary program of secession. He discovered or thought he discovered such an alternative in the theory of nullification which, before the summer's end, he developed and wrote down. Later that year, though neither endorsing his ideas nor naming him as their author, the state legislature published them in a pamphlet entitled "The South Carolina Exposition."

In "The South Carolina Exposition" he argued, with persuasive logic, to three main conclusions. First, the protective tariff was both unfair and unconstitutional. Second, the people of a state, being sovereign, had the right to nullify an unconstitutional law, such as the tariff; and the law would then be null and void in that state until the Constitution should be amended so as to give Congress the power in dispute; when and if this happened the aggrieved state could still secede as a last resort. Third, for the present the people of South Carolina should postpone the exercise of their right, so as to allow Congress an opportunity to rectify its constitutional error and relieve the suffering planters.

Calhoun had good reasons for being cautious and remaining anonymous, as he did in 1828 and for three years afterward. In 1828, while he was running for Vice-President on the Jackson ticket, nullification might well have been an embarrassment to him and his party. He hoped that Jackson, once he was in the White House, would use his tremendous influence to bring about a drastic reduction of the tariff. Thus the South Carolina Radicals, whom the nullification argument had persuaded to wait, would be finally appeased. And thus Calhoun, his fame untouched by state-rights heresy, would be eligible to go on to the presidency after a term or two for Jackson.

The Jackson-Calhoun ticket won the election of 1828, all right, but nothing else went the way Calhoun had hoped. He soon had to fend against a most resourceful rival for Jackson's favor, Martin Van Buren, the Little Magician of New York. Van Buren obtained the office of Secretary of State for himself and other choice political jobs for his friends. He made use of the Eaton affair further to ingratiate himself with, and estrange Calhoun from, the President. Peggy O'Neal Timberlake Eaton, the wife of Jackson's War Secretary, met snubs from the other cabinet wives, who considered her a loose woman and, even worse, a social climber. The gallant Jackson defended her virtue and insisted that all his followers accept her presence. Van Buren, a widower, ostentatiously did so. Calhoun, then living with his wife and mother-in-law in the latter's Georgetown mansion, could not well do the same, for his womenfolk were among those most shocked by Mrs. Eaton's pretensions. The President finally broke with the Vice-President when he received documentary proof that Calhoun, as Monroe's Secretary of War in 1817, had tried to censure Jackson on account of the Florida raid.

The two men differed on doctrinal as well as personal grounds. In the Webster-Hayne debate (January, 1830), Robert Y. Hayne of South Carolina presented the nullification doctrine on the floor of the Senate, while Calhoun in the presiding officer's chair nodded in approval. At a Jefferson Day dinner soon afterward, Calhoun along with other party notables waited for Jackson's toast, to see whether Jackson sympathized with the state-rights view. The President now made his position clear: "Our Federal Union! It *must* and *shall be* perserved!" When Calhoun's turn came he could only counter with: "The Federal Union—next to our liberty the most dear."

The next year, 1831, Calhoun came out publicly as the leading nullificationist. And the year after that, Congress finally got around to revising the tariff, after repeated urging by the President. But the Tariff of 1832 did not lower the rates a great deal—certainly not enough to placate the South Carolina Radicals.

Now was the time, they thought, to put nullification to the test, and Calhoun agreed with them. In his Fort Hill Letter (August 28, 1832) he restated his argument that the state could, and he urged that the state at last should, "interpose" to protect its people. The people, he insisted, would have nothing to fear from the army or the navy, for nullification, he repeated, was by nature "peaceable, consistent with the federal relations of the State, and perfectly efficient, whether contested before the Courts, or attempted to be resisted by force."

With Calhoun as their strategist and tactician, the Nullifiers, having got control of the legislature and the governorship, called a convention of delegates to represent the sovereign people of South Carolina. When it met, in November, the convention declared that all tariff acts, and particularly those of 1828 and 1832, were null and void within the state, from and after February 1, 1833. The anti-Nullifiers, who made up a large and respectable minority of the state's people, were powerless to stop the enthusiastic and almost hysterical onrush of the nullification majority.

To enable their top man to present their case in Washington, the

Nullifiers elected Calhoun to the Senate seat that Hayne left in order to become governor. Now (December, 1832) Calhoun did something that nobody before or since has done: he resigned from the vice-presidency of the United States. He returned to Washington and took his new place (January 4, 1833) while the rumor ran that Jackson has sworn to hang him as a traitor. Jackson thought nullification was treason and, in a proclamation to the people of South Carolina, had told them so. He asked Congress for authority to use the army and the navy to enforce the laws, and Congress began to debate a Force Bill.

Calhoun found himself in a worrisome predicament. He and his South Carolina followers faced the threat of the nation's armed might, and they faced it by themselves. Though they had sympathizers in other states, no one of these states officially endorsed the South Carolina position. Not even Georgia stood by her sister state, though Georgia in a dispute with her Indian tribes had asserted her own version of state rights and was disregarding if not actually nullifying a decision of the United States Supreme Court. After getting rid of the Creeks, the state had undertaken also to remove the Cherokees and open their lands to white settlement. Chief Justice John Marshall, in two decisions (1831, 1832), held that the Indians were "domestic dependent nations" and exempt from Georgia laws. (Georgia, unlike South Carolina, had the President on her side; Jackson was quoted as saying with regard to the Georgia case: "John Marshall has made his decision; now let him enforce it.") The South Carolina Nullifiers gasconaded and called out troops, but they did not really dare to stand, alone, against the forces that Jackson could command.

Nevertheless, on the Senate floor, Calhoun bravely defended his state's action and denounced the Force Bill as unconstitutional. He also undertook to justify secession on constitutional grounds. He said a state could "secede" from the Union as well as "accede" to it, as the states had done in 1787–88 and after. Webster rose to traverse Calhoun's arguments. There followed a Webster-Calhoun debate which, though less colorful and less celebrated than the Webster-Hayne debate three years earlier, exposed the issues far more thoroughly. Against Calhoun's subtle and intricate logic, Webster spoke as one dealing in plain matters of fact and common sense. "The truth is," he declared, "and no ingenuity of argument, no subtlety of distinction, can evade it, that, as to certain purposes, the people of the United States are one people." According to Webster, a state might secede from the Union, but it could do so only on the basis of the right of revolution, not on the basis of any constitutional right. While remaining within the Union, however, a state could not nullify congressional acts, for nullification was no right at all.

From his plight Calhoun was to be saved not by his logic or eloquence but by the ingenuity of his old associate and rival, the Great Compromiser, Henry Clay. Already Congress was considering the Verplanck Bill, an Administration measure for immediately cutting the tariff and thus pacifying the country. Neither Calhoun nor Clay wished to see that bill pass, for its passage would redound to the credit of their mutual enemies the Jacksonians, especially Van Buren. So Clay introduced and Calhoun supported a different bill, a compromise tariff that would lower rates but would do so only gradually, over a ten-year period. This bill finally passed.

Jackson signed the Compromise Tariff and the Force Bill on the same day. Calhoun was satisfied, but would all his followers be? To justify his work he had hurried back to South Carolina and to the state convention, already reassembled. Most of its members were persuaded, now that Congress was repealing its obnoxious tariffs, to repeal their own ordinance nullifying those laws. But, as if to have the last word, the convention passed a new ordinance nullifying the Force Act!

This second ordinance—whatever might be said of the first—was merely a gesture. By now the Force Act was inoperative. It had been designed to take effect only if South Carolina resisted the collection of customs duties or otherwise violated federal law. Actually, the Nullifiers at no time attempted to interfere with the customs at Charleston or elsewhere, and after repealing their first ordinance they did not even threaten to interfere. In their second ordinance they nullified a law already null.

Calhoun claimed success for both of the nullification ordinances. "I have no doubt," he confided to a Northern friend, "the system has got its death wound," and he meant the protective system, the tariff. "Nullification has dealt the fatal blow. We have applied the same remedy to the bloody act," that is, the Force Act. True, the tariff had been wounded, though not fatally by any means. And yet nullification had not really worked the way Calhoun had intended and had promised it would work. It had not been generally accepted as a legitimate and constitutional procedure—far from it. In practice the Calhoun principle had proved essentially a failure.

Though he never admitted this failure, Calhoun learned a lesson from it. He came to realize, only too well, that a single state, unaided, was powerless to interpose against federal authority. So, while retaining and even elaborating upon the nullification theory, he began to cultivate the condition he now knew was indispensable for the theory to operate. He began to cultivate, at every chance, a spirit of unity among all the Southern states. While not forgetting state rights, he gave more and more attention to fostering a sense of common sectional interests.

The religion of a people is often an accurate indication of their ideals and their weaknesses. In the years prior to 1860 the deism and philosophical liberalism of the eighteenth-century Jeffersonian South gave way to religious orthodoxy and conservatism. The greater the divergence of southern institutions from the mainstream of nineteenth-century America, the more Southerners turned to conservative religion. Most southern churches agreed that Christianity should be concerned with private morality and not with the overriding social problems. Hence, there was active opposition to drinking, adultery, and breach of the Sabbath; but slavery was defended. The abolition movement prompted a number of the southern churches to separate from their national organizations. Rosser Howard Taylor describes the churches of antebellum South Carolina.

13

"THE CHURCH
AND ITS AUXILIARIES" *

Rosser Howard Taylor

The religious scene in South Carolina in ante-bellum days was not essentially different from that in neighboring seaboard states. In the main, Episcopalians were concentrated in the Low-Country; Baptists and Methodists were in evidence throughout the State, with a preponderance of numbers in the Up-Country; Presbyterians, less numerous than the Baptists and Methodists, were widely distributed; while Lutherans were largely confined to the German groups in the city of Charleston and the town of Walhalla and to the Districts of Newberry and Lexington. There were Jewish congregations in Charleston, Georgetown, Sumter and Columbia and elsewhere in the trading centers. The Roman Catholics, with fourteen churches, possessed accommodations in Charleston in excess of those for the rest of the State. Congregationalists, Friends and a few minor sects complete the picture.

Church buildings varied in size and appearance from the stately and historic St. Michael's Church in Charleston to the crude log structures of the backwoods communities. The Episcopalians early evinced a predilection for architectural beauty in church edifices in both city and country. Constructed of brick, parish churches of the Low-Country erected in the Colonial Period stand in many instances to this day like cameos set in emerald borders of venerable live oaks draped with Spanish moss. Not all churches in the tidewater were pleasing in appearance; but outside of tidewater, with a few notable exceptions, the church buildings were more often than not plain rectangular wooden structures, with bare walls, homemade benches and with pulpits of the simplest design. The two church buildings at Conwayboro, Presbyterian and Methodist, were described

* Excerpt from *Ante-bellum South Carolina* (Chapel Hill: University of North Carolina Press, 1942), pp. 150–70; copyright, 1942, The University of North Carolina Press. Reprinted without footnotes by permission of The University of North Carolina Press.

by an English visitor, W. W. Malet, as "two long wooden buildings with green venetians and left windows," open seats and galleries for slaves. The backwoods country churches, according to Olmsted, were constructed of logs or rough boards.

A service at one of the "cracker" churches which Olmsted attended presented some singular and interesting features. The slaves were seated in the gallery, while the whites occupied the main floor. The discourse, by an uneducated preacher, was extemporaneous, and consisted, in the main, of a picturization of the terrors of hell into which the unsaved were cast before the very eyes of their relatives and friends. During the service people were going out and coming in, babies were crying and crawling about the floor with food in their hands, while just outside the building there was much conversation, neighing and braying. The bedlam described by Olmsted was probably exaggerated, but it must be admitted that in backwoods churches the service was characterized by a lack of formality. Songs, which engaged much time and attention, were generally led by a local hymnologist whose only musical aid was a simple tuning fork. Some song books contained hymns without musical notation, while others of a more popular variety, such as *Southern Harmony*, were compiled with shape notes which the musical portion of the congregation memorized in "singin' school." The Presbyterian service at Conwayboro consisted of the singing of a hymn led by an elder, a prayer by the minister, the reading of a psalm and then another hymn. Following these preliminaries, the minister delivered the sermon which was followed by a prayer and a hymn, concluding the service. The order of service in this village of about 350 people was followed with some variation in the Methodist, Baptist and Presbyterian churches throughout the State. The Episcopal and Roman Catholic services were more formal, dignified and standardized; and, accordingly, not calculated to appeal to social groups in which frontier attitudes were strongly marked.

Intelligent congregations were served by ministers of piety and learning; backwoods congregations were served, as a rule, by well-meaning but unlettered exhorters. One of the prime objects of every denomination, however, was to provide a better-trained and more godly ministry. The Charleston Baptist Association in 1818 despatched a circular letter concerning the character of the Baptist ministry to all the churches within its jurisdiction containing the following significant statement: "Men should not ordinarily be sent out to preach without going through a course of studies as will fit them to stand as intelligent witnesses of God's truth and to communicate real instruction to both saints and sinners." Further evidence of the concern of the denominations for providing a trained ministry is seen in the brave efforts made by them to found and support theological seminaries in South Carolina and adjacent states. On the whole, the requirements for ordination in the Episcopal Church were probably higher than those prescribed by other Protestant denominations for admission to the ministry. In consequence, the Episcopal Church in the 'twenties suffered from a dearth of clergymen. Due to less exacting intellectual tests for acquiring the cloth, the Baptists, Methodists, Presbyterians and other Protestant denominations were better provided with ministers of the gospel.

While earnest and devout clergymen were everywhere accorded great respect by the generality of the people, one cannot subscribe wholly to a statement of the English clergyman Malet that "great respect was everywhere paid to all ministers of the gospel." Early Methodist ministers were subjected to much ridicule in Columbia, where students once released a live goose in the meeting house. According to James Jenkins, one of the most celebrated of the early Methodist ministers, the resident minister at Society Hill (denomination unknown), used his influence to have the society of Methodists expelled from the town. In spite of opposition, the Methodists maintained their precarious position at Society Hill until some wag "fenced up the road leading to the church." The itinerant Methodist preachers were a strange lot in that they wore costumes of a queer cut, brushed their hair downward and foreswore beard and suspenders. Their zeal for the pure life led them to condemn unsparingly intemperance, cockfighting, dancing and attendance on theatres and circuses. Notwithstanding the ridicule of which they were victims, Methodist ministers, in time, by the display of great zeal and piety, came to be regarded as true messengers of the gospel.

Salaries were so meager, especially in the rural districts, as to force a minister to serve several churches in rotation and, in addition, to pursue some worldly occupation, usually farming, to supplement the dribbles received from the churches. The Reverend James Jenkins farmed and served several churches near Camden. "I had to work hard in my crop," he wrote, "but did not neglect to call sinners to repentance." Olmsted states that country churches paid their pastors an annual salary of $150 to $200. Poorly paid ministers in the rural districts found time, however, to minister to the spiritual needs of the afflicted in soul and body, to officiate at weddings and funerals and to take the initiative in reconciling brethren at variance. Churches in sizeable towns and in Charleston paid salaries which enabled a clergyman to rear a family in comfortable circumstances. For example, the Bethel (Presbyterian) Church at Walterboro paid the pastor an annual salary of $1,000 in 1827, but reduced the salary, upon calling a new pastor, to $800. A few of the older churches of the Low-Country were endowed with goods or money or both; and, besides, realized a substantial revenue from the sale or rental of pews. The Bethel Church at Walterboro owned a plantation and slaves. While these goods may not have proved a source of steady revenue, the sale or rental of pews yielded a small but steady income. The Register of Christ Church Parish indicates that in 1837 Christ Church owned 110 shares of bank stock in addition to stock in insurance companies and mortgages on real estate.

Protestant churches generally supported Bible societies, Sunday Schools, domestic and foreign missions, religious publications and education. The Bethesda (Presbyterian) Church of Camden contributed annually to domestic and foreign missions the sum of one hundred dollars divided equally between the two causes. This church also helped to support the Theological Seminary at Columbia, the American Bible Society, the Sunday School Union, the Camden Sunday School, the Commissioners' Fund to the General Assembly and a denominational paper. . . .

Frequent resort to fasting and prayer to placate the wrath of the Creator and to promote individual humility suggests a deep reliance upon the mercies of God and faith in personal abnegation. Conversion in the Baptist, Presbyterian and Methodist churches, according to John Belton O'Neall, involved a great mental and physical ordeal. The churches were provided with "mourners' benches" to which those convicted of sin came in the presence of the congregation and wrestled with their disturbed consciences, "seeking the light of personal salvation." A person under conviction would oftentimes return to the mourners' bench day after day and night after night before experiencing the change of heart incident to personal salvation. When the emotional crisis was passed, the ecstatic convert would rise and receive the heartfelt felicitations of the minister and anxious friends and relatives. Upon a public declaration of faith, the neophyte was subsequently baptized and received into the membership of the church. A religious pattern woven and transmitted by preceding generations pointed the mind to expect an experience of grace in token of divine forgiveness and personal regeneration. The ministers understood the workings of the carnal mind "and as it were, laid the sinner down on the table like an anatomist, and, taking their scapel of truth, laid bare muscle after muscle, vein after vein, artery after artery until the sinner felt that unless he could obtain mercy, he was a lost man."

On occasion, when certain reprehensible practices seemed to be in the ascendant, the churches would inveigh against the wayward and vicious courses of ungodly men. The Saluda Baptist Association, embracing a membership of 1,016, in its annual meeting in the Pendleton District in 1827 viewed "with deep regret and sorrow" the practice of electioneering "as subversive of good morals, leading the young and inconsiderate into habits of intemperance and folly." The Association placed itself on record individually and collectively to withhold votes and influence from candidates "who resort to the practice of going from place to place collecting—the vile and the vicious, the young and inexperienced and dealing out to them copious draughts of ardent spirits." The Bible Society of Greenville at its meeting in 1830 listed the following as the major sins of the people: violation of the Sabbath, taking the name of the Lord in vain, the extensive use of ardent spirits, and the use of intoxicating spirits in elections. As the evils indicated persisted, it is doubtful whether the protests of religious bodies greatly influenced the general public; but they serve, at any rate, to show that the church and its auxiliaries were alive to flagrant abuses deemed to be detrimental to the social order.

It should be noted that protests against prevalent evils emanated, as a rule, more from religious bodies in the Up-Country than from those of the Low-Country; but there the viewpoint of the people was more closely identified with the frontier. Consequently, there was slightly more intolerance and provincialism and less disposition to condone conduct which infringed upon the literal prohibitions of Holy Writ. The mind of the Up-Countryman proceeded from that of the European nonconformist which Everett Dean Martin describes as caring "little for beauty or gaiety and frowns on amusements and idleness. . . . It prizes simple goodness above either art or intellectual achievement," and emphasizes the virtues of thrift, responsibility and sobriety. The frontier state of mind of the Up-Country, however, gradually underwent modification in the direction of the cavalier ideals of the Low-Country. Two factors were mainly responsible for this transformation: the spread of cotton culture into the Piedmont and the annual exodus of the planters of the tidewater to the hills in search of health. So marked was this change, that towards the end of the ante-bellum period the most intelligent classes of the Up-Country subscribed unreservedly to the social code of the "cotton barons" of the Low-Country.

In the realm of individual behavior, the church unquestionably exercised a great spiritual and disciplinary influence over its communicants. Fear of suspension or expulsion from the church often deterred weak and halting church members from leaving the path of rectitude. The watchful eye of the church was ever upon them, and infractions of church rules involved an airing of personal weakness which usually proved embarrassing and humiliating to the offender. The records of the business sessions of most of the churches are filled with accounts of actions taken by the church in reproof of recalcitrant and erring members. . . .

Defection in orthodoxy, intemperance, immorality and profane swearing on the part of church members were common causes for disciplinary action. A person excluded from "the sealing ordinances of the church" could ordinarily, by walking circumspectly for a time, so commend himself to the brethren as to bring about his restoration to the fellowship of the church. Exclusion from the church carried a social stigma which few people cared to support; accordingly, excommunicated persons, unless devoid of a sense of personal pride or inordinately stubborn, usually strove to be restored to membership upon a statement of their intention to live comfortably. On December 16, 1815, Peter B—— was excluded from the Siloam (Baptist) Church for drunkenness, "but when he came repentant, the deacons were merciful.". . .

Women, who appear to have constituted a majority of the membership of the churches, attended the business meetings; but, as a rule, remained silent. As the "weaker vessel" who yielded to the original temptation and brought sin into the world, woman still suffered from the medieval conception of depravity. In this connection, a minute of the Siloam Church near Greenwood is of interest; "The sisters shall not be prohibited a voice in ordinary cases, but when it is judged most necessary in certain difficult matters, the whole business shall rest with the men."

The membership rolls of nearly all churches carried the names of Negro slaves; and special sections of the church, usually the galleries, were reserved for their convenience. The Register of St. James' (Santee) Parish, for example, contains copious records of the confirmation of slaves. On January 29, 1854, the following slaves belonging to William Lucas, planter, were confirmed: "Isaac, Billy, Matt, Jimmy, Jack, Mary, Bess, Grace, Fanny, Sarah, Selby, Jucy, and Rose." At Spartanburg in 1845 about one third of the members of the Methodist Church and about one tenth of the members of the Baptist Church were slaves. Of the membership of the Mispah (Baptist) Church, near Florence, in 1842, twenty-eight were white males, thirty-seven white females. In some of the parish churches of the Low-Country the black members outnumbered the whites. Outside of tidewater, however, the whites were generally in the majority.

Masters were willing and, in most cases, doubtless, even desirous that their slaves attend and join a church. Aside from the spiritual benefits to be derived from such a connection, church membership furnished a weapon for enforcing obedience to the will of the master. Threat of expulsion from the church did, in some cases, serve to make slaves more tractable; while instruction in Christian behavior imparted by the church was conducive to faithful service. The slaves found it exceedingly difficult to conform to the rigid requirements of conduct prescribed for church members. Many who were received into the church were subsequently excluded for the sin of immorality. Marriage ties rested rather lightly on the sable brethren; in consequence, they were almost constantly subjected to church discipline for the sins of fornication and adultery. In this connection, the minutes of the Siloam Church are illuminating. Black members of the congregation in 1810 numbered fourteen, of which number eight were excommunicated. Of the white membership of seventy-one only eight were not in good standing. Other church records reveal a similar situation. The Siloam Church in conference in December, 1811, excluded "Wardlaw's Abram" from the fellowship of the church "for living in the sin of adultery as we think, he having married a woman and they parted, and he taking another in her life-time." Again on February 22, 1812, the church in conference excluded Brother Ned, a Negro, from its fellowship because he was accused of being the father of a bastard child. November 17, 1818, Barnet, a black man, was "excommunicated" for drinking too much and for unbecoming conduct with "Brother Hill's Negro woman." At the Mispah Church on the fourth Sunday in August, 1838, a charge was laid against Polly, belonging to Hugh Cannon, "for having brought forth a white child." She was excluded from the church. Slaves were also disciplined by the church for running away from their masters and for stealing. Sometimes, after a period of probation, excommunicated slaves were restored to the church; but with disturbing regularity they reverted to wicked ways until the weight of years curbed physical activities. Many of the transgressions of black church members were never exposed publicly. As unbecoming conduct on the part of servants reflected a measure of discredit on masters, many slaveholders discreetly settled at home cases involving turpitude. It was a source of satisfaction to a slaveowner to have his "people" described as "well-behaved" for the reason that slaves born and reared on a plantation or farm were supposed to share at least measurably the ideals of their owners.

By and large, the church was a potent influence in shaping the ideals and attitudes of the community. The gospel it proclaimed comforted the believer in adversity as in prosperity. Resignation to the will of God, so much in evidence, brought solace to those bereaved; and reliance upon the promises of Holy Writ sustained those who struggled to overcome the world. Of simple religious faith, there was a great deal; of agnosticism and infidelity, very little. There were, of course, sinners and backsliders of the deepest dye, but these in sober moments acknowledged the hand of God in the affairs of men. South Carolina, like most agrarian commonwealths, was essentially a religious community.

Evidence of respect for the Christian church and religion is seen in the general observance of the Sabbath. On the Sabbath, the weather being favorable, people of all classes repaired to church in large numbers. Those who could not afford conveyances walked, while people of moderate means rode in wagons, chairs, sulkies or on horseback. Dr. P. B. Ruff recalled that in Newberry District many of the women had to walk to the meetinghouse. On commencing the journey, they would tie their shoes and stockings in a handkerchief and go barefooted until they were within one hundred yards of the church, at which point they sat down and clothed their feet for the entry into the church yard. The family of means and good breeding journeyed to church in much style. Caroline Gilman describes the procession which her family made *en route* to the country church on a quiet Sabbath morning. Her mother and the children rode in a carriage, her brothers rode on horseback, while her father traveled in a buggy "in which he could cross and reconnoitre two or three fields on his way." Outside the country church, before the service, men tied their horses, compared notes on the crops and discussed public questions until the ladies inside started the opening hymn; whereupon, they would file into the church with becoming reverence and sit, as a rule, apart from the women. It was not until after the service that ladies loitered on the grounds for a brief round of conversation, which included invitations to dinner. Without any pre-concerted signal, familes found their conveyances, and then a long procession of vehicles and pedestrians would swing into the serpentine road and move jerkily through the fields and forests to homes where the proverbial Sunday dinner awaited hearty appetites.

The Methodists, accounted among the strictest observers of the Sabbath, were enjoined not to make idle visits on Sunday and on no account to begin or complete a journey on the Lord's Day. Places of business were closed and people generally abstained from their accustomed labors, except in so far as necessity dictated. Here and there, in such places as Charleston Neck, disreputable characters congregated on Sunday and engaged in cockfighting, gambling and drinking to the mortification of respectable people; but such doings were rather effectually screened. Town ordinances incorporated "blue laws" to restrain those who were disposed to desecrate the Sabbath by buying and selling. The ordinances of the City of Charleston made it unlawful to sell in the public markets or elsewhere in the city on Sunday. No sports or games were allowed, and no person was to ride or drive faster than a walk when passing places of worship on the Lord's Day.

An adjunct of the church, which attained increasing importance in ante-bellum days, was the Sunday School. The primary object of the Sunday School was to provide religious instruction for children. Such schools were usually conducted under the auspices of the church; although, in some instances, they appear to have been independent establishments. For example, the Reverend John McLees noted in his diary April 8, 1838: "Began a Sabbath School in our old cotton house at ten o'clock composed of our own family with D. Simpsons, Sadlers, and Hasletts. We spent some time on McDowells Quest [questions] and appointed five Quest [questions] in the Shorter Chatechism and chose E. C. Haslett for teacher." This Sunday School closed on December 23 and reopened the following April. A Sunday School was established at Camden in 1819. Here, as elsewhere, the "scholars" were examined periodically in the catechism and the public was invited to hear the recitations. Regarding the Sunday School at Camden, a contributor to the Camden newspaper stated that "within the last twelve months forty scholars have recited 17,720 verses of scripture, answered 16,640 questions from the catechism and sung 8,240 hymns." At Greenville, when the Sunday School was reopened in 1830, males and females under twelve years of age were invited to attend. "To those who cannot afford to purchase the necessary books," ran the announcement, "they will be cheerfully given."

True enough, religious instruction of white children met universal approbation; but religious instruction of slaves provoked much discussion. Much depended upon the character of the instruction and the status of the instructor. Ordinarily, there was no objection to having the local minister preach to the slaves in the community church, but objection was raised now and then to the presence of strange missionaries on the plantations for the purpose of catechising the servants. It was held that instruction in the catechism would lead to a desire on the part of the slaves to learn to read and write. When the Rev. William Wightman of Virginia in 1838 rebuked the slaveholders of Cambridge for not properly caring for their slaves, five citizens of the Abbeville District signed a communication to the *Mountaineer* in which they alleged that a large and respectable portion of the citizens of Abbeville and Edgefield were opposed to missionary work among the slaves by the Methodists or any other sect. A short time after the Wightman episode, the Rev. Mr. Turpin, a Methodist missionary to the slaves, was by a committee of four citizens of Cambridge requested to resign. Behind the opposition to religious instruction of slaves was the widespread fear that Negro congregations would take occasion to plot against the whites; accordingly, great precaution was exercised in surrounding all religious gatherings of slaves with proper safeguards. Slaveowners, along with the entire white community, wished some guarantee against false teachers—abolition wolves in sheep's clothing—who would not scruple to use a religious meeting for sowing the dragon's teeth of sedition. In fact, any teaching which was not in keeping with the orthodox view of racial relations was suspected, and the ears of the guardians of the social order were ever alert to detect signs of defection. . . .

All the major religious denominations maintained missionary work among the plantation slaves, but the Methodists were conceded generally to be most actively enlisted in the work. In 1845 the Methodist Conference in South Carolina supported sixteen missions to the blacks, a number not exceeded by any other denomination. The Diocese of South Carolina had several clergymen devoting their entire time to religious work among the blacks, and to this work the Diocese attached great importance. The work of the Baptists, while extensive, was not well articulated. In a few instances licensed Negro exhorters of the Baptist and Methodist persuasion were allowed to harangue the black brethren, but for the most part instruction and admonition were given by the white class leaders and ministers of the gospel. Malet records that sometimes the class leaders of the blacks were Negroes. At Conwayboro he noted that Henry Wallace, a Negro class leader, preached in the Methodist Church in the afternoon. There were eight or ten Negro exhorters in the Fairfield District and a scattering elsewhere in the State, but these held meetings only by permission and under strict surveillance. . . .

The Up-Country was pre-eminently the region of the camp meeting. The people, commonly undemonstrative in the ordinary relations of life, found opportunity in the camp meeting to give expression to their religious emotions without fear of criticism. The exhibition of religious fervor on such an occasion was not regarded as an indication of personal weakness, but rather as a demonstration of the power of God over which the individual exercised little or no control. Furthermore, the camp meeting provided a means of social intercourse. Friends and relatives met on common ground to discuss common problems, while young people confusing human and divine love took advantage of the occasion to exchange compliments and pledge undying love.

Camp meetings, like revivals, were conducted, as a rule, in the late summer and early fall so as to afford the fullest opportunity for sustained attendance. Newspapers carried brief notices of annual camp meetings and newspaper correspondents reported progress achieved. It was always a matter of pride to have a correspondent report that "good order was observed throughout." A variety of motives prompted attendance. Doubtless a majority of those in attendance was motivated by a desire for spiritual uplift, but many came to satisfy curiosity and a longing for excitement. The presence of a large crowd enabled those who did not wish to appear conspicuous to witness the exercises without fear of embarrassment, while those who attended with a serious purpose could indulge their propensity for religious excitement in the general mêlée without attracting undue notice. Camp meetings lasted for several days, and those in constant attendance came equipped with food and bedding. For habitation, tents and wooden shacks sufficed. A bevy of preachers, celebrated for their forensic powers, purveyed the gospel to vast throngs of men, women and children. When the crowd was unusually large several preachers held forth at once so that those on the utmost confines of the group could receive the benefit of the service. . . .

In keeping with their purpose of working a reformation in public and private morality, the churches espoused the temperance movement. Strong drink was sold in grog shops, taverns and even grocery stores, and the drinking habit was almost universal. At muster grounds, political rallies and sales day, whiskey was imbibed freely and more or less disorder was expected and realized. "Philo," in a communication to *The* (Greenville) *Republican,* February 10, 1829, alleged that "on public days our streets are as much crowded with drunkards as formerly; during the nights there is as much rioting and noise as ever. At last fall court I heard it remarked by many persons that they had never witnessed so much noise and drunkenness in the village before." Bonded whiskey stills converted apple cider into brandy for both home and market; while tavern and storekeepers sold rye whiskey, corn whiskey, rum, wine and gin as staples, at prices which ranged from one dollar a gallon for rum to one dollar and fifty cents a gallon for peach brandy. Single drinks served over the counter could be had for six and one-half cents. Rum and whiskey were purchased along with groceries and charged to the account of the customer.

To combat the obvious evils of intemperance, the church lent its influence and facilities to the promotion of the campaign staged by the Sons of Temperance and other societies for the eradication of the vice of intemperance. At the Bethesda Church at Camden, the following resolution was adopted May 2, 1830:

Resolved that the members of Harmony Presbytery will wholly abstain from the use of ardent spirits ourselves excepting when needed as a medicine and will exert our influence by all means in our power to discourage their use with others. Ordered that the resolution be submitted to all the churches in our bounds and that every church member be earnestly enjoined to adopt it.

The Sons of Temperance, a fraternal organization with branches throughout the State, staged a procession in Greenville in April, 1852, which for fanfare and pyrotechnics exceeded a Fourth of July celebration. According to a contemporary account, "they came marching up to the Baptist Church after dark with banners flying, drums beating and torch lights illuminating the streets from one end to the other. They were dressed in all the regalia and must have looked to the drunkard more terrible than an army with banners." At the church a member offered a prayer, the temperance ode was sung and a tirade against intemperance was delivered.

The object of the temperance movement which got under way in

South Carolina in the 'twenties was to persuade people to sign a temperance pledge whereby they agreed to abstain from the use of ardent spirits and to use their influence in getting others to abstain. The temperance forces were well organized in the State and possessed an able advocate in the person of Judge Belton O'Neall. While the churches openly espoused the temperance movement, the movement did not depend entirely upon them for its advancement. The State Temperance Society held annual meetings and staged rallies in the strongholds of old John Barleycorn throughout the State. The number of temperance pledges in South Carolina in 1843, according to a credible source, was 19,211. Desertion from the ranks was all too common. Under the spell of a temperance orator, who decried the fate of the drunkard, pledges were signed freely; but, in time, the thirst for strong drink would all too often overcome solemn resolutions and good intentions. Neither the threat of expulsion from the temperance society nor the finger of scorn pointed by the drinkers of spring water availed to keep the bibulously-inclined from reverting to the ways of the flesh. So flagrant was the violation of temperance pledges, that the editor of *Temperance Advocate* was moved to state that violations among the higher classes of society were not deemed to involve a point of honor. Despite the fact that many literal-minded Christians would not support the temperance societies because they were not mentioned in the Bible, and despite almost constant defection in the ranks, the work of recruiting pledges was carried forward by zealous crusaders until the War for Southern Independence absorbed the energies of the Southern people.

Calhoun had predicted that unless the security of the minority interests of the South were guaranteed, secession would be inevitable. Still, the southern attachment for the Union was strong, and in the 1850s an internal struggle occurred between the secessionists and the unionists. For a time it seemed that the South could be secure through its influence on the Democratic Party. Such events as John Brown's Raid, however, broke up the last hopes of unity. In 1860 the Republican Party nominated Lincoln, and the Democratic Party was so badly split as to insure a Republican victory. Following Lincoln's election the South Carolina Secession Convention met, and the long-awaited separation was a fact. The state then prepared to fight its second war for independence. The following article by Charles Cauthen traces the events leading to the crisis year of 1860.

14

"THE SECESSION MOVEMENT BEFORE 1860" *

Charles Edward Cauthen

It is a commonplace of American history that South Carolina leaders did not always, in the first decades of the Union, defend the extreme state rights doctrines which John C. Calhoun so ably expounded later in the antebellum period. In the convention of 1787 South Carolina delegates played an important part in framing the Constitution. The strong nationalistic spirit which they displayed there was again evidenced in the state convention which ratified the document. And for about three decades thereafter, especially in the years immediatey following the War of 1812, there is little evidence of those extreme state sovereignty principles and sectional attitudes which led to nullification in 1832 and eventually to disunion in 1860.

In the period following 1820, however, there was a rising tide of opposition to various powers and policies of the general government, and a strong tendency for the South as a whole and South Carolina especially to seek a defense for threatened economic interests in a narrow interpretation of congressional powers and a corresponding exaltation of the rights of the state. Thus South Carolina, consistently opposing protective tariffs from the first as inequitable and blaming the tariff for the economic decline which soil erosion and destructive competition of the Southwest had more largely caused, came in the middle eighteen twenties to attack protection on constitutional grounds. In 1832 the Calhoun theory of state "interposition" was adopted in an attempt to prevent the operation of a tariff which by that time had come to be very generally regarded in South Carolina as unconstitutional. In the same period the state voiced sharp protests against the construction of roads, canals, and other internal improvements at national expense on the ground that Congress did not possess the taxing power for such purposes.

* Chapter 1 from *South Carolina Goes to War, 1860–1865* (Chapel Hill: University of North Carolina Press, 1950), pp. 1–13; copyright, 1950, by The University of North Carolina Press. Reprinted without footnotes by permission of The University of North Carolina Press.

More important than the tariff in nourishing sectionalism, state rights, and disunion was the necessity of defending a labor system which under the rise of cotton culture came to be regarded as essential to the economic well-being of the state. From the time of the debate over slavery in the Louisiana purchase and the compromise of 1820, and especially after the rise of militant abolitionism in the 1830's, South Carolina was quick to resent anything which even remotely threatened to endanger slavery and therefore her own safety. A philosophical defense of slavery was developed under which the institution was held to be a divinely established system economically beneficial to master, non-slaveholder, and slave. To it was ascribed a wholesome social and political organization which would not otherwise exist. Moreover, emancipation meant Africanization and ruin to Southern civilization in general. State sovereignty principles were seized upon as an obvious defense against interference from outside. As Francis W. Pickens expressed it, "the law of State sovereignty is with us the law of State existence." This, as Professor Wallace suggests, would no doubt have been changed to "the law of national sovereignty is the law of existence" if the slaveowner had been threatened with local opposition against which only the national government could protect him. But once state rights doctrines became firmly established, they were generally accepted and cherished without a consciousness of their economic foundation.

Disunion itself was early suggested by the more radical as a remedy for South Carolina's grievances. Amidst the anti-tariff excitement of 1827, Dr. Thomas Cooper startled the state by his famous declaration that it was "time to calculate the value of the Union." But the idea soon found many supporters. It was inherent in the "Crisis" articles of Robert J. Turnbull (1827), and in the whole nullification movement which looked to secession should nullification be resisted. That the leaders of nullification would be willing and able to carry the threat of secession into effect should the United States resort to force was believed by Joel R. Poinsett, the leader of the unionist party. And many of the unionists while denying the legality of nullification conceded at least the revolutionary right of secession. The whole episode undoubtedly tended to weaken unionism in South Carolina. The conviction that Northern and Southern interests were at variance was greatly strengthened; a majority of the people were alienated from the general government; and a disposition developed to look to secession as an ultimate necessity. "It has prepared the minds of men for a separation of the States," said James L. Petigru, "and when the question is mooted again it will be distinctly union or disunion."

Secession sentiment steadily developed in the two decades following nullification. Abolitionist literature, anti-slavery petitions before Congress, agitation for and against the annexation of Texas, continued controversy over the tariff and a national bank, "consolidation" in general, kept the state almost continuously stirred and furnished grist for the mill of Robert Barnwell Rhett who emerged from the nullification controversy as the leader of a group working for secession as a thing desirable *per se*. Calhoun, who became virtual political dictator of the state in this period, though friendly to the radical group, was much more conservative. He worked toward Southern political solidarity and hoped that the time might come when a united South, with some help from Northern or Western allies, might effect a thorough reformation of the federal government on the basis of state rights. Sincerely attached to the Union, and ambitious almost to the last for the presidency, he sometimes restrained his more radical followers as in 1844 when he used his influence to check Rhett's so-called Bluffton movement. "I had to act with great delicacy, but at the same time firmness," he said. But, however much he may have deprecated disunion as a calamity to be avoided if possible, he nevertheless schooled South Carolina and the South in the necessity of defending Southern interests by a strict limitation of federal authority and, if need be, through Southern withdrawal from the Union. An increasing number of his followers became convinced that secession was ultimately unavoidable.

The issues brought forward by the Mexican War stirred South Carolina deeply and carried her with what seemed almost complete unanimity to the very brink of secession. The Wilmot Proviso which would have prohibited slavery in any territory acquired in consequence of the war brought a determination in South Carolina that such exclusion should dissolve the Union. Calhoun, instead of restraining the radicals, became active in arousing the people. Denying that Congress had any power over slavery in the territories, he strove to unite the South on a resistance program, and spoke of secession in plainer terms than ever before. "Though the Union is dear to us," he said, "our honor and our liberty are dearer." The state legislature in 1848 unanimously resolved that the time for discussion had passed and that South Carolina stood ready to coöperate with her sister states in resisting the Wilmot Proviso "at any and every hazard."

For a time it seemed that the hoped for coöperation might be forthcoming. At the suggestion of Calhoun, Mississippi issued a call for a Southern convention. The South Carolina legislature elected delegates and resolved that the passage of the Wilmot Proviso or the abolition of slavery in the District of Columbia would be tantamount to a dissolution of the Union. But the work of the Nashville Convention (June, 1850) was disappointing to South Carolina, and Rhett, on his return from the convention, began a drive for independent action by South Carolina if other states failed to coöperate.

Meanwhile in Congress an effort was being made through compromise to avert the threatened secession of the Southern states. In January Henry Clay introduced a set of resolutions in which the South was offered the enactment of a drastic fugitive-slave law and the organization of New Mexico and Utah into territories without any mention of slavery; to the North the resolutions promised the admission of California as a free state and the abolition of the slave trade in the District of Columbia. After a memorable debate in which Calhoun made his last great plea for Southern rights, the compromise measures were adopted by Congress. But they were utterly repudiated by South Carolinians. Severely assailed from the first, the passage of the compromise seemed to increase rather than diminish disunion sentiment. The voices of a few unionists such as Benjamin F. Perry, Joel R. Poinsett, and William J. Grayson were as voices crying in the wilderness. Even Christopher G. Memminger who was soon to stand with them was saying at this time that South Carolina should secede alone if no other state would act with her.

In late 1850, however, a line of cleavage began to appear among the secessionists on the question of immediate procedure, a division which became quite clear in the legislature of 1850. Though there were only four or five true unionists, the secessionists were divided. A majority favored calling a convention for immediate secession, alone if necessary, but did not have the required two-thirds majority in the lower house. The minority was more cautious, claiming to stand for secession *ultimately* alone, if necessary, but only after an attempt had been made in a Southern congress to enlist the coöperation of other Southern states. This division between "separate state actionists" and "coöperationists" resulted in a deadlock and a compromise bill calling both a state convention and a Southern congress with elections of delegates to the convention in February, 1851, and to the congress in October.

The February elections went overwhelmingly in favor of the separate action secessionists. Of the 169 delegates elected, the *Southern Patriot,* Perry's unionist paper of Greenville, could count only 50 or

60 who were even qualifiedly opposed to secession while the secessionists claimed 127 for separate action, 32 sincere coöperationists, and only 11 "submissionists." Almost immediately, however, there was a reaction. The coöperationists organized to expose the dangers of separate action and soon the state was in the midst of its bitterest factional fight since nullification days. The separate action secessionists, or radicals, overplayed their hand in a Southern Rights convention in May by action which many regarded as an attempt to dictate the policies of the state before its people had assembled in convention. The coöperationists, skillfully led by such men as Memminger, Langdon Chevis [*sic*], James L. Orr, Andrew P. Butler, and Robert W. Barnwell, made rapid gains during the summer. They attracted into their ranks men of various opinions ranging from true resistance men holding out for joint action with at least a few other states to a group of real unionists, mainly in the Greenville area. Meanwhile the resistance program received little encouragement from the other Southern states. Virginia urged South Carolina to desist, and the fall elections in Alabama, Mississippi, and Georgia went against the secessionists. It seemed that the other states of the South would accept the Compromise of 1850 and that no Southern convention would be assembled. Nevertheless the October elections in South Carolina for delegates to the proposed Southern convention were made a test of strength between the parties and a kind of mandate to the state convention which had not yet convened. The results showed a surprising victory for the coöperationists who, by a vote of 25,045 to 17,710, elected candidates in six of the seven congressional districts. Governor John H. Means lamented: "The noble attitude of resistance which I supposed the State about to assume . . . seems to have been delayed or abandoned, judging from the popular voice, as indicated by the results of the late elections." Separate secession was indeed dead.

The state convention which assembled April 26, 1852, though containing a secessionist majority elected more than a year before, was compelled by its recent repudiation to limit its action to an ordinance asserting the right of secession and a resolution declaring

that the frequent violations of the Constitution of the United States by the Federal Government, and its encroachments upon the reserved rights of the sovereign States of this Union, especially in relation to slavery, amply justify this State, so far as any duty or obligation to her confederates is involved, in dissolving at once all political connection with her co-States; and that she forbears the exercise of this manifest right of self government from considerations of expediency only.

The more radical disunionists were disgusted. James H. Hammond thought the action "too pitiful for comment" and Rhett resigned his seat in the United States Senate on the ground that he was no longer a proper representative of his state. But Rhett's cause had almost triumphed and succeeding events were yet to bring from other states the coöperation so vainly sought in the crisis of 1850.

The political excitement of 1847–1852 left South Carolina emotionally exhausted. Factional bitterness quickly diminished and for a time the recent political alignments tended to disappear. The radicals were anxious to detach the coöperationists from their erstwhile alliance with the small unionist group in the state and to close the ranks of all true resistance men for possible future emergencies. Governor Means congratulated the state that this had been accomplished by the convention of 1852, and stated his belief that further aggressions of the North, sure to come, would rally sister states and enable the South either to "force our rights to be respected in the Union or take our place as a Southern Confederacy amongst the nations of the earth." Within the state, party division had about ended by the fall of 1852. Elections for the legislature inspired only a small vote, and harmony seemed to prevail as John L. Manning was unanimously elected governor. In 1853, admidst general prosperity, national issues were so dormant that Manning felt justified in omitting from his message to the legislature all discussion of federal relations and referred to the "distinguished head of the nation'" as a fair exponent of the political principles of South Carolina. Seemingly the state had decided to accept under President Pierce the finality of the Compromise of 1850. Certainly the political life of the state was calmer than usual in 1853 and early 1854.

Political strife soon revived, however, as James L. Orr began to organize a party whose program was the abandonment of isolation in national affairs and a close coöperation with the National Democratic party. Associated with him was the consistent unionist, Perry, and soon Preston S. Brooks, Orr's colleague in Congress after 1853. Francis W. Pickens, a recent secessionist, also associated himself with the group in 1854, as did many of the coöperationists in the struggle of 1850–52. The successor of Rhett in the United States Senate, Josiah J. Evans, also stood with this group of moderates. He wrote in 1854:

I love the Union, and hope it will be perpetual; but at the same time, I love our little State . . . and will stand by its rights when invaded, with my last breath. We have, indeed, been rather too belligerent at times, but I do not think we have lost much of national feeling, and I am sure we have lost nothing of national character.

Evans's statement seems to reflect a rather definite reaction from the extremes of 1850 and probably represents the point of view of most of those affiliated with the National Democratic party in South Carolina. Though they were denounced as nationalists, federalists, and unionists by the State Rights party, the charge in its implications was not altogether just. Some indeed did deny the advantages of disunion and believed that protection of Southern interests should be sought only within the Union. Others were in fact only coöperationists who felt that secession was no longer an immediate issue, and that South Carolina's most practical policy was to influence national affairs as far as possible through the national party. Still others believed that the National Democratic party had proved itself sound on slavery and state rights by its support of the Kansas-Nebraska bill and therefore deserved support. But the radicals made no distinction between these groups. All were bitterly denounced. In the opinion of the State Rights party the National Democratic party was not to be trusted; the South should form a strictly Southern party, nominate only sound Southern men, and if unable to control events in Washington, be organized and prepared to form a separate government.

The struggle between the National and State Rights Democrats was complicated somewhat by the appearance of the Know-Nothing party. Into its ranks went various elements. Some, trusting neither the National Democrats nor the State Rights faction, thought the Know-Nothings offered a truly national organization which might unite the sections. For example, Dr. James H. Thornwell who had been an opponent of disunion in 1832 and 1851 wrote in 1855 that if the Know-Nothings failed, the last hope for the Union was gone. Some secessionists on the other hand seem to have hoped that a great Southern party might be built up under the Know-Nothing name. Still others, fearing immigration as dangerous to slavery, were attracted by the nativist principles of the Know-Nothings. But the party had only a fleeting existence in South Carolina, largely, no doubt, because of its heterogeneous character. It was fought aggressively by the National Democrats and was opposed by the Charleston *Mercury* which feared that the state might be divided into two national parties as in 1840.

The Know-Nothings weakened, Orr proposed that South Carolina participate in the National Democratic convention of 1856 at Cincinnati, and under his influence some forty members of the legislature issued a call for a state convention to choose delegates. The secessionists greeted the proposal with scorn, and characterized the conventionists as cheap politicians, mere office seekers, and spoilsmen who would sacrifice the honor and interests of the state for selfish ambition. They accused the conventionists of sneering at South Carolina's past, and of praising the Union and praying for its preservation. But the National Democrats met in Columbia May 5–6. Delegates from the coastal region were conspicuously absent, only Georgetown and Charleston being represented, but every district of the up country save two was represented. Orr and Pickens, president of the convention, both defended the policy of participating in the national convention against the objections brought by the disunionists. To the contention of the latter that the system of representation in Democratic conventions made possible Northern dictation of candidates and platforms and that Southern interests could only be protected by a strictly Southern party, the conventionists sanely replied that the next contest would be between a Black Republican and the Democratic nominee, and since South Carolina must inevitably support the latter, the wise policy was to have a voice in his selection. Orr denied that the Democratic party was committed to popular sovereignty. He held that its Northern members were divided on the question and that the Kansas-Nebraska act itself left the matter to the courts which would surely decide against the pernicious doctrine; but even if they did not, the South was still much better off than before the Compromise of 1850 and the passage of the Kansas-Nebraka act. The federal government, he said, had ceased to be a "despoiler" of the South and had come to be its protector. In accordance with these ideas the state convention adopted a platform and elected delegates. The platform dodged the question of popular sovereignty but stated that South Carolina's participation in the Cincinnati convention was conditioned on the inclusion in the national platform of a statement that no territory should ever be closed to slavery by Congress and that the fugitive slave law should be permanently continued and enforced.

The course of the National Democrats was regarded by the State Rights party as especially reprehensible in view of the fact that the controversy over Kansas was raging at the very time of the state convention. Now of all times, it was said, Southern men should act only within a strictly Southern party. There was criticism, too, of the choice of Charleston as the next national convention city; it was a mere scheme of the National Democrats, it was said, to increase their prestige and humble the State Rights party. Though Buchanan's nomination was generally acceptable, his tariff record was severely criticized, and Rhett believed that if the tariff were not modified to the level of 1833 the Union should be dissolved. He and others proposed a Southern conference to draw amendments to the Constitution which, if unacceptable to the North, should be followed by conventions of the two sections to divide the national assets and dissolve the Union. This group also demanded that the fall elections to Congress be used to show that South Carolina, by refusing to elect "doughfaces," was not willing to follow the National Democrats.

In the contest between the parties it is probable that the more moderate conventionists represented a majority of the people of the state. The *Darlington Flag* declared:

It is time for us to awake to the full import of the deliberate popular decree promulgated in 1851. South Carolina will not secede from the Union. Nay more than this—we grieve to be compelled to say, but we cannot be blind to the fact—that a great majority of her people, in spite of the wrongs and indignities that we have received, are ardently attached to the Union . . . the overwhelmingly predominant sentiment of the people is in favor of an unreserved union with the Democaratic party.

The election of Buchanan gave general satisfaction. Only a few had hoped for John C. Fremont's election as an occasion for disunion and few suggested separate secession in case of Black Republican victory. Although the invitation of Governor Henry A. Wise of Virginia to a Southern governors' conference at Raleigh was accepted, there was slight enthusiasm for it. With Buchanan elected the legislature seemed disposed to await the results of his administration. Resolutions demanding certain amendments to the Constitution were defeated by a vote of 56 to 44 in the House and the feeling seemed to be that Southern interests might be effectively protected within the Union.

The more moderate position of the National Democrats now seemed definitely in the ascendency. Of course, all groups remained alive to Southern rights and interests, and the disunionists lost no opportunity to grumble at anything which seemed unfavorable to the South. Thus the tariff of 1857 was criticized on the ground that it forced the

South to pay tribute for the benefit of Northern manufacturers, and the Panic of 1857 was blamed on Northern speculation the baneful results of which would not have been felt had no political connection existed between the two sections. Lawrence M. Keitt wrote in the middle of 1857 that "the safety of the South is only in herself." But moderates seemed stronger in their influence. There even occurred a controversy between the Charleston *Courier* and the *Evening News* over the theoretical right of secession. Governor Robert F. W. Allston, in his message to the legislature, defended the Dred Scott decision against the resolutions of Maine and Connecticut but was rather conciliatory when he appealed for charitable judgment of one section by the other. He was willing even that South Carolinians associate themselves with the National Democratic party in nominating conventions so long as they did not pledge the state.

The strength of the moderates was also shown when Rhett received only six votes in the election for United States Senator. The radical James H. Hammond was elected over the National Democratic candidate, F. W. Pickens, but he almost immediately disappointed the ultras by a tendency to ally himself with the moderates. Very soon he was writing Perry that at the time of his election he thought the South to be in a better position than ever before in his time; with abolition somewhat checked, the bank gone, internal improvements given up, and free trade virtually adopted, the South was "on smooth water" and in a position safely to remain in the Union. In the summer of 1858 he returned to South Carolina preaching that the best policy for the South was to remain in the Union and through close coöperation control it. The radicals were alarmed at this desertion of their old leader. To them the defeat of the Lecompton constitution was positive proof that the National Democratic party could not be trusted. Orr and Hammond were therefore denounced as rank unionists, while the more radical congressmen, Milledge L. Bonham and John McQueen, were banqueted and praised. The moderates, however, retained their strength. They were unable to elect Orr to the Senate in 1858 but the choice of James Chesnut, Jr. was regarded as a victory for conservatism and a defeat of the "Congo party" which favored the reopening of the slave trade. Pickens wrote Perry from St. Petersburg, "I rejoice to see in our State more reasonable and wiser counsels prevailing than for years."

The hopefulness and what seems to have been the growing influence of the moderates in South Carolina were given a rude shock by the John Brown raid in October, 1859. Undoubtedly the effect of this incident was to drive many conservatives into the camp of the ultras. At the opening of the legislature soon after the raid, Governor William H. Gist's message was frankly disunionist. After reviewing the growth of abolitionism and referring to the Northern acclaim of Brown, he asked:

Can we, then, any longer talk about moderation and conservatism, and statesmanship, and still hug the delusive phantom to our breasts that all is well, and that the Democratic party, upon whom we have too confidently relied, will work out our salvation by platforms and resolutions?

If only the South were united, he said, "we could enforce equality in the Union or maintain our independence out of it." Let South Carolina make every effort to get the coöperation of the South but let her not yield principle, and let her not forget that she is a "sovereign and an equal" with the right to join the family of nations when she willed.

The legislature was equally stirred. No less than sixteen sets of resolutions, all radical, were introduced in the House besides a number in the Senate. One declared that South Carolina was ready to contribute money and men for the defense of the border slave states; another that South Carolina was ready for a Southern confederacy, and that the governor should be given power to call a meeting of the legislature whenever other states indicated a readiness to coöperate to that end; another that "this legislature does not hesitate to declare that this Union, of doubtful value to the South, would be scarcely an atom in the scale against the perpetual maintenance" of slavery. One looked to the establishment of a committee of public safety and of committees of correspondence. Even Perry, the unionist, offered a resolution stating that the people of South Carolina were prepared to defend the institution of slavery "at any, and every sacrifice of their political relations with the Federal Government and the Northern States, should it be invaded or assailed in any manner or form whatever," and that they felt an "inexpressible scorn and contempt at the infamous, hypocritical sympathy" expressed in the North for John Brown, "a notorious horse thief, assassin and traitor"; and that the general endorsement of John Brown would make it dishonorable in South Carolina to continue in the same government with a people whose social and moral tone "characterizes them as a nation of pirates, savages, assassins and traitors."

From the mass of suggestions a joint resolution, drawn by C. C.

Memminger, was finally adopted stating that South Carolina had declined to secede in 1852 on grounds of expediency only; that assaults on slavery and Southern rights had since increased; that South Carolina, still deferring to her sister states, nevertheless felt that a meeting of the slave states should be immediately called; that the governor request the other states to elect delegates; that a special commissioner be appointed to express to Virginia the sympathy of South Carolina and her earnest desire to coöperate in measures of common defense; and finally, that $100,000 be appropriated for military contingencies.

Memminger himself was appointed commissioner to Virginia in the belief that his reputation for conservatism would inspire confidence and render his efforts more effectual. Actually, Memminger was at this time not very conservative, as his correspondence with the secessionist William Porcher Miles of Charleston and others clearly reveals. He wrote: "My own opinion and I think the opinion of our State is that the Union cannot be preserved; and that a sectional Government such as we now have is not worthy of preservation." He added that "new terms" and "fresh constitutional guarantees" might make another Union desirable but he was apparently ready to break up the old. His reception at Richmond was courteous enough but he was disappointed to find that sentiment generally was much more conservative than he had anticipated. In his address of January 19 he made a skillful effort to arouse the Virginians, urging at least a Southern conference to discuss and propose measures which might be demanded as the price of continuing in the Union. He pledged South Carolina's willingness to abide by the decision of such a conference. "If our pace be too fast for some, we are content to walk slower; our earnest wish is that all may keep together. We cannot consent to stand still, but would gladly make common cause with all. We are far from expecting or desiring to dictate or lead." But Virginia's reaction was unfavorable. As it became clear to the commissioner that Virginia would not participate in a conference he wrote Miles: "I am brought to the opinion, that we farther South will be compelled to act, and drag after us these divided States." Only Mississippi and Alabama reacted favorably to South Carolina's conference proposal. Mississippi not only accepted the invitation but sent a commission to Virginia in support of Memminger's plea. Alabama took the advanced position of directing her governor to call an election for a state convention should the Republicans elect the

President in the fall. On this possibility the South Carolina secessionists now based their hopes.

The significance of the John Brown episode in the development of South Carolina secession sentiment was undoubtedly very great. It weakened the influence of the moderates and strengthened the hands of the radicals. Temporarily it caused even Perry and Pickens to falter in their conservatism and it made secession in late 1860 much less difficult.

Part IV:
CIVIL WAR AND RECONSTRUCTION,
1861–77

When the South seceded, the main immediate issue between
the Confederacy and the United States government concerned
the control of Union property in the rebellious states. In South
Carolina the issue soon centered on Fort Sumter in the
Charleston harbor, where Maj. Robert Anderson and a small
garrison of United States troops had holed up after evacuating
Fort Moultrie on the shore.

During the mounting crisis President Buchanan procrastinated,
but Abraham Lincoln, inaugurated March 4, 1861, soon
decided to take a firm hand in defense of Fort Sumter.
Meanwhile, Confederate emissaries in Washington, through
unofficial conversations with Union representatives, had been led
to believe that President Lincoln would evacuate Major
Anderson's forces from the fort. The new president's decision
to re-provision the fort was therefore regarded in the South as
another example of Yankee duplicity. The Confederate
authorities in Montgomery decided to reduce the fort before
the United States relief force arrived.

The dramatic story of the final tense hours in the Charleston
harbor is told by W. A. Swanberg in *First Blood: The Story of
Fort Sumter.*

15

"LET THE STRIFE BEGIN" *

W. A. Swanberg

Meekly allowing Sumter to be provisioned might lose the new Confederate government popular support. One Alabamian had warned Davis, "Unless you sprinkle blood in the face of the Southern people they will be back in the old Union in less than ten days." A sprinkle of blood, too, should bring the fencesitters—Virginia and the other border states—into the Confederate fold. There was vast indignation against the Lincoln administration that was believed to have promised to evacuate Sumter and now had broken the promise. If the Confederacy did not take Sumter, it was entirely probable that the impatient Carolinians would thumb their noses at Montgomery and reduce the fort on their own, which would be a terrible blow at the authority of the Davis government.

The state rights idea, Davis must have seen, had its drawbacks. Despite all these considerations, the burly Toombs was against resistance.

"Mr. President, at this time it is suicide, murder, and will lose us every friend at the North," he said. "The firing upon that fort will inaugurate a civil war greater than any the world has yet seen. . . ."

Prophetic words, but Toombs was overruled. War Secretary Walker telegraphed Beauregard, ". . . you will at once demand its [Sumter's] evacuation, and if this is refused proceed, in such manner as you may determine, to reduce it."

Although Beauregard got this order April 10th, he was in no hurry to execute it, being beset by last-minute troubles. He had called out five thousand more soldiers, who were now arriving in Charleston in streams, and something had to be done with them. The general did

* Excerpts from *First Blood: The Story of Fort Sumter* (New York: Charles Scribner's Sons, 1957), pp. 286–98; Copyright © 1957 by W. A. Swanberg. Reprinted by permission of McIntosh and Otis, Inc.

not trust the Washington government any farther than he could throw a columbiad after the way the commissioners had been cozened. The "provisions only" story he believed another deception, feeling sure the federals were coming with the intention of attacking and aimed to land a large force on Morris Island to take the batteries there from the rear. The only convenient way he could get men to Morris Island was under the guns of Sumter, making it necessary to keep those guns quiet until he got the men there. Charleston's shipping was taxed, getting hundreds of men and tons of equipment out to the island. One of the men was the fierce Wigfall, eager to officiate at the Union's funeral. Another was Edmund Ruffin, the "Nestor of the South," carrying a carpetbag and a musket he had obtained at the Citadel, a hoary zealot going to glory, cheered by companions young enough to be his grandsons. Morris Island soon became a chaos, glutted with equipment and recruits not knowing what to do next. Beauregard hastily sent Major Whiting, recently promoted, out to the island to restore order.

The general also was in a sweat to mount two new guns just arrived. One of them, a heavy Dahlgren, he wanted at the western end of Sullivan's Island, writing General Dunovant: "This is one of those moments when the word impossible must be ignored, for the fate of Anderson and Sumter depends upon the results of this night's firing." For all Beauregard knew, the fleet might be outside even now, the attack be made that very night of April 10th.

The other gun was a thing of beauty, the latest word in ordnance—a rifled Blakely gun just in from Liverpool, the gift of a Charlestonian in business in England, Charles K. Prioleau. On it was engraved, "Presented to the State of South Carolina by a citizen resident abroad, in commemoration of the 20th December, 1860." The Blakely, which would throw a shell or 12-pound shot with the accuracy of a dueling pistol, using only a half pound of powder, was promptly shipped to Cummings Point in the hope that it would pound holes in Sumter's gorge wall.

Out on Morris Island, Major Whiting was going frantic with more than two thousand men falling over each other, losing their muskets, getting separated from their commands, and creating unholy anarchy. "For God's sake have this post inspected by yourself, or someone else competent, before you open fire," he appealed to Beauregard. "I am expected to be engineer and everything else." Beauregard sent him a couple of officers and told him to cool off: "Things always appear worst at first sight when not perfect." The general was not as calm as he sounded. Organization was tottering just at the most critical moment. South Carolina's General Bonham, disgruntled at being left out of the picture, demanded command of all the Carolina troops under Beauregard—a ticklish point because General Dunovant would resent Bonham ranking *him*. Bonham was told he would have to wait. Beauregard, the brain of a large and complicated military movement, was sending out orders as fast as he could write them. The floating battery, too clumsy for its original purpose, would come in handy at the west end of Sullivan's Island, and he sent it there. He ordered Captain Hartstene, in charge of naval operations, to prepare barges containing great piles of wood, ready to be set ablaze at the entrance to the harbor so the enemy could not enter unseen.

Although the Confederacy now had some six thousand men surrounding Major Anderson and his minuscule command, Governor Pickens was not without fears. "I trust we are ready," he wrote President Davis with surprising uncertainty for a man who had talked of being "ready" weeks earlier, "and if they come we will give them a cordial reception, such as will ring through this country, I think. I hope we are not mistaken," adding later, "I think you will hear of as bloody a fight as ever occurred."

Charleston's streets were clogged with marching soldiers, rumbling wagons of powder, excited citizens. "Why did that green goose Anderson go into Fort Sumter?" Mrs. Chesnut wailed in her diary. "Then everything began to go wrong." Despite all the turmoil, the races were run as usual in the nearby Metairie course, Equinox beating Bettie Ward and Twilight. The Charleston *Courier* let out a blast at Lincoln's "ignorance and vulgarity," trumpeting: "We are prepared to apply the last argument. . . . We are sick of the subject of evacuation. . . . Let the strife begin—we have no fear of the issue."

That April 10th another distinguished visitor arrived at the Charleston Hotel—tall, black-haired young Roger Pryor, the Virginia ex-Congressman and secessionist who, like Ruffin, was out of patience with his own state for failing to join the disunion parade. Pryor had come to urge an attack on Sumter as the sure way to get cautious Virginia to move. A fiery orator who knew how to sway a crowd, he quickly obliged with a balcony speech when he was serenaded that night.

"I thank you," he said in part, "that you have at last annihilated this accursed Union. . . ." He poked fun at his own state for its slowness. "Give the old lady time. . . . She is a little rheumatic. . . . But I assure you that just as certain as tomorrow's sun will rise upon us, just so certain will Virginia be a member of the Southern Confederacy; and I will tell your Governor what will put her in the Southern Confederacy in less than an hour by Shrewsbury clock. *Strike a blow!*"

When April 11th dawned bright and clear, Anderson and his men received another unpleasant surprise. The floating battery had been towed from the city and firmly stranded at the west end of Sullivan's Island behind a stone breakwater that would protect it from ricochet shots. Now it added its two 42-pounders and two 32-pounders to the heavy guns already enfilading Sumter's left flank where the relief boat would anchor. If it was lucky enough to reach the fort, the boat and its occupants would be in for a screaming welcome. General Beauregard was indeed a canny artillerist. There was no help for it now. The garrison was cut off from the world, and no warning could be given to the fleet.

Captain Foster was still struggling with makeshift traverses against the unsuspected weight of metal. The remaining bread was eaten that day, leaving nothing but salt pork and a few broken crackers in the larder. Someone remembered that on the floor in one of the barracks rooms was a quantity of rice which had been dampened in shipment six weeks earlier and was spread out to dry. When the salute to Washington was fired February 22nd, the windows had broken, mixing fragments of shattered glass with the rice. The glass was now sifted out of the rice which, although a trifle mouldy, was a welcome addition to the provender. "D. [Doubleday?] found a potatoe today, and put it away," Crawford noted in his diary. "He said somebody had tramped on it, but had not hurt it much."

The harbor was alive with craft, most of them carrying men and munitions past Sumter to Morris Island. The rebels were rushing to completion still *another* battery at the end of Sullivan's Island near the floating battery, this one of one gun, a big nine-inch Dahlgren. Although he was ill and taking vile medication, Surgeon Crawford was busy arranging hospital facilities in one of the unused bombproof casemates. By Anderson's order, everybody moved their bedding from the vulnerable barracks and officers' quarters to the protection of the casemates, where they would live as well as fight. The major could see no logic in defending this fort which he considered lost anyway, but he would defend it nevertheless, resigned to what he considered sheer madness in Washington. The observant Crawford noticed an unforgettable contrast: the men working with "greatest alacrity" on their defenses, Major Anderson pacing alone in a casemate, head bowed, face grim, a man who saw nothing but tragedy ahead for the nation. Yet his report for April 11th, which might never be read, mirrored no despair but rather the determination of a soldier to do his duty.

"Although not permitted to send off my daily report," he wrote, "I shall continue, as long as I can, to prepare them, so that if an opportunity is afforded me I shall have them ready." He outlined enemy activity and his own, finishing, "The officers and men, thank God, are in pretty good health; and, although feeling aware of the danger of their position, have greater anxiety about the fate of those whom they expect to come to their succor than they entertain for themselves.". . .

Surgeon Samuel Crawford, a man with a sense of history, somehow continued to find time to dash off an occasional line in his diary. It made his Union blood race to know that an expedition was en route to fight its way into the harbor, help the garrison so long neglected, fill Sumter with fresh new men and plenty of provisions, and give the fort the strength it needed to deal out righteous punishment to the wicked inventors of secession.

"We are looking for the relief promised to us," he wrote April 11th, "and men can be seen at all hours on the parapet." They saw no warships, but at 3:30 that afternoon they spied a small boat bearing a white flag approaching from the city. Lieutenant Jefferson Davis, who had endured much joshing at the fort because his name had such a rebel sound, was officer of the day at the time. He met the boat at the wharf as Colonel Chesnut got out, followed by Captain Stephen D. Lee and Colonel Chisolm, and escorted them to the guardroom where Anderson met them. Lee, like Chesnut one of Beauregard's many aides, was a young Carolinian West Pointer who had gone with his state. Chisolm was well remembered, having once brought wine and cigars. They greeted the major and handed him a dispatch from Beauregard. In it the general said the Confederacy could wait no longer to assume "actual possession of a fortification commanding the entrance of one of their harbors," going on:

I am ordered by the Government of the Confederate States to demand the evacuation of Fort Sumter. . . . All proper facilities will be afforded for the removal of yourself and command, together with company arms and property, to any post in the United States which you may select. The flag which you have upheld so long and with so much fortitude, under the most trying circumstances, may be saluted by you on taking it down.

The three Southerners waited while Anderson summoned his officers into council in another room. He told them he had a decision to make which involved not only their position but possibly their lives. Then he read them Beauregard's message.

The phrasing was courteous, the terms generous. As Crawford put it, "was ever such terms granted to a band of starving men?" In the next breath he wrote, "we to a man unanimously refused to give up our trust." Doubleday, Foster, Seymour, Snyder, Davis, Hall, Crawford —even the young Virginian Meade, who would later join the Confederacy—all voted No. Anderson wrote his reply:

GENERAL: I have the honor to acknowledge the receipt of your communication demanding the evacuation of this fort, and to say, in reply thereto, that it is a demand with which I regret that my sense of honor, and of my obligations to my Government, prevent my compliance. Thanking you for the fair, manly and courteous terms proposed, and for the high compliment paid me,

    I am, general, very respectfully, your obedient servant,

                           ROBERT ANDERSON

                     Major, First Artillery Commanding

The major informed the three aides of the decision as he accompanied them out to the wharf. "Will General Beauregard open his batteries without further notice to me?" he asked.

Colonel Chesnut pondered. "I think not," he said. "No, I can say to you that he will not, without further notice."

"I shall await the first shot," Anderson said, "and if you do not batter us to pieces, we shall be starved out in a few days."

It was a remark which in strict military propriety he should not have made—would never have made had he considered these men enemies who must be destroyed rather than gentlemen who had a legitimate grievance. Chesnut, surprised, asked if he might report this to Beauregard. Anderson declined to give it the character of a report but said it was true. The boat pushed off.

General Beauregard did not want to shell his friend Anderson. More important, it would take some time to reduce the fort, during which time the relief fleet would surely arrive and he would have a naval enemy to combat as well. How much better if he could have the fort handed over to him intact and undamaged before the fleet arrived. He telegraphed Secretary Walker, quoting Anderson's remark and asking for instructions. At Sumter, the men kept glancing out to sea. No warships were visible. Late that afternoon three hulks were towed out from Charleston, anchored and ready to be set ablaze at the spot where the Main and Swash channels met and where the relief boats would have to turn.

Dinner that night consisted of salt pork and rice—eaten with care lest some bits of glass might remain—but it was served to the officers with customary éclat by a mulatto servant from Charleston who, along with the workmen, had been forced to remain. Over the *pièce de résistance* Anderson announced a decision that jolted his officers. He was restricting the garrison to the use of the sheltered guns in the lower casemate tier only. In view of the greatly increased enemy batteries on Sullivan's Island and the hail of metal that would whistle around the poorly protected guns on the parapet, he forbade the men to use those guns at all. He took sole responsibility for this important step. Had he had anything near the fort's proper war garrison of 650 men, doubtless he would have acted otherwise. With just about a tenth that number, his men were not expendable.

This was a blow, for the heaviest artillery was on the barbette tier, which afforded a better view of enemy emplacements and a more advantageous angle of fire. Among the twenty-seven guns there were five 42-pounders, six eight-inch columbiads, and two mighty ten-inch columbiads. Of the twenty-one guns in the casemate tier, the heaviest were three 42-pounders at the right shoulder angle, the rest being 32-pounders. The decision rendered useless the long toil expended in raising and mounting guns on the parapet as well as Captain Foster's valiant work in building a traverse to protect the barbette guns on the right flank, which must have disgruntled the captain.

That night, sentinels kept a close watch but saw no sign of the fleet. It is doubtful that Major Anderson got any sleep at all. Thirteen hundred yards south on Cummings Point, Edmund Ruffin had been made an honorary member of the Palmetto Guards under Captain G. B. Cuthbert. Cuthbert shouted to the old man, who was somewhat deaf, that the company had chosen him to fire the first shot of the fight. "I was highly gratified by the compliment, and delighted to perform the service," he wrote, and went to bed without undressing to make sure he would be ready. In Charleston, Mrs. Chesnut had attended "the merriest, maddest dinner we have had yet. Men were audaciously wise and witty. We had an unspoken foreboding that it was to be our last pleasant meeting," [sic] This brilliant woman had more forebodings than most. She knew her husband was on a climactic errand that night. "I do not pretend to go to sleep," she wrote. "How can I? If Anderson does not accept terms at four, the orders are, he shall be fired upon.". . .

At 12:45 A.M. April 12th, the Sumter sentinels hailed a boat approaching under a white flag. It was the three Confederate aides again, this time accompanied by a fourth, Roger Pryor, now an aide of General Beauregard and a quick colonel. Pryor had a sudden qualm. Recalling that his state had not yet seceded, he did not go in with the others but remained in the boat. Chesnut, Lee, and Chisolm handed Anderson another dispatch from Beauregard. In it the general said he had communicated Anderson's remark about being "starved out" to the Confederate government, and he was ordered to ask the major to state precisely when he would be forced to evacuate the fort.

Anderson aroused his officers and put the question to them. They were all tired from many a night watch and too much work for too few men. The major asked Dr. Crawford for his professional opinion: How long could the men last and do any fighting?

Crawford said the lack of food was already being felt, but estimated that the garrison could last for five days, "when they would then be three days entirely without food." There was considerable reference to Secretary Cameron's letter of instructions, so remarkably mild in tone. The secretary wrote, "Hoping still that you will be able to sustain yourself until the 11th or 12th instant, the expedition will go forward. . . . You will therefore hold out, if possible, till the arrival of the expedition." This, along with the authorization to

Anderson to capitulate when necessary, was anything but a peremptory order to hold out at all costs. The orders could be interpreted to mean that the government wished to make only a token defense before surrendering the fort to superior forces. It was now early in the "12th instant" and the expedition had not arrived. The officers debated so long that Chesnut and his companions, waiting in another room, grew impatient.

"Major Anderson made every possible effort to retain the aides till daylight," Captain Lee later wrote, "making one excuse and then another for not replying."

Possibly the major was playing for time, but it was also a hard decision to make. On one occasion when the aides pressed him for an answer, his resentment boiled over for a moment.

"You have twice fired on my flag," he said, "and if you do it again I will open fire."

At last the Sumter officers agreed that waiting until noon on April 15th, the last date mentioned by Cameron, would give the expedition sufficient time to arrive if it was coming at all. Anderson wrote a reply to Beauregard agreeing to evacuate the fort at that time unless the Confederates meanwhile made a hostile move, "should I not receive prior to that time controlling instructions from my Government or additional supplies."

Chesnut, who was instructed to act for Beauregard, read it and shook his head. There were too many conditions in it. He wrote a reply and handed it to the major:

SIR: By authority of Brigadier-General Beauregard, commanding the provisional forces of the Confederate States, we have the honor to notify you that he will open the fire of his batteries on Fort Sumter in one hour from this time.

Although he could have expected nothing else, Anderson was deeply moved. "He seemed to realize the full import of the consequences," Captain Lee wrote, "and the great responsibility of his position. Escorting us to the boat at the wharf, he cordially pressed our hands in farewell, remarking, 'If we never meet in this world again, God grant that we may meet in the next.' "

It was nearing 3:30 when the aides were rowed off into the darkness. Anderson and his officers went through the casemates where the soldiers were sleeping, arousing them one by one, giving each the same message: We will soon be attacked. Stay where you are until further orders. We will not fire until morning.

Chesnut and his mates were cutting water in the direction of Fort Johnson, where they found Captain George S. James, commander of the mortar battery. They ordered James to open fire at 4:30 with a gun that would give the signal that the crews of the forty-seven other guns surrounding Sumter had been awaiting so long—start the war.

Captain James had a full appreciation of this historic moment and his own never-to-be-forgotten part in it—something he could tell to his children and his children's children with pardonable pride. But James was a great admirer of Roger Pryor, standing there so tall and slim and eager. The captain thought a moment, then achieved a decision of real self-denial. Would Colonel Pryor be so kind as to fire it?

"You are the only man to whom I would give up the honor of firing the first gun of the war," he said.

Some thirty hours earlier the Virginian had spoken to a cheering crowd from the Charleston Hotel balcony, saying, "Strike a blow!" Yet now he was strangely agitated by the opportunity to strike it himself. "His manner was almost similar to that of Major Anderson as we left him a few moments before," observed Captain Lee, who was taking in the colloquy. After a long moment, Pryor shook his head.

"I could not fire the first gun of the war," he said in a husky voice.

So Chesnut, Lee, Chisolm, and Pryor got back into their boat and headed for Fort Moultrie while Captain James aroused his command. The four aides glided across a calm sea under a canopy of stars and scudding clouds, undoubtedly gripped by mixed emotions—relief at the end of long doubt and indecision, the thrill of impending combat, the elation of men about to settle a sore grievance combined with a solemnity in the knowledge that the settling might be painful.

They were not far north of Sumter when they saw a flash of flame from one of James's ten-inch mortars, moments later hearing its throaty roar—a sound that "woke the echoes from every nook and corner of the harbor." The shell soared in a high arc, its burning fuse spitting like a small rocket. It curved downward and burst almost directly over Fort Sumter. A few statriot watchers on Charleston's Battery later swore that when it exploded it formed a pattern in flame of an almost perfect palmetto.

Over on Cummings Point the Palmetto Guards had been aroused at four, their pieces loaded and ready. Edmund Ruffin, erect and proud, was standing by one of the columbiads of the Iron Battery when the signal gun was fired from Fort Johnson. Ruffin, with none of Pryor's qualms, jerked the lanyard and sent a shell crashing into Sumter's parapet. Then the darkness was split by thunder as a dozen batteries broke loose from various points in the harbor.

In her suite at the Mills House, Mrs. Chesnut had not slept a wink. "At half-past four the heavy booming of a cannon," she wrote. "I sprang out of bed, and on my knees prostrate I prayed as I never prayed before."

There was no stauncher advocate of secession than Robert Barnwell Rhett, editor of the Charleston *Mercury* and sometime congressman from South Carolina. For thirty years Rhett loudly clamored for disunion. But when the event was accomplished, the convention in Montgomery by-passed Rhett for any important Confederate post. Disappointed, the fire-eating editor turned again to the *Mercury*.

The war had hardly begun before Rhett, a passionate supporter of the cause, was castigating the Confederate government in Richmond, especially President Jefferson Davis. Excepting a brief abatement in 1863, his tirades continued through the war. Although Rhett's voice was the most shrill, he was not alone among South Carolina critics of Davis. The nature and rationale of South Carolina criticism is discussed by Charles E. Cauthen in *South Carolina Goes to War, 1860–1865*. On the other hand, it must be remembered that no other state more loyally supported the Confederacy than did South Carolina.

16

ROBERT BARNWELL RHETT
DENOUNCES JEFFERSON DAVIS *

Charles Edward Cauthen

The well-known opposition to the Davis administration on the part of Robert Barnwell Rhett and his mouthpiece, the Charleston *Mercury,* began almost immediately after the organization of the Confederate government. . . . The explanation of Rhett's early opposition is . . . to be found in the very enthusiasm with which he worked for the complete and permanent separation of the South from the old Union, and in his egoistic confidence in the infallibility of his own ideas on how success might be obtained. Like most successful crusaders he was prone to feel that those who disagreed with him were traitors to the cause for which he fought.

In the period between secession and the fall of Fort Sumter, Rhett's chief fear and horror was the possible reconstruction of the old Union. Fearing that some of the Southern states had seceded for bargaining purposes only, he fought throughout the period for measures which he hoped would make a restoration of the old Union impossible. He insisted, for example, on a provision in the Confederate Constitution which would exclude free states from the Confederacy. His efforts to have steps taken even before the inauguration of Davis for an alliance with England based on the commercial advantages of free trade, were also in no small degree made with the idea that such an alliance would made reconstruction forever impossible. These efforts of Rhett, however, failed, and Davis after his inauguration did not empower the Confederate commissioners to Europe to negotiate on a basis of mutual commercial concessions. Rather, President Davis and Congress seemed much more interested in the Washington mission. Rhett feared that they were hoping for

* Chapter 15, entitled "South Carolina and the Davis Government," from *South Carolina Goes to War, 1860–1865* (Chapel Hill: University of North Carolina Press, 1950), pp. 201–16; Copyright, 1950, by The University of North Carolina Press. Reprinted without footnotes by permission of The University of North Carolina Press.

a close commercial alliance, if not for some form of political reconciliation. Rhett's horror of reunion, therefore, led him early to question the policies and even the motives of the administration.

Although the Fort Sumter episode temporarily quieted Rhett's fears
of reunion he was by no means ready to accept the Davis leadership.
He was still determined on the English alliance and as chairman of
the Committee on Foreign Affairs worked hard to commit the administration to it. Failing in this he proposed a new policy under
which European nations refusing to recognize the Confederacy would
be coerced by an official embargo on the export of cotton and
tobacco. Again he met defeat. Thus neither his policy of conciliation
nor of coercion was adopted and the *Mercury* announced that the
administration had no policy.

Rhett early became convinced that the administration was also
following an unsound military policy. The *Mercury* began, therefore,
on June 1, a campaign to educate the public in the advantages of a
policy of offensive warfare hoping that public opinion would influence
the administration to abandon its policy of defensive operations. In
an editorial on "The War Policy of the South" the *Mercury* stated
that the South, though uniformly successful so far, had in every colli-
sion of arms been forced to fight. By thus assuming the defensive
the South had lost Maryland, endangered Missouri, neutralized Kentucky, and made Virginia the battle field. This was neither wise
statesmanship nor good generalship. The South should assume the
offensive. Delay was a disadvantage to the South not only from the
standpoint of numbers but also in the matter of training because the
raw troops of the South, accustomed to horses and arms, were superior
to the untrained troops of the North. The war should be carried to
Washington and into the states of Ohio and Pennsylvania. . . . After
Manassas the *Mercury* was especially critical of the failure to follow
up the victory by taking Washington, a failure which it held was due
entirely to the President. Both Congress and the generals were in
favor of a more aggressive policy, it said. When, in September, it was
announced that the army would go into winter quarters in Virginia
the *Mercury* protested bitterly against such an "absurd, flagitous and
fatal policy." The army should bivouac in Washington! In November
the invasion of South Carolina and the fall of Port Royal were blamed
on the silly policy of defensive war in Virginia.

Rhett thought that the establishment of close commercial ties with
the North was only less odious than actual restoration of the old
Union. He therefore repudiated what was called commercial recon-

struction apparently believing that it might lead to political reunion. After Manassas he seemed especially fearful that peace might be made on the basis of mutual economic concessions. To prevent this he offered a resolution in Congress on July 30 for a 15% discrimination against imports from the United States. Although the resolution failed, a committee was appointed to investigate and report at the next session what, if anything, was necessary to insure the commercial independence of the Confederacy. The *Mercury's* fear of commercial reconstruction was so great that it declared in October that "the present danger of the South is not from Yankee armies, but from the desire and designs entertained by public men of the South for commercial and financial reconstruction."

Although the *Mercury's* chief criticism of the administration in 1861 was for its defensive war policy other complaints were from time to time voiced. The provisional tariff which continued the old tariff of 1857 was criticized and a demand was made for a thorough revision. The direct tax was declared untimely though the principle of the tax was approved. The veto of a law which would have made the African slave trade a high misdemeanor instead of piracy as under the law of the United States was regretted. The War Department was criticized for its appeal to the newspapers to use more discretion in publishing military intelligence; the Commissary Department for the rations served the soldiers; and the Navy Department for its lack of energy. The early failure, as the *Mercury* supposed, to send agents to Europe to procure arms was blamed on Davis personally. Congress had given him ample powers and anyone should have foreseen the need. An agent could have been in Europe within fifteen days of the inauguration and arms could have been received within six weeks, some time before the establishment of the blockade at Charleston on May 11. By September the *Mercury* was refusing to give the Confederate government any credit at all for anything which had been accomplished. It claimed that the army was made by men volunteering and begging to be accepted; all the Confederate government had to do was to accept them and designate a field of action. The states and not the Confederacy had clothed, equipped, and armed them. The Confederate government had been totally incompetent to minister to the necessities of the wounded, sick, and dying soldiers, half of whom, but for other help, would have died from bad food and inadequate medical attention.

Enough has been said to indicate that the *Mercury* had lost all confidence in the administration by the latter part of 1861. It had

in fact become rabidly anti-Davis. It denounced the "reckless and partial manner" in which patronage had been dispensed and the evils
flowing from incompetent officials. "How much longer is favoritism
and folly to sacrifice lives and obstruct our armies?" it asked. "We
denounce this matter of personal favoritism. The COUNTRY must
be served, not personal predilections." Gradually the *Mercury* came
to believe Davis not only incompetent but also a conspirator against
constitutional liberty. In an editorial of October 30, 1861, it warned
against the tendency of executive power to increase in time of war
under pretext of military necessity. On November 4 an editorial
entitled "Another Usurpation" was highly critical of the appointment
by Davis of certain major generals, the claim being that Congress
had abolished the office and that Davis by reviving it was usurping
authority. "All free government rests upon a faithful enforcement of
the laws. The most dangerous source of this violation is the Executive," it said.

In late 1861 the *Mercury* also began its crusade against secret
sessions of Congress. The campaign was inspired when Congress,
finding the *Mercury* making reference to much that had taken place
in secret sessions, passed a resolution of censure against violations of
the rule of secrecy. The *Mercury* now began to claim that secret
sessions were simply a means of concealing the shortcomings of the
administration and that they were tending toward dictatorship and
despotism. For the remainder of the war period secret sessions were
one of the pet aversions of the *Mercury*.

There were others besides the Rhetts who disliked Davis and his
policies. As early as May, 1861, J. J. Pettigrew expressed his fear of a
dictatorship. L. M. Keitt, in June, thought "Jeff Davis a failure and
his Cabinet a farce." Hammond from the first had a very low opinion
of Davis and privately expressed it freely. In September, B. F. Perry
and James L. Petigru, the old unionists, agreed that the war would
bring a despotism. Petigru went so far as to say that it was a matter
of little consequence which side won because liberty would be destroyed in either case. Governor Pickens said to the convention in
December that it was useless to disguise the fact that the country
was under absolute military control. None of these criticisms of the
Confederate government, however, was publicly made, and only here
and there was there any open agreement with the *Mercury*. A Cheraw
correspondent wrote commending the editor for his fearless attacks
on things needing criticism at a time when other papers were
pusillanimous; and a friend of Rhett's in Orangeburg congratulated

him upon his "independence, unselfishness and courage." Such supporters of the *Mercury* were, however, apparently very few.

The overwhelming sentiment of the people of South Carolina in
1861 was that the *Mercury's* carping criticism was unfortunate. When
the Palmetto Guards in Virginia were reported by the *Mercury* to be
ready to come home in disgust at the defensive policy of the administration, they indignantly denied the report and expressed confidence
in Davis. Henry W. Ravenel, though somewhat worried about the
comparative inaction of the armies, thought the criticisms by the
Mercury were highly reprehensible. The leaders, he thought, were
better informed than the general public and should not be judged
until the war was over. H. D. Lesesne thought that almost everybody disapproved of the *Mercury's* course and wondered why no one
did anything to check the "mischievous print" which to him was a
trial "hard to bear patiently." The newspapers apparently without
exception refused to follow the *Mercury*. The most prominent of those
which came to the defense of the administration was the Charleston
Courier but various others expressed confidence in the President. The
Sumter *Watchman* thought that Davis was generally held in high
esteem, and the Spartanburg *Express* "deeply regretted the impatient
and impetuous spirit" of his critics. The Camden *Confederate* was
content to "repose the most unbounded confidence in the ability and
zeal" of Davis and his generals and referred to his annual message
as a "model in every particular." The Fairfield *Herald* took issue
sharply with the *Mercury's* editorial "Another Usurpation" and called
upon the people of the state to repudiate the *Mercury's* course. Official
endorsement of President Davis was given by the legislature. In the
called session which met to choose presidential electors, Richard
Yeadon, of the *Courier*, offered resolutions expressing confidence in
the administration and nominating Davis and Stephens for President and Vice-President. More than ten members objected to immediate consideration and Yeadon withdrew the resolutions though he
was confident that they would have passed overwhelmingly if there
had been time for their consideration. In the regular session resolutions of "full confidence in the ability, integrity and patriotism" of
Davis and in the "wisdom and statesmanship" of his administration
were passed with only one dissenting vote. The legislature, moreover, elected R. W. Barnwell, strong supporter of Davis, and J. L.
Orr, "arch-enemy of the Rhetts," to the Confederate Senate.

The military reverses of February, including the loss of Forts
Henry and Donelson and of Roanoke Island, brought a definite re-

action against President Davis in South Carolina. The Columbia *Guardian* became sharply critical, especially of appointments, and insisted that reform was badly needed. The "cup is on the point of overflowing," it said. Mrs. Chesnut remarked: "In Columbia I do not know a half-dozen men who would not gaily step into Jeff Davis's shoes with a firm conviction that they would do better in every respect than he does." H. W. Ravenel who had been criticizing the *Mercury* for its attacks, now wondered, "Why is all this neglect of preparation," when every resource of the South is at the disposal of the government? People were asking everywhere, he said, "Has our President done his duty faithfully?" Ravenel feared Davis was not the "right man in the right place." He believed that he would not receive the vote of a single state if the election were held again. James H. Hammond continued to speak bitterly of the President. "Davis's supreme imbecility has well nigh undone us. You cannot find a more signal failure in history." Hammond believed that one more defeat in Virginia would cause Davis to be deposed and a dictator appointed. Senator Orr wrote General Waddy Thompson censuring the President severely, and Judge O'Neall lamented to Perry that the country was ruined. William H. Trescot, with his bent for foreign affairs, thought that in the conduct of foreign relations the President had lost a great opportunity. Governor Pickens was correct when he wrote Memminger on April 26 that South Carolina was greatly dissatisfied with the administration. Even Richard Yeadon and Robert W. Barnwell were beginning to doubt the President's ability.

In the spring of 1862 when South Carolina as a whole seemed to be turning against the administration, the attacks of the *Mercury* increased in severity. On February 25 editorials of 1861 in which the *Mercury* had urged offensive fighting and had condemned the lack of preparation, were reprinted to show that the criticisms has been pertinent. This was followed by renewed attacks on the "lamentably shortsighted" and "feeble" efforts of the administration to build a well-equipped fighting machine. An appeal was made to the states to make up for the deficiencies of the administration by themselves importing and manufacturing the needed supplies. On February 27 the attack was climaxed by a vitriolic editorial entitled "The President and the Instrumentalities of War" in which the inadequate preparation was attributed solely to the President's "incompetence combined with arrogance and autocracy." The Richmond *Enquirer* came to the defense of the administration but the *Mercury* gave little ground and defended its whole course of "constructive" criticism. . . .

In Congress, too, South Carolina through her representatives gave evidence in 1862 of the reaction against the administration. When H. S. Foote introduced resolutions which were clearly intended to censure Secretary of War Benjamin for the loss of Forts Henry and Donelson, McQueen was the only member of the South Carolina delegation who voted with the administration. Another resolution of Foote which declared that the defensive policy should be abandoned was supported by Boyce in a long speech. Boyce thought that more energy might be brought into the prosecution of the war if a general-in-chief fully responsible for the conduct of the war, were appointed. For such a post he suggested either Toombs or Beauregard both of whom had been at odds with the President. Ayer showed his anti-Davis leaning when in a prepared speech he fought a bill which would have allowed cabinet members to speak in Congress as the Constitution permitted. He declared that there was already a tendency for the executive to encroach upon the legislative department and that the bill would further increase the executive influence. Every member of the South Carolina delegation except Senator Barnwell and Representative Miles voted against the conscription bills of 1862. Miles was, however, by no means the consistent supporter of the administration in 1862 that Barnwell was. He repudiated a newspaper statement that he was a mouthpiece of the President and at least on one occasion took exception to a remark in a message of the President which he thought cast a reflection on Congress. He also expressed his opposition to the defensive military policy.

On the whole the South Carolina delegation may be regarded as anti-Davis even in 1862. One or two of them were reported to be in favor of deposing the President. In the Senate Barnwell may be regarded as a consistent administration man but his colleague, Orr, was clearly unfriendly to the President. In the House there was no administration supporter to compare with Barnwell in the Senate and a majority was unfriendly to Davis, though Boyce, McQueen, and Miles were somewhat less so than the others.

Criticism of President Davis diminished in the latter part of 1862. This was due in part to the successes of Lee against McClellan and Pope in Virginia and more largely, perhaps, to the all absorbing nature of the executive council controversy in South Carolina. It has been suggested that a prime motive of the *Courier's* crusade against the council may have been to divert attention from the *Mercury's* attacks upon the administration. The *Mercury* itself was not entirely diverted. It occasionally restated its objections to secret sessions and it complained of too much censorship of military news. It was especially critical of the interference by Generals Braxton Bragg and Earl Van Dorn with the "freedom of the press" in Alabama. After the Peninsular campaign, the *Mercury* was on the whole less severe in its attacks. It even congratulated the House for some improvement in the matter of secret sessions. But Rhett was by no means converted to the administration. In the last session of the state convention in September, 1862, he introduced anti-administration resolutions and otherwise attacked the Davis government. The resolutions declared that free states should never be admitted to the Confederate union; that the United States should not be given any commercial advantages over other foreign nations; and that since the Constitution gave no power to Congress to establish internal improvements, the recent appropriations for building railroads were usurpations of power contrary to the spirit and letter of the Constitution. The resolutions failed. Rhett also launched an attack on Davis in opposing some resolutions of Gabriel Manigault which proposed that South Carolina prevent agents of the Confederacy from raising troops in South Carolina except through volunteering or state agencies. These resolutions Rhett opposed on the ground that they proposed to throw the state in direct conflict with the Confederacy. He declared that he was in sympathy with the principle[s] of the resolution[s] and would have supported them a year earlier but that the weakness of the administration had made conscription inevitable and necessary to prevent disaster. He insisted that the government was chargeable with weakness, vacillation, and lack of foresight and that reverses were the natural consequence of an inactive and sluggish policy. Against these charges Barnwell defended the administration saying that the South's defeats were caused by disease which had decimated the ranks. Chesnut also came to the defense of Davis. Barnwell and Chesnut were to stand by Davis until the bitter end.

At the beginning of 1863 the *Mercury* was more charitable toward the administration of President Davis than perhaps at any time during the war. The first editorial of the new year declared that the outlook for the Confederacy was bright. "Doubt and discord reign in the councils of our enemies. With us all is confidence, and unity of purpose." It praised President Davis's speech of December 26 before the Mississippi legislature and described his January message to Congress as being "decidedly the ablest and most satisfactory" that he had yet delivered. It had only kind words for the new Secretary of War, James A. Seddon, referring to him as "able and energetic" and congratulating him on his determination to enforce the conscription law.

The good humor of the *Mercury* was, however, short-lived. On March 12, in an editorial entitled "A Despotism over the Confederate States Proposed in Congress," it heatedly denounced the bill introduced by Ethelbert Barksdale of Mississippi proposing to give Davis authority to suspend the writ of *habeas corpus.* The bill, it said, would make the people slaves and subjects of the despot Davis. When the Richmond *Enquirer* defended the measure from the attacks of the *Mercury* the later [sic] accused the former of inconsistency for railing at the despotism of the United States while proposing to arm Davis with the identical powers exercised by President Lincoln. The *Enquirer* was willing to trust Davis not to abuse his powers and pointed out that he had not done so under the law of October 13, 1862. The *Mercury* replied that it would not trust a Washington with such power; that a "despotism is a despotism" whoever the despot; that if the old law had done no harm, that was proof that it had not been necessary. The *Mercury* even claimed that it had never heard of the October law and took occasion to restate its objections to secret sessions of Congress. During April it returned to the subject of *habeas corpus* again and again.

In the summer and fall of 1863 the *Mercury* became more bitter in its attacks on the administration. It ridiculed the conduct of foreign relations. It declared the tax on slaves and land unconstitutional. It complained of the gross abuse of the appointing power and of the "silly disposition of the troops." After the defeats at Vicksburg and Gettysburg, especially, it was severe in its criticism. Early in the war, it said, when an aggressive policy should have been followed, the army was kept in Virginia. Now when Vicksburg was in danger and Lee should have been kept on the defensive in Virginia while some of his forces were rushed to the West, the administration with great imbecility had sent Lee into Pennsylvania. Nothing could have been more foolish or disastrous. Davis had rightly lost the confidence both of the people and of the army. . . .

The anti-Davis group seems to have been much stronger in 1863 than in 1862. The attacks by the *Mercury* were less generally criticized by the press although a few, such as the *Courier* and the Greenville *Enterprise,* still spoke favorably of Davis. Even the *Courier* on occasion complained of government policies. For example, it took the lead in criticizing the compulsory funding act of March, 1863, saying that it was an unconstitutional repudiation which would ruin Confederate credit; the people themselves should repudiate such an "unworthy, discreditable and suicidal" policy. The *Courier* also condemned what it regarded as abuses under the impressment act. The South Carolina delegation in Congress continued to be for the most part unfriendly, and Governor Bonham, though coöperating in his official capacity, was personally unfriendly to Davis. He stated that he had no influence at all with the President.

Although President Davis was increasingly unpopular in 1863, the congressional election indicated that there was no great popular favor for the President's greatest critic, Barnwell Rhett. Rhett had not been a candidate for Congress in 1861 but after the disasters of 1863 he decided to stand in his old third district. He and his friends seem to have assumed that L. M. Ayer would step gracefully aside for a superior man. This assumption was at once corrected by Ayer in a letter to the *Courier* of September 5. From the first Ayer made the attitude of Rhett and the *Mercury* toward the administration the issue of the campaign. He was himself no Davis man and he frankly stated that he had opposed and would oppose him whenever his judgment directed. If, however, the people of his district desired "to wage war against President Davis at all times, in and out of season, and to create, stimulate and urge on a factious and most mischievous opposition" to the administration, then they should vote for Rhett, not for him. He believed that Davis needed all the support and encouragement possible. While the *Mercury* recounted the sins of the administration Rhett took the stump, and was joined by Ayer in a series of joint debates. There were no reports of the debates but the campaign apparently turned almost entirely on the relation of Rhett and the *Mercury* to the administration. On October 20 Rhett was defeated by a majority of about 500 votes.

Rhett's defeat was clearly not due to any great enthusiasm among his constituents for President Davis. One explanation is to be found perhaps in Ayer's statement that he was elected because he had looked after his sick and wounded constituents. Perhaps many people in their suffering had lost confidence in the wisdom of the man who had so earnestly preached secession. There were claims, too, that at several places in Beaufort and Colleton Districts where Rhett was strongest, the polling places had not been open. The chief explanation, however, seems to be that the people were in about the same position as Ayer; they held no brief for Davis but believed that such carping criticism as that of the *Mercury* was injurious to the Confederate cause which they wished to support.

A few days after Rhett's defeat President Davis made a three day visit to Charleston. During his stay he made a speech at the city hall, inspected the fortifications, and received all of the formal courtesies which the occasion demanded. In speaking of the successful defense of Fort Sumter and Charleston against the great attacks of 1863, Davis failed to mention the name of Fort Sumter's valiant defender Colonel Alfred Rhett, but did pay a tribute to Major Stephen D. Elliott who had only recently assumed command. He also failed to refer to popular General Beauregard. The general was offended and refused an invitation to dine with the President at the home of ex-Governor William Aiken. The *Courier* reported that the reception of the President in Charleston had been of the "warmest and most cordial" character but there was apparently much less enthusiasm than the *Courier* reported.

By the end of 1863 confidence in President Davis had been considerably impaired in South Carolina but the prevailing view was that the state should maintain an officially correct attitude and coöperate fully with the administration in the prosecution of the war. It was in this spirit that all insistence on exemptions from military service under state law was abandoned. In this spirit the people of the third congressional district refused to endorse the course followed by Rhett and the *Mercury*. It was in this spirit also that the legislature passed resolutions declaring that President Davis was "entitled to the gratitude of the people and the commendation of every enlightened patriot for his unselfish patriotism and untiring devotion to the interests of the whole country"; and that South Carolina tendered him the assurance of "unabated confidence." In the House there was objection to the word "unabated" but a motion by W. S. Mullins to omit the word was defeated 84 to 16. In the Senate, too, an amendment was offered which would have modified the endorsement but the resolutions as originally drawn were passed without a recorded vote.

Of the South Carolina press in 1864 apparently only the *Courier* remained loyal to President Davis and even it occasionally gave evidence of its waning faith in the Richmond government. The newspapers generally became so critical that little difference existed between them and the *Mercury* itself. The latter maintained its hostility throughout the year. It condemned Congress for usurping power at three "vital points": first, in making appropriations for the construction of railroads; second, in passing conscription laws which did not exempt state officers; third, in laying direct taxes on land and slaves without apportionment. Despairing of checking these usurpations during the war, it insisted that a convention must be called for reform as soon as peace was won. Though not denying the power of Congress to suspend the writ of *habeas corpus*, it applauded Brown and Stephens of Georgia for their crusade against the law of February 15 and declared that it would not support such a law if "the Angel Gabriel were our President to administer it." It congratulated the second Congress for its refusal to continue the February law and for its refusal to violate the Constitution by increasing the salary of Davis. Congress was also commended for threatening the impeachment and forcing the resignation of Secretary Memminger. With obvious reference to President Davis, Congress was reminded that by impeachment it could "strike down any portion of the Executive which it deems noxious to the interests of the Confederacy." The state legislature was chided for its failure to assert the rights of the state and for inferentially supporting usurpations by its dumb silence in regard to them. In tiresome repetition all of the sins of Congress and President Davis were paraded down the columns of the *Mercury* during the whole year of 1864.

In the last year of the war it is difficult to discover, outside of the columns of the *Courier,* any South Carolinian speaking kindly words of President Davis. In Congress Barnwell alone remained loyal. Senator Orr had been in opposition to President Davis from the beginning and described him in January, 1864, as a "weak and incompetent President" with "an imbecile cabinet to sustain him." In the House, Miles definitely went into the Davis opposition by 1864. Though never close to the President, Miles, as chairman of the important Committee on Military Affairs, had usually exerted his great influence for the war measures of the administration. Even in early 1864 he voted to leave the whole matter of exemptions to the Secretary of War but his references to Davis in his speech supporting the bill were so unfriendly as to be called an open attack. Miles came to think Davis "so stubborn and so pig-headed" that he could not be influenced except by one of his favorites, among whom, he said, he happened not to be because of having opposed him in "one or two acts of tyranny." Thereafter, said Miles, the President lost no opportunity of thwarting him. The other House members were likewise anti-Davis. Boyce and McQueen joined Miles in voting for the very limited *habeas corpus* act of February 15, 1864, but this was apparently the last distinctively administration measure which received South Carolina support. Every member of the delegation, for example, voted against efforts in the last session of Congress to pass another *habeas corpus* law; every member of the House delegation voted for the bill creating the position of general-in-chief for the armies in January, 1865. The whole delegation was reported to have called on the President early in 1865 and demanded a reform in administration.

Early in the Civil War Union forces captured and held several sea islands in the Beaufort area. Also, Charleston was under siege during much of the war. Otherwise, the state was almost free of military operations until 1865.

On December 24, 1864, General William T. Sherman, in Savannah, received permission from General Grant to invade the Carolinas. A few days later Union troops crossed the river into South Carolina. Despite rain, mud, and cold, Sherman's army slowly but relentlessly moved toward Columbia, devastating the countryside as it went. On February 16 Sherman encamped on the west bank of the Congaree.

The Confederate forces, depleted by attrition in four years of fighting, could offer only limited rearguard resistance to the invaders. Within the capital city panic reigned, as state officials, private citizens and Confederate troops tried to flee. The following day Union soldiers entered the city unopposed. During Sherman's occupation of Columbia, fires broke out and destroyed two-thirds of the city. For years afterward controversy raged over the responsibility for the fire: Sherman or departing Confederates? In *Sherman's March Through the Carolinas* John G. Barrett discusses this point and describes the awesome night when Columbia went up in flames.

17

THE BURNING OF COLUMBIA *

John G. Barrett

There is conclusive evidence . . . that at least some cotton
was fired before Sherman entered Columbia. Henry Clay McArthur
who entered the city with a small detachment of the Seventeenth
Corps forty-five minutes prior to Stone's arrival passed smouldering
cotton along the way. An escaped Federal prisoner, from his place
of refuge in a Negro cabin, saw the Confederate cavalry firing cotton
before departing the city. William Gilmore Simms, a well-known
Southern literary figure, in recording a fire at the city jail noted that
this fire "had been preceded by that of some cotton piled in the
streets." Major Chambliss, the Confederate ordnance officer, in his
official report stated that at 3:00 A.M. on February 17 the city was
actually "illuminated by burning cotton."

The origin of the early fires is still a matter of dispute. Sherman
in his official report, dated April 4, 1865, placed the responsibility
for these acts of incendiarism squarely on the shoulders of Wade
Hampton. Hampton did not let Sherman's charges go unanswered.
In a letter to the editor of the *New York Day Book,* he angrily
exploded that thousands of witnesses could testify that "not one bale
of cotton was on fire" when Sherman entered Columbia. Hampton
urged Reverdy Johnson, in the United States Senate, to set up an
"honest, tribunal" before which he pledged himself to prove that he
"gave a positive order, by direction of General Beauregard, that no
cotton should be burned; that not one bale was on fire when Sherman's troops took possession of the city. . . ." Not only did Hampton
emphatically deny "that any cotton was burned in Columbia "[*sic*]
by his order, [''] but he also completely discounted Sherman's charge
"that the citizens set fire to thousands of bales rolled out into the
streets."

General Butler substantiates Hampton's denial of Sherman's accusa-

* Excerpts from *Sherman's March Through the Carolinas* (Chapel Hill:
University of North Carolina Press, 1956), pp. 77–84, 87–93; Copyright,
1956, by The University of North Carolina Press. Reprinted without footnotes
by permission of The University of North Carolina Press.

tions. Butler, who had brought up the cavalry rear guard as it evacuated Columbia, remained on a hill outside the city for two hours watching the Federal occupation. He vouches that prior to the enemy's appearance in the capital, he saw no evidence of fire. Private Edward L. Wells, before taking position on the crest, received permission to return to Columbia in search of twelve bottles of madeira wine and to warn a lady refugee friend of his. On this trip into town and later from his location on the hill, he "saw no Confederate cavalrymen or stragglers and no fires. . . ." A lieutenant from Kentucky who rode back into Columbia after the Confederate cavalry had departed did not observe any cotton burning.

Contrary to the above assertions of Hampton, Butler, and others, the confusion in Columbia on the morning of February 17 made it impossible to enforce strictly Beauregard's orders. No doubt, in the press and hurry of evacuating the city, the burning cotton failed to register with these men.

The firing of cotton continued after Sherman's appearance in the city. Around 1:00 P.M. James Guignard Gibbes, prominent Columbia citizen, counted sixty bales on fire and later in the afternoon he saw thirty more ignited. Alderman James McKenzie and the Reverend Peter J. Shand were witnesses to this burning cotton.

For these fires any number of persons, including local Negroes, escaped Federal prisoners, released convicts, and drunken soldiers, stand as possible culprits. The most likely incendiaries in this group were the drunken soldiers who on more than one occasion were seen to light a cigar and then throw the match into some loose cotton.

In the final analysis the origin of these morning and afternoon fires is of little significance because they had all been completely extinguished by mid-afternoon. In some cases the soldiers helped the citizens fight the fires, but more often they either stood idly by or cut the hose with their bayonets. This destruction of hose eventually put all the fire engines in Columbia out of commission. On occasions the men went so far as to destroy the engines themselves. The unruly conduct of the occupying forces was not responsible, however, for the flames getting out of control. In the opinion of Major General William B. Hazen, Fifteenth Corps, the cotton fires were so completely extinguished by the middle of the afternoon that "a dozen men with tin cups could have managed it."

When the smoke from the smoldering cotton began to clear away, other columns of smoke were seen to the east of the city, two to five miles off. Sherman's incendiaries were at work. The residences of General Hampton, Dr. John Wallace, George A. Trenholm, Confederate Secretary of the Treasury, and many others, were going up in flames.

For Sherman, the afternoon passed pleasantly. He settled himself comfortably at his headquarters in the Blanton Duncan home. The command of the city had been turned over to Howard. Alone in his private room Sherman opened a piece of paper that one of the escaped prisoners had handed him at the market square that morning. It contained a song entitled "Sherman's March to the Sea" written by Adjutant Samuel Hawkins Marshall Byers of the Fifth Iowa infantry. The stirring lines of this song so impressed the General that he made its author a member of his staff.

The General's rest was interrupted from time to time by the visits of women, importuning guards for their homes. One of these callers, Mrs. Campbell Bryce, found Sherman "respectful and kindly" and quite willing to write out an order assigning a guard to her home. Mayor Goodwyn, anxious about the fate of Columbia, called late in the afternoon. He was much impressed by the polite and courteous manner with which Sherman received him and his anxiety was allayed when Sherman promised protection for the city.

The two men took a walk together. The Mayor introduced Sherman to "new and old acquaintences." In answer to a note of invitation Sherman requested they go first to the daughter of the Poyas family, whom he had known twenty years earlier at Charleston. Happy memories of his duty at Fort Moultrie had been rekindled. The General was pleased to find that the large frame house, located near the Charlotte depot, had not been pillaged and that "a general air of peace and comfort" prevailed. Much to his surprise Sherman learned that he was responsible for the "perfect safety of . . . [the] house and property." Upon entering the yard earlier in the day, the Federal soldiers had been confronted by the Poyas girl who held in her hand a book in which Lieutenant Sherman had written his name years earlier. Fortunately for the girl, one of the group verified the signature on the fly leaf. This so impressed the others that a guard was immediately stationed at the house and a young boy from Iowa was assigned the job of helping with the baby of the home. Sherman, clearly flattered by this story, paid a long social call. From here Goodwyn took the General to the home of Harris Simons, whose brother, James, had been Sherman's friend in Charleston. Sherman had also known Mrs. Simons in her maiden days as Miss Wragg.

At sundown the Mayor and the General returned to the Duncan house. Before going inside, Sherman again made it clear to his companion that Columbia was secure: "Go home and rest assured that your city will be as safe in my hands as if you had controlled it."

He did, however, acquaint Goodwyn with his plan to burn several public buildings and inquired about the condition of the city's fire engines and water works. But he went on to say that this undertaking would have to be delayed until a succeeding day when the winds were not so strong. Sherman feared the present gale-like gusts might spread the flames to private property, not "one particle" of which did he wish to destroy.

Having walked over much of Columbia during the afternoon, Sherman was tired when he lay down on his bed for a nap. Scarcely had he closed his eyes when he was awakened by a bright light flickering back and forth on the walls of his room. Fearful that the high winds had fanned the smoldering cotton fires, he sent his aide, Major George Ward Nichols, to inquire into the cause of these fire shadows. The Major returned and divulged the worst, a block of buildings in the heart of the city was on fire. But he hastened to add that General Woods "with plenty of men" was working tirelessly to bring the fires under control. Thereafter, periodic word came from Logan and Woods that the maximum effort was being exerted to curb the blazes. But man in this instance was no match for nature. The high winds were turning Columbia into a raging inferno. Around eleven o'clock, with the entire heavens lurid from the glow of dancing flames, Sherman went out himself to aid in stemming the conflagration.

Shortly after nightfall, red, white, and blue rockets, had been visible in the sky above the new state house. The sight of these flares had caused the guard at Mayor Goodwyn's to jump up and exclaim: "My God, is it coming to this" and then rush off without explanation. A minister, standing in his front yard when the first rocket went up, heard Federal soldiers near by remark: "Now you will catch hell— that is the signal for a general setting of fire to the city." If there was an organized plot on foot to burn Columbia, it is likely that the conspirators awaited these signals to begin their work since it was the general practice of the signal corps to send up rockets each night to give troop locations. Planned or not, numerous fires broke out almost simultaneously in several areas of Columbia directly after the rockets were seen in the heavens.

Among the first fires of the evening were those which broke out in the low wooden houses on Gervais Street, used mostly as places of prostitution. Presently alarms were sounded in "Cotton Town," the northwest corner of Columbia, and along the river front and to the west. In a few minutes twenty or more fires were raging in different sections of Columbia, including the very heart of the city. There can be little doubt that the capital city of South Carolina was deliberately fired by the soldiers in blue, in General Hazen's belief, "in more than a hundred places."

At dusk the hitherto deserted streets of Columbia had begun to fill up with shadowy figures carrying fire brands, cotton balls saturated in combustible material, cans of turpentine, and pockets full of matches. Prepared for the job at hand, emboldened by whiskey, and ever increasing in members, "the drunken devils roamed about setting fire to every house in every direction. . . ." The local citizens gave up all thought of sleep and watched by the red glare of burning buildings the "wretches" in blue as they walked the streets shouting, hurrahing, cursing South Carolina, swearing, blaspheming, and singing ribald songs. The horror of this scene implanted itself in the mind of young Emma LeConte, who wrote:

Imagine night turned into noonday, only with a blazing, scorching glare that was terrible—a copper-colored sky across which swept columns of black rolling smoke glittering with sparks and flying embers, while all around us were falling thickly showers of burning flakes. Everywhere the palpitating blaze walled the streets as far [as] the eye could reach—filling the air with its terrible roar. On every side the crackling and devouring fire, while every instant came the crashing of timbers and the thunder of falling buildings. A quivering molten ocean seemed to fill the air and sky.

Heart-rending cries of those in distress, the terrified lowing of cattle, and the frenzied flight of pigeons added to the pathos of the occasion.

The college library next to the LeConte home "seemed framed by the gushing flames and smoke, while through the windows gleamed the liquid fire. . . ." The other buildings on the campus, filled with three hundred sick and wounded soldiers, were soon on fire. Only through the valiant efforts of the few doctors and nurses present were those buildings saved. From the rooftops they fought the flames, while the patients as best they could, dragged themselves out into the yard. Sometime before daybreak drunken soldiers tried to storm the campus gate although a yellow hospital flag was flying and the wounded inside were both Confederate and Federal soldiers. Three of the college professors and Dr. Thompson of the hospital staff stationed themselves at the main entrance to the grounds, which were encompassed by a high wall, and warded off the intruders until a strong guard arrived.

The soldiers, foiled in their attempt to raze the college buildings, were intent upon leveling the Baptist church where the South Carolina secession convention first met. The detail sent to burn this edifice did not know its location and had to inquire of a colored man which of the many places of worship in Columbia it was. This Negro, who it is said was the sexton of the desired church, purposely directed the detail to the Washington Street Methodist Church less than a block away. Thus a faithful Negro, saved from certain destruction this symbol of South Carolina's leadership in the secession movement. Three times the Methodist Church was set on fire. The pastor, the Reverend Mr. Connor, twice put out the flames, but when the parsonage next door was fired, he had to tend his sick child whom he carried out of the house in his arms. So incensed was one soldier by this time that he tore off the child's blanket and threw it into the flames, saying: "D——n you, if you say a word I'll throw the child after it."

The Ursuline Convent suffered the same fate as the Methodist Church, even though Sherman had penciled a note to the Mother Superior promising protection for the school. His concern for the institution was based on the knowledge that this lady had once been a teacher in a convent in Ohio at the time his daughter, Minnie, was there. During the night, as the soldiers milled around the convent and sparks began to fall on the building, the Mother Superior decided to evacuate the premises. Foolishly the nuns removed none of their possessions or church valuables. Consequently, no sooner had the teachers and pupils departed than the guards, joined by drunken soldiers, began to ransack the school. A thorough job of pillage was enacted before flames destroyed the building.

A great historical and scientific loss was the home of Dr. Robert Wilson Gibbes. Soldiers fired the house of this noted man of letters and science by piling furniture in the drawing room and igniting it. The lone guard, befriended by Gibbes, tried without success to halt this lawlessness. Lost in the blaze was a large library, many portfolios of fine engravings, more than a hundred paintings, "a remarkable cabinet of southern fossiles," one of the finest collections of shark's teeth in the world, American and Mexican Indian relics, and an extensive collection of historical documents, including much original correspondence on the Revolution.

The uncontrollable fires which engulfed the city did not curb the cupidity of the soldiers. Their search for spoil continued. The men, plied with whiskey, rushed from house to house, first emptying them of their valuables, and then applying the torch. Jewelry and plate were found in abundance. Drunks staggered under the accumulation of sterling trays, vases, candelabra, cups, and goblets. Clothes and shoes, when new, were usually appropriated, the rest left to burn. Fraternal orders were not overlooked. Men absurdly attired in Masonic and Odd Fellow regalias strolled about the streets.

Many guards followed the example of those at the convent by deserting their posts and entering into the rowdyism of the night. At the Agnes Law residence the four guards conducted themselves admirably for a while. Here they were fed supper, after which one lay down on the sofa. The others walked about the yard. But when the city began to burn and Agnes wanted to remove her furniture, the guards objected on the grounds that the house was in no immediate danger. Before long these same men took lighted candles upstairs and set the curtains on fire.

More than once superhuman strength enabled an individual to salvage a heavy piece of furniture or other cumbersome possessions from a burning home. Alice Boatwright managed to get a fully packed trunk from her upstairs to her frontyard, only to have the soldiers break the lock and take what they wanted.

The Federal camps, where a few of the homeless sought refuge, were not free from theft either. The soldiers attempted to steal what little these families had salvaged. . . .

Sherman himself on the night of February 17, stopped by the Simons' home and advised the ladies to move to his headquarters where they would be safe. He ordered his own headquarter's wagon hitched up to move their personal effects.

On the main street Sherman found Generals Howard, Logan, Woods, and Hazen barking orders to the men and toiling themselves in a fruitless effort to halt the flames. Guards watched over furniture piled in the middle of the street. Sherman saw Stone's disorderly troops removed from the city and Brigadier General W. B. Woods' brigade brought in. Woods immediately began a roundup of all drunken and lawless soldiers. Three hundred and seventy were placed under arrest, two were killed, and thirty wounded. Sherman in person ordered the arrest of a drunken private and saw Colonel L. M. Dayton, his aide, shoot the man down when he resisted arrest. Woods' brigade, in spite of its hard work, fared little better than its predecessor in bringing order to the city and stemming the fires. Eventually all of Hazen's division was ordered into Columbia but only a shift of wind around 4:00 A.M. saved the city from total annihilation.

General Sherman spent the greater part of the night battling the flames but at no time did he take immediate personal charge of the fire-fighting activities. No general orders were issued by him that night because, in his opinion, his subordinates were doing all that was possible to bring the situation under control.

Many Federal soldiers, including high ranking officers, labored diligently into the early morning hours to curb the conflagration [*sic*].

The aging William Gilmore Simms admitted that this is true. Just the same, the fact stands that the small force on duty in Columbia could offer only meager efforts at stemming the raging fires. Either Sherman or one of his lieutenants should have ordered a large body of troops into the capital early in the evening. With a high wind blowing and the city full of those who did not wish to see the scene closed, "the viriest scum of the army," a force much larger than four brigades was necessary for effective action.

It seemed to the inhabitants of Columbia that dawn would never come. To them it was as though "the gates of hell had been opened. . . ." A drunken trooper "with a musket in one hand and a match in the other is not a pleasant visitor to have about the house on a dark, windy night. . . ." In the minds of the local citizenry such an individual surely must have crossed the river Styx on his journey to Columbia. When the sun rose at last, dim and red through the murky atmosphere, it shone upon a smouldering ruins that was once a beautiful and proud city. With the first light of dawn and the sound of reveille the "drunken devils" disappeared like ghosts at the cock crowing. Their work was finished. The greater part of Columbia was in ashes. From the center of town as far as the eye could reach, nothing was to be seen "but heaps of rubbish, tall dreary chimneys, and shattered brick walls. . . ." The fires had ranged over 84 of the city's 124 blocks, containing 500 edifices.

The homeless, gathered in the open spaces and parks of the city and huddled around their few belongings, were a pitiful sight. From her porch Emma LeConte looked across the street to the common which "was crowded with homeless women and children, a few wrapped in blankets and many shivering in the night air." Some were crying and despondent. A few were patient, submissive, and quiet. Others complained terribly about the "Yankees." This pathetic sight was too much for even the war hardened heart of an Illinois surgeon who entered in his diary: "I talked with some but it made me feel too bad to be endured."

Whitelaw Reid, the Ohio politician, called the burning of Columbia the "most monstrous barbarity of the barbarous march." The people of Columbia, in full agreement with Reid, were also positive that one day the Devil "with a wild sardonic grin will point exultant to a crime which won the prize from SIN." For them Sherman had out-Heroded Herod and "Beast" Butler was a gentleman in comparison.

It was the drunken soldier who was primarily responsible for the holocaust of February 17, but he was not acting under orders from his commanding general. Sherman's orders for the campaign of the

Carolinas contain no instructions for the molestation of private property in Columbia. In 1872, when called to testify in a lawsuit regarding the fire, he swore: "I gave no order at anytime to burn any private home or dwelling. . . . Nor did I give permission to anyone to set fire to any private dwelling. . . ." The question of who was responsible for the burning of Columbia was investigated by a mixed commission on American and British claims under the Treaty of Washington in 1873. The plaintiffs asked compensation for privately owned cotton on the grounds that Columbia had been "wantonly fired by the army of General Sherman either under his orders or with his consent and permission." This commission cleared Sherman's name when it found that the destruction of property in the capital was due to neither "the intention or default of either the Federal or Confederate officers."

On the night of the fire Sherman was inclined to attribute the conflagration to whiskey. In conversation with Mayor Goodwyn that evening he complained: "Who could command drunken soldiers?" The blame for what happened on February 17 was the mayor's, said Sherman, because the large stores of liquor in the city had not been removed by him. A few days reflection changed his mind. He then concluded that Hampton and cotton should bear the guilt, not whiskey. On the witness stand in one of the cotton cases he asserted:

The fire was originated with the imprudent act of Wade Hampton in ripping open bales of cotton, piling it in the streets, burning it and then going away. . . . If I had made up my mind to burn Columbia I would have burnt it with no more feeling than I would a common prairie village; but I did not do it. . . . God Almighty started wind sufficient to carry that cotton wherever He would, and in some way or other that burning cotton was the origin of the fire. . . .

Three years later in 1875, with the publication of his *Memoirs,* Sherman admitted that his charges against Hampton were designed to shake the faith of the people of South Carolina in their cavalry commander. He considered Hampton a braggart and the self-appointed champion of his people. But Sherman never wavered in his conviction that cotton fired on the morning of February 17 played the major role in commencing the fire of that evening. He did concede that some soldiers after the fire originated may have been concerned in spreading it, but not concerned in starting it.

The findings of the Mixed Claims Commission did not silence those who contended that the devastation on Columbia was carried out with Sherman's tacit consent. This group likes to quote out of context from the General's letter to Halleck, December 24, 1864, in which he used his usual intemperate language to speculate on the fate of South Carolina at the hands of his troops. By omitting the line, "I doubt if we will spare the public buildings as we did in Milledgeville" Sherman's loose words condemn him. At Milledgeville the Federal officers did amuse themselves by holding a mock session of the Georgia legislature, but they spared the Capitol as they did most of the public buildings in the town. Private homes and property were also respected. In view of this conduct, Sherman's statement that in Columbia he would probably destroy public buildings shows more clearly that he anticipated only the destruction of public property than it shows he reflected on a policy of general devastation for the city.

In the long run Sherman felt that the burning of private homes, though not designed by him, was a trifling matter when compared with the manifold results which soon followed. "Though I never ordered it and never wished it, I have never shed any tears over the event, because I believe that it hastened what we all fought for, the end of the war." This laconic statement pretty well sums up Sherman's sentiments on the burning of Columbia.

The army remained in Columbia for two days, destroying public and railroad property as ordered by Sherman. General Howard's men tore up the railroad track toward the Wateree as well as demolishing all railroad property in the city. A detail under Colonel O. M. Poe of the engineers leveled what remained of the public buildings with the exception of the unfinished state house. As one native of Columbia expressed it: "They destroyed everything which the most infernal Yankee ingenuity could devise means to destroy." The Confederate arsenal, several foundries, the gas works, and a printing establishment for Confederate money all fell before the wrecking crews. Large amounts of currency, in various stages of manufacture, fell into the hands of the soldiers who "spent and gambled with it in the most lavish manner."

A terrific explosion rocked the city on February 18 when the Federal ordnance crew became careless in dumping wagon loads of captured ammunition in the Saluda River. The accident took the lives of sixteen Federal soldiers much to the delight of Emma LeConte who rejoiced "to think of any of them being killed."

After February 17, wholesale pillage and plunder stopped, but much petty theft and rummaging in the ruins for more booty continued. The soldiers made no pretense of hiding their loot. Stolen jewelry and coin were very much in evidence on their persons as they strolled the streets boasting of having burned Columbia.

Sherman was not indifferent to the suffering of the people. From his own stores he gave rice and ham to the Poyas and Simons families.

Harris Simons' hesitancy to accept the stores from an enemy, kindled the General's temper. Eyes flashing, Sherman denounced him as a damn fool and added that he did not care if Simons starved but that the rice and ham were for his wife and children. Sherman had considerable admiration for many of the upper class. He termed the aristocracy of South Carolina men "of great honor and integrity" but for one of them to raise a point of honor at such a time was utterly ridiculous to him.

To the Mother Superior and the children of the Ursuline Convent, Sherman turned over the mansion of General John S. Preston, Wade Hampton's brother-in-law. Its occupant, General Logan, was preparing to ignite the barrels of pitch in the cellar when the white clad children arrived. Logan let out mighty oaths when handed Sherman's order but he had the barrels of pitch removed. Inside the nuns found that the evacuating personnel had left their mark. The many fine paintings and pieces of statuary which adorned the halls had been mutilated. Dignified portraits carried penciled mustaches and nude statues bore clothing.

Sunday, February 19, a delegation of local citizens went to Sherman seeking food for the city and firearms for police protection. He received them courteously but on this particular Sabbath he seemed "to be on particularly good terms with himself." He alone of the Federal officers present at the conference "appeared flushed with victory and made no effort to conceal his exultation." After hearing the purpose of the visit and expounding on the folly of war, he consented to leave behind five hundred head of cattle, one hundred muskets, ammunition, all the salt at the Charleston depot, wire enough to work a flat across the river, and medicine for the sick. The beef was poor, the arms, old, and the drugs, small in quantity, but they were better than nothing. In Sherman's eyes, an enemy under arms deserved little quarter. He saw no reason to shed tears over Columbia's plight as long as South Carolina was at war with the Union.

On February 20, to the accompaniment of hisses and boos from the people along the streets, the troops resumed their march north toward Winnsboro. As the columns in blue filed by the scattered groups of men, women, and children they were spat upon and "not a few of the women undertook to lay violent hands upon . . ." them. Moving with the army were a large number of inhabitants, both white and black, of Columbia and neighboring areas who wished to go north.

The Civil War left South Carolina destitute and broken in spirit. Marauding armies had laid waste much of the land, transportation had broken down, and federal military rule of necessity had replaced the defunct civil government. Many of the newly freed Negroes were in a state of confusion. In 1932 Francis B. Simkins and Robert H. Woody published what has since become the standard study of South Carolina during Reconstruction. The following selection from chapter 1—"The Heritage of War"—pictures conditions in the state in 1865.

18

"THE HERITAGE OF WAR" *

Francis Butler Simkins
and Robert Hilliard Woody

Any attempt to rebuild South Carolina society after the Civil War had to take into account several significant results of that war. A great amount of property had been destroyed; the Negro had been made free; and the Negro and the Northern white man for the first time had become able to compete with the native white man for the control of many aspects of local life. Accordingly, this narrative must begin with descriptions of war losses, of the freeing of the Negro, and of the ambitions and relative strength of the native white man, the Negro, and the Northern conqueror. Then the way will be open to narrate the first act of the Reconstruction drama, the attempt of the native whites to build a new political society out of the wreck of the old.

The first experience with the destructive influences of war came when Northern forces in November, 1861, captured the Port Royal area. Its entire white population fled in such haste that household belongings and slaves were left behind. The conquerors gave the Negroes freedom and allowed them to plunder their former masters' property. The freedmen occupied houses and smashed or appropriated the contents. They tore down churches and used the lumber to build cabins for themselves, and they broke open church organs and blew the pipes in the streets. A hint of the fate of the property of the planters is revealed by the reports of Northern residents. A schoolmistress found a Negro cabin she visited in 1862 "elegantly furnished" with straw matting and a mahogany bureau, and her servant carried a silver thimble and a bit of embroidered curtain as a handkerchief. A labor superintendent had this to say of the house he occupied: "The force pump is broken and all the bowls and their marble slabs smashed. . . . Bureaus, commodes, and wardrobes are smashed in, as

* Excerpt from *South Carolina During Reconstruction* (Chapel Hill: University of North Carolina Press, 1932), pp. 3–12; Copyright, 1932, by The University of North Carolina Press. Reprinted without footnotes by permission of The University of North Carolina Press.

well as the door panels. . . . We kindle our fires with chips of polished mahogany, and I am writing on my knees with a piece of flower-stand across them for a table."

Sherman's army, in its march through the state in February, 1865, destroyed on a much vaster scale. A path forty miles wide was thoroughly pillaged. The correspondent of the *New York Herald* with the army wrote: "I hazard nothing in saying that three-fifths (in value) of the personal property of the counties we passed through were taken by Sherman's army. . . . As for wholesale burnings, pillage and devastation committed in South Carolina, magnify all I have said of Georgia some fifty-fold, and then throw in an occasional murder, 'jis to bring an old, hard-fisted cuss to his senses,' and you have a pretty good idea of the whole thing." General Carl Schurz, who visited the state in July, 1865, said: "The track of Sherman's march in South Carolina, at least, looked for many miles like a broad, black streak of ruin and desolation—the fences all gone; lonesome smoke stacks, surrounded by dark heaps of ashes and cinders, marking the spots where human habitation had stood; the fences along the roads wildly overgrown by weeds. . . . No part of the South I then visited had indeed suffered so much from ravages of war as South Carolina."

The crowning act of vandalism of Sherman's men was the destruction of Columbia. "It had been a beautiful city," wrote the effusive correspondent of the *New York Herald*. "It was famed for its fine public buildings, its magnificent private residences, with their lovely flower gardens which savored of oriental ease and luxury." "The eighteenth of February," added this witness, "dawned upon a city of ruins. . . . Nothing remained but the tall, spectre-looking chimneys. The noble-looking trees which shaded the streets, the flower gardens that graced them, were blasted and withered by fire. The streets were filled with rubbish, broken furniture and groups of crouching, desponding, weeping women and children." Actually two-thirds of the town, eighty-four of its 124 blocks, lay in ashes. This included 445 stores, the old state house, eleven banking establishments and six churches. Every house except those on the campus of the state college had been pillaged. The only important edifices not destroyed were the unfinished State House, the state college, the Methodist woman's college, the lunatic asylum, and the home of William C. Preston.

Charleston had suffered terribly from a series of disasters. The fire of December 11, 1861, had cut a wide belt across the city from river to river. How this area appeared in 1865 was described as follows: "The tall chimneys, grim and charred, the dilapidated walls overgrown with moss, and cellars rank with grass, the streets without pavements, and ankle-deep with sand." The lower portion of the city showed the scars of the Federal bombardment. An English visitor described its effect as follows: "Here there was hardly a house which had not suffered more or less. To some the damage seems at first sight to be trifling; a small hole knocked in the wall is apparently the extent of the mischief, till an examination of the interior shows the injury which has been done by the bursting of shells. . . . In the next house, may be, the outside has suffered; every pane of glass is broken, the doors battered in and the handsome pillars broken short." A shell had scarred the steeple of St. Michael's Church and another had demolished the altar; the interior of the Huguenot Church had been entered by shells which had shattered the chandeliers and left piles of stones on the floor. A third disaster had devastated the upper portion of the city at the time of the Confederate evacuation—the explosion of the Northeastern Depot and the fire which followed. Some two hundred persons were killed, and "the fire spread across the city, destroying millions of dollars worth of property."

Impressions of the plight of the city are conveyed by Northern travelers. "I shall never forget," wrote General Carl Schurz, "my first impression of Charleston. . . . There was no shipping in the harbor except a few quartermaster's vessels and two or three small steamers. We made fast to a decaying pier constructed of palmetto-logs. There was not a human visible on the wharf. The warehouses seemed to be completely deserted. There was no wall and no roof that did not bear eloquent marks of having been under fire of siege guns. I was informed that when our troops first entered the city, the wharf region was overgrown with luxuriant weed, giving it the appearance of a large swamp. . . . The crests of the roofs and chimneys were covered with turkey buzzards, who evidently felt at home, and who from time to time lazily flapped their wings and stretched forth their hideous necks."

Sidney Andrews wrote: "A city of ruins, of desolation, of vacant houses, of widowed women, of rotten wharves, of deserted warehouses, of weed-wild gardens, of miles of grass-grown streets, of acres of pitiful and voicefull barrenness—this is Charleston." The churchyard of St. Phillip's, where Calhoun was buried, "symbolizes the city of Charleston. Children and goats crowd through a convenient hole in the front wall, and play at will among the sunken graves and broken tombstones. There is everywhere a wealth of offal and garbage and beef-bones. A mangy cur was slinking among the stones, and I found a hole three feet deep which it had dug at the foot of one of the graves. . . . The whole yard is grown up to weeds and bush, and the place is desolate and dreary as can be."

Sections of the state outside of Charleston and the path of Sherman showed the ravages of war. Raiding parties combed the low-country on missions of pillage and destruction. Many of them were made doubly terrible to the inhabitants because of the presence of Negro troops. A member of the Sinkler family gives an illustration of the conduct of these Negroes as enacted on her family estate, "Belvidere," at Eutaw Springs: "They broke open the smokehouse, storerooms and barns, and threw out to the Negroes all the provisions and things that they could find." Several went into the house and "began throwing things about, cursing and swearing, lashing carriage whips about our heads, and saying 'Damned rebels' very often; also kicking open doors, and thrusting their bayonets into closets and wardrobes, tearing off desk doors and evidently looking for wine and silver." Many houses were burned after being sacked. The fate of St. Andrew's Parish is thus described by a committee of clergymen: "The demon of civil war was let loose in the parish. But three residences exist in the whole space between the Ashley and Stono rivers. Fire and sword were not enough. Family vaults were rifled, and coffins of the dead forced open in pursuit of plunder."

Confederate troops were guilty of some destruction. On evacuating a position they usually destroyed cotton and other supplies and were unable to restrain the predatory instincts of the rabble. For example, on the eve of Sherman's occupation of Columbia cotton was fired in the streets; the bridge over the Saluda was burned; Wheeler's men pillaged stores; and due to the carelessness of a band of plunderers, the South Carolina Railroad Depot took fire. Moreover, Confederate raiding parties were active. "From Augusta to Hardeeville," wrote a citizen concerning the conduct of Wheeler's troops, "the road is now strewn with corn, left on the ground unconsumed. Beeves have been shot down in the field, one quarter taken off and the balance left for the buzzards. Horses are stolen out of wagons on the roads, and by wholesale out of stables at night. . . . It is no unusual sight to see these men riding into camp with all sorts of plunder. Private houses are visited; carpets, blankets and other furniture . . . are taken by force in the presence of the owners." "I am sorry to say," remarked a lady of the low-country, "that Wheeler's men have done us more damage than the Yankees. . . . I do blame them very much for their wanton destruction of property they ought to protect. It is a shame and they ought to be exposed."

The description of the effect of fire and shells on property is only a partial measure of the evil influences of war on South Carolina. There were other causes which injured economic and social life. First, there was the influence of the blockade; second, the necessities of war had prompted the neglect of processes of production essential to the normal functioning of the community; third, there was a great sacrifice of man power; fourth, most of the surplus wealth was expended in the cause of the Confederacy and the defeat blasted hopes of its future redemption; fifth, the social discipline of the community was disrupted by the destruction of slavery.

The cutting off of most foreign trade by the Federal blockade had an evil effect upon a state so dependent for many of its necessities upon the exchange of cotton. Charleston, which had been the leading seaport of the southeast, lost its air of prosperity. "We have suffered severely; we are suffering now," said the *Charleston Daily Courier,* November 25, 1861. "Property represents painfully uncertain sums. Business of all kinds is prostrated, fortunes have been swept away, and we have been forced to restrict our wants within the limits of mere comforts." Although the profits of blockade-running were high, success was rare and promoted so much speculation and extravagance that many held that more harm than good was done. Many ordinary commodities became very scarce. Patriotic citizens had felt the necessity of offering window weights and church bells to supply the deficiency of metals for war purposes, and in 1863 an advertisement announcing that no orders for a particular almanac could be filled unless fifty reams of printing paper could be purchased. "Tea," said the *Charleston Daily Courier,* "is beyond reach." The Reverend A. Toomer Porter told of children with yellow fever pleading for ice when none could be had.

The plight into which the ordinary conveniences of living fell is illustrated by the fate of means of communication. Early in the struggle the use of artificial waterways was given up, and roads and causeways, because of neglect or overuse, fell into disrepair. Toward the end of the war a few army wagons and ambulances were about the only vehicles which remained fit. Horses and mules, and the provender necessary for their support, became "scarce and dear." The railroads fell into disrepair and cars and locomotives became dilapidated. The hardships of railroad travel are illustrated by the experiences of a traveler from Richmond to Charleston. This journey, which can be made today in ten hours, then took forty-one. At Florence the traveler's train was detained by the breakdown of another, and when his was ready to move, he was forced to fight his way "into some desperately crowded cars."

A fundamental element of decay was the deterioration of the soil. This was caused by too great a concentration on staple crops, without sufficient attention either to renewal by means of fertilizers, or to soil conservation by means of such ditching and terracing as would prevent the washing away of top soil. Grass was allowed to take the fields, gates and bars tumbled down, ditches caved in, and plows became worn. Cotton seed, because of the failure to maintain the proper system of selection, became "generally defective and unreliable." These circumstances account in part for a general decline in land values of 60 per cent between 1860 and 1867, and for the fall in value of all farm properties, according to the defective census of 1870, from $169,738,630 to $47,628,175 during the ten years following 1860.

Another deplorable loss, even if considered only from an economic viewpoint, was the sacrifice of man-power made in the cause of the Confederacy. Of the state's arms-bearing population of 55,046, some 44,000 volunteered; and ultimately some 71,000, including those over and under age, entered the service. The state lost 12,922 killed in battle or died of wounds. This was 23 per cent of its arms-bearing population—a sacrifice greater than that of any other state and most appalling when compared with the 10 per cent average loss of all Confederate armies and the 5 per cent average loss of all Union armies. When it is considered that these losses came from actual or prospective bread winners, from the fathers and sons of families most of whose women were not accustomed to the pursuit of gainful occupations, and at a time when baffling social and economic problems demanded every ounce of energy, no further elaboration is needed to realize the tragic consequences. This statement is made without attempting to estimate the deleterious effect of the cutting off of the flower of white manhood on the hereditary qualities of future generations. Perhaps it can be concluded that the lack of distinctive achievements by South Carolinians since the war is in no small measure due to this loss.

On the top of other calamities was the collapse of the financial resources of the state. "It is difficult for those who are away," said the *Charleston Daily Courier,* "to understand the utter pecuniary

prostration in which the war has left this section of the country. . . .
It is as if at a single word and in a single moment the issues of every
state and national bank and of the government should prove without
value or effect, and the people, instead of currency, should find that
they had as representative of toil and years of labor and hard-earned
competency, pieces of waste paper. . . . Nearly every mode of investment shared the same fate. Confederate securities had absorbed the
greater part of the gold, and almost every representative of value. . . .
All that was practically left of the wealth in the country was the
mere lands." The *Charleston Daily News* said in a survey that
$15,000,000 in bank stock, the endowments of colleges and charitable
institutions, and all of the resources of the state's three insurance
companies, as well as the $200,000,000 invested in the state's 400,000
slaves, had been lost. This newspaper estimated that the gross property
values of the state had shrunk from $400,000,000 to $50,000,000 since
1860, that is, to one-eighth. No wonder the *Charleston Daily Courier*
said, "The condition of things has been like the dead sea fruit—fair
and bright in appearance, but within full of bitterness and ashes."

For fifteen months in 1866–67 John William De Forest, a skilled writer, served as an agent of the Freedmen's Bureau in Greenville, S.C. He was far removed from the political activities of Columbia and Washington; he had no federal troops to support him. The three counties of his district—Greenville, Pickens, Oconee—composed an area where Negroes were the fewest and Union sentiment strongest in South Carolina. De Forest was ever besieged by poor whites and Negroes for handouts. His collection of magazine articles of the time were overlooked by historians until recent years. In 1948 James H. Croushore and David M. Potter collected and edited his articles under the title *A Union Officer in the Reconstruction.* Herewith are excerpts from his chapter 4—"Drawing Bureau Rations."

19

"DRAWING BUREAU RATIONS" *

John William De Forest

It was February, 1867, and I had been over four months in charge of my sub-district, before I was driven to make a distribution of public stores.

The winter was an unusually cold one for Greenville, bringing with it ice two inches in thickness and one snowfall of three inches. I heard that the family of women and children mentioned in my former chapter as living in an unchinked log cabin had been evicted in consequence of inability to pay the rent of a dollar and a half a month, and was camping out in the snow under a shelter of pine branches. A barefooted Negro or two appeared, trampling down my sense of duty as a general principle. I slowly and unwillingly came to the conclusion that the greatest good of the greatest number must give way to the necessities of a poverty-stricken minority.

Accordingly, when an order came from the Assistant Commissioner at Charleston to make a requisition for such clothing as might be needed in my district, I remembered the aged Negroes, the soldiers' widows, and the orphan children, and demanded a supply of blankets, coats, trousers, boys' jackets, women's dresses, and shoes. Corn I would not ask for, because I considered it demoralizing. The very name of corn, the bare hope of being fed from the public crib seemed to be sufficient to change plowshares into begging-bags, and pruning-hooks into baskets.

In return for my requisition I received thirty great coats, forty blankets, thirty pairs of trousers, seventy pairs of large brogans, twenty women's skirts, and twenty dresses. Coats for men, jackets and shoes for boys, small dresses for girls were not to be had. The greatcoats, blankets, and trousers were stores originally bought for the army, but condemned as being either of inferior quality or not in accordance

* Excerpts from *A Union Officer in the Reconstruction*, ed. James H. Croushore and David Morris Potter (New Haven: Yale University Press, 1948), pp. 69–70, 71–75, 83–84, 88–90; Copyright © 1948 by Yale University Press. Reprinted without footnotes by permission of Yale University Press.

with the uniform. The brogans were the sturdiest kind of clod-thumpers, such as planters formerly provided for their field hands. The skirts and dresses, also for plantation wear, were of the coarsest imaginable cotton stuff, stiff enough to stand alone, and of a horrible bluish gray. I was grievously disappointed over my stock of "winter goods," for I had especially wanted something for women and children. There were not a quarter dresses enough, and they were "perfect frights." But the Assistant Commissioner had sent what he could get and had portioned out the various articles impartially among his subordinates. . . .

"Mornin'. How ye git'n 'long? Got anythin' for the lone wimmen?"

"Yes, ma'am. What do you need? How am I to know that you need anything?"

"Oh, Lord! I guess I'm poor enough. My ole man was killed in the war because he wouldn't jine the Rebs. They shot him in the swamp, right whar they found him. We was always for your side. And I've got two small children, and nothin' to go upon. Got any corn?"

Her old man was probably a "low-down creetur" who was executed as a deserter, having refused to join the Rebs just as he would have evaded joining any army or doing anything that implied work. But looking at her haggard face and ragged clothing, how could I find it in my heart to doubt that she was a "Union woman?" My stores, it must be remembered, were properly distributable only to freedmen and refugees, the latter term meaning Southern loyalists who had been driven from their homes by the Confederacy.

I had intended to procrastinate and be mercilessly conscientious in my distribution, giving nothing except to persons whom I knew by personal inspection to be the very poorest in the district. But the pressure of an instantaneously aroused horde of dolorous applicants rendered it impossible to be either deliberate or fastidious. Amidst such an abundant supply of poverty there seemed to be no choice; and after a few days of heroic holding on to my goods, I let go with a run. Only in the overcoat business did I make a firm stand; the weather having turned mild, I boxed them up for another winter; indeed, I counterfeited innocence of overcoats. The remaining articles, one hundred and eighty in number, were distributed among ninety-four applicants, consisting of eleven white women, forty-nine colored women, and thirty-four colored men. All but one or two of the whites were widows with families of small children; and nearly all the blacks were deformed, rheumatic, blind, or crippled with extreme age.

In vain I resolved to issue but one article to an individual, in order to make the supply go further. A venerable, doubled-up contraband would say, "Boss, I got shoes now, but dey won't keep me warm o'nights. Can't I hev a blanket, Boss?" A woman furnished with a dress would show her bare or nearly bare feet and put up a prayer for brogans. The wretched family from the brush house appeared and in its grasping distress carried off three dresses, three pairs of shoes, and two blankets. Widows of Confederates though they were, how could I look on their muddy rags and tell them that they were not refugees and had no claim upon Bureau charity? Had the Second Auditor and the Third Auditor discovered this pitiful rascality of mine, it would have been their duty to disallow my returns and stop my pay.

My little room, crammed with people of all colors elbowing each other in the equality of sordid poverty, looked as though it might be a Miscegenation Office. The two races got along admirably together; the whites put on no airs of superiority or aversion; the Negroes were respectful and showed no jealousy. There is little social distance at any time between the low-downer and the black. Two white women were pointed out to me as having children of mixed blood; and I heard that one rosy-cheeked girl of nineteen had taken a mulatto husband of fifty.

Now and then I was amused by a sparkle of female vanity. Two white widows of twenty-four or twenty-five—comely by nature, but now gaunt and haggard with the ailments which hardship surely brings upon women—charily exposed their muddy stockings of coarse homespun wool and, pipe in mouth, held the following dialogue:

"Miss Jackson, these shoes are a sight too big for me. I wear fours."

"That's so, Miss Jacocks. Fours is my number, too. And I hev worn threes."

Of my ninety-four recipients ninety-four signed with a mark; and in my subsequent issues I found that this was the usual proportion. . . .

And now the public talk was of corn. The crop of 1866, both of cereals and other productions, had been a short one for various reasons. Capital, working stock, and even seed had been scarce; a new system of labor had operated, of course, bunglingly; finally, there had been a severe drought. During the autumn and early winter I was called upon to arrange a hundred or two of disputes between planters and their hands as to the division of the pittance which nature had returned them for their outlay and industry. The white, feeling that he ought to have a living out of his land and fearing lest he should not get enough "to go upon" until the next harvest, held firmly to the terms of his contract and demanded severe justice —in some cases more than justice. The Negro could not understand how the advances which had been made to him during the summer should swallow up his half or third of the "crap."

Honesty bids me declare that, in my opinion, no more advantage was taken of the freedmen than a similarly ignorant class would be subjected to in any other region where poverty should be pinching and the danger of starvation imminent. So far as my observation goes, the Southerner was not hostile toward the Negro as a Negro, but only as a possible office-holder, as a juror, as a voter, as a political and social equal. He might cuff him, as he would his dog, into what he calls "his place"; but he was not vindictive toward him for being free, and he was willing to give him a chance in life.

On the other hand, the black was not the vicious and totally irrational creature described in reactionary journals. He was very ignorant, somewhat improvident, not yet aware of the necessity of persistent industry, and in short a grown-up child. I venture these statements after fifteen months of intercourse with the most unfair and discontented of both parties. The great majority of planters and laborers either did not dispute over their harvest of poverty or came to an arrangement about it without appealing to me.

The ignorance of the freedmen was sometimes amusing and sometimes provoking. When Captain Britton, of the Sixth Infantry, acted as Bureau officer in a South Carolina district, a farmer and Negro came before him to settle the terms of their contract, the former offering one third of the crop, and the latter demanding one sixth. It was only by the aid of six bits of paper, added and subtracted upon a table, that the captain succeeded in shaking the faith of the darkey in his calculation.

"Well, Boss," he answered doubtfully, "ef you say one third is the most, I reckon it's so. But I allowed one sixth was the most."

I passed nearly an entire forenoon in vainly endeavoring to convince an old freedman that his employer had not cheated him. I read to him, out of the planter's admirably kept books, every item of debit and credit: so much meal, bacon, and tobacco furnished, with the dates of each delivery of the same; so many bushels of corn and peas and bunches of "fodder" harvested. He admitted every item, admitted the prices affixed; and then, puzzled, incredulous, stubborn, denied the totals. His fat, old wife, trembling with indignant suspicion, looked on grimly or broke out in fits of passion.

"Don' you give down to it, Peter," she exhorted. "It ain't no how ris'ible that we should 'a' worked all the year and git nothin' to go upon."

The trouble with this man was that he had several small grandchildren to support, and that he had undertaken to do it upon a worn-out plantation. I could only assure him that he had "nothing coming" and advise him to throw himself upon the generosity of his employer. As the latter was himself woefully poor, and as it was my duty to set even-handed justice on its legs, any exaction in favor of the laborer beyond the terms of the contract was out of the question.

There were hundreds of cases like this; and there were the old, the widows, and the orphans. Although my district was a grain country, corn rose to two dollars a bushel, and bacon to forty cents a pound. In the lowlands of South Carolina the destitution was still more pinching and prices still higher. Governor Orr published a moving appeal for aid, composed mainly of letters showing a widespread want nearly approaching starvation. Evidently the hour was coming upon me when I should be obliged to make an issue of provisions. . . .

On the 30th of March, 1867, an Act of Congress appropriated one million of dollars for the relief of the destitute of the South, to be distributed under the supervision of the Commissioner of the Freedmen's Bureau. On the 15th of May I received notice that five hundred bushels of corn had been consigned to me by the Assistant Commissioner at Charleston. At the same time Governor Orr forwarded, as a gift from the state of Maryland, 250 bushels to W. K. Easely, Esq., for Pickens, and 200 bushels and one hogshead of bacon to Mr. J. M. David for Greenville. As I now had my machinery of distribution nearly complete I volunteered to take charge of the entire issue, and the offer was accepted.

The first thing to be done was to foot up my lists and assign a pro-rata allowance to each beat. The result of my calculation amazed and dismayed me. From a population of perhaps forty-five thousand persons I had received lists to the amount of about one thousand adult destitute and about eighteen hundred children under fourteen, enough to draw, as one month's ration, nineteen hundred bushels of corn and seven thousand two hundred pounds of bacon. To meet this demand I had nine hundred and fifty bushels of corn and one thousand pounds of bacon. Fortunately it soon appeared that other stores had been sent to persons in Walhalla and Pickens Court House for the relief of the western regiment of Pickens. Thus I was only obliged to supply thirty beats, containing about twenty-three hundred destitute.

Stretching my authority to its utmost once more, I issued another circular, assigning a certain quantity to each "company," and ordering the magistrates to distribute it. They were to send wagons to Greenville for the corn; raise subscriptions in their several neighborhoods to cover the expense of transportation; issue the rations on their retained copies of their lists; then forward me a statement of issues. It was laying a heavy burden on them; most of them were farmers and busy just now with their crops; many of them hardly knew how they could live until the next harvest; it was a heavy burden, but it was lifted manfully. I shall feel to the end of my life that I abused those men and that they deserve my respect and praise.

The subscription idea proved a failure, for the Southerners are not accustomed to organized benefaction. Moreover, some hard-hearted wretches, such as exist in all communities, did not want to aid in the issue, for the reason that it reduced the market value of the contents of their cribs. But the corn was all sent for, and all, as I believe, honestly issued. One distributor, an elderly man in impoverished circumstances, ground the allowance for his beat in his own mill in order to perfect the charity. Another, who told me that he did not know whether he should be able to feed his family till the next harvest, came thirty miles with his own team to get the allowance for his beat. . . .

My grand total of issue was 1,325 bushels of corn and 1,000 pounds of bacon, distributed among 1,666 poor persons, of whom 813 were white and 853 colored, including 193 men, 411 women, and 1,062 children. A far larger result could have been attained but for the superfluous minuteness of the accounting papers. As things were, it was a matter of pride to me that I had done so much without a clerk or soldier, and with only the willing aid of citizens. The manual distribution of the rations for Greenville Court House, a worrying job of three days' duration, was performed by a merchant of the village, assisted by a volunteer clerk or two from other establishments. The clerk of the freight agent at the railroad station gave out over two hundred sacks of corn to persons presenting my orders.

So far as I know I was the only Bureau agent who tried this method of issue. Other officers collected no lists of destitute and sent no loads to the farming precincts, but sat in their offices and, aided by a clerk and a soldier or two, gave out corn to the struggling crowds which came for it, filling up applications and taking receipts as they made the deliveries. They fed the strong and impudent vagrants who could march twenty miles, and I fed the old, weakly, and infantile, whose destitution was guaranteed by respectable neighbors. Theirs was the official method, and mine was not. Every time that I think of my humane and effective corn distribution I wonder that I was not fined or reprimanded or court-martialed, and I rejoice with tears in my eyes over my escape from the Commissary-General and the Third Auditor.

I found that whenever I undertook to issue without the guidance of citizens I was pretty sure to be imposed upon. For instance, three "low-down" fellows from Pickens District obtained eighteen bushels of corn on the score of having starving families, handed it over to a distiller for whisky, and went on a three weeks' bender. I could do no more than report the still to the United States revenue officer and have the proprietor (a woman) fined for carrying on her business without a license.

Even the magistrates confessed to me that they were sometimes deceived. Yet they were scrupulously careful; some of them scarcely gave out a full ration to a single applicant; to doubtful cases they issued by the half-bushel and the peck. One man made eighty bushels answer for eighty-one adults and one hundred and thirty-six children, when a full month's ration would have been one hundred and forty-seven bushels. Even in reporting the destitute to me the magistrates were particular to designate such persons as had dubious claims to charity. I remember crossing out one Negro who was described as "fond of his gun," and various women whose characters were spoken of as not fit for close inspection.

My summary of the distribution of 1867 is that it did good and harm in equal proportions. It alleviated a considerable amount of suffering, prevented possibly a few cases of starvation, seduced many thousands of people from work, and fostered a spirit of idleness and beggary. Except under the pressure of mortal famine, it will not do to run the risk of letting corn fall into the hands of a large class who "never did a lick of work" and of another large class who only "try to git, seein' it's a-gwine."

President Andrew Johnson's lenient program to reconstruct the South was initiated in the late spring of 1865, and within a few months South Carolina had a civil government back in operation. Led by Governor James L. Orr, white South Carolinians largely reconciled themselves to defeat and to the freeing of the slaves. But Johnson's mild program was quickly challenged by the Radical Republicans, whose victory in the congressional elections of 1866 left the president almost powerless. The Radicals invalidated Johnson's work and inaugurated a program of their own, which included a severe proscription of most ex-Confederates while granting citizenship and voting privileges to Negroes.

South Carolina was placed under direct military rule and ordered to call a convention to write a new state constitution. The resulting document provided increased democracy for the state government, laid the foundations for universal education, and sought to promote racial equality. Except in latter sphere, many of the features of the Constitution of 1868 were retained in the Constitution of 1895, the present frame of government for the state.

Of 124 delegates to the convention of 1868 probably as many as 74 were Negroes, 38 of whom were ex-slaves. A sizable minority of both races were from the North. The leaders among the South Carolina whites were Thomas J. Robertson, a Charleston merchant, and Dr. A. G. Mackey of Orangeburg. Simkins's and Woody's account of the convention paints a more favorable picture of its work than did earlier historians.

20

THE CONSTITUTIONAL CONVENTION OF 1868 *

Francis Butler Simkins and Robert Hilliard Woody

On the first day of the convention, Robertson, the temporary chairman, announced the purpose of the body. It was, he said, "to frame a just and liberal constitution that will guarantee equal rights to all, regardless of race, color, or previous condition." That this purpose was accomplished, in the opinion of the guiding spirits of the deliberations, was attested by A. G. Mackey, the permanent chairman, in his valedictory. He affirmed that for the first time manhood suffrage had been written in the laws of the state and all vestige of serfdom removed; that arrangements had been made for universal education; and that all dangers of rebellion had been removed by the obliteration of "that most pernicious heresy of state sovereignty." "We do not claim," he concluded, "a preëminence of wisdom or virtue, but we do claim that we have followed in the progressive advancement of the age; that we have been bold and honest enough and wise enough to trample obsolete and unworthy prejudice under foot."

The most important concern of the body was the regulation of suffrage and office-holding. The committee on franchise and elections proposed universal suffrage under certain qualifications. It suggested that every male citizen of the United States, "without distinction of race, color, or former condition," who was a resident of the state at the time the constitution was adopted, or thereafter a resident of the state for one year and the county in which he applied for voting for sixty days, should be entitled to vote, with the exception of those who should come of age after 1875 without knowing how to read and write, if physically able to fulfill this qualification, and of those who were disqualified by the national constitution. Others proposed

* Excerpts from *South Carolina During the Reconstruction* (Chapel Hill: University of North Carolina Press, 1932), pp. 95–103, 105–6; Copyright, 1932, by The University of North Carolina Press. Reprinted without footnotes by permission of The University of North Carolina Press.

that the payment of a one dollar poll tax be an additional qualification for voting. The residence proposal fitted in with the migratory
habits of the Negro and the carpetbagger and was more liberal than
any the state had ever had; the educational and poll tax proposal
fitted in with the optimistic hopes concerning what was going to be
done for popular education. All of these restrictions could have
been adopted without preventing universal suffrage from becoming
an immediate actuality.

But the convention was determined that there should be no restrictions whatever upon the political power of those who gave it
being. The right to vote, said Ransier in a discussion of the proposed
educational restriction, "belongs alike to the wise and the ignorant,
to the virtuous and vicious. . . . I hope that the music of the nineteenth century will inspire every man upon this floor to view it in
the light of progress and reason, and strike out every word that puts
a limitation upon the manhood of the citizen, so far as regards the
right to vote." Supplementing this fustian were more practical arguments. Elliott pointed out the inconsistency of the convention's attempting to limit the suffrage of those who gave it being, and Cardozo
pointed out the impossibility of inaugurating an adequate system of
schools before 1875 and that as a consequence the proposed limitation
of suffrage would prove fatal to the work of the convention. The
educational provision was deserted by its sponsors and defeated by
vote of 107 to 2. "You strike at the freedom of South Carolina,"
said Moses of the poll tax proposal. "You will allow power to go again
in the hands of the aristocratic element." It was rejected by vote of
81 to 21. Universal manhood suffrage was adopted without material
restrictions.

The convention did not stop here in its enthusiasm for political
democracy. Larceny was omitted from the list of crimes for which the
legislature might disfranchise. It was a crime of which the freedmen
were frequently guilty. Moreover, no persons could be disfranchised
for crimes committed while a slave. There should be no property
qualification for office holding, and representation in the lower house
of the legislature was no longer to be divided between property and
white population but was to be apportioned according to the whole
population. Provision was made for the popular election of presidential electors, the governor, other state officers, and the county officers
including justices of the peace. Although the election of judges by
the legislature was continued, their responsibility to public sentiment was made certain by the abolition of life tenure. Justices of

the peace were to be elected for six years and circuit judges for four. The four congressional districts were strung out in long lines of counties so as to secure "a majority of loyal voters in every congressional district." There were also to be two congressmen-at-large.

The steps taken in the direction of social equality were more nebulous than those in the direction of political equality. An elaborate declaration of rights of forty-one sections superseded the modest declarations of eight and nine sections respectively of the constitutions of 1790 and 1865. It declared that slavery and imprisonment for debt should never exist again in the state. Dueling, the sport of gentlemen, was outlawed. No person was to be disqualified as a witness, prevented from enjoying property rights, hindered in acquiring an education, or subjected to any other legal restraint or disqualification "than such as are laid upon others under like circumstances." As in Louisiana, race lines were abolished by law. "Distinction on account of race or color in any case whatever," the constitution affirmed, "shall be prohibited, and all classes of citizens shall enjoy equally all common, public, legal and political privileges." Only two definite steps, however, were taken towards applying the equality which this dictum implied. Public schools were to be open to all persons regardless of race and no provision was made for the separation of races in the militia. An attempt was made to legislate out of existence the terms by which the whites referred to Northerners and members of the inferior caste. T. J. Coghlan, a white delegate from Sumter, proposed that steps be taken "to expunge forever from the vocabulary of South Carolina the epithets 'negro,' 'nigger,' and 'yankee' as used in the opprobrious sense," but this suggestion was tabled as impractical, as was the resolution to abolish crime and poverty and establish concord.

Efforts were made to establish phases of economic equality. The landless, it was felt, should be aided in the acquirement of property and the landed aristocracy discriminated against. It was proposed that Congress be petitioned to lend the state one million dollars to be used in the purchase of land for the colored people; that the legislature be required to appoint a land commission; that homesteads up to a certain value be exempt from the levy of processes; and that all contracts the consideration of which was the purchase of slaves should be declared null and void.

The fact that Congress would not be likely to listen to a petition asking its aid in the purchase of lands did not dampen the enthusiasm with which the convention debated that question. It offered a golden opportunity for the more loquacious members to display their liking for demagoguery and reform. It was a popular measure among the land-hungry blacks. It was argued that the possession of land was a certain means of raising the new electorate to the level of responsible citizenship. "You cannot make citizens out of these people," declared Moses, "unless you give . . . land; give them houses. They deserve it from the people of South Carolina." The petition was passed by a great majority; but on the receipt of a telegram from Senator Wilson saying that it was impractical, the motion was dropped. The convention had to be content with a substitute calling on Congress to give to the freedmen lands which had been taken for non-payment of Federal taxes and with instructions to the legislature to create a commission to buy additional lands and sell them to the freedmen.

The debate over the proposal to invalidate slave contracts gave opportunity for the display of feelings against the former slaveholders. Instead of taking the statesmanlike view that it was best to say little of the errors of the past, the majority could not let pass the opportunity to rebuke the former master class. "A few years ago," declared Elliott, "the popular verdict of the country was passed upon the slave seller and the slave buyer, and both were found guilty of the enormous crime of slavery. The buyer of the slave received his sentence, which was the loss of the slave, and now we pass sentence upon the seller." The ordinance passed by vote of ninety-six to nineteen. But two circumstances prevented the rebuke from being other than moral. Punishment of the slave seller was neutralized by the freeing of the slave buyer of a debt; and it is hard to determine which of the two was the greater sinner in the eyes of the anti-slavery moralist. Second, there was great likelihood of the law's being declared unconstitutional on the ground that it impaired the obligation of contracts. This actually happened.

An act of greater sagacity was the introduction of the principle of protecting homesteads up to a certain value against the processes of creditors. The members were practically unanimous in desiring such a law, but they differed over what the amount of the exemption should be. Some opposed making it as high as two thousand dollars for fear of protecting large land holdings. The provision adopted placed the exemption on lands and buildings at one thousand dollars, in addition to furniture and personal belongings to the value of five hundred dollars.

The legal foundations were laid for a system of universal free education, the nature of which will be discussed elsewhere. It is sufficient to say here that for the first time the fundamental law of the state carried the obligation of universal education and demanded the creation of a school system like that of Northern states.

The rights of women were enlarged. The property of married women was declared not subject to levy or sale for their husbands' debts and to be disposed of as though the wives were not married. For the first time in its history the state was given a divorce law.

The principle of national unity was given a sufficiently emphatic recognition to set at rest forever the old South Carolina doctrine of state sovereignty. "Every citizen of this State," it was declared, "owes paramount allegiance to the Constitution and Government of the United States, and no law or ordinance of this State in contravention or subversion thereof can have any binding force." It was further declared, "This State shall ever remain a member of the American Union, and all attempts . . . to dissolve the said Union shall be resisted with the whole power of the State." All members of the bar, public officials, and members of the General Assembly were required to take an oath recognizing the supremacy of the national law.

Perhaps the convention's achievement of greatest permanent importance was the reform of local and judicial administration. Thereafter the judicial districts were to be called counties, the county of Oconee was created out of a part of Pickens District, and provision was made for the creation of other new counties out of areas of not less than 625 square miles. Greater vitality was given to the units of local government. Boards of county commissioners were created with jurisdiction over the highways and the supervision of the collection and disbursement of public funds. A court of probate was instituted in each county with all of the powers of the former ordinary and some of those of the commissioner in equity. A new importance was given justices of the peace by conferring on them jurisdiction in cases involving penalties or judgments not over one hundred dollars. The counties were divided into school districts and townships. All county officers were to be elected by popular vote. This was designed to stimulate the sort of interest in local affairs which Anglo-Saxons had been taught to believe would promote civic virtue.

The reforms in judicial administration, with the possible exception of the abolition of life tenure of judges, were salutary. A state Supreme Court of three justices was continued, but no provision was made for a separate court of errors. Circuit courts were continued in their old form with a few modifications. Judges were assigned to distinct districts and given jurisdiction in both chancery and common law matters. No provision was made for separate equity judges, or for the district courts of the constitution of 1865.

Not the least among the earnest considerations of the convention was the creation of devices to meet the financial obligations of the government. A committee of Conservatives estimated that $2,230,950, instead of $350,000 as had been the case before the war, would be necessary to meet for the first year the expanded functions of government outlined in the constitution. Although there is no evidence that the constitution-makers contemplated such a radical increase, they were determined to endow the state with thoroughgoing fiscal powers. Provision was made for a uniform tax on all real and personal property and for the levy of taxes by municipalities, counties, townships, and school districts. The government was obligated to make an adequate valuation of lands and improvements by 1870 and every five years thereafter. A commission composed of Chamberlain, Moses, Robertson, DeLarge, and J. M. Allen was created to investigate the financial status of the state for the guidance of the legislature. The new school system, which was expected to be the largest item of expense, was guaranteed an annual levy on all property and a poll tax.

Two acts of omission on the part of the convention were freighted with sinister possibilities. No limit was placed upon the amount of indebtedness the legislature was allowed to contract and upon the agencies to whom the credit of the state might be extended. The committee on finance and taxation suggested that the indebtedness be limited to $500,000 and that the legislature be not allowed to extend credit to private organizations. But these suggestions were voted down. Delegates professed to see visions of industrial progress through state aid. They declared that railroads, schools, and poorhouses must be built and lands distributed among the people. In a progressive age, said Wright, the legislature must do its part, and the responsibility of that body to the people was sufficient check against extravagance.

The official duties of the convention were completed with the enactment of an ordinance prescribing means to put the constitution into effect. It was ordered that an election be held on April 14, 15, and 16, at which the electorate should express their approval or disapproval of the document and choose state officers and legislators and members of Congress. Five days before the adjournment of the convention, General Canby issued an order calling the prescribed election. . . .

The manner in which the convention went about its work was almost exemplary. It finished its labors within fifty-three days, foregoing the temptation to enjoy for a longer time the eleven dollars per diem allowed each member. President Mackey and the able carpetbag leaders, assisted by the competent advice of such outsiders as D. T. Corbin and D. C. Melton, disciplined the members to their proper tasks. The loquacious were restrained, and when a member made improper mileage claims, he was reprimanded by the president. The office of chaplain was dispensed with when several members opposed "digging unnecessarily into the state treasury." An incompetent sergeant at arms was discharged. Moreover, the delegates did not create "the Negro bedlam" which tradition has associated with them. President Mackey said that he had "no unpleasant reminiscences of those acrimonious bickerings which, in all deliberative assemblies, are often incidental to the excitement of debate and the attrition of antagonistic minds." Insults were avoided in referring to the whites; there was even an inclination to respect the feelings of "the brave men" who had been defeated. The only occasion on which there was disorder was when the reporter of the *Charleston Mercury* was expelled from the floor. The newspaper had been engaged in scathing attacks on members of "the ringed, striped and streaked" convention. When an attack on the president was published, E. W. M. Mackey, his son, assaulted the reporter, and after a scene characterized by threats of mob violence, the convention voted to exclude all representatives of the newspaper. On the other hand, the *Charleston Daily News* and the *Charleston Daily Courier* were praised for the fairness of their accounts of the proceedings, and their representatives were extended every courtesy. The convention received warmly an address which Governor Orr delivered before it, and probably would have listened to other Conservatives had they been amenable.

In 1965 Joel Williamson published *After Slavery: The Negro in South Carolina During Reconstruction, 1861–1877.* As the subtitle indicates, Williamson's study centers on the Negro and not on Reconstruction as a whole. The author had access to many books and manuscripts unavailable to Simkins and Woody in 1932, thus his work is a valuable supplement to theirs and in numerous instances modifies their earlier judgments.

Traditional accounts emphasized the racial violence of the Reconstruction years and often gave a distorted picture. According to Williamson, violence fell into four rather distinct, non-successive phases: (1) July 1865–November 1866, (2) fall 1867–fall 1868, (3) October 1870–early fall 1871, (4) the campaign of 1876. The following selection from Williamson discusses the second and third phases of Reconstruction violence.

21

VIOLENCE
AND THE KU KLUX KLAN *

Joel Williamson

A second wave of violence coincided with the rise of the Negro to political power. During this period, Negroes were as often the aggressors as were the whites. In the fall of 1867, the Union League Club of Hunnicutt's Crossing in Pickens District, after killing a young man in a fight with the white membership of a local debating club, assumed control of the neighborhood. For several days, they marched about in a military fashion, bearing arms, arresting and imprisoning whites whom they accused of participating in the riot. Several months later, in Orangeburg District, "a military company of negroes" surrounded the house of a Mr. Hane who, supposedly, had shot a Negro. They held the white man as a prisoner "with the avowed intention of hanging him in case the wounded negro should die." Hane was later delivered to a magistrate, but the whites learned that the lynch rope in Orangeburg was racially impartial. As the Republicans progressed to political dominance, Negroes became increasingly restless. In several areas incendiarism was rampant, and in Williamsburg District and on John's Island large groups of Negroes were said to be organizing militarily, in the latter case "to patrol the island and keep down the white people."

Anxious elements within the white community retaliated in kind, particularly in the upcountry counties where the Negro population was not in an overwhelming majority. In its most violent form, white retaliation was an irregular campaign of terrorism against Radical leaders. Interestingly, the whites reacted violently only after the state elections of 1868 had been lost, and there was no hint at the time (though this certainly came later) that any such organization as the

---

Ku Klux Klan lay behind it. On June 1, 1868, Solomon George Washington Dill, senator-elect from Kershaw District, was assassinated in his home. When the legislature convened several weeks later, members were mysteriously warned that if they dared return to their homes after the session they would be killed. As a Northern-born Negro member later declared, on the eve of adjournment each member asked himself, "Will it be I?" Shortly after the close of the session, James Martin, an Irish immigrant who had become a Radical member from Abbeville, was "pursued by a gang of ruffians" from Abbeville Courthouse and killed. In mid-October, B. F. Randolph, a Northern-born Negro Methodist clergyman, was shot dead by unknown parties at Donaldsville, while on a speaking tour. Several days after Randolph's demise, the president of the Union League Club in Newberry, a Negro named Lee Nance, was assassinated in his front yard by a band of mounted whites.

The organization of the Negro militia was the specific Radical answer to these offerings of violence by the whites. When the legislature reconvened during the winter of 1869, it hastened to pass the law necessary to organize the militia fully. It also authorized the governor to buy 2,000 stand of arms "of the most approved pattern." However, even as the legislature acted, violent outbursts became less frequent and by late spring had virtually ceased. Politicians promptly preempted the higher ranks in the militia and the paper organization was completed, but only a few local units were actually established.

During the spring of 1870, the situation changed drastically when incumbent Governor Scott deliberately revitalized the militia and transformed it into a giant political machine for use in combatting his enemies within and outside of the Republican party. Legally, white men could have joined the militia as enlisted men; indeed, technically, they were required to join. In reality, however, whites simply refused to serve in militia companies in which Negroes were their equals or, occasionally, their superiors, and the governor refused to accept all-white companies. Therefore, whites were effectively excluded. But there was no dearth of Negro volunteers. Few young men could resist the attractions of militia service: dashing, varicolored uniforms, shining arms and clattering accoutrements, the roll of the drum, the intricate and endless ritual of the drill, and the incomparable comaraderie [sic] of fellows under arms. On the eve of the election of 1870, the militia rolls had swelled to include more than ninety thousand men. The highest ranks were of course, held by Scott's friends; but the key officers were actually the captains of local companies. Almost invariably, they were strong characters in the Negro community, sometimes noted for their prudence, often for their bellicosity. Demanding and, frequently, enjoying the complete loyalty of their men, they often failed to accord the same measure of loyalty to their nominal commanders. Some of them used their men badly, deliberately maneuvering them in ways menacing to the whites or calling out their companies to settle personal grudges.

Ultimately, the so-called Ku Klux riots of 1870–1871 occurred not because Negroes were organized in militia companies, but because the Negro militia was, in certain areas, heavily and effectively armed. From the Southern white's point of view, a well-armed Negro militia was precisely what John Brown had sought to achieve at Harper's Ferry in 1859. It was, in short, an insurrection with a high potential for disaster. The Ku Klux riots, it is true, did have a political flavor; but the flavor was of frustration, not hope. It is highly significant that the first outbreak on October 19, 1870, occurred only after the election was over. Having lost the state elections, native whites were bitter, but no white leader seemed to think that any amount of violence would recall the results of the election or improve the political prospectus for 1872. Quite clearly, the Ku Klux riots were also influenced by any number of local and personal enmities, but these were merely ancillary to the main body. Whites were also irritated and alarmed by the very existence of the Negro militia, but irritation and fear led to action only when and where the militia was armed.

This conclusion is supported by the fact that the counties which suffered most from violence were also the counties in which the Negro militia was most heavily and effectively armed. Since Scott had arms enough for barely a tenth of his force, he chose to issue the bulk of those in counties where the normal Republican majority was jeopardized by white intimidation. To the Laurens militia, he sent 620 breech-loading, rifled muskets, 50 Winchester rifles, and 18,000 rounds of ammunition, that is, roughly 10 per cent of the total distributed. It was in Laurens that the first and bloodiest of the riots took place. Comparably large quantities of arms and ammunition were dispatched to the militia in Spartanburg, Newberry, Union, Chester, York, Fairfield, Kershaw, and Edgefield counties. Each of these was also a center for large-scale violence. On the other hand, no arms were issued in the heavily white counties of Oconee, Pickens, and Greenville, and only 96 muskets were sent to Anderson and Abbeville counties together. In each of these areas, there were no significant outbreaks. The same pattern generally prevailed in the lowcountry where the

Negro population was heavy. In the Fifth Regiment, centering in Marion and Georgetown, only ninety muskets were given the militia and no riots occurred. The only exceptions were Charleston and Beaufort countries [sic] where the militia was both well organized and well armed. Here, however, the primary purpose was probably exhibitory rather than militant.

The signal importance of arming the militia in precipitating the Ku Klux disturbances was also revealed in the unerring, almost instinctive accuracy with which even the least organized white mobs focused as if by careful concensus [sic] upon the seizure of the arsenals of the militia as their goal. This was dramatically evident in the Laurens riot. Since early September, 1870, whites had been aware that a large quantity of arms and ammunition had been received by the local militia and stored by them in their armory on main street and in the fortresslike barn behind the house of their colonel. Beginning with a fist-fight between a native white and a carpetbagger on the town square, within a few minutes and apparently spontaneously the struggle grew into a shooting attack on the militia's armory. During the next few hours, the "volunteer police" managed, quite legally, to seize all of the guns in both the armory and the barn and deposit them in the courthouse. Within a day after the militia was disarmed, violence ceased. In Newberry, York, Chester, and Union counties confrontations and running battles between the Negro militia and white "citizen's committees" produced the same result. In Spartanburg, the same pattern developed over a period of several months. On September 23, 1870, in Columbia, 192 breech-loading, rifled muskets were drawn for the Spartanburg militia. On the following day, whites in Spartanburg were greatly agitated by a rumor that twenty-four boxes of Winchesters and seven boxes of ammunition had arrived for the militia and were stored in the county jail. On November 17, some twenty to fifty men, "fantasticly [sic] attired," unsuccessfully assaulted the jail. Thereafter, the arms were secreted by the authorities. During the ensuing four months a rash of Ku Klux visitations broke the peace of the county. A number of those visited were militiamen, whose houses were searched for arms. On March 22, 1871, the last large-scale raid was made on the house of a man whose son was the local militia brigadier. It was suspected that the arms had been hidden there. In Spartanburg, as elsewhere, peace was restored only after the arms were withdrawn.

To label these riots the result of a Ku Klux "conspiracy" is inaccurate and misleading. These affrays were largely spontaneous. There was no conspiracy above the very local level, and often none existed there. There were local organizations of Klansmen in South Carolina in 1870 and 1871, but it is highly doubtful that any of these were organized before this time and it is a virtual certainty that no state-wide or even widespread organization of the order ever existed. In the Laurens riot, the most murderous of the sequence, white participants made no attempt to disguise themselves in the fashion of the Klan and were not members of that society. Yet, the racial and social objects of the Klan were in perfect harmony with the objects of the white community, and it was hardly necessary for white males to swear solemn oaths, perform rituals, and wear costumes to pursue the same ends. There was a unity of feeling and action in the white community which rendered forms unimportant. Actually, all those more or less impromptu organizations which the Radicals chose to call Klans were only up-dated versions of the patrol, revitalized to meet still another "rising" by the Negroes. This was probably what the editor of the *Nation* meant when he very astutely observed that "the South before the war was one vast Ku-Klux Klan."

The published record suggests that all responsible leaders of the white community deprecated the lawlessness of the rioters. However, private correspondence indicates that the great mass of white Caro-linians were pleased by the results of a terrorist program. "It may seem very disloyal & Ku Kluxish in me, but I am exceedingly delighted at the Union & York 'outrages (?) ,' " wrote a Georgetown druggist in February, 1871, concluding that such events "will teach the misguided African to stand in the subordinate position nature intended." In Chester County, planter Robert Hemphill noted that one of his Negro neighbors was visited by the Klan for "having guns in store, & . . . acting the Big man & fool generally," and another was threatened by the Klan for having, in his capacity as overseer of a public road, "ordered out his hands, & among them some white men which gave offence." Declared Hemphill, "The K. K.s are an excellent institution if kept in proper bounds. They have been of immense benefit in our county." In Spartanburg, a small farmer hoped that the Klan would so frighten Negro legislators that they would resign and prevent his being "sold out for taxes in a year or to more." He explained: "There is a new sort of beings got up called KKs that has made a powerful show. These kks whip and kill as they pleas." One group of Klans-men fleeing across Edgefield county in November, 1871, en route to political asylum in Georgia probably never discovered that the band of mounted men pursuing them were not irate federals but local citizens fervently attempting to congratulate them upon their work. When alleged Klansmen were arrested, virtually the entire white community leaped to their defense. After several were convicted, the white community negotiated for their freedom much as if they were soldiers taken as prisoners of war. Quite obviously, the mass of native whites felt that a little Klanning was a good thing.

As an instrument for disarming the Negro militia, violence was a success. As a political tool promising ultimate victory, however, terrorism was a failure. Negroes were indeed frightened, but they were neither scared into the Democracy nor away from Republicanism. Moreover, violence simply provided more excellent grist for the Radical mill, allowing Northern Republicans to profit electorally at home by waving the freshly bloodied shirt and Southern Republicans to invoke the aid of the federal military. Finally, Negroes themselves might be driven to meet violence with violence, and in the lowcountry this could only mean disaster for the whites. Rather deliberately, the white leadership weighed the consequences of further violence and, during the winter and spring of 1871, moved to halt it. On March 13, a native white delegation waited on Governor Scott and secured his promise to recall the arms of the militia, since, as Scott asserted, "their arms provoked assaults and violence that otherwise would not have arisen." In the following month, Scott kept his promise. Responding, the white leadership took to the stump and by mid-summer, 1871, had squelched the riotous elements as decisively as if the mobs had been under their military command. Ironically, in Spartanburg, where a series of public meetings were held for this purpose, one of the speakers was a legislator who had been a local Klan leader.

The fear of some white leaders that Klan violence might lead to retaliation by Negroes was well grounded in fact. In the middle and lower portions of the state, indignation within the Negro community was marked. Late in March, 1871, a resident of Georgetown reported that the "negroes here of late have become quite outrageous in the town. . . [sic]" On July 1, 1871, in Barnwell County a group of twenty-five armed Negroes attacked the house of a white man who had reputedly wronged one of their number. They wounded the owner, his wife, and his mother and killed a white man who happened to be visiting the owner at the time of the raid. In Camden, three days later (on the fifty-fifth anniversary of a major insurrectionary threat), the Negro militia attempted to rescue one of their number from the town marshal by whom he had been arrested. A riot was narrowly averted only by the intervention of cooler heads which prevented "the street from flowing with blood."

During the summer, the white community itself put a stop to further Ku Klux outbreaks; nevertheless, in October, Scott persuaded Grant to suspend the operation of the writ of *habeas corpus* in nine counties, some of which had been the scene of only minor disturbances. The military moved in and hundreds of arrests were made. The proceedings were long drawn out. In hearings before federal commissioners, presentments of grand juries, and finally on trial before federal district courts in Columbia and Charleston, stories of Ku Klux atrocities were repeated in all their brutal and gory detail again and again. Even some conservative native whites were revolted by the awful exhibition. However, the great mass of native whites learned only one lesson: that a show of force in areas where they were numerically strong brought about similar displays in areas where Negroes were safely in the majority, and that the continued use of violence ultimately produced a crushing imposition of federal power. Under the circumstances, force was seen to be an instrument of restricted usefulness. For some five years after the summer of 1871, with only sporadic and scattered interruptions, the white community sought to gain its ends through persuasion rather than force.

The early writers of Reconstruction history usually penned their accounts in such a highly prejudicial and emotional atmosphere that even today an objective picture of the Radical Republican politicians of the era is difficult to obtain. As early as 1932 Simkins and Woody contended that the Radicals were not all rascals and that some of their political achievements were of lasting benefit to South Carolina. While taking note of a great amount of corruption, Williamson further discredits the blanket indictment of all Radical politicians. The following selections are from his chapter 13—"The Politicos."

22

REPUBLICAN LEADERSHIP
DURING RECONSTRUCTION *

Joel Williamson

The character of professional Republican politicians in South
Carolina during Reconstruction has often been debated. The Redeemers, who wrote most of the history of the period, damned them all.
The scalawags were poor whites without character, education, or position. The carpetbaggers—except those with money—were bootless
ex-officers of the Union Army and unprincipled adventurers in search
of political plunder. And Negro politicians were either Northern-
sprung zealots in various stages of mental derangement or ignorant
and deluded freedmen who moved directly from the cotton fields
into office without so much as a change of clothes. Even a cursory
survey of these groups reveals the inaccuracy of such a description.

Actually, scalawags represented—in economic status, education, and,
to a large extent, social standing—every phase of Carolina society. The
single quality found in the backgrounds of most native white Republican leaders was a spirit of Unionism distinctly deeper than that of
their neighbors. Even here, however, scalawags as a group were still
in some degree representative of the community, mustering a few
first-line fire-eaters in their ranks. Franklin J. Moses, Jr., for instance,
had been the secretary of the secession governor and had personally
hauled the United States flag down from over Fort Sumter in 1861.
Some scalawags were poor. Solomon George Washington Dill of
Charleston and Kershaw, by his own report, had always been a poor
man and identified himself with the interests of the poor. Others were
rich. Thomas Jefferson Robertson, a United States senator throughout the period, was reputedly one of the wealthiest men in the state
after the war. Precisely as South Carolina exhibited a high degree of

* Excerpts from chapter 13 of *After Slavery: The Negro in South Carolina
During Reconstruction, 1861–1877* (Chapel Hill: University of North Carolina Press, 1965), pp. 373–83, 389–94; Copyright © 1965 by The University
of North Carolina Press. Reprinted without footnotes by permission of The
University of North Carolina Press.

illiteracy in its white population, so too were there ill-educated scalawags. Dill of Kershaw, Allan of Greenville, Owen and Crews of
Laurens, and many others apparently possesed only common school ed-
ucations. On the other hand, many scalawag leaders were at least as
erudite as their conservative opponents. Dr. Albert Gallatin Mackey
graduated first in his class in Charleston's Medical School, and a Northern correspondent, visiting him in the book-lined study in his Charleston home, found him highly learned. Further, Mackey was nationally
known as a writer on the subject of Masonry, having been for many
years the Grand Master of the Order in South Carolina. The Junior
Moses, T. J. Robertson, C. D. and S. W. Melton were graduates of
South Carolina College and personally intimate with classmates from
the state's leading families. J. L. Orr completed his education in the
University of Virginia, and J. F. G. Mittag of Lancaster was an artist
of some reputation who had studied under S. F. B Morse. Doubtless
some native whites became Republicans out of expediency, but it is
also certain that many adopted the party out of principle. John R.
Cochran and John Scott Murray of Anderson and Simeon Corley of
Lexington, for instance, were Republican leaders whose principles
were above reproach even by the opposition. Although none of the
self-styled aristocracy became open Republicans, a fair proportion of
the scalawag leadership had been accepted in the elite social circle
of their own communities before becoming Republicans, and in most
cases, apparently they did not immediately lose social prestige by
crossing the political divide. Practically the whole team of scalawag
judges—Orr, Green, Vernon, Moses, Sr., Bond, and Bryan—along with
the Melton and Robertson clans and the mountain district leadership
could be described so. Indeed, very generally anti-scalawag snobbery
was much more a post-Redemption myth than a Reconstruction
reality.

Carpetbaggers exhibited the same degree of variety. John J.
("Honest John") Patterson, a Pennsylvanian, railroad manipulator,
and protégé of Thomas A. Scott, was a wealthy man before he came
to the state in 1869 to interest himself in the Blue Ridge and Greenville and Columbia Railroads. J. P. M. Epping had made himself
famous as well as rich by introducing the state to soda water in
bottles. Reuben Holmes and J. D. Bell, Beaufort's two white delegates to the Constitutional Convention of 1868, were both Northern
businessmen who had come South for economic reasons. Others, like
D. H. Chamberlain, D. T. Corbin, and Frank Arnim were young,
former officers of the Union Army. Admittedly they were on the make.

Nevertheless, they had begun to seek their fortunes in the South long before the spring of 1867, and, as a group, they were certainly not bootless adventurers when they entered Republican politics in South Carolina. And, far from exploiting the natives, Reuben Tomlinson and Justus K. Jillson contributed substantial sums of their own money to further education in South Carolina. The average carpetbagger was rather better educated than his Southern counterpart of the same age and economic background. Chamberlain, who was a graduate of Harvard and had been among the top four scholars in his Yale law class, was a man of high literary attainments. Others, like F. A. Sawyer, were well trained and experienced teachers and educational administrators. Indeed, one seeks in vain among the leading carpetbaggers for one who was ill-educated, and many of those least educated in the formal sense were, like Timothy Hurley, intelligent men of wide experience. Few political carpetbaggers were received socially by the aristocracy, but they obviously remained fully acceptable in their home communities in the North. Chamberlain, for instance, constantly drew moral strength from his New England friends, particularly from the legal community in New Haven. In 1875, he was accorded the honor of addressing Yale Law School's commencement audience. Returning North in 1877, Chamberlain became a prominent New York lawyer and a leading member of the American Bar Association. Even "Honest John" Patterson, the most notorious of bribers, returned to Pennsylvania after Redemption to win praise for his continuing success as a railroad chieftain.

The Redeemers' estimate of Northern Negroes in the South was nearly correct—they were zealots. Some, like R. H. Gleaves, came to further their material fortunes by business pursuits. Others, like Whipper and the lawyer class in general, probably saw a chance for personal profit in representing the claims of the newly emancipated. But, most of them came (or, having left the army, remained) primarily as religious, educational, and cultural missionaries, hoping to accomplish an elevation of their racial brothers which was not possible in the restricted and less populous Negro communites in the North. Just as the Massachusetts Negro regiments drew off the cream of young manhood from the Northern Negro population during the war, Reconstruction attracted the cream in peace.

The one thing that most native Negro leaders were not was fresh from the cotton fields. Of the seventy-four Negroes who sat in the Constitutional Convention of 1868, fourteen were Northerners. Of the fifty-nine Negroes who had been born or settled in South Carolina before the war, at least eighteen and probably twenty-one had been free. A dozen of these were Charlestonians. Nearly all had been tradesmen. Roughly two-thirds of this group continued to pursue their trades after the war and at least until the time of the convention. The remainder took service as Bureau teachers. T. K. Sasportas, Henry Shrewsbury, and others had risen to the educational level of the high school graduate in the North. Most possessed the equivalent of a common school education, while several were, apparently, barely literate. F. L. Cardozo, of course, having attended the University of Glasgow and the London School of Theology, was as well educated as any man in the state.

Thirty-eight of the delegates were clearly former slaves. The occupations of twelve of these are not known, but not one was described as an agricultural worker. Twenty-six were trades-, professional, or business men. Eight of the twenty-six were ministers (some being tradesmen as well), four were carpenters, two blacksmiths, two shoemakers, two had been coachmen and the remaining eight included a businessman, a businessman and steamer captain (Smalls), a tanner, a barber, a teacher, a waiter, a servant, and a carriage maker. Most of those who were tradesmen had pursued the same occupation as slaves. For instance, John Chesnut, the barber, was the son of a Camden barber whose father had been freed by the first General James Chesnut. John was born of a slave mother and, hence, was a slave but had been allowed to learn his trade in his father's shop. The degree of education possessed by these freedmen was not high. However, nearly all appeared to be literate in some degree, and a few were amazingly well read. Nash, for example, could quote Shakespeare with apparent ease and obviously read the leading Northern papers. During the war, Robert Smalls had been taught intensively by two professional educators while he was stationed for a year and a half in the Philadelphia Naval Yard. It is true that conservatives had considerable grounds for complaint against the ignorance of their late-slaves become legislators, but their charges of stupidity changed with the political climate. Early in 1866, the Camden press lauded John Chesnut and Harmon Jones as "two intelligent freedmen" for their speeches to the Negroes denying that the government was to give them lands and urging them to return to work. After 1867, when John Chesnut went into Republican politics, became a delegate to the convention which drafted a new constitution, and served thereafter in the Republican legislature, words strong enough to describe Chesnut's lack of talent were not available.

In view of the high degree of natural ability extant among leading Republicans of both races, it is barely surprising that the higher offices were filled with men who were quite capable of executing their responsibilities.

In the executive area, the abilities of such white office holders as Dr. Ensor as the director of the insane asylum and H. L. Pardee as superintendent of the penitentiary, and such Negro office holders as F. L. Cardozo and H. E. Hayne withstood the closest criticism. Although he was frequently overridden by a less careful legislature, Cardozo as treasurer of the state from 1872 until the summer of 1876 (after which his office was virtually nullified by a boycott of white taxpayers) revealed the highest capacities. Even the conservative editor of the Chester *Reporter,* after a visit to the Capitol in December, 1869, conceded that Cardozo, then secretary of state, was "courteous and accommodating," and the "most respectable and honest of all the State officials." Observing the house in action the same journalist found Henry Hayne, "a little yellow fellow," able in arguing for the sale of state lands in plots of fifty acres or less with provision made for the addition of a mule. The records themselves, particularly those of the land office and of the state census of 1875, indicate that Hayne as secretary of state from 1872 until the Redemption executed his duties well.

Even political opponents generally recognized the capacity of leading Republican legislators. South Carolina's Negro congressmen—Elliott, Rainey, Ransier, De Large, Cain, and Smalls—were usually conceded to be able enough for their posts. Though Democrats in the House scoffed, Elliott's speech to Congress on the Ku Klux was widely celebrated. Capable Negro solons also appeared in the Constitutional Convention of 1868 and in the Republican legislatures which followed. Ransier, Gleaves, and Swails as presiding officers in the Senate and Samuel J. Lee and, again, Elliott as speakers of the house were remarkably effective managers in view of their sudden elevation to their posts. There were others, like Whipper, who were virtually professional legislators and became excellent parliamentarians.

It was inevitable that combinations of intelligence, education, experience, and natural ability were in short supply among Republicans in South Carolina. After all, there were comparatively few Negroes in South Carolina who could claim to possess a high level of education or significant experience in government. In the legislature, and in local offices in many areas, there was obviously a lack of competence among Republican leaders. This absence was usually indentified [*sic*] with the presence of the Negro officeholder.

Yet, what one saw in the legislature was obviously determined by what one was conditioned to see. A liberal English observer noted that on the floor of the Senate Negro members were decorous and dignified. In January, 1869, Martha Schofield visited the new Capitol. In the senate chamber, she was the special guest of her friend, the presiding officer, D. T. Corbin, "and it was with strange feelings I sat in that body where all men were equal before the law, where those whose race had been oppressed for two centuries, were now making laws for the oppressors. . . . The colored members appear as much at ease and at home as the others," she pointedly observed. Crossing the broad entrance hall to the house chamber, the Quaker schoolmistress was delighted to see that "colored, and white, democrats and republicans were sandwiched in a way that would disturb the dead bones of many of Carolines proud sons." She heard Tomlinson speak for a bill to abolish capital punishment and De Large's answer. "London [probably London S. Langley] came to us and we had a nice chat," she continued, "also Henry Parris & Mr. Wells from Beaufort—or St. Helena." Having served in the islands during the war period, she saw "a good many acquaintances among the colored ones." "Who could have prophesied this 10 years since," she marveled. The more astute visitors, however skeptical they may have been of the results, invariably saw something vital in the proceedings of Republican and Negro legislatures in the state. "It is not all sham, nor all burlesque," wrote James Pike after his celebrated visit in the winter of 1873. "They have a genuine interest and a genuine earnestness in the business of the assembly which we are bound to recognize and respect unless we would be accounted shallow critics."

Conservative native whites were distressed by what they saw even before they entered the legislative chambers.

A Baptist minister in November, 1870, reported:

The entrance halls both upstairs and down was thronged with negroes, who were keeping up a sort of saturnalia, haw-hawing, buying and selling peanuts, candy and gumgers, 2 or 3 walking arm in arm with noisy demonstrations, one party wrestling, another tugging at each other's coattails in play, somewhat after the manner of the game of 'last tag'. . . . an uproar was kept up, which ascended through the building into the open door of the Legislative halls, and did not facilitate hearing what was going on there.

Going on was a debate over the action to be taken in answer to the Laurens riot and other "Ku Klux" activities. The clerical gentleman continued:

I heard a pretty incendiary speech from W. J. Whipper, the head negro member, in regard to alleged outrages in Laurens and threats in Edgefield against the Radical members; then a pitiful narration of his "suffrinks" from Jo Crews, who had like to have been killed several times over, and a zealous tirade from a nameless darkey who wanted to know if anybody had been punished yet of it—if they had killed any of the rioters, or tried to kill them. . . . It is a dark looking set, set off, however, with a wonderful new carpet and 5 huge chandeliers—as gorgeous as Cuffee usually delights in—when somebody else pays for it.

The proceedings of the House particularly offended whites. In August, 1868, an upcountry editor was shocked to find seven "dusky belles" seated on the platform with Speaker Moses. A year later, another observer noted that members frequently defied the chair, conversed with debaters on the floor, and, on one occasion, T. K. Sasportas answered an argument from Representative De Large with his fist. A Northern visitor in 1874 was amazed by the lack of respect accorded to some members by others. As an instance, he noted that Representative Holmes of Colleton called on the speaker for the yeas and nays on a measure, but the speaker refused to recognize him until the vote had been announced. Holmes then rose to a question of privilege and was overruled. He persisted and other members began to cough. Holmes tried to talk over the noise. The coughing grew louder. Finally E. W. M. Mackey suggested that someone call a doctor and the house roared in amusement, while the exasperated Holmes collapsed in his chair.

Capacity and incompetence frequently traveled side by side in the legislature, but incapacity was often glaringly in evidence among officeholders of the lower echelons. "Our letters are often lost now," wrote a resident of Camden to her son, "Adamson is travelling Agent to distribute the letters and Boswell and Frank Carter, Ned's son, are Postmaster[s] here." The cause, of course, was apparent: "In Columbia and elsewhere, they have negroes in the Post office, and I have no doubt our letters go astray." County and city officers elicited similar complaints. Much distressed, the grand jury of Williamsburg County, in the spring of 1871, charged that the county commissioners permitted the county's prisoners to roam the streets of Kingstree after the jail burned in 1867, kept no records worthy of the name, and had allowed the roads and bridges of the county (some of which had not been worked upon in two years) to become almost impassable. Further, they feared that the county poor farm was "calculated to do more harm to the County than good."

The great problem of the Republican regime in South Carolina, however, was not so much a lack of capacity among its leaders as it was an absence of a sense of responsibility to the whole society, white as well as black. In the idealistic days of the Constitutional Convention of 1868, Republicans often reflected verbally upon the fact that their work was for the benefit of all. Yet, within two months after the close of the convention, election results showed that, willingly or not, the Republican party in South Carolina was the party of the Negro and for the Negro. Within a short time, it also became a party by the Negro. This was a line which the whites themselves had helped to draw. There emerged among Republican leaders a new concept that their first loyalty was due, not to their total constituency, but to that particular Republican and Negro element which had put them into office. This attitude was evident in the inclination of Republicans to drive Democrats and native whites of the conservative persuasion completely out of the government. It was also evident in a certain superciliousness which developed among members of the party in power toward the opposition. In this atmosphere, the protests of the white minority became proper subjects for Republican disdain and, indeed, ridicule. "Please read where I have marked, and judge the class of men which composed the late Taxpayer's convention of South Carolina," Negro Congressman Rainey jeered quietly in a confidential communique to President Grant's secretary early in 1874. Three years earlier, while the first taxpayers' convention was in session, A. O. Jones, the mulatto clerk of the house, suggested to his partner in a corruption-laden ring of public printers that their Republican Printing Company enter a bid for the printing of "Ye Taxpayers." "R. P. C.," he jested, "That's as effective on the State Treasury as the other terrible triad is on Radical office holders—eh?" If the opposition had no political rights, they also had no economic rights. Attacks on the property by heavy taxation and then by the theft of those tax moneys was perhaps within the limits of this new morality.

Among Republican politicos in Reconstruction South Carolina, there is no correlation between intelligence, education, wealth, experience, and competence on the one hand and, on the other, integrity. The thieves included men who claimed all or most of these qualities, as well as men who could claim none. The relationship which did exist was the logical one: among those who did steal, the most successful thieves invariably combined high intelligence and large administrative talents with generous endowments of education, wealth, and experience. Petty frauds were numerous and widespread, but the truly magnificent peculations were conceived and executed by a relatively few men, usually residing in Columbia or Charleston. However, these larger schemes frequently required the purchase of the co-operation of scores of state officers and legislators, and thus corruption was spread. . . .

The average Negro officeholder realized very little profit by resorting to rascality. Those who became wealthy by thievery were few, and all the most successful were white—Scott, Parker, Kimpton, Patterson, and, perhaps, Neagle and Woodruff. These were the men who conceived, organized, and directed steals on a state-wide basis. Key figures who abetted them in their predatory operations, either as officers of the government or as lobbyists, also received substantial sums—Moses, Hurley, Leslie, Worthington, Whittemore, Elliott, Samuel J. Lee, and Swails—amounting over the entire period from scores of thousands to several hundred thousand dollars each. The average Negro legislator and officeholder, however, found that the wages of sin were pitifully small. There were only four occasions when large sums of money were passed out as bribes; other divisions were made of the printing money, and occasionally some office seeker was willing to buy votes. Senators were usually paid from $500 to $5,000 for their support on such occasions. Members of the House received much less. For voting for the Solomon claims, James Young, a Negro member from Laurens, received only $30, R. S. Tarlton of Colleton got $50, Charles H. Simons got $13 in cash and a box of provisions from Solomon's store, and Joseph J. Grant got only provisions. J. T. Gilmore, a Negro member from Richland and a farmer, was more astute. He collected a total of $250 from men working for the Solomon claims and promptly traded the money for four cows. Rivers got $500 for setting up a caucus to support the claims and for his vote in its favor.

The real profits of the corruptionists, large and small, were often much less than quoted. For instance, the bond ring sold its issues to doubtful investors at much less than par value (usually at about sixty cents on the dollar). As more bonds flooded the market and criticism of the government rose, good issues and bad dropped to fractions of their face value. One issue eventually fell to 1 per cent of its nominal value. Blue Ridge Railroad scrip, used to pay the largest bribe bill contracted during the Reconstruction Period, circulated at less than its face value. Legislative pay certificates, whether or not legitimately obtained, were usually sold at a considerable discount by impecunious members to businessmen like Hardy Solomon. Such circumstances existed because the treasury was itself perennially empty and those having claims against it had to await the pleasure or indulgence of the treasurer. While Parker held that position, large sums of tax money were sent North to Kimpton to keep the bond bubble inflated by interest payments on both good and bad issues. Local obligations were very liable to be neglected. After 1872, each claimant had to face the suspicious Cardozo, who soon became the bane of every corruptionist's existence by his miserly management of the treasury. The officers of the Republican Printing Company, to which a generous legislature appropriated $385,000 for the state fiscal year 1873–1874, had the greatest difficulty during the summer of 1874 in squeezing $250 to $300 out of the treasurer every Saturday to meet their minimum operating expenses. Lecturers in history are fond of titillating their classes with the story of how the Negro legislature voted Speaker Moses a gratuity of $1,000 for his services as presiding officer after his having lost that amount to Whipper in a horse race. Yet, Moses probably thought the gesture something less than generous since pay certificates, if the holder were fortunate enough to find any buyer, seldom sold at more than three-fourths of face value. Moreover, Moses probably considered it an ordinary reward for the extra duty demanded by his office, a burden which many legislatures, North and South, customarily eased by voting special compensation.

There *was* plush living in Columbia during Reconstruction. The senators maintained a bar in one of their cloak rooms in the Capitol and fine food, smooth whiskey, and the best Havana cigars were copiously available. The legislative halls, the offices in the Capitol, and the committee rooms located in privately owned buildings (many were in Parker's Hall, often spelled "Haul" by contemporaries) were lavishly furnished. Yet the bar, which was allegedly supported by the senators from their private resources, was closed to other officers except by invitation, and the enjoyment of the accommodations afforded by other rooms were usually limited to those who used them officially.

The average Negro representative came to Columbia on his own money. He roomed and took his meals—usually on credit—in an ordinary boarding house with a dozen or so other legislators, clerks, and legislative attachées [sic]. Many could not afford appropriate clothing.

Hardy Solomon found one member on the street so ill clad that he took him to his store and fitted him into a suit without requiring a vote in return. Occasionally some affluent Republican might offer the favorite "oyster supper" at a local dining room, or a caucus be held in which refreshments were served; but these were rare events. Such high living as was done by the legislators was done in the barrooms and, typically, on credit. "John A. Chesnut and W. J. Whipper, members of the House of Representatives from Kershaw and Beaufort," a Columbia barkeep known as "Uncle" advertised in a local paper as the session 1869 closed, "will please call on the undersigned and settle their bills at once."

Far from a jubilee, attending a session of the legislature was for many Negro members a prolonged torture. Occasionally, political excitement ran high, as during the Ku Klux troubles and recurrently during elections. But the typical legislator followed a dull, drab, daily routine. During the mornings, he attended committee meetings or caucuses, stood on the streets or about the Capitol grounds, or remained in his boarding house. Beginning at noon, he attended a three- or four-hour legislative session, most of which were uneventful and, indeed, unimportant. In the late afternoons [*sic*], he repeated the morning's performances, had his communal dinner at his boarding house, and retired. Throughout the session, he was plagued by a lack of money and by a worrying uncertainty whether he would be able to collect his pay at all, regardless of how much he voted himself, and whether he would realize from his nominal salary enough cash to meet his debts in Columbia and his obligations at home, familial and otherwise. Retrospectively, the life of the Reconstruction Negro legislator was rather monkish when compared to the annual excursions to the capital of his ante-bellum counterpart.

There are many partial explanations why Republican politicos in South Carolina stole. If prevalence of delinquency is acceptable as evidence in mitigation of crime, one has only to point northward to "Grantism" and Boss Tweed, and afterward, in South Carolina itself, to the continued success of the bond ring and the phosphate monopolists during the Redeemer period. To some extent, there was a very general loosening of moral restrictions in the state after the war. Even as the Radicals moved into Columbia during the summer of 1868, an elderly native white farmer in Spartanburg District despondently complained of "dishonesty from once honest men" without racial or political distinctions. Simple greed is an obvious reason for theft, and no doubt this existed in a large measure among corruptionists in South Carolina. Further, opportunity had much to do with it. Men who might have remained honest in other circumstances found the easy temptation offered by a Patterson or a Hurley irresistible, and their yielding made it more likely that other, more sturdy, souls would also succumb.

It is possible to construct a grand rationalization for the corruptionists. Since the whites themselves essentially had withdrawn from political participation, most Republicans felt relieved from the necessity of representing their interests in the legislature and in the government at large. The attack on the property interests of the whites was a deliberately contrived part of the Radical program; it would promote a redistribution of landed wealth and the public welfare program which their constituency wanted. From there, a quick moral slip might bring one to rationalize that anything that drove the cost of government up would promote the Republican program, the focus of one's primary loyalty. Thievery might thus become service to the party. Though no Republican ever publicized this rationale, many came very near to publicly espousing something close to it. "I believe in Mr. Cain's doctrine," cried A. J. Ransier to a lowcountry audience in 1870, " 'Get all the money you can, but vote right!' " Public morality for the Republican (and Negro) politico was thus defined by party (and racial) loyalty, and not by the ethical standards which they themselves had first established and which conservative whites, at least obstensibly, continued to serve.

A large number of legislators practiced precisely what Mr. Cain preached: they took bribes, but only after having voted "right." S. E. Gaillard, a Negro senator from Charleston after 1871, refused a $5,000 bribe to support Patterson's Blue Ridge scrip and other bills in 1872 but finally came to support a compromise measure. After the compromise was effected, he joined with other Negro senators who had promised their votes for specific amounts but were having trouble collecting. "I got in with this crowd," Gaillard later testified, "because I had supported the Financial Settlement Bill after it had been amended." He later refused an offer of $500 to support Solomon's claim, voted against it, but the ever-generous Solomon deposited $500 in his bank account anyway. Many other members testified that they had voted for the claim because it was "just," "honest," "right," and that the bribe was a "present" given in appreciation of their having voted right.

Virtually every bribe-taker felt the necessity of excusing his conduct, however specious his explanation may have been. Prince Rivers asserted that his followers began to accept bribes only after they had held office for a couple of years and that they did so then only because they learned that the lowcountry members were taking all that was offered. Moses later stated that almost every member took fraudulent pay certificates believing that each dollar collected was so much retained in the state rather than drained off through Kimpton to New York by the bond ring. Nash offered the same excuse to explain why he took $5,000 in Blue Ridge scrip after having successfully led a fight to give Patterson less than half of what he wanted. "I was supporting these Bills because I thought," he swore, "after hearing the arguments of these men, that it was right, and I merely took the money because I thought I might as well have it and invest it here as for them to carry it off out of the State." In the fall of 1877, he still had the scrip in his possession, obviously being very certain that it remained in South Carolina. A few members described their motive as simple economic necessity. After having voted for Corbin for United States senator in the fall of 1876, L. J. Keith, a Negro representative from Darlington, admitted: "I would have voted for any other candidate under the same circumstances. I was pretty hard up and I did not care who the candidate was if I got $200."

Part V:
FROM RECONSTRUCTION TO WORLD
WAR I, 1877–1914

The hard-fought and bitter political campaign of 1876 ended in a deadlock, as both parties claimed victory. Finally, in April 1877 President Hayes withdrew federal troops from Columbia, whereupon the Republican regime of Daniel Chamberlain collapsed. General Wade Hampton III and his Democratic cohorts took undisputed control of the state. Thus began thirteen years of political domination by conservative Democrats, often called "Bourbons."

Once assured of clear-cut authority as governor, Hampton immediately concerned himself with harmonizing race relations. Although a believer in white supremacy, he was anxious to grant Negro citizens economic and educational equality, justice before the law, and some voice in political affairs. Such a policy, he felt, was only fair to the Negroes and would win Negro support for the Democrats.

During the campaign of 1876, Hampton had appealed to Negro voters by pledging acceptance of the Thirteenth, Fourteenth, and Fifteenth Amendments. Now he was determined to honor his commitments. On the other hand, many Democrats, led by Gen. Martin W. Gary, disapproved of Hampton's policy of conciliation. Instead, they favored repression of Negro rights as the best means to insure white supremacy.

The story of Governor Hampton's struggle to end discord and redeem his pledges is described by Hampton M. Jarrell, who concluded: "Rarely . . . have political pledges been better kept by a leader or kept under more difficult circumstances. . . . Hampton in two years accomplished more for both races and more nearly harmonized the two than has any other leader, North or South."

23

"HAMPTON'S ADMINISTRATION" *

Hampton M. Jarrell

The quality of Hampton and the men who supported him insured the rapid return of South Carolina to the ante-bellum standard of honest, efficient, and economical government. But we are concerned not with that process but rather with the continuing division of white men in the state into hostile factions, largely on the issue of the Negro.

Two conditions dominated the politics of South Carolina during the decade following the victory of seventy-six. One was the absolute need for white unity against the Negro vote—about that, right or wrong, there was no dispute. Hampton was credited (or discredited) with saying, "An independent is worse than a Radical." Whoever said it, it was the *sine qua non* of South Carolina politics, the one guarantee against the return of Negro supremacy. The second condition during the decade was the high prestige of Hampton himself with all classes throughout the state. As the luckless Gary was to prove, open opposition to Hampton meant political death. Therefore hostility towards him and his supporters was self-suppressed. When it did break out a decade later, its bitterness and intensity amazed all observers. The ever-present threat of the Negro vote prevented, of course, the normal development of two-party government. Although Gary led the opposition to the Hampton faction, this opposition usually had to conform to the party line and vote for men and measures it did not approve.

Shortly after the departure of federal troops from the State House, Hampton called a special session of the legislature. Immediately the need became apparent for a rigid Democratic caucus to prevent indirect domination by the Negro minority in the legislature. The constricting force of absolute conformity thus became the essential but

---

* Excerpts from chapter 6 of *Wade Hampton and the Negro: The Road Not Taken* (Columbia: University of South Carolina Press, 1949), pp. 124–30, 132–39, 150; Copyright 1949 by the University of South Carolina, Columbia. Reprinted without footnotes by permission of the University of South Carolina Press and the author.

baneful condition of continued white supremacy, that is, of the prevention of a return to Negro supremacy.

The first violent disagreement arose over filling the vacancy in the Supreme Court caused by the death of Chief Justice Moses, father of the robber governor. Hampton backed the candidacy of Associate Justice Willard, a Northerner and a Republican, but an upright judge and, as senior associate justice, the logical successor to the Chief Justice. Fulfilling his pledge that his victory was not of party or race but of honest government, Hampton insisted on Willard's election. In the resultant Democratic caucus the contest was long and hard, with Gary leading the opposition in favor of General McGowan, a distinguished and popular South Carolinian. During the election itself there was the ironic spectacle of most Democrats sourly voting for Republican Willard, but the Negro Republicans, to complicate the issue, voting for Democrat General McGowan.

Disagreement over the election of Willard as Chief Justice—"conciliation of Radicals"—was by no means the only point of conflict between Hampton and Gary. Hampton called a special session of the legislature for April 24, 1877, shortly after federal troops were withdrawn. In his first message to that body he strongly recommended immediate action to provide for the public debt, as he had pledged that he would do.

In a speech on May 25 Gary met Hampton's request with a frontal attack on the platform and pledges of the campaign of 1876, particularly on the pledge to uphold the Consolidation Act of 1873 and the pledge of a constitutional amendment to provide a two-mill tax for the education of both races. His argument was that the Democratic Executive Committee had had no right to make such pledges and that therefore all such pledges were binding on no Democrats except the members of the committee. Gary wanted to relieve the state of the debt accumulated by the Republican administrations, which he considered to be fraudulent. After extended discussion and investigation, a compromise was agreed on which met the spirit if not the letter of Hampton's pledge in regard to the debt of the state.

In this controversy Gary bitterly attacked those who were insisting on what he called "Quixotic schemes of public honesty." In a style that Tillman was later to make famous, he lashed out at those "elegant, smooth-mannered, oily-tongued bond holders, bond speculators, bankers and members of the financial boards who have produced a magical influence upon the law makers of this General Assembly."

On May 2 he had already attacked the ruling class of the state: "It was this same spirit of aristocratic exclusiveness which . . . established an aristocratic ring, who ruled the affairs of this State with such a proscriptive spirit as to drive many of her most gifted sons to seek their fortunes in the West, because the accident of birth did not place them within the charmed circle."

Gary also opposed Hampton's recommendations in regard to education, particularly the education of Negroes, which *The Nation* described as "all that could be asked for by the most exacting advocate of free schools and equal rights." He wanted no appropriation for education—only the proceeds of the poll tax for the public schools and no state support for the University. Sheppard summarizes a speech made by Gary shortly after the close of this special session:

Continuing his plea for economy and retrenchment in government, Gary announced his opposition to ratification of the annual tax of two mills upon all property of the state for educational purposes. Nine-tenths of this tax would be paid by white people, and three-fourths of it would be spent in educating piccaninnies. This was discrimination. He advocated education, but the impoverished condition of the people was a handicap in furnishing schools for white children. He was unalterably opposed to taxing whites to supply the teachers for blacks.

Hampton, however, had his way in this regard, as on most other issues. The constitutional amendment providing a two-mill tax for the education of both races was ratified, and an act was passed

that his Excellency the Governor and the Board . . . shall . . . devise plans for the organization and maintenance of one university or school for the white and one for the colored youths of the State, which said universities or colleges shall be kept separate and apart, but shall forever enjoy precisely the same privileges and advantages with respect to their standards of learning and the amounts of revenue to be appropriated by the State for their maintenance.

Thus Hampton, during the special session of 1877, established his political control of the state, and Gary, whose unsuccessful bid for the United States senatorship won by General M. C. Butler laid him open to the charge of being a disappointed officeseeker, became the recognized leader of a generally unpopular opposition—unpopular more because of Hampton's high personal standing in the state than because of any grass-roots opposition to Gary's views.

Thus had Gary blazed many of the trails that Tillman was to follow a decade later, when Hampton's personal power had so faded as to no longer be the dominant political factor in the state. Gary probably came closer than Hampton to expressing the convictions of a majority of the white voters of the state, and he was defeated because of his opposition to Hampton rather than because of his political views. If he had lived through the next decade, he would probably have received the support that went to Tillman. As it was, he had won the fighting loyalty of those who were close to him, many of whom were to provide leadership for the Tillman revolt. And Tillman inherited from Gary not only many political convictions and the foundations for a strong party, but also an accumulation of resentment against the Hampton faction which gave the populist movement in South Carolina its unexpected tone of violent bitterness.

A speech delivered in April of 1878 by Major Tom Woodward, the man who in 1867 had plaintively asked why "Southern nigger-worshipers" like Hampton did not leave the Negroes alone and let them do their work, reveals this odd combination of objection to Hampton's conciliatory policy and of personal loyalty for Hampton himself that was characteristic of many citizens:

> When Governor Hampton . . . brought to bear his great influence against men like McGowan . . . in favor of a Carpetbagger, I thought then, and I think now, that he did violence to the sentiments of Straight-out Democracy and went beyond any pledges I heard him make in his brilliant and unparalleled campaign.
>
> When he appointed Gleaves, the vile Negro mulatto ex-president of the most infernally infamous Chamberlain Senate, to the position of Trial Justice, I said then, and say now, that he temporarily lowered the standard of Democracy. . . .
>
> When the Legislature, through what I now believe to have been the influence of Governor Hampton . . . seated the dirty, thievish blackguards of the Mackey House, I asked, "In God's name, are these the fruits of the Democratic victory. . . ."
>
> When again, Mr. Chairman, the good citizens of this county . . . prayed a Democratic Legislature not to seat the member, Prince Martin, who was known to be the most corrupt and scoundrelly Radical in the state, and found themselves checkmated, as I believe, by Governor Hampton, I cried aloud. . . .
>
> But, sir, despite all this, and more that can be alleged, I honor and love this man. I know, personally, that he possesses those magnetic attributes of head and heart which will endear him to this people, and will keep the

honor of the old Palmetto State and the welfare of its citizens uppermost in his mind.

In his efforts at achieving conciliation—an end to old animosities—Hampton was faced not only with dissent within his own party and long-standing racial and party hatreds within his state; he had to reckon with honest suspicion in the North as well as with the conventional bloody-shirt waving of the extreme Radical press. His restraint and good judgment had gained him much favorable opinion, and the justice of his administration won him many more friends and admirers in the North.

Many Northern papers, Republican and Democratic, were praising his work during 1877 and 1878. His address at the Winnebago County Fair, Rockford, Illinois, in September, 1877, was a forthright and manly plea for an end to sectional animosities, and somehow he struck the right note to awaken an enthusiastic response throughout the country.

During the spring of 1878, E. P. Clark, managing editor of the Springfield, Massachusetts, *Republican,* visited South Carolina, travelled over the state, and wrote a shrewd, well-informed estimate of Hampton's accomplishments during the first year of his administration. Dated Columbia, April 10, and copied in the Columbia *Register* for April 19, 1878, his account serves both as a statement of what Hampton had done and as evidence of well-informed liberal Northern Republican reaction to his administration.

Clark first called attention to the changes "nothing less than wonderful" which had resulted from a year of Hampton's administration. A year before, the people of South Carolina had been "divided into two opposing parties—the Democrats flushed with their long-delayed victory, the Republicans embittered by their final defeat and genuinely distrustful of the future." Racial relations, too, were dangerously tense. "The negroes saw at last the success of that party which they had been sedulously taught for years would signalize its accession to power by relegating them back into slavery. . . ." The close of the year, Clark continued, "finds everything absolutely changed. The political excitement which had long kept the state in turmoil has disappeared, and complete peace prevails. Financial distrust has given way to a feeling of growing confidence. . . . The relations of the two races have steadily improved, till a far better feeling is already reached than was ever before known."

Although he considered himself "somewhat familiar with the course of events," Clark was surprised at the universal Republican admiration for Hampton that he found in the state. He made a careful survey of Republican opinion, Up-country and Low-country, Negro and white, high and low—judges, postmasters, the Collector of Internal Revenue as well as the Negro "I might chance to have for my driver," so that he had "sounded all phases of Republican feeling."

The concurrent testimony of all these Republicans, white and black, is the most sweeping commendation of Governor Hampton's course and the most implicit confidence in the man. Said Dr. Boseman, Postmaster of Charleston, "You may quote me as expressing absolute confidence in Governor Hampton and entire satisfaction with his course. . . . He has kept all his pledges." Said Postmaster Wilder of Columbia, "Governor Hampton has done everything we could have asked. . . ." The striking testimony of these colored men is reechoed by their white associates.

Clark continued his political analysis with the observation that Hampton's "victory over the malcontents in his own party has been no less complete." For the benefit of his Northern readers he explained the division of the Democrats in the state into two factions, the Gary Group (whom he calls Bourbons), "which looks regretfully and longingly at the past," and the Hampton group, "which cuts loose from that past and fixes its eye on the future." . . .

One further reconciliation was essential if Hampton was to secure for South Carolina the complete peace for which he was striving. Throughout the eight years of Grant's administration there had been virtual war between the President of the United States and the white men of South Carolina; Hampton wanted peace and mutual trust. Fortunately he discovered in President Hayes another moderate and patriotic statesman, and very soon the two men trusted one another so well that they could work together for the welfare of the state and nation in spite of outraged extremists in both sections. In South Carolina Gary, of course, urged that the people "unseat the usurper"— that is, President Hayes—thus, oddly enough, taking the same ground as Radical extremists like Conkling. Hampton, he said, was guilty of "consorting with, aiding and abetting one Rutherford B. Hayes in his usurpation upon the Presidency of the United States." Hampton, on the other hand, defended Hayes: "He did not propose the Electoral Commission, and is not responsible for its results. The Democratic party is responsible for the Electoral Commission. . . . The Commission gave Mr. Hayes the office and the Democrats were a party to it, and in accepting it he did as any American citizen would have done, and it is well for us that he did. . . ."

The cordial relations that Hampton soon established with the President, which benefited both the state and the nation, caused the Gary faction to suspect some venal deal between the two men, and Sheppard in *Red Shirts Remembered* advances every possible argument for such a conspiracy. If one accepts the theory that there was fighting war between Democrats and Republicans, then Hampton *was* guilty of communication with the enemy. If, however, one admits that there was a state of peace, Hampton and Hayes were acting together for the best interest of all concerned. Gary, like extreme Radicals in the North, probably sincerely believed—or felt—the former alternative; Hampton and Hayes accepted the latter.

The story of Hampton's relations with Hayes is an essential part of an account of the Governor's administration. The accusation that early in the election of 1876 Hampton had been "willing and anxious" to betray the Democratic Party in the Presidential race in return for a guaranteed victory in the state has been disputed above. Furthermore, Hampton had no part in the much-misunderstood "bargain" between Southern Congressmen and friends of Hayes. The point of the Southerners' agreement is not that they "sold their Party down the river," but that they agreed to abide by the decision of the Electoral Commission, a method of reaching a decision between Tilden and Hayes that the Democrats, North and South, had strongly supported. When the blind partisanship of the commission became clear, however, extreme Northern Democrats in the House wanted a filibuster to prevent a decision by Inauguration Day. The Southern Democrats blocked such a maneuver. The very probable alternative was war, and Southerners of that generation knew too well the cost of civil strife. Hampton agreed that his party should abide by the commission's decision. Indeed, on December 23, 1876, even before Congress had decided on the Electoral Commission, he had written to both Tilden and Hayes that it was the "firm and deliberate purpose" of the people of South Carolina "to condemn any solution . . . that involves the exhibition of armed force or that moves through any other channel than the prescribed forms of the Constitution, or the peaceful agencies of law."

Before Hampton and Hayes met face to face, each distrusted the other; afterwards, there is every evidence of mutual confidence and respect. Hampton's three letters to Hayes which immediately preceded this conference are therefore coldly formal, so much so, in fact, that Hayes' biographer complains of "questionable taste."

There is no record of what transpired in the first meeting between the two men, but they took each other's measure and liked what they saw. At last, moderate and courageous men, North and South, men with the power to implement their convictions, were consulting as to the status of the Negro in the South. As has been true throughout the course of our history, such men could find essential agreement on every important point; tragically, though, the course of our history has rarely given them a chance. The Sumners and Stevenses, the Garys and Tillmans—not the Hamptons and Hayeses—all too often have forced political action on the Negro question by the concentrated intensity of their convictions. For just a little while after 1877, moderate men controlled the destiny of the Negro in South Carolina. The result merits most careful and thoughtful consideration; it has received only the scantiest attention.

In a letter immediately following the conference, Hampton wrote to Hayes what he conceived to be the essence of their agreement:

. . . you sincerely desire to see a peaceful and just settlement of the questions which are distracting our people and injuring so seriously the material interests of our State and I trust that you are equally convinced of my earnest wish to aid in accomplishing this happy end. . . . if Federal troops are withdrawn from the State House, there shall be on my part, or that of my friends no resort to violence. . . . With the recognition of the perfect equality of every man before the law, with a just and impartial administration of the laws: with a practical secure exercise of the right of suffrage: with a system of public education which will open the services of knowledge to all classes we may hope to see our State soon take the position to which she is entitled.

This mutal trust and respect between Hampton and Hayes meant much in the settlement of vexing problems between state and federal governments during the next two years. That Hampton and Hayes could work together with confidence and understanding made far easier South Carolina's hard road back to true statehood.

A need for understanding soon arose. About eight hundred South Carolina Democrats were under federal indictment as a result of the activities of United States Attorney Corbin during the campaign of '76. Since an "ironbound" test oath excluded from federal juries "all who voluntarily participated in rebellion," such juries were virtually limited to Negroes and carpetbaggers. Trial before these juries under the federal election laws then in operation was no light matter. Moreover, three South Carolinians were still in federal prison as a result of the Ku Klux trials, and many others were prevented from returning to the state for fear of arrest.

On the other hand, many Republicans who had participated in the state Reconstruction government were manifestly guilty of various crimes, and a few had been tried and convicted. Most people in the state quite naturally wished for and expected the prompt punishment of numerous Radicals, particularly those whom the current investigation showed to be worst offenders.

Hampton knew, however, that such trials would arouse old animosities and would set off hysterical demands for retaliation in the Radical press, which was objecting even to the investigation of frauds, conducted by a committee with a Republican chairman, as a violation of Hampton's pledges and as political persecution. In his Anderson speech in March, 1878, Hampton publicly stated his purpose:

> I think the wisest statesmanship is amnesty. I want the cases in the United States courts against our people dismissed—the Ku Klux, Hamburg and Ellenton and revenue cases. If we give general amnesty, we shall have amnesty for our own people." [sic]

Negotiations to that effect had already begun ten months before in a telegram from Hampton to Hayes, dated May 11, 1877, accompanying a concurrent resolution of the General Assembly. Hayes' reply, dated May 12, contained a guarded agreement that "a general amnesty should extend to all political offenses except those which are of the gravest character."

A long letter from Hampton to Hayes, marked "personal" and delivered by South Carolina's Attorney General Youmans (dated March 25, 1878), indicates how far Hampton's policy had progressed during the intervening ten months.

Hampton began his letter with an explanation of what he had done to minimize prosecution of Radical offenders in the state. He had sponsored in the General Assembly "a resolution authorizing me to 'nol pros' any of the cases which are regarded as political" since it "is very desirable that all agitation should cease in the state" and he desired "as full amnesty as can be granted." There had been "but three trials of cases of this sort, though there is evidence sufficient for two hundred," and Hampton had arranged for the pardon of the three men convicted.

In return, Hampton urged Hayes,

You can strengthen my hands in carrying out the policy of amnesty greatly by the exercise of executive clemency in behalf of those who are charged with violation of the U.S. laws and I appeal to you to do so. . . . I feel sure that you could do nothing which would be more grateful to our people, than to end at once all this irritating source of anxiety. Public opinion would then sustain me in the course I wish to pursue here and all political causes of dissension would be removed.

Hampton explained to Hayes the difficulties that had faced him during the first year of his administration: "My position has been a very difficult one, for besides the opposition to me from political opponents, I have had to meet and control that of the extreme men of my own party. That this latter has been bitter, the enclosed article published here will show you, but I can crush out all opposition, if you can grant amnesty to our citizens."

As an indication of what his policy could accomplish in the state, Hampton reviewed his accomplishments towards securing peace and good will:

> It is very gratifying to me to learn that I have gained the confidence of the Republicans here, by my administration of the government, for this proves that justice has been done. A Republican Senator offered resolutions endorsing the course I have pursued, saying that I had redeemed every pledge made, and every Republican in the legislature voted for them. The colored people urge me to be a candidate for the next term, and assure me that there shall be no opposition if I will run. We have peace throughout the state, and goodwill between the races is growing up. As you have seen, the people and the volunteer troops respond readily to my orders to assist the Revenue officers, and the laws are enforced everywhere. You have been largely instrumental in bringing about these happy results, by your policy to the South, and I feel therefore that I can approach you in full confidence that you will sympathize with my objects. We have in this, a common end in view, and if you will trust my judgement in the matter, you can accomplish a great work, one that will do much towards pacification.

Not until 1884 were all legal knots formally and publicly untied, but by the middle of June, 1878, Hampton could write to a friend that "your brother and all others concerned with the Ku Klux troubles, can return to the State, with perfect safety. Mr. Hayes promises that no action shall be taken against any of these parties. . . . It is not desirable to make any public announcement as to the action of the President just at this time. . . ."

The state *quid* for this federal *quo* made a distasteful pill for South

Carolinians to swallow. The idea of refraining from prosecuting the bribe givers and bribe takers, the forgers and embezzlers who had bankrupted the state, was a hard one to take, and many and loud were the complaints. But Hampton had his way—surely, all things considered, the best way. The letters from Hampton to Hayes reveal how difficult politically for both men this "exchange of prisoners" really was, and how impossible it would have been without the mutual trust that they had achieved.

A potentially troublesome conflict between state and federal governments over the collection of internal revenue—"revenuers" in the mountains—and acts of illegal violence by both moonshiners and revenue officers, also yielded with a minimum of excitement to the personal communications between the two men, thus removing another dangerous source of hatred and strife.

Early in the fall of 1877 President Hayes toured several Southern states to promote reconciliation, the first such gesture since the war, the federal government having been more prone to send troops than Presidents into the South. Hampton accompanied the President, who introduced him to a Kentucky audience as "a noble and patriotic man." As Hampton said of Hayes, ". . . he serves his party best who serves his country best. . . ." Hampton and Hayes worked faithfully together, one in Washington and the other in South Carolina, to end the animosities of war and Reconstruction. Both men jeopardized their political fortunes in the service of their country, and the result was good.

In December 1878, while dangerously ill from an accident that cost him a leg, Governor Wade Hampton was elected to the United States Senate. Thereafter he had little influence on the policy toward the Negro in South Carolina. Gradually the Bourbon leaders shifted toward the repressive measures advocated by the Gary wing of the party. By various means, legal and illegal, the Negro vote was minimized, and increasingly the blacks experienced discrimination in many walks of life.

The small white farmers, while generally favoring the Bourbons' Negro policy, were otherwise disenchanted with their leadership. The Bourbons, largely representing a planter–lawyer–businessman–ex-Confederate brigadier clique, apparently had no viable program to alleviate the economic plight of the agrarians. And after General Gary's death in 1881, the yeomen farmers had no leader. As depression lay heavy over the farm belt and grumbling increased, Benjamin Ryan Tillman came forward in 1885 to champion the small farmers' cause.

The agrarian discontent of the 1880s is described by Francis B. Simkins in his biography *Pitchfork Ben Tillman*. The following passage is taken from chapter 6—"The Background of Tillmanism."

24

"THE BACKGROUND OF TILLMANISM" *

Francis Butler Simkins

The disintegration of the old social order was accompanied by the emergence of new classes of whites. The pronounced increase in the number of farms indicates the partitioning of great estates into small rentals and perhaps the actual increase of small proprietorships. The old slaveholding families, unable to adjust themselves to new conditions, in many instances deserted the land. Many men of distinguished names preferred the overstocked professions of law and politics to the difficulties of land management.

Others, however, who before the war had been unable to compete with the planter and his slaves, took advantage of these changes. This new element found landownership less difficult because of the prevailing low prices, the elimination of the necessity of large capital investments in slaves, and the expansion of credit facilities for the carrying on of farm operations. There was a great development of small-farm cotton culture, especially in the Piedmont region, marked by an increased use of commercial fertilizers.

After the war, towns and villages multiplied strikingly at strategic points along the railroads, and in these settlements a significant new mercantile class emerged. These merchants became the wealthiest men in South Carolina by charging high interest rates on crop liens and other types of advances. Their wealth often gave them dominant positions in banking, in the church, and in political life. They ruled the

* Excerpt from *Pitchfork Ben Tillman, South Carolinian* (Baton Rouge: Louisiana State University Press, 1944), pp. 72–81; Copyright, 1944, by Louisiana State University Press. Reprinted without footnotes by permission of Louisiana State University Press.

community as supremely if not as glamorously as ever did the antebellum planters.

Another evidence of aristocratic decay was the rise of the more democratic upcountry at the expense of the low country where the devastation of war and the demoralization of the Negro had been greater. Rice, before the war the chief staple of the low country, had, by 1883, declined to one third its former value, and was soon abandoned altogether. In the upcountry, on the other hand, the extensive use, after 1865, of commercial fertilizer turned exhausted sand and hill lands into valuable cotton fields. Likewise, there was a rapid increase of cotton manufacturing in the upcountry, while the one great industry of the low country, the mining of phosphates, had only a temporary prosperity. Charleston, the commercial center of the low country, suffered a relative decline. This was due to the absence of water power suitable for factories, to the decentralization of cotton marketing, and to the use of rail routes to ports farther north by interior industrial centers.

These economic and social changes did not cause the immediate overthrow of the traditional political leadership. Conditions existed, however, which were preparing for the rise of a new and more democratic leadership. Consider the political reforms achieved during Reconstruction; the nature of the Hampton victory in 1876; the unsatisfactory solution of the problem of Negro suffrage; the failure to solve acute problems of agricultural distress; and the manner in which public offices were distributed. All these factors served either to create unrest or to make easier the assertion of discontent.

The constitutional conventions of both 1865 and 1868 facilitated a wider degree of popular participation in government. The first body apportioned legislative representation to the advantage of the upcountry and abolished property qualifications for officeholding. the second provided for the popular election of most officers, for the reapportionment of legislative representation every ten years, and for the principle of universal education.

The methods by which the campaign of 1876 was won were not in all respects satisfactory to the Bourbons who gained the offices.

Contrary to the advice of the low-country conservatives, the contest was directed along lines of mob violence by bold upcountry leaders. Hampton was "woefully mistaken" in believing that his policy of persuasion swung enough Negro voters to account for his election. This was really won by the rifle clubs keeping blacks away from the polls. The white masses who composed these organizations, knowing that they had done the work, would at a later date transfer to their own shoulders the toga of political control.

Notwithstanding the fact that all sorts of successful expedients were adopted to lessen the influence of the Negro in politics, the degree of reaction did not satisfy the riotous white public consciousness created by the victory of 1876. A resolution calling for a constitutional convention, through which the stigma of living under a Negro-made constitution could be removed, was defeated at successive sessions of the legislature. The only plan of suffrage restriction which that body could be induced to enact, as a substitute for the necessity of white men standing over the polls with their guns, did not entirely exclude the Negro from office. Black South Carolinians could still be seen in Congress and the legislature as representatives of the coastal counties, and it was deemed necessary to allow them a limited part in the councils of the Democratic party. A full policy of anti-Negro reaction was prevented by a sense of responsibility to the Negro, whose suffrage Hampton had promised to protect; by fear of Federal intervention; and by the timidity of the overdiscreet leaders of the black counties.

The white masses desired a system of government which completely excluded the Negro from politics. Unashamed of their anti-Negro opinions, they were dissatisfied with the halting manner in which their leaders stated their position. When opportunity came to justify South Carolina race attitudes, ample evidence was advanced to prove the venality of Negro government, without a word concerning the methods used to restore white supremacy. Cautious leaders were reluctant to expose practices to which they felt they had been driven by necessity. The cultured upper classes disapproved of the violence with which the lower classes disciplined the blacks. The press and the pulpit, motivated by the patriotic desire to have South Carolina live up to the standards of the more civilized communities, cried for "law enforcement" and stridently exposed the doings of lynchers, duelists, murderers, and other men of violence. The legislature outlawed dueling and tried to suppress lynching and pistol toting. The thousands who participated in or were sympathetic toward ruffianism were irritated by these harsh criticisms. They wanted a leader who would justify what they considered necessary oppression of the blacks.

In the 1870's the South Carolina farmers met with economic reverses. The fall in the price of cotton, the great increase in the number of liens on unharvested crops, and the purchase of farm supplies on credit from usurious merchants at prices 20 to 100 per cent above cash charges, caused much complaint and a searching for remedies. Many farmers between 1872 and 1875 joined the National Grange of the Patrons of Husbandry, an organization of national extent which, through its co-operative program of buying and selling and its demands for state regulation of railroads, promised relief. But as may have been expected, the Grange was of little practical benefit to the South Carolina farmers. The attempt at co-operative trading was wrecked by faulty management and the impatience of the average farmer with such slow means of betterment. Although Governor Hampton and his successors were sympathetic toward the demands of the farmers, they were able to do little. Their theories of the limited functions of government prevented notable ventures in paternalistic legislation. They did, however, create a department of agriculture and the office of railroad commissioner, and laws regulating the railroads were passed. Officers of mediocre ability were placed in charge of these agencies; the earning power of the railroads did not warrant such reductions of rates as would have materially lightened the burden of the farmers. After 1875 the Grange rapidly declined in membership; what was left of it joined hands with the conservative Agricultural and Mechanical Society to hold summer meetings in the various villages of the state.

But the Grange was not without lasting effects. It taught the farmer to be class-conscious and to turn to the government for the redress of his ills. This in connection with the decline in value of staple crops in the 1880's, the failure of efforts to establish a cash basis of tenancy, and the forfeiture by 1887 of over one million acres of land for non-payment of taxes, created an atmosphere of unrest and resentment. Between 1875 and 1885 there was a drop of six cents a pound in the price of cotton; and this measured the difference between easy living and the pinch of poverty.

Of course, this condition was caused by circumstances for which no particular group should be held responsible. Overproduction of cotton resulted in ruinous prices; and one-crop specialization meant the purchasing of foodstuffs and other commodities which should have been produced at home. As a consequence the farmers fell in debt to merchants who took liens on their crops. These were uncertain risks naturally bearing high interest charges. Bad debts were numerous, and only the shrewdest merchants avoided losses.

The discomfited farmers turned on the merchant-creditors as the authors of their woes. Interest on loans ranged from 10 to 15 per cent, and the high prices charged for corn, bacon, clothing, farm tools, fertilizers, and even mules and horses purchased on credit or under the crop lien system were equal to interest charges of 25 to 100 per cent. The farmers, while enduring their own impoverishment, witnessed the enrichment of the merchants. They even saw merchants acquire mortgaged farms and operate them with Negro labor for whose services they outbid the older class of farmers. No wonder the prevailing credit system was regarded as "commercial extortion or legalized robbery of the farming, and, in general, the poorer class."

The merchants of Charleston became the special butt of the up-country farmers. To inherited prejudice against that ancient center of supposed social and political tyranny was added envy of the profits of the city's bankers and cotton and fertilizer merchants. It was the "money center" whose usurers mulcted the country merchants, who in turn mulcted their farmer-debtors. Through the "endless tolls in one way or another" it was said that Charleston cotton factors, without the mediation of the country merchants, extorted great gains from the farmers. And this city was the seat of the profiteering fertilizer industry.

Likewise, the farmers complained against the conduct of their state government. They said taxes were too high; they suspected corruption and believed that a state officer's salary of $2,100 was flagrant robbery.

These accusations were supplemented by more convincing charges of sins of omission. The farmers called their rulers Bourbons, men who neither learned nor forgot anything; and indeed the hidebound South Carolina leaders adhered to the theory that the state should be content with a minimum of intervention in social and economic matters, discoursing in the meantime on their heroic services in the cause of the Confederacy, on the time-honored doctrine of tariff-for-revenue, and on economy in expenditures, and "viewing with alarm" the encroachments of the Federal government upon spheres of action marked out for the states.

In another sense, however, they were not Bourbons. They were attuned to the progressive sentiments expressed in Henry W. Grady's definition of the New South. Without sacrificing their party or Southern principles, they wanted closer union with the North and the suppression of the crasser Southern prejudices. They fostered the growth of business and industry by low taxation, by a careful maintenance of the state's credit, and by avoiding restraining social legislation. Unlike Georgia's leaders, they did not corruptly mix business in politics; most of them remained almost pathetically poor; but they did participate in a sort of "Little Barbecue" not unlike the "Great Barbecue" attended by politicians and businessmen in more opulent commonwealths. They allied themselves with the business leaders of the day, lending them the prestige of aristocratic names and glamorous reputations gained in war and politics. They were wined and dined by the rich men of Charleston and Columbia; they served as corporation lawyers; and by acts of omission encouraged the growing power of industry.

Although this alliance was too subtle for the farmers to recognize, they saw obvious injustice in the office-grabbing tactics of the Bourbons who granted appointments exclusively to themselves and their friends as though public salaries were their private property. Perhaps the Bourbons discharged public trusts with more than average merit. Yet farmers and others, in times of economic distress, were envious of their positions and capable of developing the emotions necessary to give a righteous bias to efforts to oust them from office.

Even during the early years of the Hampton regime there were "mutterings of discontent," "one or two spasmodic efforts to overthrow ring rule . . . where there was a majority of white voters." The Greenback party in 1880 made a slight dent in the solid wall of Democratic strength, and noisy protests were made against the Fence Law, by which the landless were forced to confine their stock. In 1882 a legislative candidate in the upcountry won a large vote by attacking useless offices and the appropriations for state colleges.

Thus in the 1880's were circumstances prepared for a revolt from Bourbon control of South Carolina. The Civil War had shattered the social and economic bases of aristocratic privilege. The reforms of Reconstruction removed legal barriers against popular government, and the manner in which the Reconstruction regime was overthrown proved that the white masses of the state were capable of effective exercise of their franchise. Economic distress coupled with the ineptitude of the Bourbon government made the farmers discontented. All that was needed for this discontent to find expression was for a leader of intelligence and courage to emerge.

Although having no program to alleviate the farmers' ills directly, the Bourbons hoped to bring prosperity to South Carolina by encouraging the growth of industry. Their conservative philosophy, which promised low taxes and political stability, coupled with a vast non-union labor supply seemed to offer the proper inducement. Fortunately, too, the nation emerged from a severe four-year depression as Reconstruction came to an end. Once more, capital began to move freely.

South Carolina had long had a small textile industry. Graniteville, the best known and largest pre-war factory, dated back to 1845. But in 1880 there were only 14 plants, employing about 2,000 workers. Between 1880 and 1900 the textile movement began in earnest. By the latter date the state had 115 mills, employing about 30,000 workers. Steady progress continued henceforth. Poor farmers, many of them tenants, poured in from the piney woods, the piedmont, and the mountains of North Carolina. Most found wages and living conditions in the mill villages more rewarding than on the farm and thus remained in their new locations.

The story of life in a cotton mill village in the 1880s has been told by William E. Woodward, a noted writer who grew up in Graniteville. His description appeared in his book *The Way Our People Lived,*

25

"A COTTON MILL VILLAGE IN THE 1880's" *

W. E. Woodward

Compared with other Southern cotton mill communities in the 1880's Graniteville was a model town. The typical mill village of that period was a sun-baked collection of hovels on a hillside. In some of them the workers lived in barrack-like structures that housed eight or ten families in a common atmosphere of flies, dirt and foul odors. At election time the men, in some mill towns, were given the names of the candidates for whom they must vote and an official of the mill stood by the ballot box to inspect each vote. If a worker insisted on voting for a candidate not on the list he would bring down a lot of trouble upon himself.

One Carolina factory village was surrounded by a high wooden fence; no one was allowed to enter or leave this stockade without permission of the management. Some of the mills made employees sign a contract when they were hired that absolved the company for any blame or penalty in case of accident to the worker. This contract also contained a clause under which the company withheld two weeks' wages. These the worker would lose altogether if he quit his job without giving two weeks' notice in writing.

In Graniteville there were no hovels or human rabbit warrens. Wages were not held back, and every man might vote as he pleased. The people were all poor, and could not afford even the simplest of luxuries, for the cotton mill scale of wages—not only in Graniteville, but also in every other factory town—was too low to permit any kind of extravagance. But the Graniteville operatives got plenty to eat, decent clothes to wear, and fairly comfortable houses to live in.

Every mill family was provided with a cottage that stood apart from the neighboring houses. These houses all had gardens that were

* Excerpts from *The Way Our People Lived: An Intimate American History* (New York: E. P. Dutton, 1944), pp. 326–43; Copyright, 1944, by E. P. Dutton & Company, Inc. Reprinted by permission of Harold Ober Associates Incorporated.

large enough to grow most of the vegetables needed for the family larder. There was a chicken yard also where the wife kept ten or twelve hens; and in the pig sty at the far end of the garden a pair of porkers were fattened until November, which was the hog-killing month.

The mill cottages varied in size to fit the conditions. The typical cottage of four rooms—and there were many of these in the village— consisted of a sitting room, two bedrooms and a kitchen. In front of the house there was a porch and space between the house and the street for a flower garden. The cottages had no cellars or basements, but the entire house, resting on brick pillars, stood about three feet above the ground. The space underneath the house was often used in rainy weather by the children as a playground.

The houses were without running water, plumbing, gas or electric light. They were simply large boxes, covered by a plain ceiling and a shingle roof, with windows and doors. But the rooms were all light and airy and much larger than the rooms in workers' flats in the large cities. Most of the houses were painted white, but here and there one saw a brown, gray or yellow cottage.

There were hundreds of these cottages in the village when I was a boy, and some ten or twelve more elaborate houses in which the "quality" lived. Under this descriptive heading may be classed the superintendent of the factory, who was the most important person in the community. He and his wife were at the head of the village aristocracy. Next came the three or four managers of important departments of the mill, a couple of village merchants and two or three families that were not connected financially with the village in any way and they lived—apparently—on income from investments.

The factory employed about five hundred hands altogether—men, women, boys and girls—and the total population of the village was around two thousand.

There was not a wealthy person or family in the place—not one. A salary or income of as little as one hundred dollars a month put its possessor into the "quality" class. The social distinctions were sharply defined and the atmosphere of the village was quite as snobbish as that of Newport or Tuxedo. Even among the mill hands there were upper and lower classes.

The pomp and pride of the three-dollar-a-day men were among the interesting features of life in the village in that decade. About a score of these men were employed in the mill. They were not bosses, or department managers, nor did they belong to the white-collar office contingent, but they were capable and skilled mechanics, such as loom fixers, engineers and machine repair men. It is no exaggeration to say that they kept the plant going. Without them to look after the machinery the factory would have been tied up in snarls of one kind or another in forty-eight hours.

These workmen were on the pay roll for eighteen dollars a week, which was a straight salary, while most of the operatives were paid on a piecework basis. This rate of pay was more than twice as large as the earnings of the average mill hand.

Their friends and acquaintances pointed them out to strangers, and frequently they pointed themselves out by saying to new-comers "I'm a three-dollar man" by way of introduction.

They took pride in being extravagant in various ways, just to show off, on the same principle as that of a newly rich millionaire who builds a far larger house than his family needs, or puts a hundred thousand dollars' worth of diamonds on his wife.

One three-dollar man made a practice of smoking three or four ten-cent cigars in the course of an evening, and of handing out one occasionally to his poor acquaintances. "Have a cigar on me," he would say, "I buy 'em by the box." Another one always bought his clothes in Augusta, which is twelve miles from Graniteville. "They cost more," he said to a group of card-room hands, who were listening in admiration, "but they not only look better; they wear longer. My Augusta tailor won't let a suit leave his shop unless it's a perfect fit."

Among these free-handed spenders was one who hired a horse and buggy every Sunday to take his best girl out for a drive. "We usually drive over to Aiken and eat dinner there at the hotel. It don't leave much left out of a five-dollar bill, what with the meal and the buggy hire, and everything, but what's the diff?" He snapped his fingers. "We live only once anyway, and when we die we're dead a long time."

The three-dollar men stood at the top of the list of manual workers in the factory; at the bottom, in respect to earnings, were the doffers in the spinning room, who were little boys of ten or twelve—some even younger—and their daily wage was twenty-five cents. At that time there was no child labor law in South Carolina. The work done by these children was easy; it required neither strength nor skill. They took off or "doffed" the bobbins when the spinning machine had filled them with thread and in their places they put fresh empty bobbins. The doffers had to be present in the factory for the full twelve hours each day but they worked only part of the time. The doffing could be done in a few minutes and the bobbins were not full again for some time. In the meantime they could amuse themselves, or even take a nap in a sort of rest room on the spinning-room floor.

Duke Ross, a three-dollar man, owned the first bicycle I ever saw and the first one ever brought to Graniteville. This was in 1887, I think, or it may have been 1888. It was of the high front-wheel type, known as a Columbia. Everybody in the village knew that Ross had bought a bicycle, and it had been the chief subject of conversation for a week before he brought it out on a Sunday to learn to ride the contraption. About two hundred men and boys stood by to watch him, and there they remained the whole afternoon. After repeated failures, headlong falls, tumbles and breakdowns, he did actually ride the machine home just before nightfall, when supper for all the spectators was waiting and growing cold. Ross was a mass of bruises from head to foot, and his clothing was torn. I wondered then, and I still wonder why the early bicycle makers thought it necessary to make the front wheels of their machines so high.

The wages and salaries were low, but the cost of all living necessities was low in proportion. A four-room cottage rented for four dollars a month. I know this sounds incredible—a four-room house and a large garden all for a little less than a dollar a week—but when we look into the matter closely it does not seem to have been such a wonderful bargain, after all.

The land on which these cottages were built had cost around three dollars an acre when it was purchased by the company back in the 1840's. A four-room, one-story house could be put up for about two hundred dollars. The material used was pine, and the company owned several square miles of pine forest. The carpenters, bricklayers and painters were paid the local scale of wages; not one of them got more than twelve dollars a week, and some were paid much less.

The most attractive features of the village were its airy spaciousness and its shade trees. Widespreading elms and oaks grew in all the streets. They made the place fairly cool and comfortable on the hottest midsummer days. We had live oak trees around our house; in very warm weather my mother used to spread a table under one of them, and there we would have our dinner.

There was plenty of food for everybody but it was lacking in variety. Nearly all meat was fried. I am sure that I never saw or tasted a piece of roast beef, or roast ham, until I left Graniteville and went to college. Occasionally—but rarely—we would have baked chicken when the fowl was too large and too old for frying, but even large and old poultry was more likely to appear on the table in the form of a stew.

At breakfast the usual fare was corn meal mush with sugar and cream, fried ham and eggs, pancakes and coffee. Dinner was the mid-day meal. Meat loaf or chicken giblets with flour dumplings were commonly the principal part of the repast, though we often had fried chicken or sausage. Among the mill hands fried or boiled pork was a staple food. Boiled rice was a part of every midday meal, and usually there was pie for dessert. Sweet potato pie was almost always a part of the day's menu. In the summer we had watermelon every day. One could buy a twenty-pound melon for five cents.

Oysters were a prized delicacy, but they were sold only in cans, as the village was too far from the sea to get them fresh. The canned oysters came in large square tins, which were about eight inches long and six inches wide and three inches deep. On these tins there was no label of any kind.

Corn bread stood in high favor as a developer of muscle, strength, and height. I preferred then—and still prefer—bread made of flour, but my parents insisted that I eat corn bread at every meal. "It will build you up," my father said, "while that pale flour bread that you like so much has no strength in it. Look at Negroes working on a farm. They don't get wheat bread more than once or twice a year but they have corn bread every day, and they're as strong as oxen." This corn-bread fetish existed at that time all over the South. It was thought that bread made of white flour should be eaten only by delicate ladies and old people who had no particular need for musclar strength.

Early to bed and early to rise was the rule for the mill hands of that factory town in the 1880's. The working hours ran from six in the morning until six-thirty in the evening, with half an hour off at noon. It was a twelve-hour day for five days a week and nine hours on Saturdays—a sixty-nine hour week.

At five o'clock every morning the "waking" bell tolled, rung by the night watchman at the mill. A powerful and deep-toned bell, its solemn notes seemed to run through the village and in and out of the houses like a living thing. It was still vibrating when lights began to shine through the windows of the houses; the wives were up and preparing breakfast for the mill hands of the family.

At six o'clock the bell rang again—three strokes—and the gates of the factory swung shut. Any worker who arrived after six in the morning—even one minute after—found himself staring at a locked gate. He could come again at noon and work the rest of the day, but he would be docked half a day's wages.

By nine o'clock in the evening, winter or summer, most of the houses were dark. People who rise at five in the morning and work twelve hours a day need sleep and they go early to bed. But homegoers might be met occasionally in the streets until midnight, young men and girls who had been to a party. Prayer meetings were popular, for these religious assemblies had a social atmosphere. Young men attended them with the hope of meeting a girl there and escorting her home, and the girls—or some of them—went to the meetings with the same general idea in mind.

The young fellows usually tiptoed out of the church before the services were over, if they went in at all, and stood lined up on each side of the entrance. The etiquette of the occasion demanded that the young man approach the girl he had selected, tip his hat, and say, "Miss So-and-so, may I have the pleasure of seeing you home?"

If the girl liked him and wished to encourage his attentions she nodded pleasantly, gave him her arm, and they went homeward together. But if she did not care for him she would turn her back on him and say coldly, "I don't require your company."

The young man so treated was said to be "kicked." Next morning everybody in the village—all the wives and young women, at any rate—would hear about it. . . .

The company did not employ negroes in the factory, but they were hired to clean the streets, to work around the mill yard, and for other menial tasks. No negroes lived in the village, for the company, owning all the land and the houses, would not rent a house to a negro family. The colored folk lived in Madison, an incorporated hamlet which may be described as a suburb of Graniteville. Madison, which had a population of perhaps five hundred people—three-fourths of whom were negroes—was about half a mile south of Graniteville. It stood just outside the company's land.

The sale of liquor in Graniteville was banned, but in Madison there were three saloons. Like everything else in the factory community, the liquor sold in the saloons was low in price. A drink of corn liquor, rye or bourbon, cost ten cents, and a large stein of beer could be bought for a nickel. A man could get pleasantly drunk for fifty cents and dead drunk for a dollar.

Saturday was pay day, and the big drinking took place that night. For many a mill hand getting drunk on Saturday night was a regular custom. Around midnight the noisy topers could be heard coming home from Madison, screeching and singing, sometimes quarreling and fighting.

Besides the liquor sold across the bar the saloons carried on an extensive bottle trade. Each of the three liquor dealers had a messenger who went around quietly taking orders and delivering the whisky. Many women bought liquor in this manner, and among the masculine purchasers were some of the leading citizens, whose consciences were so highly moral that they would not think, even for a moment, of entering a saloon.

No doubt there would have been less drinking if the people of the village could have had some form of popular amusement within easy reach. But there was nothing, except hunting and fishing. Motion pictures did not exist in the 1880's, nor did the radio. Theatrical companies never came to Graniteville.

There was a theater in Augusta, across the Savannah River, and only twelve miles from Graniteville, but it might as well have been a hundred miles, for the only way that a Graniteville mill hand could attend a performance was to go to Augusta on the afternoon train and stay there overnight, coming back to village on the next morning's train—unless he owned a horse and buggy. But what in the world would a mill hand do with a horse and buggy when he had to work indoors twelve hours a day? For nine-tenths of those who lived in Graniteville the attractions of Augusta were virtually nonexistent.

Before the automobile era traveling for even short distances was so uncertain and expensive, and took so much time, that most people— not only in Graniteville but everywhere else—stayed at home when they were not at work.

In the little cotton mill village liquor drinking was a refuge from the utter dullness and boredom of life.

Anything new, or any harmless playful activity that promised diversion, became wondrously popular almost at once. In 1886, or 1887—I do not remember exactly when—a photographer set up his studio in Graniteville. His success was phenomenal. He took tintypes only and charged twenty-five cents a picture. On Sunday afternoons anyone who desired to "have his likeness taken," as the operation was known in popular speech, might have to wait two hours, sitting on one of the benches in the garden around the photographer's house, until his turn came.

Some of the factory girls, the good-looking ones, had their likeness taken many times, and in various poses. A new dress meant a new picture also. They took as much pride in the murky little tintypes as the movie stars of today have in their photographs.

In the absence of other diversions the people of the village went in for music, and in a big way. Every mill family that included young people had an organ if the family could afford to buy one—and most of them could, for the organs were sold on tiny monthly installments. In the afternoons and evenings, and all day on Sunday, the notes of organ music floated through the silence that always lay over the village. The few families that belonged to the "quality" had pianos, but a good many families of mill hands had what was called a "cottage organ." To learn to play an organ was part of a factory girl's domestic education.

Among the men the fiddle was the favorite musical instrument. Some of them were wonderful fiddlers. They could pay *Turkey in the Straw* in a way that would start even the bearded deacons to dancing.

There were also skilled accordion players, and the young boys all tried to learn, and many did learn, to play the harmonica. This last-named instrument was called a mouth organ in Graniteville; I never heard the word "harmonica" until I was grown and far from that village. . . .

There was a bitter division of sentiment in Graniteville over the moral aspect of dancing. Many of the older people and a few of the younger ones looked upon any kind of dancing as immoral, more or less, but most of the young men and women liked to dance and saw nothing wrong in doing so.

The waltz was then unknown in small towns; it did not become popular until late in the 1890's. The popular dance in our little mill town was the quadrille, and of course the jig. Almost every Saturday night there was a dance at Thorpe's Hall, which had the only floor large enough for a dozen couples. I was too young to dance but I would often go to the hall and look on. Sam Arthur, his moustache bristling and his face dripping with perspiration, always furnished the music. The tunes were usually *Money Musk, Pop Goes the Weasel, Arkansaw Traveler, Peas on a Trencher,* and *Old Dan Tucker.*

One of the young men acted as a figure-caller. I remember one whose voice could be heard at least a quarter of a mile as he sang out "Choose Partners, Sashay All, Swing and Change, Ladies Chain, Balance All." And there was the sound of clattering feet that could be heard afar, disturbing the deacons and elders as they lay in bed and causing them to have poor opinion of the younger generation.

Twice a year the sleepy little town was stirred into a kind of frenzy by revival meetings. These campaigns for bringing Christianity back to Graniteville and thus increasing the membership of the churches lasted about two weeks. They were conducted by professional revivalists, assisted by the local pastor, who played a minor role for the time being.

These professional groups went from one town to another the year around. In the make-up of the organization one man was an organist, another played a powerful trombone that filled one's ears, the church and everything else with a reverberating din. There was also a singer whose voice, very tuneful, luscious and emotional, was strong enough to make all other human sounds sink into the class of whispers. Besides these musicians, there were usually two preachers in the outfit.

The revival crusade began always on a Sunday evening, and there was a meeting thereafter every evening for two weeks. For the first few days the revival services were subdued and wholly unemotional. The sermons were short and clear expositions of the Christian doctrine. Before and after the sermon the preachers would go about the body of the church, among the congregation, meeting people, shaking hands with them, and conversing in a rather jovial, good-natured manner. I was always patted on the back and given a word of welcome. "And you, my little man," the preacher would say, "it's fine to see you here."

The sermons and the accompanying music acquired more and more warmth as the campaign went on. These experts in revival tactics were skillful in building up the emotional basis for mass hysteria. Young as I was, I could see that their chief instrument of persuasion was not love of God but fear of Hell.

Yet, notwithstanding all the hell-fire element of this discourse, I must say that I heard one of them, a Reverend Mr. Evans, preach a sermon that he called, *How Easy It Is to Go to Heaven,* which remains in my memory today as the best sermon I have ever heard or read.

Mr. Evans declared that all you have to do to reach Heaven is just to be a decent fellow. You must believe in God, and in God's holy word, the *Bible.* You must join God's church. All that is easy to do, isn't it? Now here's the next easy step. You have heard of the Ten Commandments? Sure, you have. Many of you know them by heart. Well, to go to heaven you must follow every one of the commandments. Is that a hard task? I should say not. Well, what else? The rest is simple enough, said Mr. Evans. Just treat everybody as you would like to be treated. Don't lose your temper, don't drink liquor, don't abuse your family. Always be kind and generous. That's easy, isn't it? Live that way and you'll go straight to heaven. I've always wondered, Mr. Evans continued, why sinners put themselves to so much trouble to go to hell. To sin you have to go out of your way, while it is perfectly natural to be decent and good at heart and in action.

Some of the hell-fire sermons were calculated to make one's hair stand on end. They described the tortures of the damned, their screams and the howling that rose from the burning lakes of hell. "Have you ever touched a red-hot iron?" I heard a preacher demand from his audience. "Have you ever held your hand, even for a second, in a live flame? Have you ever spilt a drop of molten lead on your flesh? In hell the damned live in flames, they walk on red-hot iron; the fiends give them molten lead to drink."

He paused a moment and held a handkerchief to his eyes as if he could not bear the sight of the damned. From around the altar came the sobs and groans of the mourners who had left their seats and gone forward when sinners and repentant souls had been invited to approach the altar and kneel.

"You wonder why they don't die under all that torture," the preacher continued. Then he shouted at the top of his voice, "They don't die because in hell there is no death. They must exist forever in a lake of fire. The suffering they have to endure would kill anyone here on earth in ten seconds but the damned souls in hell cannot die."

From the prostrate forms around the altar came a chorus of moans, and a woman's voice, calling loudly, "God save me, a sinner!"

"As long as you are on this earth, you can repent and be saved," the reverend gentleman declaimed, his voice filling the church as water fills a pail. "But you cannot repent when you are in hell; then it will be too late. God doesn't hear the prayers of those who are burning in eternal fire. Souls in hell do not belong to God; they belong to Satan, and he laughs at their suffering."

At the close of every meeting the mourners at the altar rose and with the rest of the assembly joined in singing a hymn. Many of them became members of the church then and there. . . .

There was a constant flow of share croppers and poor folk from the country to the cotton mills. The long hours and low wages did not seem long and low to the hillbillies and poverty-stricken plow hands. To these people life in Graniteville was wonderful and thrilling.

"Why, where I come from, over in Lexington County," I heard one of them say to my father, "I never had as much as five dollars of my own from one year's end to the other. Now I get money every Saturday, what with me and my three gals at work in the mill."

"I suppose you were a share cropper," my father said, "and had to turn over most of the cotton you raised to the landlord. That right?"

"No, sir—only half the crop went to the owner. I'd pick the cotton, me and my gals—I got three daughters—then the owner would come and take his half, and after that storekeeper down in Batesburg where I got my supplies would come and take the other half to go on account of the debt I owed him."

"Were you always in debt to the store?"

"Sure I was. Never out of debt, because, you see, the storekeeper could put up the prices on every blessed thing I got from him, and I couldn't stop him, for what would I do if he'd shut down on my credit? So that's the way it worked out. Sometimes I'd have from two to five dollars left over, and that's all the cash I'd see in a year."

"You like it better here in Graniteville, don't you? What about the working hours—the twelve hour day?"

"I worked jes' as long when I lived in the country," said this ex-share cropper, "and it was harder work, too. Anyway, I don't know what to do with myself when I ain't at work.

"I like it here. We live in a nice house, lots better'n than that cabin in the country. And there's always people around to talk with. Me and my gals—between the four of us we make from twenty-five to thirty dollars a week, and that ain't to be sneezed at, lemme tell you. And we get it in good, hard cash every Saturday, without any ifs and ands about it. The ol' woman stays at home and keeps house; me and the gals bring in the money.

"And when one of the gals needs a shawl or stockings or a dress she goes over to Miz Ethridge's store, buys it and pays cash."

Tight corsets were fashionable. Some of them were laced so tightly that it seemed hardly possible for the woman who wore them to live and breathe. The girls who worked in the factory did not wear these strait jackets on week days, or they would not have been able to work at the machines, but they did their best to make up for it on Sundays. Girls bound up in this fashion ate and drank very little for their bodies were so compressed that they had little or no room for food. Upon coming home Sunday afternoon the corset wearers would hasten desperately to get out of the corsets in the quickest possible time. Then they would lie on a bed or sofa and pant with relief.

Snuff using was an almost universal habit among the Graniteville women of that period, as it was everywhere else in the Southern states, except among women of the higher classes.

In using snuff a woman would take a large pinch of it, about half a teaspoonful, and deposit it between her lower lip and her teeth. Eventually, after years of constant use, the snuff caused that part of the lip to stick out permanently, so that from the outside it looked like a bump or swelling.

Every user of this form of tobacco owned a snuff brush, which was easily made of a twig of willow or of any soft wood. One end of the twig was frazzled into a brush-like form. With it the snuff could be moved around to reach all parts of the mouth. Snuff users were encouraged to continue the habit by the mistaken notion, widely circulated, that women who used snuff never had any trouble with their teeth.

Nearly all the men chewed tobacco, but smoking was a rare habit, because—one may suppose—it could not be done during working hours by the mill hands. The lighting of a match anywhere within the cotton factory was then, and is now, an offense on the order of high treason, murder and child-stealing. The match lighter would have been expelled from the premises and ordered out of town at once. But tobacco chewing was not under the ban, though the chewers were warned not to get tobacco juice on the cotton yarn or cloth. Cuspidors were provided.

Cigarette smoking in Graniteville in the 1880's was condemned right and left by everybody of authority, a term which included the preachers, the doctors, the factory managers and the schoolteachers. No grown man would have ever dreamed of smoking a cigarette, and an imputation that he did actually smoke cigarettes secretly would have been considered an insult.

It was exclusively a boys' vice. There was some little difficulty in buying cigarettes, as no storekeeper in the village sold them, but they could be bought in Madison, and that was only half a mile away. The price was five cents for a pack of ten, and with each pack the buyer got a small picture of some celebrated actress of that period. Fifty of the pictures—all different—formed a series, and many of the boys strove to accumulate the whole lot.

I remember smoking some of the cigarettes, and after all these years I recall the vileness of the tobacco with which they were made. The smoking was done in secret, of course, not only by me but by all the boys.

At that time many people in Graniteville believed implicitly that young men and boys addicted to cigarette smoking went insane eventually. The wise men of the village declared that they had heard of such cases. Neither my father nor my uncle took any stock in this theory, but they were both opposed to my smoking, and as I was opposed to it myself, I stopped after I had consumed ten cents worth of cigarettes and had pictures of two ladies in stage costumes. My father, who chewed tobacco all his life, said if I had to use tobacco, then "why not chew it like a man instead of sipping at those filthy little cigarettes?" But I was not a chewer, so tobacco did not cut much figure in my young life.

The Bourbons' reputation for retrenchment in government expenditures was nowhere better illustrated than in public education. During Governor Hampton's administration the state spent an average of $2.70 per pupil per school year. By 1890 the amount had been reduced to $2.03. And there was opposition in some quarters to even this paltry amount. This miserly attitude extended to higher education, albeit state appropriations for the University of South Carolina were increased from $12,500 in 1882 to $20,700 in 1885. At that time the university came under heavy attack from two sources: denominational colleges—resentful of the free tuition system at the more prosperous university, and the farmers—demanding improvement in agricultural education.

The friends of the university successfully defended free tuition in the 1885 legislative battle but shortly it appeared that the agrarians and churchmen would combine to overwhelm the partisans of the university. Under the leadership of President John M. McBryde, the university compromised with the denominational colleges and then successfully blunted the farmers' attack until the death of Thomas G. Clemson in April 1888. His will paved the way for a separate agricultural college. During the fray The Citadel also came under fire, for Benjamin R. Tillman, the farmers' leader, wished to abolish that institution.

The following selection is taken from a vivid description by Daniel W. Hollis, official historian of the University of South Carolina.

26

"THE DEFEAT OF THE
SECOND UNIVERSITY, 1885–1890" *

Daniel Walker Hollis

As the summer wore on, the president of the College became more and more disheartened. Eighteen eighty-six was an election year, and the supporters of the church colleges, refusing to admit the permanence of their defeat in the legislature in 1885, made free tuition a major issue of the campaign. The sectarians won a sweeping victory, and R. R. Hemphill, the College's old antagonist from Abbeville, advanced to the senate. To make matters worse, Governor Hugh S. Thompson, a supporter of free tuition, resigned in July to become assistant secretary of the treasury in Grover Cleveland's cabinet, and his successor, Lieutenant Governor John C. Sheppard, was known to be opposed. Weary of the unending struggle, McBryde turned an attentive ear to overtures from the University of Tennessee, which had deeply regretted losing him in 1882. On September 2, he wrote O. P. Temple, chairman of the Tennessee trustees, that the outlook was dark in South Carolina. At the next session of the legislature, the free-tuition privilege would be abolished. "I do not wish to be connected with such a fossilized institution as this will necessarily be," he said. "There is no danger of its being closed, but the State has already a useless military college and will probably have a separate agricultural college. It is ridiculous for a small and impoverished State to attempt three State colleges—all will necessarily be weak." A few weeks later, he accepted Temple's tentative offer of the presidency of the University of Tennessee, pending election by the board of trustees in January, 1887.

Meanwhile, the fight against the South Carolina College continued, and McBryde mustered his energy for another battle in the legislature.

* Excerpts from chapter 7 of *College to University* (*University of South Carolina*, Vol. II) (Columbia: University of South Carolina Press, 1956), pp. 138–45, 148–58; Copyright © 1956 by the University of South Carolina Press. Reprinted without footnotes by permission of the University of South Carolina Press and the author.

Realizing that the College could not continue a war on two fronts, he urged the trustees to compromise with the denominationalists, who at the moment appeared the stronger of its adversaries. Free tuition would have to be given up, but perhaps the College could retain the income from fees—especially for the law school, whose professor must have his salary of $450 a year supplemented. With the church colleges mollified, a firm stand could be taken against Tillman. McBryde's annual report indicated the strategy: stating categorically that there "was no superior virtue in separate colleges of agriculture," he said that the finest work in this kind of education was being accomplished at Cornell and the University of California, both of which had developed technical programs within liberal-arts colleges. Twenty-four of the thirty-eight states taking advantage of the Morrill funds had established agricultural schools as part of their universities. He heaped scorn upon Stephen D. Lee's Mississippi college, which Tillman held up as an example. Such colleges attracted students because their terms of admission were low, because "they advertise, they are liberally supported by the legislature, and make a great show of equipment," and because their manual-labor feature enabled them to offer virtually every matriculate a scholarship paying from $40.00 to $80.00 per session. But the majority of students were "utterly indifferent to the advantages of an agricultural or mechanical education and only anxious to obtain a collegiate education on the cheapest possible terms." McBryde questioned the value of the education provided by grubbing stumps and "pitching manure." His argument was double-barreled: agricultural education at a separate college would be not only inferior, but more expensive. He hoped to wound his opponents with the first blast and annihilate them with the second.

Probably unknown to McBryde, Tillman, who realized that the expense of a separate agricultural college was the weakest link in his armor, was being assured of eventual invulnerability at this point of attack. During the fall of 1886 Clemson called Tillman to Fort Hill; the two men talked over plans for the establishment of a separate agricultural college; and the Edgefield farmer was informed of the terms of Clemson's will. Accounts of the meeting vary, but Tillman must have left with the feeling that in the long run he would be victorious. The conference resulted, says Tillman's biographer, in "a merging of forces in common cause for the sound principle to which both individuals were already converted. Clemson's special contribution was the land and the money; Tillman's, the force of his agitations." It was a potent combination, but one whose full force depended, ironically, on the death of the senior partner. Shortly after Tillman's departure, Clemson rewrote his will, making even more emphatic and specific his intentions for the founding of a State agricultural college at Fort Hill. This time it was not James H. Rion who made the draft, but R. W. Simpson, who had earlier looked forward with pleasure to the day when the walls of the South Carolina College would be torn down and sold for brick.

If McBryde realized, as the legislature assembled, how much depended on the slender thread of an old man's life, he did not show it. In face of a multiple attack by the College's enemies, he "strained every nerve. . . ." As he later wrote, "I lobbied and wire-pulled, which filled me with indignation, for after our great success I could but consider it an insult and degradation to resort to such measures." In rapid succession, Governor Sheppard announced his opposition to free tuition, the sectarians proposed to require the College to charge a fee of $60.00 a year, and the Tillmanites introduced a bill to establish a separate agricultural college, diverting the Morrill funds from the South Carolina College to the new institution. As a means of putting pressure on McBryde to surrender the free-tuition privilege, the denominationalists entered a bill to remove judges from membership on the University board of trustees—retaliation at Justice McIver for his part in the controversy—while the agrarians tempted the president by offering him, in all sincerity, the top administrative position in the proposed new college. Both loyalty and a conviction that the State was too poor to support another institution made McBryde refuse.

The progress of the session showed that the president had judged the strength of his opponents correctly. N. G. Gonzales, reporter for the *News and Courier*, wrote that there was considerable sentiment for the agricultural college, but that there was little chance for it, since there were no funds available. The continuing need for economy prevented the bill from passing. The denominationalists were stronger. Senator B. W. Edwards of Darlington, an alumnus of the College and author of the tuition bill, contended that charging of fees would not really injure the institution, since many students could afford to pay them and any poor boy worth his salt could work his way through school and be all the better for it. "The Senator devoted much time and considerable pathos and eloquence to praise the sweet uses of adversity, and the value of thorns in the flesh as developers of character," Gonzales reported. Supporters of the bill radiated confidence:

"I think we are going to whip you this time," exclaimed Senator James A. Sligh of Newberry.

Finally, as the sectarians and agrarians threatened to join forces to reduce the University appropriation, the friends of the College agreed to compromise. Tuition fees were fixed at $40.00 a year; and an amendment, offered by Senator E. B. Murray of Anderson, allowed the College to remit fees "to such competent and deserving youths of this State as may be unable to pay the same." Except in the case of the law school, income from fees would not go to the College, as McBryde had hoped, but after October, 1887, to the State treasury. Judges were to remain, however, as members of the board of trustees, and the appropriation was increased to $23,000.

Propitiated by the surrender of the College on the free-tuition question, the denominationlists henceforth desisted from further frontal assaults, although from time to time they continued to snipe at the immoral institution in Columbia. McBryde, encouraged by his success in the legislature and learning that the University of Tennessee might be in even more critical danger than the South Carolina College, began to reconsider his decision to depart. On January 14, 1887, he wrote Temple: "I am willing to endure a present ill here to escape a worse there." Nevertheless, the persistent Temple would not accept a refusal, and the passage of the Hatch Act by Congress in February, 1887, brightened the picture at Tennessee. The act provided each state or territory in which an agricultural college had been established under the Morrill Act $15,000 annually for the support of agricultural experiment stations; and Tennessee offered McBryde, at a salary of $5,000, both the presidency of its university and the directorship of its experiment station. Assured that Tennessee was no longer beset by the difficulties he encountered in Columbia, he formally accepted early in April. Submitting on May 4 his resignation (effective September 30, 1887) as president of South Carolina College, he devoted during the ensuing weeks a considerable amount of time to planning a reorganization of the University at Knoxville. News of his resignation aroused consternation in South Carolina, where even Tillman and the agrarians had never attacked him personally; and the University trustees, resolving that his resignation was an "incalculable loss to the College," appointed a special committee of John Bratton, J. C. Haskell, and J. H. Rice to persuade him to remain.

Meanwhile, bad health intervened. In May and June, 1887, McBryde suffered from a protracted illness, aggravated by overwork; and his physician strongly urged him to remain in the State where he was already established. South Carolina would also receive Hatch Act funds, and the *News and Courier* was already advocating that McBryde be made director of the State's experimental station. For these and other reasons, he agreed to stay. . . .

Within ten months the prospects of the College had changed completely. In September, 1886, McBryde had foreseen a "fossilized institution" in the offing. In June, 1887, the trustees, overjoyed at the decision of the president to remain, and with their eyes focused on the Hatch funds, adopted a resolution stating that "the Educational Interests of South Carolina would be . . . promoted by the elevation and expansion of the State University so as to establish and include Colleges of Literature, Law, Agriculture and others complete" and recommended the concentration of all available funds for this purpose.

In the fall of 1887 the State Board of Agriculture appointed McBryde director of the State agricultural experiment station created by the legislature in 1886, and implied that he would also be made director of the station to be established with the Hatch Act funds as soon as the General Assembly passed the necessary legislation. A special meeting of the University trustees was convened to discuss McBryde's acceptance, since the by-laws stipulated that members of the faculty must not engage in other remunerative pursuits. "It should be clearly understood," the president informed the trustees, "that my acceptance commits the University to a policy of determined opposition to the proposed agricultural college and it will be taken as a declaration of war by Mr. Tillman and his allies." It was not too late, he added, to come to terms with Tillman by giving up the Morrill funds and by making no effort to secure the Hatch funds. Otherwise, there would be open and prolonged hostilities. "Should we lose it will be *vae vietis*," he warned. The trustees approved his acceptance, and the die was cast.

Tillman watched with growing anger and frustration, but there was little he could do, so long as he was confronted with the seemingly insoluble problem of raising the $100,000 necessary to finance his college. In a letter to the *News and Courier* he declared that the "long-headed board of trustees intend to keep their grip on the land script fund and name 'agricultural' if they can, so as to fall heir to other national appropriations. . . ." In August, 1887, he compared the College to the dog with the bone in his mouth that waded across a creek, saw his reflection in the water, and lost his bone snapping for another. He warned of impending revolution, if plans for expansion and for securing the Hatch funds were further pursued by the friends of the College: "Don't they know that the masses of the people don't love it anyway, and only need leading to destroy or cripple it badly?"

McBryde and the trustees, long accustomed to such threats, calmly prepared for the fall session of the legislature. General John Bratton wrote a public letter to the *News and Courier* advocating a "centralized unified system" over a "diffused diversified system" of higher education with separate colleges. Colonel John C. Haskell presented the University plan to a farmers' convention, calling their attention to the fact that it included a greatly enlarged agricultural unit; and the *News and Courier*, again changing its mind, on this occasion endorsed the proposal.

The General Assembly was asked for an increase of $13,500 to enable the trustees to create a University, and the annual legislative battle began. Tillman, who was not a member of the Assembly, fought the proposal as effectively as he could from the outside. At his instigation, a Marion County farmers' convention asked their legislators to vote against it, and Tillman announced that he was not afraid "to tackle Colonel Haskell, President McBryde, or anybody else as to the superiority of the separate college over the annex system." The enlarged annex at the University, he said, would be merely "a greater humbug." In the legislature itself, denominational opposition was led by Senator Hemphill, in a struggle that saw the University bill progress inch by inch to final passage. On one occasion, a measure of comic relief was provided by Professor Joynes, who sent Hemphill a beautiful bunch of violets from the College greenhouse. Gonzales reported that the senator, who had never been accused of "extreme devotion to the University scheme," pinned one of the flowers in his lapel and was known for the rest of the day as "a college dude."

The Act of 1887, written largely by McBryde, provided for a University at Columbia with six schools and colleges and permitted the trustees to set up other departments as they might later see fit. The Citadel and the agricultural and mechanical college at Orangeburg remained technically parts of the University, although there was still no coordination among the separate branches. The members of the State board of agriculture (ten in number) were added to the board of trustees as ex officio members. Section 2 of the statute complied with the terms of the Hatch Act and entrusted the funds to the University trustees. The 1887 appropriation of $37,000 was even larger than the amount requested, and the income from tuition fees, about $5,000 per year, was to be retained, instead of being remitted to the State treasurer.

Thus the second University of South Carolina was established. . . .

Tillman was so exasperated by the failure of the legislature in 1887 to establish his agricultural college and by the passage of the University bill that he wrote a "Farewell letter" to the *News and Courier* and retired from the lists. He flayed the University with its "$97,800 income" (here he included not only the total appropriations of the University, The Citadel, and Claflin, but also the Hatch fund, most of which went to the experimental station). Poor farm boys, he wrote, could not afford to attend the South Carolina College, "I beg pardon, University." He drew a devastating comparison between beneficiary cadetships at The Citadel and the work-scholarships at the Mississippi Agricultural and Mechanical College. The people, he warned, would not take much more: "If they submit to such injustice; if they allow the 'military dude factory' to live after this, and the grand 'University' . . . too, I am sadly mistaken." To the triumphant University officials, these statements must have sounded like the sour grumblings of a beaten man. And indeed, Tillman during the months of January and February, 1888, must have felt that Thomas G. Clemson by delaying death so long had cast away the only hope of victory.

Then, early in April, Clemson died, leaving a cash endowment of about $80,000 and his Fort Hill estate of 814 acres to the State of South Carolina for the establishment of a separate agricultural college. Another spectacular reversal of fortune, so typical of the events in the University's history, had taken place. Tillman immediately ended his brief retirement and resumed his crusade. . . .

With the chief obstacle to the separate agricultural college—its initial expense—removed by Clemson's will, Tillman in April, 1888, could see the way clear before him. The first step was to get the State to accept the bequest; the second was to wrest control of the Morrill and Hatch funds from the University. Tillman's opening move came later in the month at a State farmers' convention, which adopted his "Address of the Executive Committee" denouncing the "consummate cunning" with which the University trustees had built up "that wonderful ten-student 'annex'" by robbing the farmers of the land-scrip fund—whereupon they "stretched forth their greedy hand and grabbed the Hatch fund also." In May he carried his standard into the stronghold of his enemies—the State Democratic convention, which met in the State House. Denouncing the convention system, he demanded the nomination of governmental officials by direct primary. "Two years from now when there is a full head on," he warned the conservative delegates who tried to shout him down, "you will be swept before the flood." Referring to the second College and the second University as an example of the "financial extravagances" and "tricky practices" of the existing regime, he declared that the Redeemers had gone back on their pledge of 1879 to establish an agricultural college. The representatives of the farmers in the legislature had been "bamboozled or affected in some way by Columbia water or whisky or by Charleston brains."

Tillman's primary plan was rejected, but his proposal that candidates for office tour the State and appear in public debate was accepted. There was thus ushered into South Carolina political life a distinctive institution that has enabled candidates who, like Tillman, excel in the ability to awaken popular passion and prejudice, to bring hitherto untapped power to their support. Tillman was not a candidate for public office in 1888, but he stumped the State with those of his supporters who were, and made acceptance of the Clemson will a major issue in the campaign. These forensic contests filled a genuine recreational need in South Carolina, whose populace was overwhelmingly rural and liked its religion and politics red-hot. On such occasions farmers rode for miles to assemble at courthouses, churches, or schools for all-day meetings with dinner on the grounds, in eager anticipation of hearing rival candidates belabor each other. It was here that the fate of the institutions of higher education in South Carolina was determined.

In the heated public debates of 1888–1890 the politically aroused farmers tended to mistake prejudice for truth, passion for reason, and invective for documentation. The conservative opponents of Ben Tillman—including such South Carolina College alumni as Wade Hampton, John Peter Richardson, Matthew C. Butler, John Bratton, Alexander and John C. Haskell, and Leroy F. Youmans—were completely outclassed by the Edgefield farmer in appealing to the electorate. On one occasion, when a heckler persisted in asking him questions, Tillman demanded the man's name. The heckler replied that it was Calhoun. "Aw, hell!" exclaimed Tillman, "all the Calhouns I ever heard of who were worth a damn have been dead nearly fifty years!" The Euphradian and Clariosophic societies had not prepared their orators for infighting like this.

The first debate occurred on July 20 at Hodges Depot in Abbeville

County. Tillman repeated the old charge that the board of trustees had engaged in a conspiracy against the agricultural interests of the State. According to Gonzales' report, Tillman said that, in his opinion, "President J. M. McBryde is the man who stood more in his (Tillman's) path than any other. He might do Mr. McBryde an injustice, and some other man might be the 'head devil' of the opposition, but he believed him to be the man." He next directed his withering sarcasm to an issue of the *South Carolina Collegian*, the campus magazine, in which a student essayist had painted an idyllic picture of scholastic life in Columbia. The article described a "typical day" at the College that began with janitors bringing water, shining shoes, and arousing sleepy students for a leisurely breakfast. Tillman contrasted this with life at the Mississippi Agricultural and Mechanical College, where the boys rose at the crack of dawn and put in an arduous day on the farm, in the shops, and at classes. The rural audience roared in delight. The trouble with the University students, he said at Chester on August 1, 1888, is that "they don't sweat none the four years."

The students watched the emergence of the "Agricultural Moses" with dismay. Some of them were sons of well-to-do lawyers and merchants, but the majority were poor; and all resented his labeling them as lazy, pampered aristocrats. One of the more prosperous students, W. W. Ball, later reminisced that at the time he was "boarding at ten dollars a month and getting on handsomely on three hundred and fifty dollars a year, wearing a 'frat' pin and dancing at least one night a week." He added that David F. Houston, a classmate, had "possibly two hundred and fifty dollars a year."

During the 1888 campaign Tillman successfully mustered support for the Clemson bequest, and when the legislature convened in November a bill to accept the provisions of the will passed both houses, in spite of the efforts of such alumni as William H. Brawley and J. C. Haskell, who opposed it to the end. Governor Richardson, however, withheld his signature on the ground that since the will was contested by Clemson's granddaughter, Floride Lee, it would be unwise to commit the State until its legality had been determined. In May, 1889, the will's legality was sustained by a United States Circuit Court, one of whose judges was Charles H. Simonton. A supreme irony in a story full of ironies is that this should be the last appearance of Simonton in the University's history. More than any other one man he had sustained his Alma Mater during its most troubled quarter-century. His personal sense of honor dictated that he should consider only the high principles of law, as he watched the downfall of his beloved University.

In the following November, Governor Richardson signed the bill accepting the Clemson bequest; and forthwith a measure was introduced to establish the Clemson Agricultural College, whose trustees were to become custodians of the Morrill and Hatch funds. Again, University alumni, led by Brawley and Haskell in the house and by Fitz William McMaster in the senate, exerted every effort to defeat the measure. It is worth noting that they were joined by some of their old denominational antagonists. Senator McMaster directed a bitter attack upon Thomas G. Clemson, whom he described as "a poor vanity-stricken, miserable agnostic in Oconee, who desired to perpetuate his name." The establishment of Clemson College, he stated, would destroy the University, and he urged the senate to refrain from pulling down an institution that even Sherman had spared. McMaster went too far, and Senator Buist of Charleston, long a loyal supporter of the University, warned that if McMaster's opinions were typical, the institution would have to be saved from its friends. The measure passed.

Transfer of the Morrill and Hatch funds meant that the agricultural annex at the University would cease to exist in June; but even at this late date, after four years of incessant attack, there was still a possibility that the University, shorn of its agricultural department, might be preserved. This hope disappeared on January 23, 1890, with the appearance of a political philippic known as the Shell Manifesto, a statement by the executive committee of the Farmer's Association of South Carolina signed by its president, but actually written by Tillman. Tillman, disappointed that the legislature had not carried out many other features of his program, had determined to run for governor in order to accomplish his objectives. The Manifesto contained the harshest strictures he had yet leveled against the University. It assailed the "aristocratic coterie who were educated at and sought to monopolize everything for the South Carolina College" and warned the farmers that they could not relax, even though they had secured their college, for the Bourbons would strike back and undo the work of 1888-1889. Senator McMaster, the Manifesto pointed out, had said that he hoped to see "the infernal Clemson College sink out of sight next year."

A farmer's convention met in Columbia on March 27, 1890, and nominated Tillman for governor. Opposing representatives of the rising generation, who more than their elders stood to lose or gain by the outcome of the campaign, were a feature of the occasion. "Four of Orangeburg's plough boys, who was [sic] compelled to leave their native state to attend an institute [Alabama Polytechnic], such as your Patriotic Association has so nobly contended for," were ushered on the stage to present a gavel to President G. W. Shell. A number of University students also attended and exhibited their hostility to Tillman by hissing in the gallery and by following him to his hotel, singing to the tune of "John Brown's Body"—"We'll Hang Ben Tillman on a Sour Apple Tree." Five of Tillman's political lieutenants wrote a public letter to McBryde protesting the actions of this "organized mob." The *News and Courier* did not blame the students, especially in the light of the abuse Tillman had heaped upon them; but the Columbia *Daily Register* predicted that Tillman would inevitably make political capital of the affair.

The *Register* was correct. Shortly thereafter, Tillman charged that fifty University students had ridden to Ridgeway, with faculty endorsement, to heckle him at one of the debates: "That school teaches the aristocratic right that those boys are the inheritors of power. . . . Egged on by the politicians these very boys talked about hanging Ben Tillman to a sour apple tree." "That has given you many a vote," cried one of his stalwarts. The contention of University officials that only five well-behaved students went to Ridgeway was ignored.

Tillman's opponents in the 1890 gubernatorial campaign were General John Bratton of Winnsboro and Joseph H. Earle of Sumter. Bratton was a graduate of the class of 1850, a Confederate brigadier, and a University trustee. He possessed many of the finest qualities of the old regime, but he and his values appeared hopelessly out of date in 1890, and Tillman disposed of him with a withering characterization: "He sees through ante-bellum spectacles. His gaze is toward the grave." Earle, a Furman graduate, was a more effective antagonist and defended the University ably, if to no avail. Although the University was by no means the only issue in the campaign of 1890, it was the most prominent, and the pages of the *News and Courier* are filled with accounts of Tillman's relentless attacks. He won a sweeping victory, and when the State Democratic convention assembled in September, it nominated him for governor. The platform pledged liberal support to the South Carolina College as a classical and literary institution.

When the new legislature convened, it was well understood that the fate of the University was sealed. Although the outgoing governor, John Peter Richardson, asked for its preservation, Tillman in his inaugural address stated that "the people have decided that there is no use for a grand University. . . ." He recommended that its agricultural and mechanical departments be liquidated and the proceeds transferred to Clemson. He did urge, however, that the institution in Columbia be granted $30,000 a year to insure its maintenance as a liberal-arts college. To the surprise of many observers, he did not recommend that The Citadel be closed, although he had repeatedly threatened such action during the years 1885–1890. "There are too few lights in South Carolina," he said, to permit any of them to be put out; but he added that The Citadel would have to show better cause for its continued existence as "a charity school for military training."

The 1890 legislature contained only fifteen alumni of the College—five senators and ten representatives. This was a far cry, indeed, from ante-bellum days. In 1858, for example, there had been at least nineteen alumni senators and fifty alumni representatives. On the day after Wade Hampton was defeated for reelection to the United States Senate, Representative David E. Finley of York introduced Tillman's bill to reorganize the University of South Carolina. The 1890 statute repealed the act of 1887, and the University was divided into three branches. The unit at Columbia was stripped of its mechanical department, graduate school, normal school, and pharmacy school. Agriculture had already been removed by the act of 1889. All agricultural and mechanical equipment at the University was to be sold or transferred to Clemson, and the South Carolina College and The Citadel were directed to confine themselves to theoretical science, law, literature, and the classics. The University trustees were directed to reorganize the Columbia branch in 1891 to conform with these stipulations. The elected members of the board of trustees were increased from seven to nine and were to serve six years instead of four. The number of ex officio trustees was reduced by relieving the members of the State board of agriculture of this duty; but the governor, the justices of the supreme court, the superintendent of education, and the chairmen of the house and senate education committees continued to serve.

Thus the second University ended its brief three-year career. . . .

Undoubtedly, 1890 was the year of disaster for the University. Even more than defeat in the Civil War and occupation by the Radicals, the Tillman revolution undermined the morale of the institution at Columbia. The earlier crises had come from without. They had been overcome with much trial and tribulation; and success, almost as unexpected as it was brilliant, had come with the flowering of McBryde's University. The very height of this success made the fall more devastating, and the chief perpetrator of the deed was a native of the State. Senator McMaster was right; what Sherman had left undone, Tillman did not hesitate to do. In June, 1890, a distinguished Columbia lawyer and former member of the University board of trustees, who had just seen the Edgefield farmer in action, exclaimed in anguish: "In the very presence of Hampton, I have heard this man strike with poisoned tongue at the vitals of our civilization." He spoke for the University and the entire Redeemer regime. To them, Tillman seemed out to destroy everything that they held dear.

Tillman, however, scoffed at the idea of " 'existing institutions' which must remain inviolate . . . the South Carolina University, Citadel. . . . These pets of the aristocracy and its nurseries are only hoping that the people will again sink into their accustomed apathy. . . . South Carolina has never had a real Republican Government. Since the days of the 'Lords Proprietors' it has been an aristocracy under the forms of Democracy. . . ." What did the ordinary man care about the preservation of a system that seemed to ignore him?

And that, when all is said and done, was the weakness of the University. The Redeemers had failed to convince the common man of South Carolina that the institution had anything of value for him. The University—with its weight of history dating back to 1801, its Prestons, Hammonds, and Hamptons, symbolizing the dominant antebellum group—would have to go through many years of humiliation before the descendants of the Tillmanites would turn to it, help it to rise again, and make it their own. In the meantime, they would go to Clemson—as did over four hundred during the very first session that college opened its doors.

Elected governor in 1890, Benjamin R. Tillman ("Pitchfork Ben") served two terms as a colorful chief executive of the state. But despite his bombast, Tillman's program was mainly one of modest educational and tax reform and the establishment of government dispensaries for the sale of liquor. Additionally, he lent his efforts to constitutional disfranchisement of Negroes.

Wade Hampton's departure for the United States Senate in 1879, as noted earlier, had opened the door for increased fraud against Negro voters. The best known device to reduce black votes was the "Eight Box Law" of 1882. This act ostensibly provided a literacy test, for the voter had to choose by label the box for his ballot. Election managers could always instruct illiterates who would vote "right." Through this and other means of fraud and intimidation the Republican vote of 91,870 of 1876 was reduced to 13,740 in 1888. Some white leaders, however, were worried over the moral effect of such encouragement to lawlessness. They wished to find constitutional means of minimizing the Negro vote. It was at this juncture that Tillman captured control of the Democratic Party. The attempt by the Haskellites to use the Negro vote against Tillman in 1890 convinced him too that a constitutional convention was needed to eliminate Negro suffrage in South Carolina. George B. Tindall tells the story in his *South Carolina Negroes, 1877–1900.*

27

"NULLIFICATION OF THE FIFTEENTH AMENDMENT" *

George Brown Tindall

Tillman's influence could not secure the passage of a measure for the calling of a convention during his first term as governor. It was only after the election of 1892 that he had a sufficient stranglehold on the General Assembly to choke out the two-thirds vote necessary for the passage of a joint resolution to provide for a referendum on the calling of a convention. After the resolution was passed in 1892 the issue was dormant until the beginning of the election campaign in 1894, the year in which the popular referendum was scheduled.

The state Democratic executive committee in 1894 played upon emotion and fear by pointing out in a pronouncement to the Democrats that the potential colored voting population of the state was about forty thousand more than the white and that white independents intended to capitalize on it to carry the state in 1896. "Fortunately, the opportunity is offered the white people of the State in the coming election to obviate all future danger, and fortify Anglo-Saxon civilization against every assault from within and without, and that is the calling of a constitutional convention to deal with the all important question of suffrage."

The committee also assured the voters that it was possible to disfranchise the Negroes without denying the vote to any white man and, what was more important, without violating the United States Constitution. It was generally understood that this could best be done by something like the Mississippi Plan, the chief feature of which was a literacy qualification with a property alternative and an "understanding clause."

When Tillman himself was asked what measures were in view for

* Excerpt from chapter 5 of *South Carolina Negroes, 1877–1900* (Columbia: University of South Carolina Press, 1952), pp. 74–89; Copyright 1952 by The University of South Carolina Press. Reprinted without footnotes by permission of the University of South Carolina Press and the author.

accomplishing a limitation of the suffrage, he replied in a statement remarkable for its dictatorial tone:

That's my secret. Let the people of the state . . . trust me. Let them vote for the convention. The time to discuss the method for reducing the Negro majority is after the convention has been called. . . . If the plan then suggested does not meet their approval they can elect men pledged not to incorporate it in the new Constitution.

At the same time he reviewed the horrors of Reconstruction and expressed alarm at the continued tendency of white men, in spite of this memory, to split into factions and appeal to the Negro vote. Not since Reconstruction, he said, had the issue of the Negro vote come so much to the fore, because not since then had the white people been so dangerously divided.

The white opposition to the convention represented no positive movement to protect Negroes in their political rights. But the Republicans quietly permitted the brunt of opposition to be borne by the Conservatives within the Democratic party. The opposition from this group came from a fear of what the Tillman-controlled convention might do, and to some extent a feeling that the suffrage issue was a sleeping dog that might better be let alone.

As the campaign progressed the pressure became so strong that it was obvious to all that the vote on the convention would be extremely close, although the Tillmanites were assured of winning the gubernatorial and senatorial races by comfortable margins. the [*sic*] final official vote in the referendum was 31,402 for and 29,523 against the convention, a slim majority of 1,879. The general picture was one of Low Country opposition and Up Country support, with exceptions in scattered counties.

The leading Conservative papers of the state claimed fraud, the Charleston *News and Courier* headlining the election news, "A Machine Election—White Men Cheat White Men in South Carolina." Four days after the election the same paper carried accounts of fraud charges in Greenville, Darlington, Aiken, Fairfield, Florence, Orangeburg, and other counties. Samson Pope, independent candidate for governor, issued a statement calling upon the people to "remember that a Constitutional Convention has been called through fraud of the blackest character." The Columbia *State* likewise flatly charged fraud and carried reports from many parts of the state to back up its accusations.

The nearest thing to a formal investigation of the charges can be found in testimony on three contested congressional elections held at the same time as the vote on the convention. This approach is unfortunately indirect, but damaging evidence was presented. On the basis of one of these investigations the second district seat was declared vacant on June 1, 1896.

While the Democrats were organizing for the election of convention delegates in August, 1895, there was an unusual degree of political stirring among Negroes and Republicans, greater than had been seen since the stormy days of 1876. On January 4 a call went out for the Republicans to meet in a state convention on February 6, warning that "the very life of suffrage in this State is at stake and other cherished rights and interests are imperiled."

About one hundred delegates, among them twenty-five whites, assembled in Columbia on the day set. Ellery M. Brayton, the party chairman, called upon colored ministers to explain the intricacies of registration to the voters and to encourage them to vote. At the same time he made a direct appeal for fusion with the Conservatives.

The convention stated in its platform that the party was not seeking a return to power but merely the preservation of the citizenship rights of its members. It adopted four planks for the constitution: (1) the document should be submitted to the people; (2) it should make no discrimination against any class of people; (3) it should not reduce taxes for school purposes; and (4) the two major parties should participate in election management. The platform also rehearsed the broken promises of the Democrats in 1876, and the quiet submission of the Republicans to their rule "with docility and faithfulness and hope which must challenge the admiration . . . of the world." It quoted Tillman's charge that white governments up to 1890 had been characterized by "corruption, bribery, political leprosy and imbecility," as well as similar countercharges against the Tillman administrations. "The cries of white supremacy and negro rule," said the platform, "are simply exhausted bugaboos which will frighten no man who thinks, and are used by shallow partisans for purposes of deceit."

Negro ministers at the same time were active on their own initiative. In January a call was issued by twelve Negro ministers for a convention to meet February 14 in Columbia with the objective of securing unhampered citizenship rights at least to the "intelligent" of both races, as well as good government and good schools, but above all "for the purpose of getting the Negroes registered to a man and standing ready to vote for any set of men, regardless of their party name, who are in favor of an honestly managed government and opposed to racial, class or impracticable measures being encouched in the new constitution." The call asserted that the ministers who preach "thou shalt not steal" should see to it that the Negro be not robbed of his right to the franchise. The Democrats were likened to an embezzler who started with small sums and gradually became bolder and bolder. The "sugar-coated pledges made by Hampton" in 1876 had by now been broken and the constitutional convention was to be the climax in the process of robbing the Negro of suffrage.

On January 31, a different group of fifteen to twenty Negroes issued a cleverly designed statement after a meeting in Columbia. They called first for the cooperation of "that class of white men whom we know to be too proud, broad and humane to take advantage of the weak." They admitted that disfranchisement might have been justifiable twenty years before, but held that colored taxpayers now paid five times as much property tax as then and that Negro teachers and professional men compared favorably with the whites. The cry of Negro domination, not the Negro, they said, had brought the state to its bad condition.

Fifty preachers appeared for their scheduled meeting on February 14 at Calvary Baptist Church in Columbia. A state executive committee was chosen and it was proposed to organize Negroes all the way down to ward and precinct levels. In addition, the meeting urged colored citizens to put forth every effort to register and to secure accurate information about the requirements for registration and about the candidates.

Later the Negro Ministerial Union, formed at this meeting, issued an even stronger statement calling upon the national government to intervene and keep a small desperate minority from trampling constitutional rights underfoot.

Meanwhile, the Beaufort *New South*, edited by S. J. Bampfield, son-in-law of Robert Smalls, reminded readers that "unless some prompt action is taken these white supremacy howlers . . . will succeed in fastening upon the people an oligarchy of fraud that will keep the machine in power and the honest people of the State under their heels for the next half century." "There is clearly a conspiracy against the purity of the ballot box," it warned, "and a determination to continue the system of fraudulent elections that have disgraced South Carolina for so many years and brought reproach upon the people of the State. Indeed there is no longer even an attempt to disguise it. . . ."

During March the Negro Congressman, George W. Murray, set forth on a tour "to canvass the state and educate and arouse our people up to a realization of the situation and what they can do to help themselves." There is evidence that he was well received, being heard by mixed audiences of whites and Negroes in some towns. Murray himself reported "splendid success" and asked a friend in Washington to secure contributions to help in the campaign "to break the chains which are forged and are being forged for all colored Carolinians" by bringing suit against the registration act.

An anomaly in the campaign was the one substantial white citizen, Colonel John J. Dargan, editor of the Sumter *Freeman* and a Red Shirt leader in 1876, who raised his voice in support of the political rights of Negroes. He ran in Sumter as an independent candidate for the convention and in a speech in the courthouse at Columbia proclaimed that he was "not fighting for white supremacy, but for the supremacy of right and justice, first, last, and all the time." He pointed to Georgetown as the most encouraging example of interracial cooperation in the state, where the offices were divided between whites and Negroes. "If we try this in South Carolina," he said, "it will cure the disease of the State."

Later in the campaign, Dargan, with more courage than caution, invaded the bailiwick of Tillman. A committee, led by the county sheriff, informed him that he would not be permitted to speak in Edgefield, and in the streets he was surrounded by an angry mob that attempted to provoke him by insults into striking the first blow. Dargan managed to make the first train out of town before any violence occurred. The following week, admitting that he had been wrong in stirring up Edgefield unnecessarily, he wrote the Charleston *News and Courier* that he was nevertheless

more than ever . . . impelled to go forward with my missionary work, proclaiming; Prepare ye the way for a higher and better civilization; a civilization of liberty, equality, and justice for all; justice and equality under the law, and freedom of thought and speech.

That was the last heard from Dargan in the campaign.

During the brief period of registration for the election of delegates a statement was presented to Governor John Gary Evans by a committee with George W. Murray as chairman in which it was complained that "not more than 10,000 electors were registered within the entire state and . . . many more than 100,000 after unparalleled exposure, suffering, and sacrifices remain unregistered and disfranchised." A special session of the legislature was proposed to provide additional periods for registration. Evans naturally was not disposed to lend an ear to any plea for more registration.

In May the Democratic state committee ordered that a primary be held in each county to select party candidates for delegates. Candidates were required to file at least ten days in advance a pledge to honor the results of the primary. The possibility of independent revolt was effectively squelched by this means, although a number of Conservatives, including Wade Hampton, advised their followers to stay out of the primary.

Hampton's statement came in a letter from Washington to the editor of the Spartanburg *Herald*. It would carry little weight in all probability, he admitted in a tone of injured pride, but added,

> . . . I have no fear of Negro domination—a cry used only to arouse race prejudice and to put the incoming convention under control of the Ring which now dominates our State. The negroes have acted of late with rare moderation and liberality, and if we meet them in the same spirit they have shown, they will aid in selecting good representatives for the convention.
>
> I for one am willing to trust them, and they ask only the rights guaranteed to them by the constitution of the United States and that of our own State. "Corruption wins not more than honesty," and I advocate perfect honesty, for defeat on that line is better than victory by fraud.

A meeting of Conservatives in Columbia also advised the people to stay out of the primary and perfect an independent organization. The group included Edward McCrady, A. B. Williams, and N. G. Gonzales. Its influence in the end was nil, not one county outside Charleston sending a solidly Conservative delegation and that group elected on the Democratic ticket.

The primary on July 30, as had been expected, resulted in a sizable victory for the Tillman forces. Membership was settled finally in the general election which left the count of delegates 112 Tillmanites, 42 Conservatives, 6 Republicans. All of the Republicans were Negroes, one coming from Georgetown on a fusion ticket and the other five from Beaufort on a straight Republican ticket.

The dominant figure of the convention was Ben Tillman, who more than any other one person was responsible for the calling of the convention and for the form which the new constitution took. Other important white delegates were John Gary Evans, John Laurens

Manning Irby, George Dionysius Tillman, and John Pendleton Kennedy Bryan.

The six Negro delegates were Robert Smalls, Thomas E. Miller, William J. Whipper, James Wigg, and Isaiah R. Reed, from Beaufort; and Robert B. Anderson, from Georgetown. . . .

Since the major objective of the convention was disfranchisement, the most important standing committee of the convention was the Committee on the Rights of Suffrage, which was appointed on the second day with eight Tillmanite and three Conservative members. Ben Tillman was appointed chairman.

The suffrage article proposed by this committee forced each voter to run the gauntlet of numerous suffrage restrictions. First, it provided suffrage for male citizens who could meet the qualifications of age, residence in the state two years, county one year, precinct four months, and payment of the poll tax at least six months before the elections. These were calculated to eliminate many Negroes because of their migratory habits and to disfranchise them in November for not paying their poll taxes in May, a time when ready cash was least available to farmers. But the chief trap was the literacy test, a requirement that each registrant prove to the satisfaction of the board that he could read and write any section of the Constitution. There were two alternatives to the literacy requirement: ownership of taxable property assessed at $300 or more, or ability to "understand" the constitution when it was read aloud. The latter provision was the only permanent registration, but voters were required to qualify under it before January 1, 1898. The other registrants had to renew their registration every ten years. The final obstacle between the prospective voter and the ballot box was to be the local election manager, who was to require of every elector proof of the payment of all taxes assessed against him the previous year.

Additional measures against the Negro vote were provided by a list of disfranchising crimes, including those supposed by the whites to be most frequently committed by Negroes and also those of the most heinous nature. Others disfranchised were idiots, the insane, paupers supported at public expense, and persons in prison.

Two provisions of the committee report did not find their way into the final draft despite Tillman's plea for them. One granted a right of appeal to "any court" when one was denied registration. This was changed to a right of appeal to the Circuit Court of Appeals only. The other defeated proviso was for minority representation on registration and election boards. Tillman tried to re-incorporate the proviso, making an earnest plea that the nation was watching South Carolina to see if she were willing to make adequate safeguards against fraud. The suffrage committee, he said, unanimously favored the principle of minority representation, but the convention voted it down by 74 to 51.

Discussion of the suffrage provisions for the new constitution brought eloquent speeches from the Negroes for the preservation of unrestricted suffrage. Miller, who made the first speech, reviewed the history of Negroes in America, citing the martyrdom of Crispus Attucks and favorable comments by Charles Pinckney and Henry Laurens as character evidence for the race. Negroes were not aliens, he reminded the delegates, any more than Caucasians. "A residence of our foreparents of near 300 years; birth and rearage here; our adaptation to the wants of the country; our labor and forebearance; our loyalty to the government—are all these elements indices of an alien race?" He made an adroit appeal to those who feared the disfranchisement of the poor whites, quoting remarks by J. L. M. Irby that the $300 property qualification would not be a sufficient alternative for those who were poor as well as illiterate. This point he illustrated with a story about a boy, exploring the banks of the Salkahatchie River, who chanced upon a moccasin and catfish trying to swallow each other. The moccasin was successful in getting the catfish down, but his fins cut the moccasin's throat. The moccasin personified the Tillmanites, he said, and the catfish represented the Conservatives who were achieving their objective of disfranchising the poor whites. Twitting the votaries of the Lost Cause tradition he said:

The majority of you blame the poor Negro for the humility inflicted upon you during that conflict, but he had nothing to do with it. It was your love of power and your supreme arrogance that brought it upon yourselves. You are too feeble to settle up with government for that grudge. This hatred has been centered on the Negro and he is the innocent sufferer of your spleen.

Wigg renewed the appeal for a straight literacy qualification, indicating that an additional or alternative property qualification would be acceptable.

You charge that the Negro is too ignorant to be entrusted with the suffrage. I answer that you have not, nor dare you, make a purely educational test of the right to vote. You say that he is a figurehead and an encumbrance

to the State, that he pays little or no taxes. I answer that you have not
and you dare not make a purely property test of the right to vote.

He bluntly attacked the doctrine of white supremacy with the
argument that it was sheer fallacy. Every white delegate, he said, had
been pledged to the false doctrine of white supremacy, to the securing
of it by either honest or dishonest methods. "Beneath this yoke,
humiliating as it is, each one of you had to pass; to this pledge each
one of you had to subscribe before you could have the privilege of
being counted as a delegate to this convention."

The following day Smalls and Whipper were heard. Smalls charged
fraud in the committee's suffrage article. The suffrage plan, he said,
might fool "the crackers" but no one else as to its essentially fraudulent nature. He dared Tillman to accept a straight literacy qualification which would leave a white majority of fourteen thousand in the
electorate. Appealing to the white desire for cheap farm labor, he
warned that the Negroes might leave the state if things became too
hard for them.

Whipper devoted the first part of his remarks to the denial that
Negro government had ever existed in South Carolina, pointing out
that Beaufort County offered an example of Negro willingness to accept white officeholders even where they outnumbered the whites by
twenty to one. He charged bodies like the convention with inciting the
crime of lynching and derided white supremacists for trying to show
their superiority by defrauding old slaves.

Pleas by the lesser known and less experienced Reed and Anderson
were presented on October 29. Reed deplored the unfair administration of justice to the Negroes, but held that Negroes were perfectly
willing to let the "intelligent" rule, many having in fact voted for
Wade Hampton, Johnson Hagood, and even B. R. Tillman for governor. In conciliatory tone he reminded the whites that they trusted
Negroes in many vocations. "You have suffered the negroes to harness
. . . your costly steeds; you have suffered them to serve the delicacies
of your festal boards; in short, you have suffered them to attend many
other vocations of life which come nearer to your honor, nearer to
your person and nearer to your property than casting a ballot."

Anderson, the school teacher, pointed with pride to the great strides
of progress made by Negroes in the past thirty years and pleaded that
he was asking for the suffrage on behalf of 100,000 patriotic citizens.
". . . I am constrained to raise my voice in protest against the passage by this convention of the political scheme . . . proposed by the

committee on suffrage. A scheme that will forever rivet the chain of disfranchisement upon the colored people of South Carolina. A scheme that was conceived in equity [iniquity?] and born in sin."

Senator J. L. M. Irby, "the poor man's friend," followed the Negroes two days later with a presentation of his objections to the suffrage scheme. Formerly an ardent Tillmanite and still chairman of the Democratic state committee, he predicted bloodshed if illiterate whites were disfranchised while educated Negroes were permitted to vote. The suffrage article, he said, "builds bombproofs and fortifications for the educated and property owning class . . . while it leaves the poor white man to risk and endure the tests of a hostile court." The understanding clause in his opinion was unconstitutional and would give the ballot to the illiterates only until it came to a test in the federal courts.

Such telling blows had been landed by the Negroes that Tillman felt the necessity for delivering a full dress reply with his one eye cocked to the national audience. He was prepared on October 31 and delivered his speech immediately after Irby's. Most of the speech was concerned with the swindles of Reconstruction days and especially with the taint of fraud that hung about the reputations of Smalls and Whipper. His objective was to answer Whipper's contention that there had never been "Negro government" by proving the responsibility of the Negro race for corruption under radical administrations. The radical constitution, made by the "ring streaked and striped carpetbagger convention," had been ratified by Negroes and Negroes had "put the little pieces of paper in the box that gave the commission to white scoundrels who were their leaders and the men who debauched them. . . ."

The difficulty of his task Tillman recognized and confessed, when the question of the poor whites arose, "If there was any way under high heaven by which we could do more than we have done, in God's name I would glory and honor the man, and bow down and submit to his leadership if he could show us."

As for the methods to be used by registration boards, he said in reply to a query by Irby:

I said last night that the chalice was poisoned. Some have said there is fraud in this understanding clause. Some poisons in small doses are very salutary and valuable medicines. If you put it here that a man must understand, and you vest the right to judge whether he understands in an officer, it is a constitutional act. That officer is responsible to his conscience and his God, he is responsible to nobody else. There is no particle of fraud or illegality in it. It is just showing partiality, perhaps, (laughter) or discriminating. . . .

After the Tillman speech Smalls made a denial of his connection with any of the frauds charged against him. The whole matter had been dragged into the debate "to inflame the passions of delegates against Republicans and force them to vote for this most infamous Suffrage Bill, which seeks to take away the right to vote from two-thirds of the qualified voters of the State." Concluding passionately, he proclaimed that his race needed no special defense.

All they need is an equal chance in the battle of life. I am proud of them, and by their acts toward me, I know that they are not ashamed of me, for they have at all times honored me with their vote.
I stand here the equal of any man. I started out in the war with the Confederates; they threatened to punish me and I left them. I went to the Union army. I fought in seventeen battles to make glorious and perpetuate the flag that some of you trampled under your feet.

Thomas E. Miller, against whom no fraud was intimated, made the point in reply to Sheppard and Tillman that the corruption of one Negro could not be the valid basis for generalization against the race any more than Boss Tweed or T. J. Mackey could be for the entire white race. Tillman's emphasis was laid on fraud in the period 1869–1873 when the Negro was still innocent and incompetent, he claimed. The Negroes began to clean out the corruption in the period of 1873–1876 after they had become more experienced. They had started the investigations and repudiations of bonds that had been continued by the Democratic administrations.

William Henderson of Berkeley, exasperated at the talk by the Negroes and Conservatives of the need for fair elections and perhaps confused by Tillman's irony about "showing partiality," declared frankly:

We don't propose to have any fair elections. We will get left at that every time. (Laughter) Who will be the managers? Won't they be Democrats and Republicans, and don't you see that will be a bar to the Democrats? I tell you, gentlemen, if we have fair elections in Berkeley we can't carry it. (Laughter) There's no use to talk about it. The black man is learning to read faster than the white man. And if he comes up and can read you have got to let him vote. Now are you going to throw it out (Laughter).
. . . We are perfectly disgusted with hearing so much about fair elections.

Talk all around, but make it fair and you'll see what'll happen. (Laughter)

Late on November first the suffrage article passed the second reading by 69–37 with only eight Conservatives voting against it. After the elimination of the provisions for minority representation on the boards of registration and for appeal to any court, the measure passed the third reading by 77–41.

The final vote on ratification of the constitution as a whole came on the afternoon of December 4. The convention, with thirty-four delegates absent, voted 116 to 7 for the new constitution. Only two white conservatives joined the five Negroes present in voting against it. Despite two motions by Thomas E. Miller to have the constitution submitted to the people for ratification, the document was promulgated to become effective on January 1, 1896.

The most important factors in the disfranchising arrangements were the restrictions hedging registration. These were utilized quite freely by registration officials and were not put to any serious test by Negro citizens, more impressed than ever with the futility of attempting to vote. In October, 1896, it was reported that 50,000 whites and only 5,500 Negroes had registered in the state. Only Georgetown County had a majority of Negroes registered, and there it was only a majority of 861–814, which was wiped out in subsequent years. A resident of Beaufort County reported in 1903 that although literate male Negroes in that county outnumbered the white voters by 3,434 to 927, ". . . registration officials do not allow registered Negro voters to outnumber the whites."

Tillman stated on the floor of the Senate in 1900 that there were about 114,000 registered voters, of whom 14,000 were Negro. Later he told the Senate, "We of the South have never recognized the right of the negro to govern white men, and we never will." James H. Tillman, Ben's nephew, stated in his 1900 campaign for lieutenant-governor, "It is no crime for a supervisor of registration to deny a negro a certificate. . . ."

Some doubt has been expressed by students of the state's history as to the importance of the Constitution of 1895 in disfranchising Negroes. Figures on the decline of the Republican vote would indicate that disfranchisement already had been substantially accomplished. The psychological impact of the convention and the provision for a new registration may have been important in accelerating the existing trend, but the chief instruments of disfranchisement were still what they had been before the convention—intimidation, violence and fraud. In the face of the Fifteenth Amendment this was the only means of securing white majorities in those few areas where literate Negroes outnumbered literate whites. Fraud was still practiced in the count, too. Nearly a decade after the turn of the century a Charlestonian told a traveller of an election in which he and other Negroes cast Republican ballots, but the result as announced showed not a single Republican vote.

The Democratic primary, which was first held on a direct state-wide basis in 1896, soon became the real election. It has already been indicated that the Tillmanites had inaugurated in 1890 a rule that no Negro should vote in the Democratic primaries unless he had voted Democratic in 1876 and ever since. The quiet establishment of the statewide white primary served to bulwark more strongly than the Constitution of 1895 the achievement of disfranchisement. Already eliminated from any prospect of influencing general elections, Negroes were thus eliminated completely from the only election that had any real meaning.

At the end of the nineteenth century cotton was firmly entrenched as South Carolina's number one crop—but not a profitable one. Prices were low and tenancy was high. Tobacco growing was still in its infancy, whereas rice was rapidly vanishing. The most important economic change was in the growth of the textile industry. The revolution in cotton manufacturing was shortly accelerated by a revolution in the production of electric power. Dr. Walker Gill Wylie furnished the idea and tobacco tycoon James B. Duke the money.

Henry Savage, Jr., one-time mayor of Camden, recounts the story in his *River of the Carolinas: The Santee.*

28

THE REVOLUTION IN ELECTRIC POWER *

Henry Savage, Jr.

One of "Buck" Duke's feet, already famous for their outlandish size, was giving him a lot of trouble in the late summer of 1904; so much so that by early fall the restless, aggressive tobacco magnate was forced to call in a doctor to treat it. From his humble origin on a small tobacco farm in the hills of central North Carolina, red-haired, raw-boned, fifty-eight–year–old James Buchanan Duke had come a long way. By dint of ceaseless work, a boundless thirst for power, an uncanny ability to seize opportunities before others saw them, all coupled with an ample share of the ruthlessness of the day, he had already become the tobacco tycoon of the world, counting his riches in hundreds of millions—when, to his disgust, his sore foot began seriously to hamper his activities.

The doctor he summoned to treat his foot was another transplanted Carolinian, who in his profession had also achieved great fame. The amazingly versatile Dr. Walker Gill Wylie in 1904 enjoyed an international reputation in the fields of surgery, gynecology, and hospital design. Since treating sore feet, erysipelas as it turned out, was not among the doctor's specialties, it is likely that he was Duke's choice because they were both of that numerous group of Carolinians who had physically transplanted themselves from the "tight-belt" post-war economy of their native section to the greener fields of New York but had never succeeded in entirely moving their hearts from the farms of their boyhood. Be that as it may, it is certain that when Dr. Wylie called on Duke, although both men had long been nominally New Yorkers, both were still essentially Carolinians with plans to return "home."

* Excerpt from *River of the Carolinas: The Santee* (Chapel Hill: University of North Carolina Press, 1968), pp. 346–56; Text © 1956 and 1968 by Henry Savage, Jr. Reprinted by permission of The University of North Carolina Press and the author.

So it was natural that when the doctor came to Duke's house day after day to change the dressings on the ailing foot much of their conversation carried them back to their Carolina hills. It was also natural that they talked of another common interest. Both men as a hobby were experimenting with the possibilities of using water power to generate electricity. Duke had built a small hydroelectric plant to light the buildings of his country estate on the Raritan River in New Jersey. Dr. Wylie had employed a young engineer, William States Lee, a kinsman of his who lived in Lancaster, across the Catawba from the doctor's home in Chester, South Carolina, to build a small hydroelectric plant on his plantation. He told Duke of Lee's boundless enthusiasm for the possibilities of hydroelectric power. George Westinghouse and Nikola Tesla, a few years before, had demonstrated the possibility of transporting electricity over long distances by stepping the voltage up very high, so in the future the plants consuming the hydroelectric power would not have to be located at the powerhouse. The limitless opportunities offered by this discovery had been quickly grasped by Lee. With enthusiasm he had told Dr. Wylie of a future day when up and down the whole Catawba-Wateree there would be a series of great dams with their powerhouses all linked together by high tension lines, with other lines carrying the power to factories and towns all over the Carolina Piedmont. Duke was fascinated by the doctor's account of his kinsman's dreams. This sort of thing was just his meat—building on an imperial scale. His reaction was immediate: "Get that young fellow up here."

A few days later Lee returned to South Carolina with two checks, each for $50,000—one from Dr. Wylie and one from Duke—to purchase the site for the Wateree Dam near Camden. He had also a verbal promise from Duke of all the millions necessary to develop the Catawba-Wateree from the mountains to the fall line. Thus was born the Southern Power Company, the world's pioneer major hydroelectric, superpower system, which in the next two decades transformed the turbulent Catawba-Wateree into the country's most highly developed major power river, a distinction it would carry for years—until the free flow of government money and the Tennessee combined to give that river the crown.

Arrangements were soon made to take over the languishing small-scale development at Catawba, near Rock Hill, and a little later construction was begun on a dam to provide a seventy-one–foot head at Great Falls. Before the latter was completed, a dam to create a fifty-eight–foot head at Rocky Creek was under way. Others undertaken in that first busy decade of the mammoth plan were the seventy-eight–foot project at Lookout Shoals east of Hickory, a sixty-eight–foot one at Fishing Creek below the old Catawba project, a seventy-two–foot one at Wateree near Camden, and the hundred-thirty-five–foot one up against the mountains near Morganton. At this last site a great lake of extraordinary beauty, then known as Bridgewater but later called Lake James, was created by three towering dams, one across the Catawba River, another across Paddy Creek, and the third across the Linville River where the powerhouse was located. By 1926 the harnessing of the Catawba-Wateree was completed (except for one potentital [sic] site above the Mountain Island Reservoir which remains undeveloped) by the addition of a seventy-eight–foot project at Mountain Island near Charlotte, and seventy-one–foot one at Dearborn near Great Falls, a sixty-foot–one at Rhodhiss, northwest of Hickory, an enlarged seventy-foot dam at the original Catawba site, an additional 45,000 KW powerhouse on the Cedar Creek side of the Rocky Creek dam, and a ninety-foot dam at Oxford above the Lookout Shoals project. The combined heads of all these projects utilized 768 of the 1,051 feet which the river falls in its course from the headwaters of Lake James to the tailrace at Wateree. The chain of lakes created by these dams transformed more than 140 of the once turbulent 215 miles between these points into quiet hill-girt lakes, individually varying in length from a few miles to more than twenty-five for the larger ones.

Meanwhile to the westward on the Broad at 99 Islands, a seventy-five–foot dam had been built and incorporated into the system.

The combined generating capacity of the completed hydro system was a whopping (by the standards of the day) 460,000 KW. Almost from the beginning the company had been confronted with the problem of getting customers for the power it had for sale, a problem which kept growing in magnitude as each new generating plant was completed. Duke himself substantially assisted in solving this problem by building electrically driven cotton mills near several of the hydro installations, and by engaging in a widespread pump priming in the form of financial assistance to and investment in many others in return for contracts to use his electric power. His activities in that field provided a substantial added impetus to the already rapidly growing textile industry of the Carolina Piedmont. Widespread extensions of the high tension transmission lines fully solved the customer problem so that by 1925 when the last of the dams was completed there were customers waiting for its power.

That same year there came a record-breaking drought and a drastic shrinkage in the flow of the river. In an effort to meet the customers' power demands, the water level in the chain of reservoirs kept dropping lower and lower until thousands of acres of sun-baked, stump-studded mud surrounded the diminished reservoirs, and a lesson was emphatically driven home to those who had placed too much reliance on nature's staying "normal" over an extensive period: That without reservoirs of impractical hugeness rivers cannot be relied upon to produce a steady "normal" supply of power. The drought had demonstrated that, to produce a dependable supply of power, auxiliary generating plants would have to be added to the system. Although the company had at the time two small steam generating plants, the unified system of mutally supplementing steam and hydro plants of today's system was born of the 1925 drought. Larger steam generating plants were soon under construction to bear the load in times of low water. By 1930 a fourth of the power sold was produced in steam plants.

In recent years with the coming of accelerated prosperity and rapid industrial expansion in the Carolinas the demand for electric power has multiplied phenomenally. Since the power output of an already harnessed river does not grow, all the added generating capacity necessarily was provided by steam power plants. By 1953 but a ninth of the power produced came from the hydro installations. They had become the auxiliaries of a gigantic steam generating system. Now any one of four of the steam plants of the company produces more power than all the eleven great dams of the hydro system. Although the water-power system is now but a relatively small auxiliary to a great steam-electric system, it is still essential for the production of electricity at a minimum of cost. Water power is capable of almost instantly answering a call to inject additional power into the transmission system. The operator has but to open the gate to start the turbine which turns the generator at full speed almost immediately. On the other hand it requires nine hours and an enormous consumption of fuel to heat a boiler of a modern steam plant before it can operate at all, for the steam has to first be heated to 950 degrees. So water power facilely and economically takes care of the above-normal fluctuations in the power demands made upon the system such as occur during those hours when housewives are cooking and ironing and the factories are at the same time making their top demands for power.

Similar efficient, dovetailing dual generation systems utilize other parts of the Santee system. Involving other rivers and other power companies, these systems, all connected and dovetailed, are in operation all over the Carolinas.

With the final evolution of the dual hydro and steam system came great changes along the river. As long as water was the primary source of the required power, the reservoirs were called upon to supply that water even when the river flow was insufficient to replace the demand. The lake levels then rapidly fell, exposing the sediment clay so that the slightest wave action against that mud soon reddened the entire lake expanse. The turbid waters and the repeated exposure of their breeding beds made fish life almost nonexistent. In spite of the attractive surroundings of all those reservoirs, few people were attracted to them. Now, with a full or almost full head of water being carefully maintained [so] that the maximum power may be obtained during the relatively few hours of peak demand, the reservoirs stay filled. Except in times of flood they are beautiful clear green lakes, meccas for tens of thousands of fishermen. On sites liberally leased by the power company, thousands of summer cottages have suddenly dotted their shore lines. Now, all over Carolina, boat and trailer rival television antennae in their ubiquity.

However, the river yet remains an essential ingredient of the region's electric-power system—even of the now primary steam generating plants. The steam plants themselves are tied to the river they invariably stand beside, for they require enormous quantities of water for their operation. A large modern steam plant, such as the Lee Station on the Saluda, Cliffside on the Broad or Riverbend on the Catawba, uses daily for cooling its steam condensers about the same amount of water required by a city of two million people.

There is one more episode in the story that started with Mr. Duke's sore foot. In 1924, shortly before his death, he set up the Duke Endowment Fund, starting it with $40,000,000 in assets—much of which was stock in the power company, which had by then become the Duke Power Company. Consequently most of the profits of that momentous involvement of an industrialist, a doctor, a young engineer and a river flow back to their fellow Carolinians in the form of charitable and educational works in the two states.

The hydroelectric story of the Santee only begins with that of the Wateree-Catawba tributary. Even the Broad, the least developed of the Santee tributaries, has its notable installations. In the Blue Ridge is the three hundred-foot dam across the Green River which creates

Lake Summit and on the Broad itself is one hundred-foot deep Lake Lure at the mouth of spectacular Hickory Nut Gorge. Below these on the Broad and its tributaries, the Second Broad, the Pacolet, the Tyger and the Enoree are the 99 Islands and Parr Shoals projects and some eighteen more installations, most of them supplying the power for a single cotton mill.

In point of time the story of the hydroelectric development of the Santee system should have begun with the Saluda, for far up that tributary, at Pelzer, stands the first dam to generate electricity for transmission elsewhere for use. In 1882 a group of Charlestonians had built a water-powered cotton mill in an all but unpopulated spot near Wilson's Bridge. The venture prospered greatly and kept expanding. A dozen years after the first plant was opened the fourth and largest unit was being planned. Its power was to be furnished by a damsite about three miles below the existing mills and village. Up to that time it had always been necessary to set the mills close by the power supply. Since the Pelzer officials very much desired to locate their new plant alongside their village, the best electric power talents of the country, among them being Charles Steinmetz, were called on for a solution to the problem. In 1895, the same year that Westinghouse was demonstrating the feasibility of cross-country transmission of electricity, the new fifty-five–thousand–spindle, electrically operated mill was built several miles from its powerhouse, a feat made possible, in the absence of step-up transformers, by directly generating high voltage current. So in 1895 on the banks of the Saluda stood the world's largest electrically operated cotton mill, receiving its hydroelectric power from one of the first, if not the first, cross-country industrial electric-transmission lines.

A score of miles downstream from Pelzer begins the twenty-five-mile long reservoir of Lake Greenwood, the "Buzzards' Roost" development of Greenwood County.

Below Lake Greenwood is the Dreher Shoals development of the Lexington Water Power Company. Here the mile-and-a-half-long, 211-foot-high Saluda Dam, having a base 1,100 feet thick and covering 100 acres, is one of the largest earthen dams in the world. It impounds the Saluda to form Lake Murray, one of the world's largest power lakes, covering 50,000 acres and having a shore line of more than 500 miles. Its 175,000 horsepower plant more than doubles the capacity of any other hydroelectric installation on any of the Santee tributaries.

All these power developments add up to a bountiful supply of electricity in the Carolinas with rates substantially below the national average. Consequently Carolinians, although they are still near the bottom in per capita wealth, regularly use in their homes half again as much electricity as does the average American—an intimate factor and boon in everyday living in which Santee waters have played a major role.

The Constitution of 1895 called for a re-organization of South Carolina public school districts and for additional financial support. The state thereafter slowly pumped more money into the system. And beginning in 1907 the legislature provided for state support to public high schools. Seemingly, nearly every community hurriedly set up a high school—over 100 within a year.

The state high school inspector until 1919 was Prof. William H. Hand, of the Department of Education, University of South Carolina. He seriously went about his duties as inspector, and his highly critical and sometimes caustic annual reports clearly revealed the inadequacies of the new program. Hand was also unsparing of his criticism of the South Carolina colleges—too many, too poor, too mediocre.

The selections below are taken from his report of 1910, an inauspicious year, for Cole Blease, no friend to public education, had just been elected governor. However, Hand's annual "blasts" undoubtedly were responsible in some measure for the pronounced improvement in the quality of South Carolina education after World War I. Looking back from the vantage of 1970, the high schools were indeed in a "sad state" in 1910.

29

THE SAD STATE OF
THE HIGH SCHOOLS IN 1910 *

[William H. Hand]

Inexperienced Principals. Some successful experience is demanded in undertaking the management of everything—but a school. To put a wholly inexperienced teacher at the head of a school is hazardous and may be ruinous. To put a principal without a day's experience in a schoolroom in charge of from three to ten assistants, as is frequently done, is to invite disaster to both the school and the principal. This raw recruit is often put in charge of the work of assistants who know more of teaching and school management than this novice will know when he is ready to leave the schoolroom for some other vocation. The inconsistency of the thing becomes the more glaring when he is paid twice the salary of his most experienced and successful assistant. Here are two instances for illustration: A school board put at the head of its school with ten teachers and 350 pupils, a young man who had been graduated from college in June prior to taking charge of the school in September. Another board put a June graduate in charge of 5 teachers and 175 pupils. Two of his assistants had had more than ten years' experience.

Some of the blame for this playing with fate rests upon over-zealous and indiscreet college presidents and professors who recklessly recommend their raw graduates for these positions. Some of their letters of recommendation have fallen into my hands, and it is hard to understand how men, with a proper sense of their responsibility, can give such endorsements to wholly untried men for positions so responsible. In bold contrast stand other college professors who absolutely refuse to recommend any inexperienced young graduate to any but subordinate positions. May their tribe increase!

* Excerpts from the *Forty-Second Annual Report of the State Superintendent of Education of the State of South Carolina, 1910* (Columbia: Gonzales and Bryan, 1911), pp. 135–39, 141–46, 147–50.

Change of Principals.—No school can be developed or be of much permanent service to a community so long as it changes principals every year or so. Of the 162 high schools here reported, 58 had one high school teacher, or one teacher and part time of a second teacher, while 104 schools had two or more high school teachers. Of the one-teacher schools, 27 changed principals at the end of the year, and of the two-teacher schools and more, 49 changed principals at the end of the year. Usually the smaller the school the more frequent the changes in the teaching force. This fact alone is a strong argument for the consolidation of little weak schools of whatever grade.

A change of principals usually involves a change of organization and policy in the school. The changes are not necessarily improvements. The new principal often lays all the shortcomings of his school to the bad organization of his predecessor, forgetting that his successor is doing the same thing somewhere else.

The High School Teaching Force.— . . . Certainly the time has come for requiring of a high school teacher something more than the ability to get a first grade teachers' certificate issued by a county board of education under our present law. Certificates issued on the diplomas of low-grade colleges promise little more. While we have some excellent high school teachers—some as good as can be found anywhere, we have others who are wholly incompetent to teach the subjects they attempt. Under a regulation of your Board, your inspector has within the past four years quietly notified several high school boards that no more State money would be given with certain teachers retained in these schools. In each case the teacher was quietly dropped at the end of that year, and in several instances the same teacher dropped from one school would be employed in another school the next year.

I feel safe in saying that the poorest teaching in the high schools of this State is that in the subject of English. It has the least definite aim and organized purpose in it. Next comes Latin, and the root of the whole matter is that men and women who know no Latin are attempting to teach it. Latin is attempted in every high school in the State, and it is attempted in many of the little rural schools with but one teacher, yet there is absolutely no examination of the teachers' fitness to teach it. In many of the schools history is either a grind in unfamiliar names and meaningless dates, or it is a line for line repetition of some textbook. These remarks naturally lead to the consideration of the certification of teachers.

Certification of Teachers.—Acting under instructions from this Board, I have made some investigation as to the certification of teachers. I am loath to criticize public officials, many of whom I count among my best personal friends. Besides, it is ungrateful to criticize an official whose duties are somewhat onerous and whose remuneration is contemptible, as is the case with the county superintendent of education in this State. Nevertheless, the certification of teachers is a matter of so grave importance to the whole school system, that candor compels me to discuss it here. With a full realization of the meaning of my words, I assert my belief that were an investigation made of the administration of the present law in regard to the certification of teachers, the conditions in some of the counties would be found little less than scandalous. In some of the counties the flagrant and open violation of the law is all but amazing. Indeed, in some places but little show is made of enforcing the law or respecting it. It is safe to say that in some counties one-fourth of the teachers in the public schools are teaching and being paid public funds illegally, since they are doing so without valid certificates. Many of these teachers are entitled to certificates upon diplomas which thy [they] hold from accredited colleges, but have never secured them. Some of this class have been teaching for ten and fifteen years. There are numbers of others who have been teaching as long as ten years without certificates, and who are not entitled to them. There are others still who are teaching on certificates several years out of date. . . .

Improved Courses of Study.—Many of the schools have materially improved their courses of study within the past two or three years. This has been done chiefly by attempting fewer subjects at a time, and by a closer articulation of those retained. Poorly organized and poorly articulated courses have been sources of decided weakness in our high schools, and there is yet much room for improvement. It is but just to say that most of the principals who have had any considerable experience, and who have made a study of high school curricula, have at least reasonably good courses. But much is lacking in the courses of many of the inexperienced principals. They are not to be blamed too severely; many of them have had no preparation whatever for the responsible positions to which they have been called.

The high schools of this State are radically weak in two particulars: 1. The lack of four-year courses with sufficient teaching force; 2. The lack of parallel courses from which pupils may select the one best suited to their needs. The remedies for both these defects are discussed under the heading Standard High Schools.

The One-Teacher High School.—I have for several years watched with intense interest the vicissitudes of the little one-teacher high schools. A large number of communities are depending upon them for the preparation of their boys and girls for college and for the duties and responsibilities of life. Since so many places have only this type of high school, I have endeavored to anchor my faith to them, although my judgment admonished me not to do so. Results justify my judgment. The one-teacher high school itself is, from force of circumstances, inefficient, and it is almost always maintained at the expense of the common school. The high school department is inefficient because in nine-tenths of the cases the one teacher is given three grades to teach. It is a physical impossibility for any teacher to handle three high school grades with any degree of thoroughness. At once two evils arise: The pupils are not getting what they ought to get, and the whole community is misled into believing that it has a real high school. Both these are serious matters, and they may retard the educational sentiment of a community for years to come. Elsewhere I have called attention to how the common schools are robbed to establish and maintain a little high school annex. One teacher is given 15 or 16 so-called high school pupils, while two other teachers are given 75 to 100 pupils below the high school. Or half-prepared pupils are taken out of the lower grades to fill up the so-called high school grades. In addition to all these evils, the so-called high school after a struggle of several years is no stronger in the preparation of its pupils or in the number of its pupils.

Delmar, Ebenezer, Gold Hill, Taylors, Williams, and Willis each organized a one-teacher high school and was given State aid. Delmar dropped the high school, because it was unwilling to run eight months. Gold Hill, Taylors, and Willis dropped out for various reasons. Ebenezer never reached the required 15 enrollment, and was dropped. Williams struggled for two years, and dropped out because it had not the required 15 pupils. White Plains has been State aided two years and is asking aid for 1910–1911, yet the school has been in session eight weeks without reaching the required enrollment of 15 pupils.

Ehrhardt was State aided in 1909–1910, reached an enrollment of 16, had an attendance of 12 last February, and after eleven weeks in session the enrollment has not reached 15 pupils. Shiloh has been aided one year, after running five weeks this year has not reached the required enrollment. Oakway has been State aided three years and asks aid the fourth; after seven weeks the school had not enrolled 15 pupils. In February, 1910, a blank was sent out to high schools asking for the attendance for that month. Bowman reported 9 pupils, Ridge- way reported 12, White Plains reported 11, Lamar reported 12, Wil- liams reported 8, Crocketteville reported 13, Travellers Rest reported 11, and Reidville reported 12.

Jefferson established a two-teacher high school, later dropped to a one-teacher basis, and finally dropped out. Mauldin, Zoar, Townville, Lebanon, Ridgeway, Ruby, Reidville, and Rembert each established a two-teacher high school. Ruby has had to abandon the high school for lack of pupils. Each of the others has had to drop to a lower basis. Olar has not enough pupils at the end of eight weeks to continue on a two-teacher basis, and Rowesville required eight weeks to enroll the required 25 pupils. The attendance last February was 17 in Summer- ton, 20 in Cameron, 22 in Chesterfield, 19 in Inman, 22 in Williams- ton, 23 in Kershaw, 21 in Elloree, 18 in Hampton, and 22 in Jonesville. Cameron has not after eight weeks the required 25 pupils. Bethany has abandoned the high school.

In 1910 each of the following places voted high schools, and their applications for State aid are now on file: Bethune, Cherokee, Dacus- ville, Brightsville, and Swift Creek. So far, December 15th, not one has enrolled the required pupils.

As a further evidence that these small high schools are maintained at the expense of the elementary schools, let me call your attention to more figures: In 24 of these high schools, each with two teachers below the high school, there were enrolled last year below the high school 2,377 pupils. These 48 elementary teachers had an average enrollment of a little more than 49 pupils to the teacher, while the high schools were struggling to gather in 15 pupils each.

The schedule . . . [on p. 310] gives a fair idea of what these one-teacher high schools undertake[.]

One teacher is here undertaking as much work as two can possibly do well. In three years pupils are carried through arithmetic, algebra and plane geometry, in less than one-half the teaching time given

Subjects—First Year.	Recitations Per Week.	Length of Recitations.
Arithmetic	5	20
Algebra	5	25
Physical Geography	4	20
English History	5	20
Latin	5	20
English	3	20
Subjects—Second Year.		
English	5	25
Algebra	5	20
Latin	5	20
English History	5	20
Arithmetic	5	25
Subjects—Third Year.		
English Grammar	5	20
Latin	5	20
Rhetoric	5	20
Geometry	5	20
Physics	4	20
Business Methods	3	20

to this group of subjects in a standard high school. In this school, and in many others like it, all the classes in mathematics are on recitation at the same time. The same is true of other subjects. One is compelled to ask how much Latin can be read in such a school in three years, and how much physics, geometry, and rhetoric can be accomplished. When one remembers that the pupils in these schools have not had sufficient teaching force below the high school grades, he is prepared to appreciate the inferior results in the high school.

It is exceedingly unfortunate that such schools are called high schools at all, and it is to be hoped that some appropriate name can be found. If these one-teacher high schools are to continue to receive State appropriations, I earnestly recommend that they be required to confine their work to two high school grades. To continue to foster three-year courses taught by one teacher is to prostitute the high school movement. The money is not economically spent, and such schools mislead the people as to the meaning of a high school. All over the State are scores of little schools with fewer than a half dozen pupils above the seventh grade, calling themselves high schools, and the people believe that they are high schools.

Time for Increased Efficiency.—Your Board has made it the invariable rule to give no aid to a high school, unless the school added something to its efficiency in return. From the facts enumerated in the previous paragraphs, it ought to be patent that you are now aiding a number of schools that have made little, if any, growth in two or three years. Even some of the two-teacher schools have added nothing to their efficiency since they first received State aid. It would seem that the time has come to demand some additional efficiency on the part of at least some of these schools, before giving them further aid. From year to year the State appropriation should be used to stimulate local effort and growth in places willing to grow, and not to foster the habit of looking to the State for support that should be given locally.

Further, there are several places in the State that have been receiving State appropriations for their high schools, but are not supporting their schools even to patronizing them. In these places it is difficult to keep the pupils through the third high school year, to say nothing of keeping them through the fourth year. In my report for 1908–1909 I showed that a number of places are sending their pupils away from home to school at an expense exceeding the total cost of the home high school, and at the same time asking the State to help support their schools at home for the remainder of the pupils. I am fully persuaded that the time has come for your Board to take this matter into account. If these places are not going to use the money to give their children better schools, then it is time to give it where it will be used to advantage.

The State Appropriation.—It has been exceedingly difficult to get the people to appreciate the purpose of the high school appropriation. From the first the notion took possession of the people at large, and of a few members of the General Assembly, that it was to be used to pension needy schools—a "pork barrel" to be divided out among the hungry. Trustees and other officials ask for State aid solely on the ground that their schools are in need of money, though they have no high school pupils and no reason to hope to maintain a high school. Districts with not more than a half dozen pupils above the seventh grade hold high school elections, and send applications for State aid. It would be eminently wise and safe to accept no high school until it had run one year on its own resources after measuring up to the State's requirements. This would give some evidence of the good faith of the people and the possibility of maintaining a high school. A high school should never be established, unless there is good reason to believe that it will be a permanent affair.

Some have clamored for State aid to be given to schools with only ten high school pupils. To do so would be a waste of the people's money, and a check to building good high schools. On the present basis of appropriation to a 15-pupil high school, the State is giving $20.00 per pupil. The State can not afford to do more. It would be cheaper to the State to send the high school pupils to a boarding school than to give State support to 10-pupil schools.

In our short-sightedness we have made a blunder in taxing larger aggregations of wealth and population for the sole benefit of smaller aggregations. There is absolutely no economy, justice, statesmanship, or patriotism in the present high school law in discriminating against the larger towns. If we are to develop a system of high schools that will be of the highest value and service to all the people, we must rise above the selfishness of the pie-hunter. Under the present law eighteen places in which high schools of the best type could be maintained, are debarred from participating in the privileges of the high school law, on account of population. . . . These towns are contributing to the schools outside their own districts $80,917.84, or 41 per cent of the total revenue from the 3-mill school tax collected upon their taxable property, then support their own schools by a local levy, yet they are debarred by law from using one dollar of the $60,000.00 high school appropriation. . . .

Standard High Schools.—At this stage in the development of our high school system, we are in great need of standard schools, by which is meant four-year schools with sufficient teaching force to offer several parallel courses of study to pupils of widely different tastes and needs. The high school offering a single course, usually leading to college, is an anachronism. The high school of the future must offer more than one course of study. Barring the question of parallel courses, the State has very few four-year schools. Only look at the pitiably small number of fourth-year pupils—250 in a State with upward of three-quarters of a million white people! And some of these are in schools with wholly inadequate teaching force.

A four-year high school with but one course of study cannot properly be taught by fewer than three teachers. On this basis South Carolina has but thirteen four-year public high schools—Abbeville, North Augusta, Anderson, Bamberg, Charleston (2), Darlington, Summerville, Johnston, Winnsboro, Marion, Mullins and Bennettsville. The State needs at least 50 good standard high schools, and they can be easily had by abandoning the multiplication of the little one-teacher schools, and by consolidating many of those already established. It will pay the people to do so. By consolidating two one-teacher schools each with 15 to 18 pupils, one good two-teacher school could be maintained. Such a school should be restricted to a three-year course. Occasionally three small schools could be combined. In many places a one-teacher school and a two-teacher school could be consolidated. In either case a good four-year school could be maintained.

Our present plan is wasting money, working an injustice to the pupils by giving them inferior schools, and clogging the progress of high school development. In order to show the force of these statements, I have inserted an outline map of Laurens County, giving the location of its eight State aided high schools. These eight schools employed the full time of fourteen high school teachers at a combined salary of $8,610.00, and one superintendent (doing no teaching) at a salary of $1,500.00. It is correct to say that these schools cost $10,770.00, of which the State paid $3,000.00. The salaries ranged from $315.00 up. Four of these schools are housed in buildings that could be erected for $600.00 to $1,000.00 each. All eight of these schools reported maps and charts, for both common school and high school departments, at $185.00. All eight teach physical geography. Three teach physics, while the total value of the apparatus is reported at $5.00. In the eight schools were enrolled last year 144 pupils in the first high school year, 119 in the second, and 75 in the third. Six schools have each three high school grades, while two have two grades. Is Laurens County or the State of South Carolina spending money economically, providing properly for these pupils, or developing a high school system?

Of the 338 high school pupils in these eight schools, not one can find a fourth-year class in the county, and in this particular the county is no better off than it was five years ago. All the teaching apparatus reported in these schools would not equip one good high school. Most of the maps and charts are for the elementary school work. Three schools attempt the science of physics with $5.00 worth of apparatus! Physical geography is taught without any better equipment. Beyond these two subjects none of these 338 pupils has the opportunity to study any elementary science.

What is the remedy? Consolidation. Reduce these weak schools to a few strong ones, give each school from two to five high school teachers, offer at least one four-year course in each school with three or more teachers, offer in the largest schools at least two parallel courses of study, and equip each school to do real high school work. Unless some such plan is adopted, five years hence will find Laurens County no better equipped in high schools than today. Can it be done? Yes. Will it be done? It will, if the people can be made to see what a first-class high school means as compared with a make-shift. It will, if the people can be made [to] see that this is the only way by which first-class high schools can be supported. It will not be done so long as every school district that can enroll 15 pupils above the 7th grade, insists on having its own little starving so-called high school taught by one teacher paid in part by a dole from the State treasury. What has been said of Laurens is applicable in varying degrees to nearly every county in the State, making due allowance for the sparseness of population in a few counties. The situation in Anderson, Greenville and Orangeburg counties is almost identical with that in Laurens.

The State's money should not be frittered away on little schools that never can become permanent factors in the educational system of the State. Instead, it should be spent on schools in which there are pupils to be educated, on schools which are capable of being made permanent and efficient. There can be no doubt that far better results would accrue, if the State were to put the $3,000.00 into two high schools in Laurens instead of into eight as now. These two schools should be at such places as would furnish adequate buildings and sufficient and competent teaching force, and would maintain four-year courses of study. Of course these schools should be at accessible points in the county, and should be free of tuition to any pupil in the county. This plan would do away with attempting to run high schools with $40-women teachers and $75-men teachers—something that must be done, if we are ever to have high schools worthy of the name.

In 1908 Senator Tillman suffered a stroke of paralysis, followed two years later by a cerebral hemorrhage. Thereafter, he was forced to take a backseat in state politics. In his stead emerged a new leader of the masses, Coleman Livingston Blease. Although greatly different in personality from Tillman, Blease originally supported the fiery agrarian and adopted his demagogic methods.

The ambitious "Coley" ran for public office in nearly every election from 1890 to 1938. He gradually built up a loyal following among the textile workers and small farmers, but only thrice were they able to elect him to high office, the governorship in 1910 and 1912 and the United States Senate in 1924. The infirm Tillman broke with Blease in 1912 and helped frustrate the outgoing governor's bid for a Senate seat in 1914.

David D. Wallace, South Carolina's foremost historian, closely followed Blease's political career. In the following selection from *The History of South Carolina,* Dr. Wallace compares "Bleaseism" with "Tillmanism" and describes Coley's first term as governor.

30

COLEMAN LIVINGSTON BLEASE—
TEMPESTUOUS GOVERNOR *

David Duncan Wallace

The Nature of Tillmanism and Bleaseism—The administrations of Governors Heyward and Ansel were an interlude in a movement which took definite shape by 1885, and is yet unspent. Its early leader was Tillman; its later representative Blease. Particular leaders merely rode the waves of the modern nation-wide (and even world-wide) democratic movement as it surged through South Carolina with a frothy fury determined by our somewhat rigid social structure. Tillmanism and Bleaseism are misleading terms unless understood merely as indicating the noisy bubbles on the current as it dashed against their angular personalities. It is the misfortune (or good fortune, as one prefers) of our profound discontent of the past fifty years that South Carolina has never had a leader combining unselfish heart, intellectual stature, and effective personality to give adequate expression to the aspirations of modern democracy. Tillman and Blease possessed the externals of political leadership. Richard I. Manning, who best expressed the ideals of modern democracy without its crudities, was handicapped by origin, surroundings and personality, which made him seem a benevolent patron rather than one who could become the darling of the people. It is the inconsistency of the profound force back of Bleaseism and the persistent office-seeking of the individual in the position of leader that prevents its devotees and opponents from understanding each other. The former grasp passionately upon the only leader they find available; the latter see nothing but the violence and selfishness of the demagogue.

Tillman's office-seeking and abusive speech alienated many friends of the original farmers' movement. Blease's platform and some of his measures looked fair enough; but his conduct and associations

* Excerpt from *The History of South Carolina*, 4 vols. (New York: The American Historical Society, Inc., 1934) , III, 424–30; Copyright, The American Historical Society, Inc., 1935. Reprinted without footnotes by permission of R. M. Wallace.

rendered his attempt to revive the name "Reform party" a mockery. Tillman overwhelmingly controlled the State, ruled the legislature, and was never defeated for office. Blease was repeatedly defeated, never won high office except by small majorities, and never had a majority in the legislature. His forceful personality, oratorical talent, ability to make and hold personal friends and inspire the devotion of the tenant farmers and factory operatives gave him a personal prominence far beyond his influence on legislation. The poor and ignorant felt profound disappointment at the outcome of Tillmanism, and waited for a new agitator. But so undeveloped and unorganized were their ideas that they pressed few demands. The strength of Blease's appeal was not any platform of measures, but his personality and viewpoint. He not only offered no program of benefits to labor, a program which was still repugnant to South Carolina individualism, but won favor by railing against measures which labor where organized and informed demands. He associated with the masses intimately, and gave them what they valued more than measures— recognition and equality. They did not want legislation, but they did want to be treated with respect, and felt that Blease was making them a force in the State. Men paying no taxes shouted when he denounced high taxes. In the semi-socialistic program of social reform that makes the taxpayer sweat for the benefit of the proletariat neither he nor his followers had any part. Without rendering them any benefits, he held large masses through their ignorance, individualism, and personal devotion. With all his violence of speech, pardons, and tolerance of lawlessness, Mr. Blease was a thorough conservative in legislative policy.

Of this fact some cool men of big business were well aware, and occasionally supported him in revenge for sympathy with strikers, etc., by anti-Blease leaders. Blease's opposition to the American Federation of Labor for textile operatives, and his proposing local unions instead, was welcome to cotton mill executives. His cousin, Mr. B. L. Abney, the able attorney for the Southern Railway, lived in the executive mansion, and numbers of officials of the system were understood to be for Blease. Self-interest of another sort brought him the support of a large group of experienced and able politicians; for, aside from State politics, where his stamp was always of doubtful value, in many counties the Blease vote was essential to success.

Tillman, in condemning Bleaseism in 1914, was right in attributing its strength to class antagonism. The social scorn toward the cotton mill operative by the revived Bourbonism thinking itself alone fit to rule, said Tillman, drives them to Blease for revenge. "You can tell a crowd of B[l]easeites as far as you can see them," was a common gibe. Said an illiterate citizen of Berkeley in 1912, who knew little of either candidate, "I know I ain't goin' to vote for no aristocrat"; and a candidate in Dorchester County in about 1900, turning to some of that hated class, shouted, "You think we were laid by a buzzard in a hollow stump and hatched by the sun." They were determined to assert themselves as being as good as anybody. It was a passionate defiance of the whole class that they conceived to have looked down upon them.

Blease as Governor—Mr. Blease in pandering to this feeling represented himself as more common than he really was. Born in 1868 of good middle class English descent on both sides (the father's ancestors having come from near Liverpool), he had the advantage of collegiate education. Intensely ambitious, his career at the South Carolina University had been terminated by plagiarizing an essay for a prize. Soon entering the legislature, his parliamentary ability made him a conspicuous leader. As a member of the committee investigating the dispensary, he had been regarded as the friend of the men under charges of corruption. His scoring 41,000 to Ansel's 60,000 on the latter's race for the traditional second term foreshadowed his victory in 1910. The hate he had inspired was expressed in the cartoon in *The State* of September 8, 1910, representing him as a buzzard with wings marked "Dispensary grafters, ignorance, race prejudice, lawlessness, blind tigers, injustice, class prejudice, demagogy," while South Carolina stood guard armed with a sword, "the ballot." The gross cartoon doubtless swelled Blease's vote; but his unexampled organization and his opposition to prohibition operated strongly for him. Charleston, set against prohibition, represented by C. C. Featherstone, gave Blease 3,565 to Featherstone's 820—a large proportion of his majority of 5,645, the largest which he ever received.

Blease was largely made by the newspapers; for his style of saying and doing things made them "news." His enemies made the tactical blunder of circulating incredible falsehoods, often easily proved untrue, instead of confining themselves to criticism founded on fact. He was said to have engaged in a drunken orgy the night before his inauguration; whereas he was carried to Columbia, ill, upon a cot and spent the night with a physician at his side. The exposure of such a slander disarmed a hundred legitimate criticisms.

Governor Blease's inaugural opposed compulsory education, the use of white taxes for negro schools, any further laws regulating child or adult labor, and urged marriage certificates or registration, the separation of the races among convicts, and the privilege of a county's choosing high license as well as dispensary or prohibition, and liberal though not extravagant grants for education, etc., on the ideal of "a poor government and a rich people, in place of a rich government and a poor people." He interpreted his election as vindication against the newspapers and the preachers, all but two or three of the former and nearly all the latter having opposed him.

The new Governor's autocratic spirit at once found expression in his refusal to appoint as special Judges the persons nominated by the Supreme Court, as directed by law. "A large majority of the people of South Carolina elected me Governor," he wrote the Chief Justice February 2, 1911 (referring to his victory by a margin of 5,645), ". . . and I expect to see that my friends receive at least some consideration from this administration." He then demanded that the legislature give him power to appoint special Judges independently of the court, lest there be conflict. The Governor also defied the law by appointing as township commissioners in Beaufort persons of his own choice instead of those nominated by the county delegation— action which was unanimously condemned by the Supreme Court. When his negro chauffeur was twice fined $3.75 for speeding, he pardoned him. The city authorities disregarded the pardon and imposed $15.75 for a third offense on the ground that, although never decided here, the courts of other States denied that the pardoning power extended to persons punished by city courts. The Governor retaliated by placing extra liquor constables on the city payroll and promising another for every time his chauffeur was "persecuted" on account of his employer's politics.

"The statute outlawing race track gambling," remarked the Charleston *Post,* "went into effect July 1, 1912." But the manager of the races, to prevent the repetition of which the law was enacted, remarked to the Cincinnati *Enquirer* that the racing would proceed despite the law, as Charleston was peculiar in taking its own way with laws it did not like. The racing interests, said the Anderson *Daily Mail,* would feel safe after Attorney-General Lyon's retirement, January 14, 1913.

Governor Blease said in his second inaugural (January, 1913), "They are yelling, 'What is the Governor going to do about the Charleston races?'" "Do they expect me to dress up like a preacher and beg them not to race?" Said Bishop Guerry in a powerful sermon in St. Philip's Episcopal Church, Charleston, March 2, 1913, representative citizens declined his request to take part in protests against race track gambling and blind tigers, because they belonged to clubs that were legally blind tigers. "The situation is indeed serious when our most respectable citizens are aiding and abetting the spirit of lawlessness in our midst which threatens to overturn the very foundations of our civilization, and is making our fair city a bye-word [*sic*] and a reproach to the whole country. How can you blame the professional gambler, or those who make their living by unlawful practices, when the most respectable element in the life of the city tells you 'their hands are tied' through their own failure to keep the law?"

The *News and Courier* said editorially in the same issue that this powerful sermon should be pondered in the face of "the lethargy that exists in Charleston today in the face of moral conditions which have made this city a bye-word [*sic*] and a reproach from one end of the land to the other." The reproach for the fact that Charleston had more vice dens than any other city of its size in the country, as the editor states is reliably said by those in position to know, is due to the class whom the Bishop holds responsible, said the editor.

For these disgraceful conditions the city and county government, and the portion of the public profiting by the presence of visitors, good and bad, must share the responsibility. The racing stopped after four meets of about two months each as a matter of course immediately before the inauguration of Governor Manning.

Governor Blease's relations with the legislature, in which he never had a majority, were tempestuous. His numerous vetoes were generally overridden. He denounced two of its leaders as North Carolinians born and another as of Northern parentage. Factionalism was so strong that anti-Bleaseites revolted at supporting even his recommendations which they approved, and were actually in danger of being proclaimed Bleaseites if they did. Physical combat between the Governor and various opponents actually within the legislative chamber or capitol was repeatedly immanent [*sic*]. Several messages were devoted to charges that the father of one of his Senatorial enemies had commanded negro troops, that the Senator was trustee of a negro school, and that a negro was a trustee in Beaufort. I have no fear of negro contacts, said the Governor, "neither for me nor any of my family—for each of them, I am proud to say, is physically able to pull a trigger whenever it should become necessary. But I am pleading for the white girls and white women of my State."

With a few exceptions, non-Bleaseites were excluded even from being notary publics. Commissioner of Agriculture E. J. Watson, of exceptional ability and fidelity, was told that unless he stopped running around the United States he would be discharged, to which Mr. Watson humbly replied that his recent trip had been discussed with the Governor, to whom he had pledged coöperation and his hardest work. The legislature promptly made the office elective by the people.

We must go back almost two hundred years to Governor Nicholson for such hostility as Governor Blease's to the press. In vetoing a bill to modify the severe libel law, he used the word "lie" thirty-three times, "liar" eight times, strewed along "cowardly," "slime," "scurrilous blackguard," "low down," attacked newspapers by name, branded the newspaper fraternity as a dirty set of liars, and glorified Jim Tillman's murder of Editor Gonzales. The House expunged all but the essential parts of the message, as self-respect forbade such language in its records. The Senate refused to record the accompanying exhibits, and the *News and Courier* felt restrained by court decisions from printing some of the passages. In 1913 following the Governor's recommendation that imprisonment be imposed on reporters or editors publishing candidates' speeches so as to give a false impression, a follower introduced a bill which, it was said, would imprison an editor for publishing facts of an officer's wrecking a bank, as it would "injure his standing in the community."

Never before in the State's history had there been an individual who so fully made his own personality and interests the center of politics. Amid the welter of personalities and passion Governor Blease made little systematic effort to press any consistent program, although the statement of a writer sympathetic with his professed aims that he left not an act for the benefit of the masses might be considered extreme. He did contribute to some measures for the unfortunate, as separating the races on chain gangs, the abolition of the penitentiary hosiery mill as unhealthy, the establishment of the State tuberculosis sanitarium, and adopting the Medical College in Charleston as a State institution. He insisted on better provision for common schools, a special tax on hydro-electric companies, and the assertion of the State's rights in the Columbia Canal. On the other hand, he was the strongest dependence of the liquor element, and opposed factory inspection, compulsory education, and the medical examination of school children. The latter he represented to credulous ignorance as endangering female modesty and threatening to blast reputations by doctors tattling that girls were not pure. He would telegraph a pardon, he declared, to any man who killed a doctor violating his daughter's modesty.

The Governor's opposition to factory inspection incurred the displeasure of organized labor (which, however, then included few cotton mill operatives), who could not understand why tens of thousands of free operatives should not have as good protection against unsanitary conditions as the Governor insisted upon for a few score convicts working under constant government supervision in the penitentiary. But Governor Blease was an extreme individualist, and he knew that the individualism of the unorganized operative was stronger than his realization of the need of modern social protection. He would veto any law, he declared, for improving the conditions of adults, who were free to work where they pleased; that he knew more about factory workers than organized labor did, and that persons mistreated must see him in person. When the Columbia Federation of Trades condemned him, he promised to inspect factories by liquor constables.

PART VI:
RECENT SOUTH CAROLINA

While South Carolina's attention was firmly fixed on the antics of unpredictable Governor Cole Blease, near the end of his second term war broke out in Europe. President Wilson announced a policy of American neutrality, and South Carolinians continued about their affairs in a routine manner. Richard I. Manning succeeded to the governor's chair, while Blease unsuccessfully challenged Ellison D. "Cotton Ed" Smith for his seat in the United States Senate. Two years later the undaunted Blease made a futile bid to oust Governor Manning from the executive office. Meanwhile, the American government found itself gradually being drawn into the European holocaust. In April 1917 President Wilson asked Congress to declare war against Germany.

The advent of World War I coincided with important political events in South Carolina. Before the war had run its course, Blease was in temporary eclipse due to two successive political defeats (1914, 1916), and veteran Senator Ben Tillman had died (July 1918). New leaders took over, and the state got on with the war effort. One of South Carolina's chief functions was to serve as a training ground for American troops destined for Europe. Large military camps were established at Columbia, Greenville, and Spartanburg. The story of a New York National Guard division at Spartanburg is recounted in the WPA's *History of Spartanburg County.*

31

YANKEE SOLDIERS INVADE SPARTANBURG IN 1917 *

Fronde Kennedy

Settling into Camp—The men of the Twenty-Seventh Division went South as fast as trains were available. Leaving Fifth Avenue and Van Cortlandt Park, they arrived at a small country station in the woods. The famed Twenty-Second Engineers with its elaborate equipment was the first regiment to arrive. Then followed the equally famous Seventh, popularly designated in New York as the "Silk Stocking Regiment." It was one hundred and six years old. This regiment reached Spartanburg with 1,825 members, proud of having lost 178 of its men to the Plattsburg Officers' Training School. Silk stockings notwithstanding, these men set cheerfully to work chopping down trees, laying off streets, and pitching their own tents.

Day after day men poured in by the thousand. The camp presented to observers a scene of infinite variety—lines of men marching from the Fairforest station to their assigned rectangles, and upon arrival pitching their tents; squads installing lights and spigots; cavalrymen, artillerymen, quartermaster's motor trucks, spectators, all scurrying here and there. Within two weeks the New York Engineers were beautifying their camp so that it soon appeared more like a park than a camp. They moved trees from the woods, planted grass plots, gathered white stones with which they marked their company numbers, and even transplanted small evergreen trees to make hedges.

Camp Life—At once the soldiers began to gather pets. Within two weeks the 10,000 men in camp had dozens of pets of every sort—especially dogs of every known breed. The Forty-Second had a bear, which later was well-known in Spartanburg. Company mascots included roosters, pigs, goats, burros, mules, opossums, raccoons, and cats. One enterprising man bought a captured opossum—an animal new to him. He was so fascinated with the creature's pouch that he put into it his gold watch. The startled animal, in frantic alarm,

* Chapter 23, entitled "The Twenty-Seventh Division at Camp Wadsworth," from *A History of Spartanburg County*, Writers' Program of the WPA, Fronde Kennedy, supervisor (Spartanburg: Spartanburg Branch of American Association of University Women, 1940), pp. 242–51.

clawed the soldier's face, causing him to turn loose the chain by which he was holding his new pet. Whereupon Brer 'Possum plunged wildly across the camp and escaped into the nearby woods, probably the first opossum in Spartanburg County to carry a timepiece.

Within a few weeks the cavalrymen found that they were to be transformed into a machine gun unit. Sadly the First Cavalry made its last parade, and the men turned their horses over to the remount station. The following morning before three o'clock, about three hundred of these horses broke their corral and headed for their old picket line, two miles away, across the camp reservation. The thundering of hoofs awoke the cavalrymen and from their tent doors they saw their mounts approaching over the parade ground in columns-of-fours formation, as if on parade. The horses rounded the headquarters and proceeded down the company street to their old picket line, where, after milling about for a few moments, they took their accustomed places. This procedure had aroused the whole regiment, and soon the men were dressed and about the job of welcoming, feeding and watering their beloved steeds, many of them bred in the cavalry service and as perfectly trained as their masters.

As cold weather set in, the problem of fuel presented itself as serious. In the haste necessary to clear the camp, great piles of wood, brush, and stumps had been burned. Wistful thoughts now recalled these fiery sacrifices to temporary expediency, for the quartermaster was buying wood from farmers all over the county, with the proviso that details of soldiers would cut and haul it. One farmer took a squad to his wood lot and designated certain trees which were not to be touched. "Si, si, Signor," he was told. Not a man in the detail spoke English well enough to grasp the farmer's instructions; and as a result the trees reserved for their value as lumber were the first to fall under the axes. City men nearly froze trying to make fires in the little camp stoves with poorly selected wood, often green, sobby, or wet.

Dramatic Incidents—Reporters roved through the camp invading the privacy of millionaires, celebrities, and men of affairs in search of "human interest" stories. They found a multi-millionaire using as his office a fly tent with a dirt floor, and for its sole furniture two camp chairs. That was Colonel Cornelius Vanderbilt. They were equally fascinated by the situation of young Cornelius Vanderbilt, who was a buck private in his father's regiment, in a company of which his former chauffeur was captain. The Vanderbilt family supplied the reporters with many stories. Mrs. Vanderbilt and her daughter Grace paid a visit to Colonel Vanderbilt and Cornelius, Jr., and lived in a private car on the railroad siding in a cotton field. In that car Grace celebrated her eighteenth birthday. A "Squaw Camp" of portable houses was established by some of the New York officers that they might have their families near them during their brief respite from possible death. In such quarters lived several families of railroad presidents, newspaper owners, New York business and professional men of substance.

One New York woman provided a folk saga which, with such variations as may occur to the mind of the individual narrator, has been repeatedly told by the "old inhabitants" about the camp. The tale runs that this woman, determined to be as near her son as possible while he was in training at Camp Wadsworth, visited the camp, selected a house in the vicinity, knocked at the door, and announced that she wished to rent the house. The owner, startled by so novel an idea, said the family had always lived there, and their people before them, and the house was not for rent. The lady insisted; money was no object. Some narrators report that she offered $500 a month for the house, others say $600, and one imaginative soul insists she paid $1,000. Whatever the price, she got the house, with the stipulation that such improvements as she deemed necessary must be made at her own expense. The owners moved into a tenant house close by, where, unfortunately for their peace of mind and pride, they had to see their cherished home "magicked" before their very eyes into a residence adapted to the tastes of a sophisticated New Yorker. The hearts of the owners burned within them with resentment that what had been good enough for three generations of a good Spartanburg County family would not serve a rich Yankee for a few months. This tenant appeared in the fall, did her bit to make her son and his friends happy, and in May, when he was sent overseas, presented to the owners all the improvements she had placed in their house and returned to New York.

The local Spartanburg papers kept reporters at Camp Wadsworth, as did most of the New York leading dailies. Every day produced its crop of stories. The New York *World* had thirty-eight employees in service at Camp Wadsworth, each of whom received from the paper each month a check covering the difference between his army pay check and his salary on the paper.

The soldiers began to publish their own papers; Company A, Seventh Regiment, published *Att-A-Boy* every Saturday. Company B followed with *The Bee Hive. Trench and Camp* appeared October 8, published at Columbia as the official paper of Camps Jackson and Wadsworth. Later the Twenty-Seventh Division had its own official weekly paper called *The Gas Attack,* heralded as a rehabilitation of the *Rio Grande Rattler,* which these same men had published on the

Mexican border. The first issue, with twenty pages and a colored cover, appeared in November.

The Twenty-Second Engineers had a highly trained orchestra, for which Colonel Vanderbilt bought a piano. On October 2, 1917, this orchestra gave its first entertainment, a concert in "the red schoolhouse on the National Highway between the camp and the city." The camp had its first wedding October 18, with a colonel to give the bride in marriage and the colonel's lady to act as dame of honor. The groom was a sergeant, and the bride traveled down from Asbury Park, New Jersey, to marry him. The chaplain used the ring ceremony, and the newly married couple passed from the chaplain's hut under the crossed rifles of the groom's company. The groom had a leave of absence, and the pair went to Asheville for their honeymoon. A year later an equal excitement was felt over the first christening in camp. Weddings had become commonplace.

Reorganization and Drill—Such was life at Camp Wadsworth during the early months. Meanwhile the great machine which was the Twenty-Seventh Division was being constructed. Orders came from the War Department for a reorganization, to facilitate cooperation with French and British units. Hearts burned when old companies and regiments were broken up or done away with. A regiment would parade for the last time; officers and men would have a dinner, gifts and compliments would be exchanged, and the members would report to new assignments or adopt new numbers as their insignia. Visiting French officers appeared to direct bayonet drill; English officers supervised practice in trench and tank warfare. These visitors bluntly warned the Americans, "You are going to kill or get killed. You must know your rifle and your bayonet."

The first World War trenches in America were constructed at Camp Wadsworth, and were first used on the night of November 19, 1917, when "2,000 men marched into the labyrinth of trenches under cover of darkness, there to remain for twelve hours." Calisthenics, drills, marches, cross-country runs, memory tests, lectures, first-aid instructions kept the men busy all day. By the end of September more than 20,000 men were actually in camp, and every day was bringing in more. The quartermaster reported that the monthly bill was more than two million dollars, $600,000 for food alone.

The Artillery Range—In August 1917, Major Michel, representing the Southeastern Department of the United States Army as an artillery expert, inspected a proposed artillery range and pronounced it "a most satisfactory location, the character of the land being just such as we like to have for artillery work." The tract selected extended over a mountainous area about seven miles long and from two to three miles wide along the outlying ridges of Hogback and Glassy mountains. It lay entirely in Greenville County, distant twenty-six miles from Spartanburg and two and a half miles from Landrum, the nearest railroad station. The topography was adapted to all sorts of artillery practice—range firing, barrage fire, or the moving of guns from point to point.

Paul V. Moore and Baylis Earle arranged all the details preliminary to occupation; and, September 24, fifty men of the Twenty-Second Engineers moved in, with ten big army trucks carrying supplies and tents. The next day the two thousand men who were the first to be trained began arriving. Along with them went newspaper reporters, who interviewed veterans of Manassas, the Wilderness, Chancellorsville, and Appomattox. They wrote of New York men who for the first time drank spring water from gourds; of the mountaineers' comment that soldiers wore blue uniforms and brass buttons and that these men in camp wearing butternut jeans were just workmen; of the mountain cabin in which a New Yorker found, over the mantel, in close juxtaposition, an old-fashioned pistol and a gaudy framed motto, "Prepare to Meet Thy God." The camp at once became an objective for sightseers from many miles around, and the roar of cannon and the whistling of shells became familiar sounds.

Spartanburg Hospitality—The Red Cross, the Young Men's and Young Women's Christian Associations, the City Federation of Women's Clubs, the Country Club, the fraternal lodges, the churches, the colleges, the Rotary Club, the Chamber of Commerce—all the city's agencies worked wholeheartedly to extend hospitality to the men at Camp Wadsworth. Wofford dormitories housed the Reserve Officers until the camp could provide them with quarters. The city raised a fund of $27,500 for War Camp Activities.

A letter written by a New York woman for the New York *Times* and reprinted in the *Herald* of November 11, 1917, depicted vividly some phases of the enterprise, as seen through a woman's eyes. She wrote of the crowded conditions; the dazed, bewildered housekeepers overrun with would-be paying guests and distracted by demoralized servants; of block-long lines of soldiers waiting their turn to get to the soda fountains; of drug stores taking in $1,200 a night and having to restock daily from New York and Atlanta; of the excellence and insufficiency of the food; of the hospitality of local housekeepers whose best hand-embroidered bed linen was not withheld from their country's defenders or their womenfolk; of the churches with doors and grounds and kitchens wide open to the guests; of the bridge games, country club parties, and Saturday night dances for the soldiers. "When the military band strikes up 'Over There,' and all the soldiers sing as they dance, the sight is one never to be forgotten," the letter ran; and its concluding passage read:

> If it were not for the heavy cloud of war, time in Spartanburg would pass very pleasantly. It may be, however, that life becomes more precious when at stake. The men and women feel that they would make the most of this crowded hour of glorious life, so they seize each minute when they can be together. When the soldiers are at work in their all-day drills or trench digging, the women can sometimes motor out and watch them do their bit with enthusiasm. As one Spartan lady remarked: "We know now as eye-witnesses that New York has given her best."

The imagination of the people of Spartanburg had not prepared them for the numbers or the requirements of the soldiers' relatives. Houses and rooms were not sufficient to supply the demand. The school enrollment showed a twenty per cent increase. It appeared that citizens and soldiers alike sought refuge from reflection by filling every moment not assigned to duty with organized recreation. Parties, dances, barbecues, watermelon cuttings, banquets, concerts, old fiddlers' conventions, community singings, spirituals sung by Negroes, plays, and musical shows in which soldiers and townspeople cooperated, concerts by the military bands, parades, teas—always something was doing somewhere.

The Spartanburg County Fair Association and the Community Fair Association responded to the stimulus of prospective visitors from another State. Chesnee, Landrum, Wellford, Reidville, and Poplar Springs all held community fairs and also entered their exhibits at the county fair which was held October 30-31 and November 1-3, 1917. Pauline held a Dahlia Show of such excellence that a permanent Dahlia Club grew out of it. Saxon, being so close to Camp Wadsworth, enjoyed an especially good patronage for its community fair.

Camp Hospitality—But Camp Wadsworth presented much more interesting exhibits to Spartans than anything they could offer in return. The Converse College girls, escorted in a body through the underground trenches and dug-outs, pronounced the experience "thrilling." Band concerts, parades, drills, and teas drew hundreds of civilians to camp as spectators every day the weather permitted. Musical and drama-loving Spartans reveled in the contributions made to their pleasure by the soldiers' amateur theatricals and by the military bands and individual musicians. Soon after the camp was organized, General O'Ryan issued a special order permitting camp bands and orchestras to participate in civic programs when invited. Singers gave their services to the local church choirs; and many of them were men of exceptional talent and professional status in New York.

The Over There Club, a social organization composed of enlisted men who were former students of Yale, Harvard, and Columbia universities, presented a musical comedy entitled *Swat the Spies,* which fascinated Spartans. The play was written by Lawton Campbell, formerly of the Princeton Triangle Club. His assistant, L. P. Hollander, who wrote the lyrics and arranged the musical numbers, had been interested in dramatics at Exeter and had belonged to the Harvard Dramatic Club. The scene of the play was laid in the Cleveland Hotel dining room, and the intricate plot centered around some papers which a German spy obtained from a general at Camp Wadsworth, who was under heavy financial obligations to the German. Private Cornelius Vanderbilt, Jr., played the leading role.

Christmas at Camp Wadsworth—All sorts of plans were proposed for the celebration of Christmas. Spartanburg had been impressed by the lavish flow of money, and the many stories of wealthy New Yorkers and their extravagant demands. That there was another side to the picture was brought home to the readers of the *Herald,* December 16, 1917, by a letter to the editor signed "One of the Northern Visitors." This letter pointed out that there were many very poor men at Camp Wadsworth who could not spend even the quarter it cost to get to town, and who were forced to make long marches in the snow, gloveless, because of their poverty. Characterizing the proposal to spend $2,000 on a Christmas pageant for the men at Camp Wadsworth as merely "a personal display for a few people," she demanded tartly:

Is this the spirit of Christmas? Is this what we want Christmas to mean to 40,000 men, not children? What do they care about floats and expensive decorations, while their hearts are back home thinking of little Susie's stocking? . . . The men in the camp need warm things. There are many men there too poor to receive gifts from home, men the families of whom will pass a sad Christmas, not just because of loneliness, but because money is scarce. Santa Claus will not come down many a chimney for a little child back home, while here at Camp Wadsworth a wonderfully planned pageant will take place.

The weather prevented a pageant; the roads were slushy with half-melted snow, and it was bitter cold. Lighted Christmas trees and carols and concerts cheered town and camp. Northerners were shocked by the typically Southern celebration of Christmas with fireworks—and Spartans were shocked to learn that such a mode of celebration was not universal. The 105th Regiment Infantry had a "Regimental Gala Night" in the Harris Theatre, December 24, arrangements for which were made by men of influential theater connections and experience, who gave New Yorkers and Spartans an evening of New York vaudeville.

Hardships and Disappointments—Camp morale was high. The discipline was severe, but the men found it interesting. Many among them had seen service overseas and could therefore help others visualize what was ahead of them. Numbers of the experienced French and British officers serving as instructors were maimed, and the sight of their heroic bearing challenged similar courage in the men.

So sensational were the rumors in circulation as to the suffering in camp that Chief of Staff Colonel H. H. Bandholtz made, December 22, 1917, an official statement to the press concerning camp health conditions. A New York paper had published a story that six men had frozen to death in the trenches at Camp Wadsworth. Colonel Bandholtz stated that not even one death had occurred from trench service, and that only eleven deaths had occurred among the 31,000 men at Camp Wadsworth during the entire four months of its operation.

Winter had set in early and was cold, rainy, and snowy. Snow fell December 12, much earlier than usual in this section. The soldiers really suffered extreme discomfort—and so did Spartans. There was a coal shortage. The hastily built roads did not stand up well under the stress of bad weather and constant heavy hauling over them. Townspeople and soldiers were equally embittered by the difficulties of transportation between camp and city. The electric interurban company was confronted with a problem impossible of immediate solution in the sudden demand for increased facilities in three camp towns—Greenville, Charlotte, and Spartanburg. Private taxi fares were exorbitant.

The soldiers, if they did manage to get into Spartanburg, were often doomed to disappointment in their search for pleasure. There were not enough picture shows, lodge rooms, soldiers' clubs, restaurants, ice cream parlors, in the town to accommodate them all. Worse still, few of the available amusements satisfied the cravings of sophisticated men used to the gaieties of New York.

Jarring notes crept in, but not enough of them to destroy the harmony. Although everybody had a great deal more money than before, it soon began to appear that everything cost a great deal more too, and there were complaints of extortion. Men and women used to New York often found Spartanburg annoyingly "small town"—and some Spartans confronted with this attitude manifested peevish resentment. Not everybody fell in gracefully with the sugar allowancing, the meatless days, the wheatless days requested by Food Administrator Hoover. One lively old lady voiced her disgust at the parade made of it all. She said that during the sixties people were really driven to desperate makeshifts—parched potatoes and oats for coffee, sorghum or honey for all sweetening, burned corncobs for soda, wheat flour only on Sundays. Then good manners required that makeshifts be ignored and forbade any unpleasant comment on the food. But now she found every meal made hideous by calculations of calories and citations from the Hoover Card as to what one must eat or refrain from eating.

Difficult situations grew out of conflict between the rigid requirements of military etiquette and civilian ignorance of its details; and sometimes democratic scorn of its irritating inhibitions. The soldiers chafed when crowds failed to remove their hats on proper occasions, and some of them attributed such failure to "Unreconstructed Reb cussedness" instead of to ignorance of military conventions. The Bank of Spartanburg distributed a helpful pamphlet showing the significance of military etiquette and insignia—bars, stripes, chevrons, hat cords; the crossed sabres of the cavalry; the crossed rifles of the infantry; the crossed guns of the artillery; the wings and serpent of the medical corps; and so on. Eventually even little boys and girls in Spartanburg could glance at a soldier's uniform and determine his exact status, and few people failed on the proper occasions to remove hats or stand at attention.

In November General O'Ryan's continued absence from camp occasioned surmises and comments. When he reappeared December 6 and disclosed that he and Colonel Bandholtz had been in Europe inspecting the European war front and conferring with General Pershing, excitement rose high; for the men anticipated orders to move any day. During November the camp had visits from Governor Whitman and Senator Wadsworth of New York and Governor Manning of South Carolina—visits which entailed many parades, dinners, banquets, reviews, and speeches; and heightened the men's eagerness to go "Over There."

Not until April was this desire satisfied; and in the interval drill and discipline were increasingly rigorous. So closely guarded were all plans that before Spartans realized it, the Twenty-Seventh Division was gone. A committee of citizens followed General O'Ryan to New York and presented to him and the division, on behalf of the city of Spartanburg, a silver bowl.

One of the facets of the "Jazz Age" following World War I was
the movie craze. South Carolina was affected much the same
as the rest of the nation. By 1930 every town of any consequence
had a picture show house, well attended by avid screen fans.
A harbinger of this popular movement was the appearance
of Hollywood's first significant movie, *The Birth of a Nation*.
Based on Thomas Dixon's novel and play *The Clansman, The
Birth of a Nation* glorified the role of the Ku Klux Klan in
"liberating" the South from Radical Reconstruction. John
H. Moore describes South Carolina's reaction to both the play
and the movie.

32

SOUTH CAROLINA VIEWS
THE BIRTH OF A NATION *

John Hammond Moore

Beginning in October 1915 when Spartanburg was the first community in this state to see the motion picture based on Thomas Dixon's *Clansman,* thousands of South Carolinians thrilled to the stirring scenes of *The Birth of a Nation.* Men who once wore gray uniforms, white sheets, and red shirts wept, yelled, whooped, cheered, and on one occasion even shot up the screen in a valiant effort to save Flora Cameron from her black pursuer. A carnival atmosphere reigned whenever this movie came to town. Special trains brought in throngs from outlying farms and villages. Some South Carolinians saw this epic over and over. At the end of his eleventh consecutive show, a Charleston man told the *News & Courier* he had enjoyed each one "immensely." Although few displayed such extreme devotion, an overwhelming majority of white citizens wholeheartedly endorsed *The Birth of a Nation.* Whenever it returned, as it would periodically until 1930, this precedent-breaking film was greeted by packed houses.

This does not mean everyone approved of what they saw. Many applauded this technical triumph while rejecting its strident, racial message. Although few Negroes actually saw the movie in this state, it was not long before they knew the story it was telling. In December 1921 a man who grew up in Sharon—a small community near old Yorkville where much of the action in this movie takes place—recalls that he and his brothers and sisters were bundled into the family buckboard before daybreak. They drove to Rock Hill, saw this movie, and returned home after dark. Each child was cautioned *not* to tell where he had been or what he had seen for fear Negroes working their spacious farms might be offended.

* Reprinted from *The Proceedings of the South Carolina Historical Association, 1963* (Columbia: South Carolina Historical Association, 1964), pp. 30–40, where it was entitled "South Carolina's Reaction to the Photoplay, *The Birth of a Nation.*" Reprinted without footnotes by permission of the South Carolina Historical Association.

In the spring of 1923 *The Birth of a Nation* finally came to York's Star Theater. A gracious lady who had been among those taking a special train to Charlotte to see the movie eight years earlier flatly refused to let her children attend. Why? Because they were too young? No, because it was "just too horrible. . . . I was afraid it might upset their views on race relations." Ironically, in 1915 this was precisely why members of the NAACP and northern liberals tangled with policemen, threw eggs at the screen, and protested so vigorously that within a month of its debut some 170 scenes were deleted.

While South Carolina Negroes did not grasp the full impact of *The Birth of a Nation* when it first appeared here, from the outset some newspapers in this state were restrained in their praise. Although promoters purchased column after column of advertising, free publicity of the sort such expenditures usually warrant is missing. Actually, this has little to do with the movie itself. It stems from a deep-seated antipathy to the Reverend Thomas Dixon, Jr., author of *The Clansman, The Leopard's Spots,* and an amazing variety of works attacking not only the Negro, but socialism and communism as well.

The feud between Dixon and the South Carolina press—specifically the Gonzales-edited Columbia *State*—began in 1905, the year in which *The Clansman* appeared. In this novel and *The Leopard's Spots,* which was published in 1902, Dixon develops his controversial thesis: the Ku Klux Klan saved the South from the Negro, scalawag, and carpetbagger. By freeing the South from unjust rule, the Klan made it possible for the South to remain pure. And, to keep it pure, the Negro must now go back to Africa. Education of this "human donkey" would merely complicate the race problem.

As a result of these views, Dixon in June 1905 launched a bitter attack upon Robert Ogden, president of the Southern Education Board. He accused Ogden, manager of Wanamaker's and benefactor of Hampton Institute, of being a "Negro lover" who walked about his Manhattan emporium with an arm draped around Booker T. Washington, the noted colored leader. As for the Southern Education Board, it was nothing but "an insidious, dangerous movement against southern sentiment." Both the *State* and the *News & Courier* asked Dixon to prove his charges. Dixon accepted the challenge, but his reply was weak.

To add fuel to the fire, in September, Dixon published an article in *Collier's,* "The Debt of the Law to the Lawless." Once more he presented his controversial thesis in a fashion difficult to misinterpret: "When Goth and Vandal overran Rome and blew out the light of ancient civilization, they never dreamed the leprous infamy of raising the black slave, a thick-lipped, flat-nosed, spindle-shanked negro, to rule over his white master and lay his claws upon his daughter. . . . And so a lawless band of night raiders became the sole guardians of society, brought order out of chaos, law out of lawlessness, and preserved our race in America from extinction at last in negroid mongrelism."

In October Dixon's stage production of *The Clansman* packed full of racial equality, mixed marriage, and other explosive subjects began a southern tour. Reaction was far from favorable. The author quarreled with reviewers in Richmond and Norfolk. On October 9, five days before the play appeared in Columbia, the *State* called attention to the *Collier's* article and dubbed *The Clansman* "a fairy tale." How could a sensible man write such a book! Solid citizens of South Carolina fought for and saved this state long after the Klan faded out of existence. There was no Klan here after May 1871, emphasized the *State,* yet Negro rule continued until 1876. "The soul of the superior race prevented its descent to mongrelism; its spirit precluded submission. Wade Hampton and the men who wore red shirts in the broad light of day and the women who blessed them redeemed South Carolina from Negro rule. Let us not surrender the heritage of our achievement for a tinsel setting to a sensational drama!"

Three days later the *State* censured North Carolina's governor for endorsing Dixon's play as "truthful." The *State* reviewed the history of the Klan, admitting it did some good, but eventually got out of hand and committed outrages: "As is every case where there is recession from law, there were needless excesses and unwarranted outrages. The Klans then ceased to 'right grievous wrongs'; they perpetrated them. Such acts were doubtless often committed by those not members of the organization, but operating in its name."

On Saturday, October 14, *The Clansman* appeared in Columbia. At one point a score of policemen had to restrain inflamed patrons from mobbing a white member of the cast playing the role of a Negro lieutenant governor. Yet, in a brief curtain speech Dixon emphasized he was not trying to revive bitter memories: "My play is an attempt to build a lighthouse of historic facts on the sands of Reconstruction. Its scene is past. Its purpose is present and future. I am seeking to unite the nation in a knowledge of the truth. The race question is a worldwide one. The southern man who walked the way of sorrow from 1865 to 1875 has a message for the world in this crisis. I have tried to speak it in this play without one weak, lame, or halting word. . . . Every scene and incident of my story is founded on fact!"

Reverend Dixon vowed he had sworn testimony to back up his claims and would give $1,000 to anyone who could disprove his "facts." Unfortunately, several young-men-about-town hissed Dixon as he spoke. He in turn called them "scalawags." After the show they went to his hotel to demand an apology, but Dixon and his wife slipped out and caught a train to Savannah. Since then, the Yorkville *Enquirer* noted a few days later, "tongues have been wagging!"

Actually, more than tongues were wagging. The telegraph wires between Columbia and Savannah were searing hot as Dixon and W. E. Gonzales of the *State* ripped into each other. Gonzales suggested that an impartial board investigate Dixon's "facts." Dixon agreed, recommending a twelve-man board from the American Historical Society. (The *State* concluded he was thinking about the American Historical Association.) In addition, Dixon said, if his play was indecent—a charge which apparently had not been raised—let the Columbia chapter of the United Daughters of the Confederacy decide this matter. The *State* countered with its consistent charge that the play was historically inaccurate. Dixon evidently told the wire services Gonzales inspired the hissing incident. Gonzales asked Dixon to reply collect whether he had released such a tale. Dixon answered that he accused Gonzales of something much worse—circulating the story that he (Dixon) had said Gonzales inspired the affair. This exchange of telegrams ended with the editor calling the minister's statements "a cold lie."

Meanwhile, *The Clansman* appeared in Charleston where the *News & Courier* summed up its thesis: "Hate the Negro; he is a beast; his intention is to rob and murder and pollute; he should be transported or annihilated!" The *Evening Post* denounced posters featuring a Negro in chains about to be lynched for rape. Dixon is, the *Evening Post* concluded, "a man with a firebrand."

As Dixon and his troupe moved on to Atlanta and more trouble, the Yorkville *Enquirer* termed Dixon's novel "sensational . . . an idealistic story of Ku Klux times . . . interesting and very inaccurate as to facts and not altogether wholesome as to doctrine." The *Enquirer* thought both the play and the controversy it was creating would soon be forgotten. Late in October, however, this weekly announced it would soon begin publication of *The Clansman* in serial form. "Much of the story," the editor emphasized, "is based on events that actually occurred in York County."

In Atlanta Dixon suddenly discovered a local man had inspired him to write *The Clansman,* an honor previously conferred upon Ben Tillman. The Atlanta *Journal* called the dispute with Gonzales merely a publicity stunt to create interest in a mediocre play. Meeting at Johnston, the South Carolina Women's Christian Temperance Union lashed out at alcohol and narcotics, and denounced "in unmeasured terms the unspeakable play, 'The Clansman.'" On November 5, the *State* revealed its disagreement with Dixon was still very much alive. After summarizing the whole affair, Gonzales let his adversary have it with both barrels:

It may be appropriate and dignified for a minister of the gospel, a shepherd of the flocks (God save the lambs!) and the self-chosen leader of the Southern people, to travel through the country and in speech and interview meet arguments by offers to wage $1000, by referring to opponents as 'jay editors,' and by assuming that adverse critics are liars. That may be meet and proper for those of the Rev. Thomas Dixon calibre. The bigotry and egotism of the man, sharpened by intense hunger for money-making notoriety apparently render him incapable of comprehending that men may differ from him and still be honest and patriotic; that men may differ from him and still never have their minds polluted by thought of the low plans and conspiracies for his undoing with which he credits them; and that there are men who do not play to the galleries even for the worshipped dollars; that there are men having an inherent aversion to the mountebank and his ignoble methods.

A short time later this same newspaper gleefully headlined proof that Dixon was nothing but a "rampant, anti-South Republican" who had endorsed McKinley and gold in 1896. And, it asked readers: "Is the South so poor in patriots that no less ignoble spokesman for Southern sentiment can be obtained? Is the South so poor in sense as to confide in the clatter of the showman and demagogue, double-faced and unscrupulous?"

Early in 1906 *The Clansman* opened at New York's Liberty Theater, lasting only six weeks. It also had a brief run in Washington, where one reviewer concluded that if the topical drama has arrived theater goers must be prepared for plays about railroad rebates, graft, and tariffs. In October 1906 the production was banned in Philadelphia after one noisy performance; and, in 1911—the same year in which Dixon tried unsuccessfully to film *The Clansman*—the city fathers of Orangeburg also refused to permit the play to be seen in their town.

It is apparent that Dixon's activities in the early 1900's—his attack on Ogden, his inaccurate interpretation of South Carolina history, and his violent debate with Gonzales—did little to pave the way for the reception of *The Birth of a Nation* in this state. Actually, this remarkable motion picture was not his creation, but the brainchild of David Wark Griffith, the Kentucky-born son of a Confederate colonel, "Roaring Jake" Griffith. As a stage-struck youth Griffith saw *The Clansman* and was greatly impressed with its powerful message.

From 1905 to 1914 Griffith lived in New York City where he became a prominent figure in the early film industry, turning out countless two-reelers which he contemptuously dubbed "sausages." Then, early in 1914 he began to talk with his cameraman, Billy Bitzer, about filming *The Clansman* on a huge scale. Bitzer was confused: "Griffith acted like here he had something worthwhile. . . . Personally I did not share the enthusiasm. I had read the book and figured out that a negro chasing a white girl was just another sausage after all, and how could you show it in the South?"

Nevertheless, throughout the spring of 1914 Griffith could talk of little else. He met with Dixon, discussed problems involved in filming his story, put together a script of sorts, and late in June set out for California accompanied by Bitzer and his camera. Fantastic as it may sound, only *one* camera was used throughout the entire production. Shooting commenced on July 4 and lasted about two months. During these weeks Griffith and his cast faced many problems. Because of war clouds in Europe it was difficult to obtain horses, mules, and cotton. Although the script was at times non-existent, some scenes were rehearsed twenty-two times before the camera rolled. In midsummer Griffith ran out of money, and at that moment Dixon showed up demanding the $2,500 promised him. Griffith eventually talked the author into accepting 25% of the profits instead. This reluctant decision would make Dixon a millionaire for this would be the most successful film ever made. Meanwhile, Griffith's backers dug up $60,000, and *The Birth of a Nation* was completed. In all, it cost $110,000, although advertisements and subsequent publicity would proclaim a figure of half a million.

Despite many obstacles, Griffith had at least two advantages: a superb cameraman and a dedicated cast. For the first time audiences would see extensive close-ups, night shots, and panoramic scenes. The cast, although not well paid (Lillian Gish worked for only $35 per week), became infected with the director's enthusiasm. The idea of a *twelve* reel movie fired their imagination.

During the fall months Griffith and Bitzer cut and spliced 140,000 feet of film into 12,000 feet of actual footage. The result was unveiled at Clune's auditorium in Los Angeles on February 8, 1915. That same day it was copyrighted in Washington as *The Birth of a Nation*. A short time later this original version, containing some 1,500 prints, was rushed to New York for a private showing to Dixon, the backers, and a group of very reluctant distributors. After all, they asked, who would pay *two dollars* to see a mere movie? Who would sit through twelve reels? However, the reaction, according to Dixon's unreliable memory, was electrifying. As the lights came on, he recalls jumping to his feet and shouting that it was "the birth of a nation!" Hence, the name of this great epic. This, however, overlooks the copyright filed several days earlier.

Nevertheless, distributors remained sceptical. The movie was too long, too expensive, too controversial. Then, Reverend Dixon's flair for publicity came into play. He recalled that at Johns Hopkins he had known Woodrow Wilson. If the chief executive approved of this movie, how could others object? So, Dixon asked his old friend if he would like to see a movie. On February 18, the president, his cabinet, and a few guests saw *The Birth of a Nation* at the White House. The following day the Supreme Court and members of Congress viewed the film. Wilson was greatly impressed. "It was," he said, "like writing history with lightning!" As Griffith relied heavily upon Wilson's *History of the American People* for some scenes, his approval comes as no surprise. Actually only the last half of the movie is based on *The Clansman*. The first half is a patched-up, southern-oriented tale of how slavery came into being.

On March 3, 1915, *The Birth of a Nation* opened at New York's Liberty Theater, the same place where *The Clansman* appeared nine years before. The movie, however, did much better, lasting forty-seven weeks. It was a tremendous success, but stirred up a violent controversy. Hundreds rioted in Boston, and irate patrons in other cities "egged" the screen, usually as Gus was chasing Flora Cameron. Early in April Dixon and Griffith were summoned to the office of New York's mayor where they met with two influential Negro leaders. Under pressure they agreed to delete some 170 prints from the film. Nevertheless, some critics were not satisfied. The NAACP threatened to produce its "answer" to *The Birth of a Nation*—"Lincoln's Dream." It appears to have been just that, a dream. There is no indication that such a film was ever made.

Most northern reviews, while lavish in praise of this technical triumph, branded the tale as a false, distorted appeal to race hatred.

Outlook said: "Mr. Dixon has a 'single track mind' and that track leads only through a very unpleasant country. He is a partisan, and a dangerous one. He can see questions only in broad splotches of black and white. He knows but one side of southern life, the sex problem of Aryan and Negro. The evil in *The Birth of a Nation* lies in the fact that the play is both a denial of the power of development within a free Negro and an exaltation of race war."

By autumn eight copies were being shown throughout the nation, and one of these opened a three-day run in Spartanburg's Harris Theater on October 21. The Spartanburg *Herald* hailed it as "the most remarkable moving picture ever thrown on the screen." The audience was "almost hysterical." Yet, the reviewer found nothing objectionable. True, several scenes might be called "sensational," but certainly not "harmful." The *Herald* saw Griffith's epic as a "plea for universal peace."

Three weeks later the controversial motion picture came to Charlotte, North Carolina. Several hundred York citizens went by special train to see what Dixon, a frequent visitor in their midst, had created. Some who attended recall only how exhausted they were when they returned at 4 A.M.; others remember the brilliant music. For, during its first circuit about the nation, Griffith's extravaganza had an orchestra of some thirty pieces, a score of people to manage sound effects, its own projection machine and screen—in all, two carloads of equipment accompanied *The Birth of a Nation*. It was, in fact, a mixture of stage production and motion picture. After all, you had to give folks someting 'extra special' for their two dollars! Like the Spartanburg *Herald*, the Charlotte *Observer* found no basis for northern criticism. Commenting editorially on Flora's efforts to elude Gus, the *Observer* noted: "One scene is devoted with tremendous realism to the ever-living terror of The Menace. O, Heart of the South! And, even that scene does not depict the full agony!"

On October 24 *The Birth of a Nation* opened in Columbia. Its arrival was heralded by a ten-day advertising campaign which never mentions the setting of this epic. In fact, references to South Carolina in advertisements appearing throughout this state are rare. This, coupled with wide-spread endorsements by local historians, indicates promoters were fully conscious of Dixon's troubles here ten years before. D. D. Wallace of the Wofford College faculty called the movie "stupendous." He said anyone who lived through war and reconstruction would understand those years better after seeing *The Birth of a Nation*. "Yes, there are some horrible things in it; but there are some horrible things in life, and I don't know that we are going to get rid of them by pretending that they are not there. Taken all in all, it is something that no American, certainly no Southern man or woman can afford not to see. I took the whole family except the baby, and if it comes along after she's big enough, I'll take her, too." J. A. Tillinghast of Converse College saw the movie twice when it appeared in Spartanburg and concluded that Griffith had done a great service by showing the horrors of war.

Late in January 1916 *The Birth of a Nation* played a week-long engagement at Charleston's Academy of Music. The *News & Courier* agreed it was a "remarkable picture" and essentially true. Perhaps the mobs of Klansmen were a bit large. But, this newspaper asked, "Will it do any good?" The editor was not sure. "The people of this section scarcely need the enlightenment which this photoplay has undoubtedly helped bring many people of the North."

During April, May, and June *The Birth of a Nation* appeared in numerous South Carolina communities, among them Orangeburg, Sumter, Darlington, Anderson, Chester, and Rock Hill. The pattern in each was the same: huge advertisements, reduced railroad rates, exhortations to read the book and see the movie. The Orangeburg *Times-Democrat* said that the movie's message was certainly plain and should be clear to any man who attempts to put the Negro into politics. "It is a great motion picture drama. As a work of art it stands preeminent in its field, but as a historical treatment of Reconstruction, and as the message of the South to the world then, and now, it has even a greater value."

The Anderson *Intelligencer,* one of the few South Carolina newspapers to give the movie extensive free publicity and relate it to the Piedmont region, had this to report:

A hush of expectancy swept across the vast audience as the curtains rose and the orchestra began to play a tune that harmonized with the opening scene. . . . In many parts of the theatre women were seen to weep and even the men repeatedly wiped their eyes and blew their noses like trumpets to hide their real feelings. . . . Before the picture ends, when the spectator has enjoyed nearly three hours of mingled emotions—happiness and sorrow —a feeling of repugnance to war creeps into the breast and when the Civil War comes to a close and the South's freed of carpetbaggers and evil Negroes, there goes up a shout of approval from every side, and one leaves the theatre in a happy frame of mind.

The Opera House in Chester received mail orders from over fifty miles away, and the Chester *Semi-Weekly News* had high praise: "To say that it exceeded all expectations for grandeur, thrills, and throbbing heart interest would be expressing it mildly. To dwellers of Carolina it falls little short of being a sacred epic in film and music and should be seen by every person in Chester County."

In Rock Hill there was the same circus-like atmosphere. The movie was scheduled to play three days, but remained for five. A local resident who as a youth sat through every showing recalls the difficulties faced by the troupe. Friedheim's Opera House was really nothing but a dance hall. Wiring was faulty, windows had to be darkened, seats provided. The reaction of the traveling group was one of deep despair. One member turned to a local resident and asked: "Gosh! Is this where you raise kittens?"

Five years later when the movie returned to South Carolina for a second time it showed at regular movie houses for about half as much. Top price was $1.00. In 1923 when it finally reached York—the community Dixon tried to re-create in *The Clansman*—tickets were only fifty cents. Throughout the twenties *The Birth of a Nation* continued to appear throughout the South, frequently with the solid endorsement of the local Klan. One of the bizarre by-products of Griffith's extravaganza was a re-kindling of interest in the Ku Klux Klan. This interest did not, however, extend to South Carolina. The revived Klan got little support in this state.

What *was* South Carolina's reaction to *The Birth of a Nation*? Clearly it was one of almost unanimous approval—unrestrained and enthusiastically so in most regions. Yet, there are indications that the major newspapers in this state, still somewhat irked by Dixon's flamboyant personality, withheld all-out endorsement. The advertising campaigns reveal an awareness of this anti-Dixon sentiment. His name is played down, there are few references to the movie's South Carolina setting, and endorsements of local historians are prominently featured—endorsements which presumably would dilute or erase haunting memories of Dixon's "historical license." And, although difficult to substantiate, it is apparent South Carolina Negroes soon learned about the message *The Birth of a Nation* was spreading.

This epic evidently found its most devoted fans among the Thomas Dixon-David Griffith age group—that is, those too young to remember the horrors of war and Reconstruction but young enough to support Ben Tillman and his avowed policy of white supremacy. For these folks and thousands of youngsters strongly indoctrinated in the Confederate tradition this was an unparalleled emotional experience. It was Christmas morning, circus day, and victory for the home team over its arch rival all rolled into one. A Rock Hill resident compares the impact to that of John Glenn's space flight. People could talk of little else. The daily business routine was forgotten. A lady in York, laughing as she recalled the exhausting train trip to Charlotte in 1915, exclaimed: "You know, it was the biggest thing ever to hit this town . . . up to that time, that is!" Perhaps this best sums up South Carolina's reaction to *The Birth of a Nation*. It was truly a memorable event. And, if not "the biggest thing to hit town," *The Birth of a Nation* certainly looms large in the memory of all who saw it.

Stump speaking in South Carolina during the 1930s varied little from that of "Pitchfork Ben's" day. Large crowds gathered wherever the candidates spoke, and a festive atmosphere prevailed. Moreover, the old type spellbinders were often still successful at their trade. Best known in the 1930s were Governor Olin D. Johnston, who had grown up as a poor boy on the farm and in the mill village, and Ellison D. ("Cotton Ed") Smith, the senior senator from Lynchburg, South Carolina. By contrast, there was the dapper and dignified junior senator, James F. Byrnes. Not only different in personality, Byrnes differed greatly from "Cotton Ed" on political issues. Byrnes, a staunch supporter of Franklin D. Roosevelt's measures to alleviate the depression, shortly became the most influential South Carolina politician in Washington since John C. Calhoun. On the other hand, Senator Smith was an outspoken foe of Roosevelt's "New Deal." Yet, Palmetto voters insisted on keeping both men in the Senate, "Little Jimmy" being re-elected in 1936 and "Cotton Ed" in 1938.

The following selection is *Time*'s report on the Byrnes campaign in 1936.

33

"PALMETTO STUMP"—
'THIRTIES STYLE *

Only a very few highly literate and exceptionally inquisitive South Carolinians know who Joseph Warren ("Tieless Joe") Tolbert is. Those who do recognize this unkempt, unshaven oldster from Ninety Six as the Republican leader of the most overwhelmingly Democratic State in the Union, regard him with political scorn and social contempt. To most decent whites he is guilty of South Carolina's supreme sin: trafficking with Negroes for political purposes. Nevertheless, in one day last week "Tieless Joe" Tolbert and his black-&- whites turned a trick the like of which it takes the State's Democrats more than two months to achieve. Meeting in Columbia Boss Tolbert and his Republican committee quickly nominated his nephew, Joseph Augustis Tolbert of Greenville, to stand for the U. S. Senate this November.

South Carolina Democrats will pick their Senatorial nominee in next week's primary—and simultaneously the next Senator from this once aristocratic State. To most of them the only question to be settled by a prolonged campaign is whether two anti-New Deal Democrats opposing President Roosevelt's personal friend, Senator James Francis Byrnes, can make a sufficient dent in his majority to injure the prestige of the New Deal in the country at large.

Unique is South Carolina's method of campaigning for a primary election. In 1890 Benjamin Ryan ("Pitchfork Ben") Tillman, out for Governor, charged that only a man of wealth could reach the people through the Press, stumped each & every county in the State in person, won a great victory. Two years later the anti-Tillman faction sent its candidate out to dog the Governor around the State. Thus the custom developed of having all the candidates in a State-wide primary travel together, speak in the same place at the same time. This system is hard on office-seekers but easy on the voters who have to

* Reprinted from *Time*, XXVIII (August 24, 1936), 17–22. Courtesy TIME, The Weekly Newsmagazine; Copyright Time Inc. 1936.

turn out only once to hear all the candidates. To enter such a Democratic primary, each & every candidate binds himself to obey the party's rules, one of which is to follow the State-wide campaign itinerary drawn up by the State committee.

This year's Senatorial campaign began at Lexington, across the Congaree River from Columbia, on June 9 and rolled on, a county a day, through the west central part of the State. After two weeks an adjournment was taken so that candidates could attend the Democratic National Convention in Philadelphia. By July 4 the tour had covered the southern "low country" counties along the coast, then skipped to the Piedmont. In mid-July the stumpsters knocked off for another week to allow voters time to harvest their tobacco crop, resumed their speech-making in the northeastern tier of counties.

The routine of the meetings in each county is the same. On the scheduled day fields and cotton mills are deserted, Fords and Chevrolets, new when AAA bounties were largest, fill the courthouse square, and sunburned countrymen and linty mill hands gather to judge the candidates at first hand. The candidates arrive separately, take separate rooms at the town hotel, generally eat at separate tables. At the appointed hour each, in rotating alphabetical order, mounts the platform with exactly 30 minutes to speak. Afterwards there is hobnobbing and hand-shaking with admirers outside the courthouse.

To his two touring companions this summer dapper, little Jimmy Byrnes never referred by name. In his speeches they were "a former Mayor of Charleston," and a "retired officer of Marines." The first was Lawyer Thomas Porcher Stoney, who is not a U. S. District Attorney because Senator Byrnes failed to get him the appointment. The Marine is Colonel William Curry Harllee, whose chief service to the service was replacing enlisted men with civilians as servants. Colonel Harllee retired a few months ago without the generalship which he expected, because Senator Byrnes failed to wangle it for him.

Rather better, however, than the average run of disappointed office seekers were Senator Byrnes's two opponents. Candidate Stoney, born 46 years ago on Midway Plantation in Berkeley County, is a fiery stumpster, full of gags and gusto, with an impressive shock of iron-gray hair and a rafter-raising bellow. Candidate Harllee, tall, bald, gaunt and aging, was born in Florida, spent years in the Philippines, China, Hawaii, Cuba, Santo Domingo, Haiti. Because of his South Carolina ancestry, however, he fished for votes by traditionally invoking the shades of the State's particular heroes: John C. Calhoun,

Senator, Secretary of War, Secretary of State, Vice President of the U. S.; Wade Hampton, Confederate General, ("Hampton's Legion"), first Democratic Governor after Reconstruction, Senator; Ben Tillman, Governor, longtime Senator, rabble-rouser. A Harllee invocation: "I am a Democrat of the old-fashioned brand. . . . I shall be guided by the beacon lights kindled on the altars of our ancient faith . . . and kept aglow by . . . that paragon among Democrats, John C. Calhoun . . . and the noble Wade Hampton who will stand ennobled as long as sacrifice and service to mankind measures the standard of nobility among Christian men and Christian women."

To his roots in South Carolina, Colonel Harllee pointed when he campaigned at Dillon: "Near Little Rock, on the banks of the Little Pee Dee, in our family cemetery where, to use the words of my beloved kinswoman, Mrs. Hattie Dillon David, for whose father Dillon County was named, the lovely willows and the cypress cast their soft shadows and the dogwood and the plum trees brighten the spot with their wealth of blossom in springtime, rest three preceding generations of my forefathers."

Born in Charleston 57 years ago to a poor, widowed mother, James Francis Byrnes learned shorthand, served as a court reporter in the Aiken Circuit, was elected to Congress in 1910. Ambitious, he ran for the Senate in 1924, was beaten by Coleman Livingston Blease, whose appeal to South Carolina "red necks" was then irresistible. Moving to Spartanburg to practice law, Byrnes reversed the result on Senator Blease in 1930. Opening his campaign for re-election last June he declared: "What South Carolina needs is not a good political campaign but a good rain."

Senator Byrnes studiously ignored the attacks of his opponents, stuck to the proposition "Roosevelt will be elected and so will Jimmy Byrnes." He would not even stay to hear their speeches. At one of the early meetings Candidate Stoney demanded: "Is Senator Byrnes in the house?" Fingers pointed to Byrnes standing in a rear doorway.

"Come and sit down here, Jimmy," roared Stoney, "I want you to hear this."

"No thank you," the Senator shot back, "I'll take it standing up."

Nub of the South Carolina fight was the New Deal and the slavish support Senator Byrnes has given President Roosevelt. To charges of New Deal extravagance Senator Byrnes countered at every meeting by repeating the story of a farmer who promised himself to economize but, just as he started, his wife fell desperately ill. She could be saved only by an operation, but her husband went to her and said: "I am economizing. An operation would cost far too much. You'll have to die. Goodby, my love, goodby." Candidate Stoney said he had heard this sad tale so often that he felt like calling a doctor for the poor woman and paying the bill himself.

A prime campaign statistic which Senator Byrnes used to his advantage: South Carolina received $242,000,000 in relief, AAA benefit payments, etc. from the New Deal, while only $10,000,000 of Federal taxes had been collected in the State. This prompted Candidate Harllee to cry:

"Who has fouled the nest of the Democratic Party? It is those who would prostitute its good name by such acts as the boasted plundering of the people's treasury on the '250 million for ten million' scale. . . . O shame, where is thy blush!"

When Senator Byrnes quit the campaign tour in mid-June to attend the closing of Congress and the Philadelphia convention, Candidate Stoney made much of his absence, boasted he could beat "Little Jimmy" if he could get him back on the stump. While absent, though, the Senator did some of his most effective campaigning, got Admiral Standley, Acting Secretary of the Navy, to guarantee no reductions of personnel at Charleston's Navy Yard, got Harry Hopkins to raise South Carolina's relief wages $2 a week. But his visit to the Democratic Convention at Philadelphia backfired on him when he returned to the South Carolina campaign.

Two familiar items in most South Carolina campaigns are "Niggers" and "Catholics." Senator Byrnes's mother was a devout Catholic, as is his first cousin, famed Washington Lawyer Frank Hogan. Though Byrnes was never an out-&-out Catholic, his early connections with that faith were used against him in 1924 when pamphlets saying, "Remember when Jimmy Byrnes was an altar boy" flooded the State. Now, to the great disgust of South Carolina's few Catholics, the Senator is a thoroughgoing Episcopalian.

This year the "Nigger issue" has been raised against Byrnes, who once in Aiken unsuccessfully tried to get a grand jury to indict a white man for shooting a blackamoor. At the Philadelphia convention South Carolina's Senior Senator Ellison D. Smith made headlines by walking out in protest when a Negro preacher prayed over the assembled Democrats (*Time*, July 6). Senator Byrnes, busy on the Resolutions Committee, did not walk out. Back in South Carolina Candidate Stoney on his tour passed around pictures of the Negro preacher, paid tribute to "courageous Senator Smith," declared, "Little Jimmy Byrnes is not the man we sent to Washington as a Senator, else he would have walked out too."

Croaked Candidate Harllee, "Our State has had plenty of experience with the kind of harpies who consort with colored people to control the Government."

If an outsider had listened to the campaign speeches of Colonel William Harllee, unsuccessful candidate for the Senate in 1936, or "Cotton Ed" Smith in 1938, he might have thought himself back in the mid-nineteenth century. He would have heard, among other things, a glorification of Confederate heroes and detected a nostalgia for the Old South.

This affinity for the "Lost Cause" was commonplace throughout South Carolina, at least until World War II. It is best expressed and explained by Ben Robertson in *Red Hills and Cotton,* first published in 1942. Robertson, Pickens County native, was reared amidst a number of older relatives who had fought under the Confederate banner. He had frequently listened to their war stories. From his red hills he had moved on to become a fine journalist and war correspondent before his life was tragically snuffed out in a plane crash at Lisbon, February 1943.

34

CLINGING TO THE "LOST CAUSE" *

Ben Robertson

It is lost wars that age a people in their country, and we have lost more than one struggle in South Carolina. We were beaten by Spaniards in 1702 and by Indians in 1761; we have lost costly campaigns to the English and have been overwhelmed by the Yankees. Of course we have won some wars; we have whipped Frenchmen in our state, we have whipped Spaniards, Indians, and Englishmen, but successful wars are forgotten—they are like other kinds of fulfillment. You have accomplished something you have started to accomplish, it is finished. It is defeat that lives on and takes the years to smother. Of all people in the world, we in the South should have been forewarned about the Germans—we should have known what defeat would do to the German nation. We should not have forgotten our successful war of 1918 with its half-defeated peace. We of all people should have known we should either have demolished the German Empire or have restored it to glory.

We should have been forewarned in 1918 because twice within one century our own state was pillaged and burned by enemy armies. Our state is pocked with battlefields—Cowpens, Kings Mountain, Eutaw Springs. Old Charleston, fragile and chilled with beauty, was until 1914 one of the most bombarded and besieged cities in existence. The mellow bells in St. Michael's white tower have been back and back again over the ocean. And then there is Columbia on the high hills of the Congaree—the city that Sherman burned. There are still scars on our Statehouse in Columbia from the cannons of Sherman—damaged stone that for eighty years we have refused to repair. We are too proud to repair those battlemarks, so we have just left them as

* Excerpt from chapter 1 of *Red Hills and Cotton: An Upcountry Memory*, 2nd ed. (Columbia: University of South Carolina Press, 1960) , pp. 23–30; Copyright 1942 by Ben Robertson; Copyright © 1960 by the University of South Carolina Press. Reprinted by permission of the University of South Carolina Press and Mrs. Julian Longley, Sr.

Sherman left them, and have placed bright bronze stars beside each one of them to fix the attention of the stranger. Trouble and defeat have been with us so much in our state that we have turned trouble into a glowing virtue. Trouble is made to shine in our sky. One of the sayings my Grandmother Bowen used to quote us was: "Shrink not from facing sorrow—she is the messenger of God to thee."

Hard times either embitter you or leave you mellowed like crab-apples and turnips after the iciness of frost. Troubles have given us perspective in our country, a kind of sorrowful sympathy and under-standing—a view of all life as alternate capture and release. We know in Carolina that nothing lasts forever—neither victory nor defeat, nor spring nor summer—and no matter what comes up, we can usually find within our rich experience some precedent to steer us. We know if the cotton fails that the corn will probably prosper. If there is drought and the young begin to worry about all the crops, the old will tell us not to give up hope—it can't be worse than 1845, when the rivers dried to a trickle and even our cows died. If the summer is cold—there was the year it frosted on the 6th of June; if the winter is mild—well, the roses once bloomed at Christmas. We have been at the top and at the bottom in South Carolina. We almost alone in our small Southern state directed the history of the American Union from 1830 up to 1860—one brilliant Carolinian after another was produced as we needed new leaders. We have been down now for the last eighty years. We have tried radicalism and have failed, we have tried impatience. Now, whenever we come to any new crossroads, both our white people and our black people are apt to advise caution. We are conservative because of our troubles and because of our age. We are old, but at the same time we are tough; we are a branch of Americans, beaten so many times that we are not appalled any more in the slightest by any kind of dire prospect—not by five-cent cotton nor by forty-cent meat, nor even by another gigantic foreign war. We have hung on in spite of every-thing for so long now that I cannot think of any sort of threat to America that would ever make us quit.

When we were growing up, our Southern country and all of our older people were still grieving. We had lost the Southern cause—the kind of country we had wanted, the sort of life we had created out of the earlier Revolution. We had lost everything that to us and Thomas Jefferson had been so high and holy, we had been nailed by a Northern economic system to a sort of Northern cross; almost we were strangers stranded in our own country. Always and everywhere as I was growing up, there was the lament: we had lost, we had lost. Among our own kinfolks our Confederate soldiers could not bear to think that so many of our fine and promising and dear relations had died on the battlefields for nothing more than failure. They could not bear to let the lives of so many of our kinfolks sink into such futility and little use. They could not bear that—so they resurrected all the dead. The Confederates who came home from the war spent the rest of their lifetime telling a generation of Southern children and a generation of Southern grandchildren about the men who had died for the South in the Civil War. They gave those dead young soldiers a new life in a glowing personal legend. I don't suppose there ever was an army that lived on individually as the Confederate army has lived for these last eighty years throughout the South. Today I know a great deal more about my Great-Uncle Joel, who was killed at Fredericksburg, than I know about his namesake, my Uncle Joel—and I knew my Uncle Joel well. My Grandfather Bowen and my Great-Uncle Bob, the one who was shot in the hip at Missionary Ridge—these two veterans sat for years on our wide piazza and told us about the men who had been killed in the battles. We would sit in the warm Southern darkness and the katydids would cry in the oak trees, and the tale would grow and grow. They told us so vividly and in such detail that sometimes I feel I have taken part myself in half the campaigns of the Confederate army.

Like most Southerners, I visit battlefields. Southerners will visit almost any battlefield anywhere, but we are especially fond of the Civil War scenes because we know who fought where and how they did their fighting. Once at Fredericksburg, I heard my Uncle Wade correct a professional guide—a man hired by the government to show visitors about the field. The guide said so and so had happened, my Uncle Wade said he was mistaken. Uncle Wade said: "Uncle Alf said this was the way."

I enjoy walking across battlefields, thinking of other men in other times, facing their trouble. I cannot keep back the tears even now at Chickamauga and at Manassas. I am overwhelmed at Appomattox— I remember how my grandfather said he had felt there, hungry and tired and beaten. How sorry he said he had felt for General Lee. How broken-hearted for the South. To me one of the holiest of the world's holy places is the field at Gettysburg across which the army of Pickett charged—their gesture was like so many of the world's great gestures, a defeat for the spirit. It is the devotion of the

Confederate army that stirs me at Gettysburg and all those places, the bravery, the courage, the manner of the dying.

The past that Southerners are forever talking about is not a dead past—it is a chapter from the legend that our kinfolks have told us, it is a living past, living for a reason. The past is a part of the present, it is a comfort, a guide, a lesson. My Grandfather Robertson was captured in 1865 and walked after the war was over from a prison camp on the Hudson River all the way to South Carolina, a hard long journey in those days. He was ragged when he got there. Sixty-two years later, during the depression of 1932, I was working in New York, and I said to myself I need not worry too much if I lost my job—what my grandfather could do in 1865, I could do in 1932. I had the same valley to return to that he had. Both of us had the hills and the fields and home. And when I had to be bombed in England in 1940, I said to myself that I had come to my Gettysburg, and what my grandfather had gone through, I could go through. I feel now about London as my grandfather felt about that town in Pennsylvania—I have fought over every inch of the ground. The past encourages us Southerners at all times of crisis.

Often I am a sort of Confederate—often I try to be my grandfather's grandson. I even find that I have a queer way of translating the Confederacy straight into the present United States. I in my generation am Southern, but it is the army of the United States that is my army, and I find that it has always been my army. It seems to me it was the North and not the South that seceded, it seems to me that we were the Union, and that the Union went with us—the uninterrupted strain of the United States moved along to Richmond and then back again to the north bank of the Potomac. I cannot imagine any United States that we were not always a part of. Lee and Jackson were our generals and Lincoln was President of our United States. It was Sherman whom we fought, and Sherman was not of America at all; Sherman was like Santa Ana [sic] and Cornwallis—he was foreign. Once my Great-Aunt Narcissa told us she hoped William Tecumseh Sherman burned forever in the hottest stove in hell.

I am so unconsciously Southern that even today it surprises me to hear officers of the present United States Army describe movements that Federal troops made during the battles of the Civil War. It startles me to realize that there are Americans who study what Grant and Sherman did. It is just like reading Tolstoy and learning what the Russians did when Napoleon was marching toward Moscow. It is like hearing a Filipino discussing the Philippine insurrection from

am born so Southern that
co, I was astonished when
1 of the Thirtieth United
h Georgia. My army play-
re surprised had it struck
conscious Southern mind
he Confederate army that
cause—my grandfathers
f God, they have assured

In the latter part of the nineteenth century lynchings were quite common in South Carolina, fifty-two occurring in the 1890s alone. Not infrequently high public officials openly condoned mob action against alleged criminals, and seldom did a sheriff make a serious effort to protect the intended victim. By the 1920s, however, public opinion had slowly undergone a change; lynchings had noticeably decreased. In fact, only eleven occurred during the entire decade.

Nearly all victims of "Judge Lynch" were Negroes, invariably accused of crimes against whites. Rarely did law enforcement officials make arrests or indict the lynchers. In any event, there were no convictions. But as South Carolina passed through the Great Depression and World War II, public opinion veered still further from lynch law, as evidenced by the case of Willie Earle.

Earle, a Negro, was arrested in Pickens County on February 16, 1947, charged with the murder of Thomas Watson Brown, a Greenville taxicab driver. The following night a mob forced jailor Ed Gilstrap to surrender the prisoner to them. Later his body was found just inside the Greenville County line. Investigation by South Carolina law enforcement officers, aided by the FBI, led to the arrest of thirty-one persons, twenty-eight of whom were taxicab drivers and friends of the dead Brown.

To arrest a large group of persons for allegedly lynching a Negro was novel for South Carolina and unusual most anywhere. But if the accused were somewhat concerned by their indict-ment, they must have been genuinely shaken when Governor Strom Thurmond sought a vigorous prosecution of the case. Luckily for the accused, confessions they had made at the time of their arrests were ruled inadmissible evidence at the trial, thus weakening the state's case. The jury acquitted the defendants, as it might have anyway. Nevertheless, as of this writing, no person has been lynched in South Carolina since Willie Earle.

The Earle case attracted nationwide attention, and national news media sent reporters and photographers to Greenville to cover the story. Among the reporters was Rebecca West for the *New Yorker*. The following selection is excerpted from her account of the trial, and entitled "Opera in Greenville."

35

"OPERA IN GREENVILLE" *

Rebecca West

Near the center of Greenville there stands an old white church, with a delicate spire and handsome steps leading down from a colonnade—the kind of building that makes an illusion of space around itself. This is the First Baptist Church. In there, on Sunday evenings, there is opera. The lovely girls with their rich hair curling around their shoulders and their flowered dresses showing their finely molded throats and arms sit beside the tall young men, whose pale shirts show the squareness of their shoulders and the slimness of their waists, and they join in coloratura hymns with their parents and their grandparents, who sing, like their children, with hope and vehemence, having learned to take things calmly no more than the older characters in opera. As they sing, the women's dresses become crumpled wraps, the men's shirts cling to them, although the service does not begin till eight o'clock at night. But undistracted by the heat, they listen, still and yet soaring, to the anthems sung by an ecstatic choir and to a sermon that is like a bass recitative, ending in an aria of faith, mounting to cadenzas of adoration. In no other place are Baptists likely to remind a stranger of Verdi.

In the Court House, also, there was opera. This is a singularly hideous building, faced with yellow washroom tiles, standing in Main Street, next to the principal hotel, which, it should be noted for those who want to understand the character of Greenville, is cleaner and more comfortable and kinder to the appetite than most of the great New York hotels at this moment. The courtroom is about the size of the famous court at the Old Bailey, in London. In the body of the courtroom there were chairs for about three hundred white per-

* From A TRAIN OF POWDER by Rebecca West. Copyright 1947 by Rebecca West. Originally appeared in The New Yorker [XXIII (June 14, 1947), pp. 31–34, 36–40]. Reprinted by permission of The Viking Press, Inc.

sons. The front rows were occupied by the thirty-one defendants who were being tried for lynching a Negro early on the morning of February 17th of this year. With the exception of three young men, one a member of a wealthy mill-owning family, one a salesman, and one a restaurant proprietor, these defendants were all Greenville taxi-drivers. Many people, including a number of Greenville residents, some of whom desired them to be acquitted of all charges on the ground that lynching is a social prophylactic, talked of them as if they were patently and intensely degraded. As a matter of fact, they covered a wide range of types, most of them very far from repulsive. Some were quite good-looking and alert young men; most were carefully and cleanly dressed; some were manifest eccentrics. The most curious in aspect was a young man of twenty-five who must have weighed about three hundred pounds. The contours of his buttocks and stomach suggested that they were molded in some ductile substance like butter, and his face, which was smiling and playful, was pressed upward, till it turned toward the ceiling, by an enormous accumulation of fat under the chin and jaws. His name was Joy, and he was known as Fat Joy. The most conspicuous by reason of character was Roosevelt Carlos Hurd, Sr., who was a taxi-driver also working as a taxi dispatcher, a man of forty-five with hair that stood up like a badger's coat, eyes set close together and staring out under glum brows through strong glasses, and a mouth that was unremitting in its compression. He looked like an itinerant preacher devoted to the worship of a tetchy and uncoöperative God. In his statement, he had declared that his education had stopped in the second grade. This did not necessarily imply that he was of weak intelligence. When he was a boy, there were no laws against child labor in the State of South Carolina, and it is probable that he went to work. Several of the statements made by other defendants alleged that Mr. Hurd was the actual trigger man of the lynching, the man who fired the shot that killed the Negro.

Nearly all these defendants were exercising a right their state permits to all persons accused of a capital offense. They had brought their families to sit with them in court. Many had their wives beside them, young women, for the most part very young women, in bright cotton and rayon dresses, their curled hair wild about them. A number of these women had brought their children with them; one had five scrambling over her. All the children were plump and comely, and though some were grimy, all of them were silent and miraculously court-broken. Mr. Hurd, though married and a father, was accompanied only by his own father, a thin and sharp-nosed man, his eyes censorious behind gold-rimmed spectacles, the whole of him blanched and shrivelled by austerity as by immersion in a caustic fluid. It was altogether plain that at any moment he and his son might become possessed by the idea that they were appointed God's arm and instrument, and that their conception of God would render the consequence of this conviction far from reasonably bland. . . .

Behind the defendants and their families sat something under two hundred of such white citizens of Greenville as could find the time to attend the trial, which was held during working hours. Some were drawn from the men of the town who are too old or too sick to work, or who do not enjoy work and use the Court House as a club, sitting on the steps, chewing and smoking and looking down on Main Street through the hot, dancing air, when the weather is right for that, and going inside when it is better there. They were joined by a certain number of men and women who did not like the idea of people being taken out of jail and murdered, and by others who liked the idea quite well. None of these expressed their opinions very loudly. There were also a number of the defendants' friends. Upstairs, in the deep gallery, sat about a hundred and fifty Negroes, under the care of two white bailiffs. Many of them, too, were court spectators by habit. It is said that very few members of the advanced group of colored people in the town were present. There were reasons, reticently guarded but strongly felt, that they did not want to make an issue of the case. They thought it best to sit back and let the white man settle whether or not he liked mob rule. But every day there went into court a number of colored men and women who were conspicuously handsome and fashionably dressed, and had resentment and the proud intention not to express it written all over them. They might be put down as Negroes who feel the humiliation of their race so deeply that they will not even join in the orthodox movements for its emancipation, because these are, to their raw sensitiveness, tainted with the assumption that Negroes have to behave like good children to win a favorable report from the white people. In the shadows of the balcony the dark faces of these people could not be seen. Their clothes sat there, worn by sullen space. The shoulders of a white coat drooped; a hat made of red roses tilted sidewise, far sidewise. The only Negroes who were clearly visible and bore a label were two young men who sat in the front row of the balcony every day, cheerful and dignified, with something more than spontaneous cheerfulness and dignity, manifestly on parade. They were newspapermen from two Northern Negro journals. They had started at the press table down in the front of the court, for the newspaper people there, Northern and Southern, national and local, had made no objection, and neither had the judge. But one of the defense attorneys said that it was as good as giving the case to him to have a nigger sitting at the press table along with white men and women, and this remark was repeated. Also, the local Negroes intimated that they would take it as a favor if the Northern Negroes went up into the gallery. So they took their seats up there, where, it may be remarked, it was quite impossible to get anything like a complete record of the proceedings. Then there was a very strong agitation to get them to come back to the press table. But that turned out to be inspired by the defense. Such was the complication of the case.

It was complicated even to the extent of not being a true lynching case, although the man taken from prison was a Negro and the men charged with killing him were white. Or, rather, it was not a pure lynching case. The taxi-drivers of Greenville are drawn from the type of men who drive taxis anywhere. They are people who dislike steady work in a store or a factory or an office, or have not the aptitude for it, have a certain degree of mechanic intelligence, have no desire to rise very far in the world, enjoy driving for its own sake, and are not afraid of the dangers that threaten those who are on the road at night. They are, in fact, tough guys, untainted by intellectualism, and their detachment from the stable life of the community around them gives them a clan spirit that degenerates at times into the gang spirit. The local conditions in Greenville encourage this clan spirit. In every big town, the dangers that threaten taxi-drivers as they go about their work are formidable and shameful to society, and they increase year by year. In Greenville, they are very formidable indeed. A great many people are likely to hire taxis, for there are relatively few automobiles in the region; two-thirds of the people who are likely to hire a Greenville taxi live in small communities or isolated homes; it is so hot for the greater part of the year that people prefer to drive by night. Hence the taxi-drivers spend a great part of their time making journeys out of town after dark. In consequence, a large number of taxi-drivers have during the last few years been robbed and assaulted, sometimes seriously, by their fares. The number of these crimes that has not been followed by any arrest is, apparently, great enough to make the taxi-drivers feel aggrieved. The failure to make an arrest has been especially marked in cases in which the assailants were supposedly Negroes, for the reason, it is said, that Negroes are hard to identify. The taxi-drivers therefore had a resentment against fares who assaulted them, Negroes in general, and the police. In defense of the police, it is alleged that investigation of these crimes is made difficult because a certain number of them never happen at all. Taxi-drivers who have got into money troubles have been known to solve them by pretending that they have been robbed of their money by fares, whom they describe as Negroes in order to cash in on racial prejudice.

On February 15, 1947, an incident occurred that drew the taxi-drivers of Greenville very close together. A driver named Brown picked up a Negro fare, a boy of twenty-four called Willie Earle, who asked him to drive to his mother's home in Pickens County, about eighteen miles from Greenville. Mrs. Earle, by the way, had given birth to Willie when she was fourteen. Both Willie Earle and Brown had been the victims of tragedy. Willie Earle had been a truck driver and had greatly enjoyed his occupation. But he was an epileptic, and though his mates conspired with him to conceal this fact from his employer, there came a day when he fell from the truck in a fit and injured himself. His employer, therefore, quite properly decided that he could not employ him on a job in which he was so likely to come to harm, and dismissed him. He could not get any other employment as a truck driver and was forced to work as a construction laborer, an occupation that he did not like so well and that brought him less money. He became extremely depressed, and began to drink heavily. His fits became more frequent, and he developed a great hostility to white men. He got into trouble for the first time in his life, for a sudden and unprovoked assault on a contractor who employed him, and was sent to the penitentiary, from which he had not been long released when he made his journey with Brown. Brown's tragedy was also physical. He had been wounded in the first World War and had become a taxi-driver, although he was not of the usual type, because his state of health obliged him to take up work that he could leave when he needed rest. He was a man of thoughtful and kindly character. A Greenville resident who could be trusted told me that in the course of some social-service work he had come across a taxi-driver and his wife who had suffered exceptional misfortune, and that he had been most impressed by the part that Brown had played in helping them to get on their feet again. "You could quite fairly say," this resident told me, "that Brown was an outstanding man, who was a good influence on these taxi boys, and always tried to keep them out of trouble. Lynching is just the sort of thing he wouldn't have let them get into."

Willie Earle reached his home that night on foot. Brown was found bleeding from deep knife wounds beside his taxi a mile or two away and was taken to a hospital, where he sank rapidly. Willie was arrested, and put in Pickens County Jail. Late on the night of February 16th, the melancholy and passionate Mr. Roosevelt Carlos Hurd was, it was said, about certain business. Later, the jailer of the Pickens County Jail telephoned to the sheriff's office in Greenville to say that a mob of about fifty men had come to the jail in taxi-cabs and forced him to give Willie Earle over to them. A little later still, somebody telephoned to the Negro undertaker in the town of Pickens to tell him that there was a dead nigger in need of his offices by the slaughter-pen in a by-road off the main road from Greenville to Pickens. He then telephoned the coroner of Greenville County, whose men found Willie Earle's mutilated body lying at that place. He had been beaten and stabbed and shot in the body and the head. The bushes around him were splashed with his brain tissue. His own people sorrowed over his death with a grief that was the converse of the grief Brown's friends felt for him. They mourned Brown because he had looked after them; Willie Earle's friends mourned him because they had looked after him. He had made a number of respectable friends before he became morose and intractable. . . .

The men who took Willie Earle away were in a state of mind not accurately to be defined as blood lust. They were moved by an emotion that is held high in repute everywhere and especially high in this community. All over the world friendship is regarded a sacred bond, and in South Carolina it is held that it should override nearly all other considerations. Greenville had at first felt some surprise that one of the defense attorneys, Mr. Thomas Wofford, had accepted the case. It was not easy for a stranger to understand this surprise, for the case might have been tailored to fit Mr. Wofford; but all the same, surprise was generally felt. When, however, it was realized that the group of defendants he represented included the half-brother of a dead friend of Mr. Wofford, his action was judged comprehensible and laudable. It is not to be wondered at, therefore, if in Greenville a group of very simple people, grieving over the cruel slaughter of a beloved friend, felt that they had the right to take vengeance into their own hands. They would feel it more strongly if there was one among them who believed that all is known, that final judgment is possible, that if Brown was a good man and Willie Earle was a bad man, the will of God regarding these two men was quite plain. It would, of course, be sheer nonsense to pretend that the men, whoever they were, who killed Willie Earle were not affected in their actions by the color of Willie Earle's skin. They certainly did not believe that the law would pursue them—at least, not very far or very fast—for killing a Negro. But it is more than possible that they would have killed Willie Earle even if he had been white, provided they had been sure he had murdered Brown. The romances in statement form [their signed confessions] throw a light on the state of mind of those who later told of getting Willie Earle into a taxi and driving him to a quiet place where he was to be killed. One says that a taxi-driver sat beside him and "talked nice to him." He does not mean that he talked in a way that Willie Earle enjoyed but that the taxi-drivers thought that what he was saying was elevating. Mr. Hurd described how Willie Earle sat in the back seat of a Yellow Cab and a taxi-driver knelt on the front seat and exhorted him, "Now you have confessed to cutting Mr. Brown, now we want to know who was the other Negro with you." Willie Earle answered that he did not know; and it appears to be doubtful that there was another Negro with him. The taxi-driver continued, in the accents of complacent pietism, "You know we brought you out here to kill you. You don't want to die with a lie in your heart and on your tongue."

Brown's friends were in the state of bereavement that is the worst to bear. Brown was not dead. He was dying, and they could do nothing to save him. They were in that state of frustration that makes atheists at the deathbed of their loved ones curse God. "They then drug the Negro out of the car," said Mr. Hurd in his statement. ("Drug" is certainly a better word than "dragged.") Nobody speaks of doing anything there beside the slaughter-pen; they all speak of hearing things. One heard "the tearing of cloth and flesh," another heard "some licks like they were pounding him with the butt end of a gun." Some heard the Negro say, "Lord, you done killed me." Some saw as well as heard. "I saw," stated one, "Hurd aim the single shotgun towards the ground in the direction of where I judged the Negro was laying and pulled the trigger; I then heard the shot fired. I then heard Hurd ask someone to give him another shell." But Mr. Hurd also is among those who heard but did not do. He did not even see. "When I seen they were going to kill the Negro," he stated, "I just turned around, because I did not want to see it."

People can become accustomed to committing acts of cruelty; recent Europe proves that. But the first act of cruelty disgusts and shames far past the unimaginative man's power of prevision. The men who had joined the lynching party in the mood of righteous men fulfilling a duty did not, according to their statements, enjoy the actual lynching. "I only heard one report from a gun because I immediately drove away," stated one. "I have worked only one night since then," stated another. Fat Joy, another says, was overcome by terror on the way home, and drove up to one of the taxis and said, "Let's drive side by side; I think the law is coming." But it was only the civilian car that had been with them all night. Of their return to the town, another states, "I got out at the Southern depot and went into the Southern Café. I got a cup of coffee. The man George, a Greek, behind the counter said, 'Did you get him?' I said, 'Who do you mean?' He said, 'You know.' I said, 'I don't know what you're talking bout.' " It was so little like what they had expected that even Mr. Hurd informed the F.B.I. that he thought it had all been a mistake, and recalled that he had never been in trouble for anything before. That the deed sickened them was proved beyond a shadow of doubt in the Court House. When Sam Watt, the assistant but more conspicuous prosecuting attorney, read from the statements the details of what had been done to Willie Earle and described them as the detestable horrors that they were, the defendants were ashamed. They did not like their wives to hear them; and indeed their wives were also sickened. Mr. Hurd's father himself, whose loyalty to Mr.

Hurd will be unshakable in eternity, looked down his long nose; so might an Inquisitor look, suddenly smitten with doubt of the purging flame. That hour passed. There were those at the trial who saw to that. But in that hour the defendants surely hated evil and loved good.

As South Carolina legislators found no legal way to frustrate the Court's decision in *Smith* v. *Allwright,* the Democratic primary was opened to Negro voters in 1948. However, the pronounced conservative reaction was strengthened by a civil rights plank added to the national Democratic platform of 1948. Many South Carolina Democrats and those of other southern states balked at this. Unable to block President Truman's renomination, they refused to support him for re-election. Instead, they organized the Dixiecrat Party, with South Carolina's Governor J. Strom Thurmond as presidential nominee. Governor Thurmond carried four southern states in a losing battle.

Thurmond, with somewhat of a liberal image when elected governor in 1946, was henceforth known as a staunch conservative. He was not alone. James F. Byrnes, former "New Dealing" senator, Supreme Court Justice, and secretary of state, had likewise turned against the national Democratic administration. In 1950 he came out of political retirement to run for governor, winning easily. In his autobiography *All in One Lifetime,* Governor Byrnes gives an account of his administration.

36

A SENIOR STATESMAN
COMES OUT OF RETIREMENT *

James F. Byrnes

It may have been because of my discussion of the problems of state governments that letters came to me from people in all walks of life throughout the state, urging me to become a candidate for Governor. Some pointed out that while I had spent many years in the service of the federal government, I had served my state only for two years as prosecuting attorney in my early life.

Whether it was the old horse in the Fire Department responding from habit to a fire alarm or just susceptibility to flattery, I announced my candidacy. As I had been away from the state so much during the war years, it was surprising that, with three opponents, I received nearly 80 per cent of the votes in the Democratic primary. This was equivalent to election, since I had no opponent in the general election.

When a man has been honored as I have been by the people of my state, every problem that confronts them is of concern. However, this is not a history of the state or its people, and I shall comment on only a few of the many problems that occupied my attention while Governor.

In my inaugural address in January, 1951, I referred, among other things, to the Ku Klux Klan, which had been active in an area near the North Carolina border, and in some instances had arrogated to itself the authority to punish several persons thought by the Klan to be violating the law. I urged the enactment of a law making it a criminal offense for persons over sixteen years of age to "parade on the streets or highways while masked," and also prohibiting such persons from "entering upon the premises of a citizen to threaten or intimidate him." Declaring that we must have a government of the people under law, I said that I did not need the assistance of the

* Excerpts from *All in One Lifetime* (New York: Harper & Brothers, 1958), pp. 406–13, 419–21; Copyright © 1958 by James F. Byrnes Foundation. Reprinted by permission of Harper & Row, Publishers.

Ku Klux Klan, nor did I want interference by the National Association for the Advancement of Colored People.

The General Assembly took but a short time to enact the legislation requested. The Klan resorted to leasing private property for meetings, but our state law enforcement officers were so active in policing the meetings that Klansmen in a border county took a man across the state line into North Carolina to administer punishment in the mistaken belief that officers of that state might not be so diligent as those at home. They were arrested and convicted in North Carolina. The leader, who really possessed some qualities of leadership, announced from jail that he would quit the Klan, and when he was released he lived up to his promise. Since then there have been attempts to revive it, but today there is no effective Klan organization in South Carolina.

Between the time of my nomination in June and inauguration the following January, my study of the revenue problem had convinced me that the only source from which we could raise the money necessary to improve our educational facilities was a sales tax, which had previously been urged and rejected. It is a burdensome tax, but one of the few sources of revenue left to the states.

Therefore, in my inaugural address, I urged that adequate school facilities must be provided through a state-wide program which would require the issuance, over a period of twenty years, of $75 million worth of bonds.

Outlining the necessity for levying a sales tax of 3 per cent, to be used only for public school purposes, I stated, "It is our duty to provide for the races substantial equality in school facilities. We should do it because it is right. For me, that is sufficient reason. If any person wants an additional reason, I say it is wise."

I called attention to the fact that laws on segregation similar to our laws existed in seventeen states of the Union and said, "except for the professional agitators, what the colored people want, and what they are entitled to, is equal facilities in their schools. We must see that they get them."

Fortunately, at the time I submitted the school building program, there was a legislative committee which had been appointed at the previous session and had given study to the school problem. The committee agreed to the necessity for the sales tax; the legislature adopted it. It provided for improved bus transportation and authorized the consolidation of school districts. To carry out the educational program we established the State Educational Finance Commission, of which the Governor was chairman. Later, the limit of the bond issue was increased.

Our program was rightly called an "Educational Revolution." In our little state we had more than 1,200 school districts, which we reduced to 102. That required the consolidation of many districts and the abandonment of many inadequate schools. At the end of four years we had eliminated 824 totally inadequate schools in rural areas. . . .

At the end of four years, our Commission reported that $124,329,394 had been allotted from the proceeds of bonds sold and the sales tax—Negro schools receiving two thirds of the amount, even though Negro pupils comprised only 40 per cent of the total enrollment. This was over and above funds from local taxation for school purposes, the only previous source of funds.

In collecting the sales tax some unfriendly merchants would ask the customer for "Jimmie's tax." It was not calculated to increase my popularity but I am proud of what the tax accomplished in our educational program.

There was now at least one first-class high school for colored students in every district, and in many instances these schools were better than those provided for white students because they were newer.

There were also adequate elementary schools for both races. Almost immediately it became apparent that the improvement in elementary schools in rural areas would result in students' continuing in school for more years, and certainly we would require additional high schools. It also became apparent that the vastly improved high schools with increased attendance would stimulate a greater demand for college training.

At the 1953 session of the General Assembly it was evident that at the end of the fiscal year the state would have a surplus. I called to the attention of the legislature that if we were to attain a balanced program of public education, the colleges must be properly supported, and urged the allotment of most of the surplus to the colleges. Because legislators, as a rule, are more interested in appropriating funds for schools attended by the masses, rather than for colleges attended by relatively few, it provoked a hard fight but we won.

At the same session I urged, and the legislature authorized, the issuance of revenue bonds by state educational institutions under certain restrictions. The bonds were payable primarily from funds the colleges derived annually from tuition fees. Later they were authorized to issue revenue bonds payable out of dormitory revenues. The funds from these sources made it possible for the state university and the state colleges so to improve their physical plants that today returning graduates cannot recognize the place of their studies or the scenes of their crimes. But more important than the building program has been the increased funds made available by the General Assembly for faculty salaries. Now I am proud of our educational system and particularly proud of the improvements at the State College for Negroes.

Another program that made my service as Governor seem worth while was the improvement at the state hospital for the mentally sick. When elected, I was ashamed of our state hospital; now I am proud of it. That institution had no alumni to solicit support from legislators for improvements, but the legislature responded generously to my appeals and we provided not only modern buildings and equipment but highly skilled psychiatrists and staff. It was heartening because at times I fear the mentally sick are the forgotten people—forgotten even by relatives.

To enlist the co-operation of legislators in the building program for the mental hospital, I appeared at a joint session of the two houses and invited all members to join me in visiting the hospital. We first visited an old building occupied by the more violent patients, which I wanted to have replaced. I was gratified that approximately 150 legislators were with me, but I was told by an attendant that my enthusiasm was not shared by a patient on a second-floor balcony who, when he looked over the large group approaching, headed by the resident physician and me, excitedly exclaimed, "Good Lord, we are overcrowded now; we can't take in all those nuts!"

In 1950 we had an excellent training school for mentally defective white children, but mentally defective colored children were sent to to the hospital for insane colored persons. There were just as many, or possibly more, mentally defective Negro children, but most of them were in the rural areas and in most cases the parents were not willing to let them leave home.

There was no appeal to me from any organization of colored or white people for a school for mentally defective Negro children, but I made it my pet project. Because of the terrific demands upon the legislators for funds for many deserving purposes in the closing days of the legislature, the conferees on the appropriations bill eliminated the funds to construct this school.

I still smile at what followed. When informed of that action, I met with the conferees. They said that they had eliminated the item in order to maintain a balanced budget and not because of opposition to the school. When I asked whether they would restore the item if I should find the necessary funds, they agreed, the chairman asking in which pocket I had a million. To their surprise I was able to tell them that on the books of the state treasurer there was a special fund of nearly a million dollars that could be used to start the building. That fund had been established in 1943, out of a surplus that year, to invest in revenue bonds of some state colleges issued some years before and then selling at a discount. By wise handling of the fund, a profit had accumulated. Accordingly, language was written in the bill transferring the special fund to the general fund, and the appropriation was restored to the bill to start Pineland School for mentally defective colored children. Later, additional funds were appropriated, and the school has now been operating for several years.

It was surprising that I should be called upon to give so much time to the effort to obtain industries for the state, but it was rewarding. A prudent businessman moving a plant for any reason makes a careful survey before deciding on a new location. I recall working with one prospect for three years before he reached a decision. In fact, he did not actually start construction until my term had expired. This effort to "sell" the state as the best place for the location of an industry provided some interesting experiences.

On one occasion, while urging upon the president of an industrial enterprise who was a guest at luncheon the soundness of our state government, I told him that under the rules of our House of Representatives the bill providing appropriations to operate the state government could not be passed unless the total of appropriations was less than the revenue estimated for the next fiscal year. My visitor immediately asked why, during my long service in House and Senate in Washington, I did not have the federal government adopt that policy. I did not try to answer that one.

Because this guest was a good friend, as we approached the end of our luncheon I told him the state had a balanced budget because it was economical even in little things. To illustrate, I said that the colored maids and butler who were waiting on the table were not paid by the state; that they were prisoners who, as a reward for good behavior, had been trained for housework and then were assigned by the superintendent of the penitentiary to the Governor's House for this much-sought-after service. He asked, "What are they in for?" When I told him, "murder and manslaughter," he expressed surprise— and I thought some fear—so I assured him that the five who were at the Governor's House had only committed crimes of passion, the two men having killed their wives and the three women having killed their husbands. However, when I told him one of the women had poisoned her husband, I wondered thereafter if he was sincere when he said, "I never eat desserts."

At first I did not like the idea of having prisoners at the Governor's House, but later realized it might contribute to their rehabilitation. We came to like them, and they must have liked us because every Christmas morning since we left the Governor's House, by permission of the present Governor, they have come to visit us, and, with my wife playing the piano, we all join in singing Christmas carols and Negro spirituals.

After I had started our educational program, counsel for the N.A.A.C.P abandoned a suit that had been previously brought in Clarendon County for equal facilities in a school district and brought a new suit asking the court to declare unconstitutional the laws requiring separation of the races in public schools. A three-judge court upheld our segregation laws and this judgment was sustained by the Court of Appeals for the Fourth Circuit.

When the case was appealed to the United States Supreme Court, President Truman directed his Attorney General to intervene in the name of the United States and urge the Court to declare our laws unconstitutional. In the original suit, E. S. Rogers had represented the school district. When the constitutionality of our laws was attacked, Robert McC. Figg, Jr., was employed by me, as Governor. When the case reached the Supreme Court, I requested the Honorable John W. Davis of New York to argue the case for us. Davis was in the U. S. House of Representatives when I was first elected and I regarded him as the ablest constitutional lawyer of his time.

After studying the record, he said he would make the argument because, in the light of previous decisions of the Supreme Court on the subject, he believed the judgment of the lower courts right. After the argument he declined to accept any compensation, and on his next birthday the State of South Carolina presented him with a beautiful silver service.

At the time there were four similar cases pending in the Court. The case for the plaintiffs was argued by Thurgood Marshall, counsel for the N.A.A.C.P., and by an attorney representing the Department of Justice. While only four states and the District of Columbia were directly affected, similar segregation laws existed in seventeen states and would be affected by the decision of the Court. But the Court could not reach a decision and after many months invited counsel to reargue the cases at the next term. . . .

It was not until May 17, 1954, that the Supreme Court filed a decision setting aside the provisions of the constitutions of seventeen states requiring segregated schools. Two years before we had established a committee to recommend a revision of our school laws. Under the intelligent leadership of Senator Marion Gressette, the committee recommended many changes, including procedure in assignment of students, which were adopted by the legislature.

After I left the office of Governor in January, 1955, the legislature enacted a law providing that if, by, or in consequence of an order of a court, state or federal, a student was transferred from a school to which he had been assigned by education officials to some other school designated by a court, all appropriations for both such schools should immediately cease. There are similar laws in other states. No such court orders tranferring students have been sought by colored students in South Carolina, and thus far we have escaped the serious race riots and disorders that have occurred elsewhere.

I am confident that our foresight in 1951 in adopting a program providing modern and splendidly equipped schools and improved transportation for colored students has contributed to their satisfied attitude. But most credit for our peaceful conditions must be given to the conservative Negro citizens who, expecting to continue to live by the side of their white neighbors, have resisted the efforts of agitators from other states to force prompt integration in the schools. They know it would undo all that has been done during the last fifty years by leaders of both races to bring about improved relations. The educational and economic progress of our colored citizens during that period is something of which I am very proud.

Of course the problem is not solved. It has been suggested that if as a result of a court order a public school is closed in any community, the state should make an allotment to parents to cover tuition fees paid to private schools. Even with aid for both races, it will be difficult for colored citizens to establish and operate private schools, particularly in rural areas. However, thoughtful white Southerners are agreed that the education of the colored children is essential to any wise solution, and they are determined to find a way to ensure that innocent colored children are not denied an education. They believe the school problem is a local problem. They believe that people who advocate immediate integration everywhere are more interested in what they believe to be a desirable social reform than they are in advancing the education of the children of both races.

I fear that in any community in which race tension is such that classrooms have to be equipped with guns and students supervised by the United States Army, as at Little Rock, or by the police, as has been proposed by a grand jury in Brooklyn, there can be no educational progress.

Under the most favorable conditions, it is frequently difficult to get children to study. The presence of soldiers and guns may cause them to study two R's—race relations—but will not encourage them to concentrate on the three R's.

The routine of administering state affairs was broken in 1953, when the President appointed me a representative to the General Assembly of the United Nations. After the first week, it was difficult to believe that it was 1953 and not 1946, when I had spent most of the year negotiating with the Soviets. I commented to Leonard Meeker, a staff member, that we had the same issues, the same actors, and the same frustrating methods employed by the Soviet Union and its satellites. I found myself again making a speech about the outrageous action of the Soviets in refusing to return to Germany and Japan the hundreds of thousands of soldiers held as prisoners of war and the thousands of civilians who had been taken to the work camps of Russia on the pretext of being war criminals. Vishinski was just as vigorous, and vindictive! At the end of the session I had to admit that little real progress had been made toward putting an end to the cold war and to the threat of another world war. . . .

On January 18, 1955, I left the Governor's office and public life. Within me was the satisfaction that comes from the consciousness that through the years I had faithfully tried to discharge my duty. I knew I had made mistakes, because I am human. I knew I had made political enemies because I had taken positions on controversial issues and fought to sustain those convictions. But there was compensation in the knowledge that I had made countless friends whose under-standing and sympathy had enriched my life.

As I thought of the past, overriding all thoughts of personal rela-tions was my realization that this country is truly the land of oppor-tunity. Now as I think of the future, my hope is that my experiences may encourage others to dedicate their talents and energies to public service, for I believe with Tolstoi that "The sole meaning of life is to serve humanity."

As noted, Governor Byrnes secured a 3 percent sales tax
for improvement of South Carolina education. He vainly
hoped that equalization of the public schools for both whites and
blacks would influence a pending Supreme Court decision on
racial segregation in a Clarendon County school district.
Nevertheless, in the case *Sweatt* v. *Painter* (1950) the Court
had already outlawed racial segregation at the University of
Texas. Thus, its decree of May 17, 1954, outlawing enforced
segregation in tax-supported schools, came as no surprise.

The Supreme Court did not immediately implement its
decision. All over the South delaying tactics were put into
effect. In South Carolina the legislature in 1956 passed a series
of laws designed to thwart the decree of the tribunal. Luckily
for the peace of the state, no further lawsuits were soon pushed
to a conclusion as in Nashville, Little Rock, and Oxford,
Mississippi. In these and other places segregation gave way to
token integration, sometimes with violence. As time went on,
however, it became increasingly clear that South Carolina
must sooner or later yield or close its colleges and public
schools. The showdown came at Clemson University (then
College) in January 1963. Newsman George McMillan tells the
story.

37

"INTEGRATION WITH DIGNITY" *

George McMillan

At 1:30 P.M. on January 28, 1963, a bright but cold day at Clemson College in the Piedmont hills of South Carolina, some 160 TV, radio, magazine and newspaper reporters waited quietly for the first Negro student to enroll in a white school in South Carolina.

The Negro's name was and is Harvey Gantt, and many people expected his imminent arrival to bring on one of the nation's worst racial explosions. In fact, of course, it did nothing of the kind—as everyone who has followed the case is aware. But behind that amazing fact lies a complex and fascinating story that has never been told until now.

For the peace with which Harvey Gantt entered Clemson was no mere lucky happenstance. Violence did seem clearly in the cards. South Carolinians are notoriously passionate when it comes to defending the South or southern "customs." The logic of South Carolina's history and the force of her traditions argued that Clemson would be another Oxford, Mississippi.

South Carolina was the spiritual, cultural and financial center of the South when Mississippi was still Indian territory. The fact is that South Carolinians created the South as a politically self-conscious region, led it out of the Union, and then fired the first shot of the Civil War.

Elaborate security precautions had been made to protect Gantt at Clemson, and his routine for the day had been scheduled with the precision of an astronaut shot. He was to arrive at Tillman Hall, the old brick administration building, any minute now. He was to go inside and register, come out another door, walk 35 yards to his dormitory, visit his room briefly, and then walk another 750 yards to the

* Reprinted from the *Saturday Evening Post,* CCXXXVI (March 16, 1963), 15–21; Copyright © 1963 by The Curtis Publishing Co. Reprinted by permission of William Morris Agency, Inc.

architectural-school building to be interviewed by the dean. The press
—more than waited for James Meredith at the University of Mississippi—was ready.

At 1:33 P.M., only three minutes behind schedule, a black 1959
Buick sedan came slowly up the drive, parked in front of Tillman,
and Gantt stepped out.

There was a frantic jostle. Tripods clanged as they were hastily
dragged into position. Cameras whirred and clicked. Voices began to
be heard talking sententiously into microphones.

But that was the action, all of it. It was one of those moments
when the paraphernalia of coverage overwhelms the event. It was excitement without substance.

The only sign of an "angry mob," aside from the press, was an as-
semblage of about 200 students, standing with their jacket collars
turned up against the wind, laughing at the antics of the reporters.
There were still 100 or so of them around when Gantt came out of
Tillman. But by the time Gantt emerged from his dormitory, only a
handful were there to watch him start his walk to the architectural
building. The reporters who had been following Gantt fell back,
leaving him to the TV and radio men, who kept sticking microphones
in front of the young Negro's mouth, insisting, "Come on, Harvey,
say something!" But he was silent, and the campus was now deserted.

For the press, the day was over. And nothing had happened. Not
one thing. South Carolina, emotionally the deepest Deep South state
of them all, had met and peaceably passed its most serious racial
crisis since the Civil War.

Why hadn't something happened? What was the explanation for
this astonishing turn of events? Had South Carolina learned a lesson
from Oxford? Or was it something else? The question was important;
if South Carolina could keep the peace, so could any southern state.

The answer is this: When South Carolina's turn came to face the
inevitable fact of racial change, its responsible people, its leadership
group, its "power structure" took the initiative and handled the
crisis with dignity, dignity for the Negro as well as for the white man.
This is why the South Carolina story is one of the most significant—
and reassuring—stories in the recent history of race relations in this
country.

The story begins on July 1, 1961, a day so hot that the Spanish
moss seemed to be sweating. At the annual Watermelon Festival in
the small Black Belt county seat of Hampton, the biggest businessman

in South Carolina stood up and delivered himself of these somewhat astonishing sentiments:

"The desegregation issue cannot continue to be hidden behind the door. This situation cannot satisfactorily be settled at the lunch counter and bus station. We have a definite obligation to increase the productivity of our Negro citizens, to provide them with good jobs at good wages and to continue to assure them of fair treatment. . . . By raising their education and economic status, we could raise the whole economy of the state."

Charles Daniel, the speaker, knew what he was doing even if his audience of stunned cotton planters and restless beauty queens did not. Tough, hard-boiled, self-made and ultraconservative, Daniel had hewn together in three decades the largest construction company in the Southeast. Now he had struck the opening blow in a carefully planned effort to save Clemson College. He had joined the ranks of a handful of shrewd, influential and determined men who, in that summer of 1961, pledged themselves to see to it that Clemson stayed open and unharmed, even if it had to integrate.

The little group included besides Daniel: Robert Edwards, Clemson's president, a hard-driving textile executive who had been brought to Clemson originally as vice president in charge of development; Edgar Brown, chairman of Clemson's board of trustees, state senator from Barnwell County, president pro tempore of the state senate and the Daddy Rabbit of South Carolina politics; John K. Cauthen, executive vice president of the South Carolina Textile Manufacturers Association and the most skillful lobbyist in the state; Ernest F. Hollings, the handsome young governor of the state, who was making new industry the focus of his administration's effort; Wayne Freeman, editor of the Greenville *News* and one of the five nonlegislative members of the Gressette Committee, the state's clearinghouse for racial problems, named for State Senator Marion Gressette.

It was a loose, informal coalition; the five men never met as a group. If there was an understanding between them, it was that each would do what he could in whatever way he thought best to fulfill their common intention.

The seed of this understanding was planted in the spring of 1961 when Edwards called Cauthen about something else. Before hanging up, Edwards asked Cauthen if he thought the state's businessmen would be willing to share some of the responsibility for the problems that would arise if Harvey Gantt, who had applied for admission to

Clemson in January, 1961, was finally admitted to the school on court order.

A "monster" to be stopped.

Cauthen was sympathetic, and he went to work. South Carolina is a small, unusually cohesive state, and the lines of communication between its seats of political and economic power cross and recross at dozens of points. Cauthen sent feelers and messages along these interior lines, found support not only from businessmen but also from men like Hollings and Freeman and Brown, who are not.

By the end of the year Cauthen, Daniel, Edwards and the others had, in "talking around," let it be known that there was an important body of opinion in the state that firmly believed in law and order at all costs.

This was a solid achievement. But it was still an "inside" one. When Governor Hollings toured the state in the fall of 1961 he was shocked at the kind of talk he heard. He told me, "People thought I ought to have some magic to stop the monster that was about to gobble us up, or else they expected me to go to jail. It looked to me like it was high time we started sobering people up before it turned out to be too late."

Having been turned down on his first application, Gantt reapplied for admission to Clemson in January, 1962.

It was Hollings's custom to hold an off-the-record press briefing the week before the General Assembly convened, and he seized that moment to strike a blow.

"Before 1962 has passed," he told newsmen that January 9, "South Carolina's legal defenses will fall like a house of cards. You might as well start preparing your readers for the inevitable. We are not going to secede."

Not long after this the authoritative Columbia *State* began to give extensive, detailed coverage to Gantt, forcing by its example other newspapers in the state to treat the story as fully and as fairly. They did.

But there wasn't much news about Gantt and Clemson during the spring and summer of 1962. It was election time in South Carolina. Hollings ran for the U. S. Senate, trying to unseat the wily old veteran, Olin D. Johnston, in the Democratic primary, and got clobbered. Donald Russell, a wealthy Spartanburg lawyer who had served in Washington as an assistant to James F. Byrnes when the latter was Secretary of State, was elected governor to succeed Hollings, to take over in January, 1963.

Gantt's second application had never been formally acted upon, and the young Negro, represented by N.A.A.C.P. attorneys, filed suit in Federal Court on July 7, 1962. What this meant did not hit hard in South Carolina until September 30, when rioting broke out at Oxford, Mississippi.

Mississippi indirectly called for help, and there were South Carolinians—plenty of them—who felt that Governor Hollings should go at once to Governor Barnett's side. A member of the state house of representatives, A. W. Red Bethea, insisted that Hollings lead a motorcade of South Carolinians to Oxford. Hollings refused—and was rewarded with a batch of insulting telegrams.

Other South Carolinians began to back up Barnett. Russell praised Barnett's "courage and resolution," and said he was "hopeful that Barnett's conduct may be invaluable to us in demonstrating the strength of Southern conviction." State Senator Marion Gressette, Mister Segregation in South Carolina, the man who is chairman of the state committee set up to "discourage" integration, called on the South "to rally to the support of the great state of Mississippi."

Hollings's silence stood out and annoyed some South Carolinians. Farley Smith, longtime executive secretary of the Citizens Councils of South Carolina, remarked, "It is inconceivable to me that South Carolina, of all southern states, has not, through its governor, made its position crystal clear."

A few days later, in the first week of October, a reporter cornered Hollings. Would Hollings, or would Hollings not, be willing to go to jail to prevent integration of a South Carolina school? "If it works out like Mississippi," Hollings replied, "jail would certainly be the safest place."

He was due to attend the Southern Governors Conference at Hollywood, Florida, the next week. "Faubus and Patterson [Governors Orville Faubus of Arkansas and John M. Patterson of Alabama] were waiting for me to head up a movement to wire and welcome Ross Barnett to the conference," Hollings said. He refused.

If Hollings did nothing to "help Mississippi, he did something to help South Carolina meet *its* forthcoming crisis. He sent Pete Strom, head of S.L.E.D. (South Carolina Law Enforcement Division), to Oxford. He told him to study that situation and to come back home and work out with Harry Walker, his legal counsel, a security plan for Clemson.

He laid down three guidelines for Walker: (1) The plan must be foolproof; there should be no question of the need for U. S.

marshals; (2) it should be designed to prevent even the possibility of allowing a crowd to gather, and (3) a carefully thought-out schedule must be arranged for controlling the movement of the press.

Through the late summer and fall Gantt's attorneys and South Carolina engaged in a series of legal maneuvers, but by November it was clear that Clemson sooner or later would have to admit Gantt. It was just a matter of time, and there was not much of that.

Meanwhile Cauthen had not been idle. He was "talking around" in those key places he knew so well. One day in the fall, for example, he and Clemson President Edwards went to Hartsville to see A. L. M. Wiggins, the elder statesman of South Carolina's business community. A former railroad president and Under Secretary of the Treasury, Wiggins was head of the Governor's Committee on Higher Education. "Mr. Wiggins was very strong on our side," Cauthen says.

Up to now, none of the little group had taken a public stand on the case of Harvey Gantt, but the hour was obviously near when somebody must speak out clearly. The occasion arose at the end of December, when a Charleston newspaperman called Clemson board chairman Brown and put to him one of those have-you-stopped-beating-your-wife questions: "Now that it is pretty certain that the Clemson board is going to admit Harvey Gantt, what explanation would you give to the people who elected you, in the event of such a decision?"

Nobody had said that Clemson was going to admit Gantt, but Brown took down the reporter's question in shorthand and promised to give him an answer later.

He called Cauthen in Columbia, Edwards at Clemson. Both agreed to meet Brown in Barnwell the next morning. They talked it over, then Cauthen drafted a statement. Brown released it that day to the Charleston newspaperman but at the same time sent it to the press associations.

"Your premise is false," Brown's statement noted. "If the ultimate decision of the Federal courts directs that Harvey Gantt should be admitted, my position is that the board of trustees and the administration at Clemson College will not tolerate violence on the Clemson campus."

Brown had set the strategy with Cauthen months ago, when he told Cauthen not to hold an open meeting of businessmen, but rather to assemble his forces quietly. Now the strategy was about to pay off. Now the power structure of the state was agreed upon, if not yet openly committed to, a policy of admitting Gantt to Clemson and preserving law and order on the campus at the same time.

The newspapers of the state quickly joined behind Brown, and the opposition was caught flatfooted. The kind of people who might favor making a "protest" had taken it for granted that everyone in South Carolina would agree with them when the time came. They were not organized, not prepared. The Citizens Councils had been, as executive secretary Smith explained to me recently, "mainly a stand-by organization in South Carolina." Present membership is probably "less than 10,000" by Smith's estimate, and these "are not very active." This is not to say that the Citizens Councils favored violence; Smith insists they did not. But in this sense nobody in the South *plans* violence. What some groups do is stalemate and neutralize local and state law-enforcement agencies so that the relative handful of racists who will be violent can come in from the country, often from across state lines, and create chaos.

Half, maybe more, of the battle had been won without a word's being fired in anger. It was not over, not by any means. But men as savvy in the ways of Palmetto politics as Brown and Cauthen knew where their opposition lay.

The trouble might come from any one or all three of these powerful men:

1. James F. Byrnes. Still, in his 80's, the same dapper little man with gray felt hat whose picture was once frequently taken on the White House steps, Byrnes is today "a bitter man," according to those who are close to him. When Byrnes returned to South Carolina in the 1950's and became governor, he convinced the legislature that it ought to levy a sales tax, and he undertook an extensive program of school-building designed to create separate and equal school systems in South Carolina. "He thought the Supreme Court would recognize this," I was told. "He had convinced himself the Court would rule five to four in favor of South Carolina in the Clarendon Case [concerning public-school segregation in Clarendon County]. When it voted nine to nothing against, he turned bitter." As a member of Clemson's board of trustees, Byrnes "wouldn't say yes, and he wouldn't say no," about Gantt. His attitude in board meetings was such that some of the others on the board felt that Byrnes might, if Gantt were admitted, make an independent statement that would, considering his prestige, do serious damage to law and order.

2. State Senator Marion Gressette. Gressette was No. 2 in seniority in the senate, a man whose sincerity and integrity have never been questioned in the legislature. Every bill that might affect or be affected by a change in the status quo in segregation went to the Gressette

Committee. From Calhoun, a Black Belt county in the Low Country, Gressette announced to the press that he was praying every night over the Clemson situation, and it is significant that not even the worst cynic doubted his statement.

It was almost solely their confidence in Gressette that caused groups like the Citizens Councils to stay dormant. For Gressette to go along with a plan that called for admitting a Negro to Clemson without some kind of protest would be a severe wrench for Gressette personally and for all the people who had had complete confidence in him as an anti-integration warrior. If Gressette came out publicly against admitting Gantt, all the hitherto latent forces of disorder in the state would come alive.

3. A. W. Red Bethea. Bethea is the most forthright racist in South Carolina. If Bethea went to Clemson to lead a "protest," as, in fact, he threatened to do, it would be hard to turn him away. He was both a member of the legislature and a Clemson alumnus.

Cauthen moved quickly to get business support on the line for a public announcement. Eighteen of the state's top textile executives met for lunch at the new, luxurious Palmetto Club in Columbia on January 3, 1963. When they had finished their business, Cauthen passed out three-by-five file cards, read them a statement he had drawn up. It read in part: "The major business and industrial interests of the state strongly approve the announced [Note: it had *not* been announced then] determination of the board of trustees and the administration of Clemson College to maintain law and order at all times." Cauthen asked the executives to vote Yes or No on the cards, and to hand them in without signing their names. He got 18 Yeses.

The next day the Chamber of Commerce followed suit. Polled by telephone, 70 South Carolina businessmen—52 were members of the Chamber's board of directors, 12 were former presidents and six were officers—unanimously approved the statement. The state bankers' association and the broadcasters' association followed in quick order.

Nowhere in the South in the recent history of racial change had the business community taken such a strong stand *in advance*. Clemson President Edwards on January 3 had a "very serious" meeting with Gressette and some members of his committee. Without acrimony Edwards made it plain that if he was not supported in admitting Gantt and handling the whole situation with dignity, he would resign. He got down to brass tacks with Gressette about the effect of violence. One of the nation's largest manufacturers had made overtures about building a multimillion-dollar plant in Gressette's county.

The state makes its choice.

"Senator, if there's a ruckus at Clemson those people won't even plant scrub oak in Calhoun County," Edwards said passionately.

On January 9, Governor Hollings spoke out, in a farewell address to the state legislature.

"As we meet," he said, "South Carolina is running out of courts. This General Assembly must make clear South Carolina's choice, a government of laws rather than a government of men. We must move on with dignity. It must be done with law and order. The state's institutions and all law-enforcement agencies have been charged with their responsibilities."

When Hollings was halfway through, Bethea rose in his seat, took a step as if to leave, but then changed his mind and sat down. The rest of the joint session gave Hollings an ovation. "They were *impressed*," a legislative correspondent told me later.

The next night Hollings called Attorney General Robert Kennedy and outlined the security plan which by now had been worked out. He told Kennedy that U. S. marshals would not be needed. Kennedy promised not to send them.

On January 12 Hollings held a meeting in his office for a final review of the security plan. Donald Russell Jr., son of and assistant to his father, the incoming governor, was present and took a copy for his father to see.

The plan is probably the most complete and carefully thought-out one ever drawn up in the United States to meet the threat of racial violence. None of its details have ever before been made public.

It warned all officers of the law: "The state of South Carolina has assumed responsibility of maintaining law and order as a state function, and the state is capable of carrying it out." It told them to "tolerate verbal abuse or similar harassment . . . but, when faced with violation of the law, to perform duties with efficiency and dispatch. . . . If trouble occurs," the instructions said, "remove troublemakers quickly to detention areas set aside for large numbers of persons."

A S.L.E.D. aircraft was to patrol from the sky, police photographers were to be on the campus to take movies and photographs, the sheriffs of adjoining counties were briefed; magistrates were put on duty so that they could issue warrants; fire-fighting and medical equipment was made ready; and a central command post was set up to coordinate all the activity.

An elaborate program of briefing was set up for the Clemson student body and faculty. The student body was to be policed by its own student government. Supervisors were given the right to send students to their individual dormitory rooms.

Students were warned that "gatherings which indicate unnecessary curiosity . . . will be avoided. Counseling, advising and frank discussion should solve most problems. Situations requiring more forthright action will be dealt with firmly and effectively."

The courts began to move quickly. On January 22 District Judge C. C. Wyche complied with the Appellate Court ruling and signed the order admitting Gantt to Clemson. That same day State Senator John D. Long of Union County rose in the upper chamber of the legislature on a point of personal order. It was "cowardly" of Clemson to admit Gantt without a fight, he said.

"I would prefer that my children be raised in ignorance—not knowing 'B' from Bullsfoot—than to see them cringing and bowing before tyranny," he cried out.

Word of the debate reached the house, and Bethea and many of his colleagues came over to the senate, packed the galleries. Senator H. H. Jessen of Dorchester County joined in on Long's side. "South Carolina should not lie down and let itself be walked over," he said.

The time had come for Gressette to take his stand. He rose and began to speak slowly, sadly. "A lot of things happen in life," he said. "We have disappointments. Sometimes I feel like making a speech like my two friends made. We have lost this battle but we are engaged in a war. But this war cannot be won by violence or by inflammatory speeches. I have preached peace and good order too long to change my thinking."

If the legislature now felt that he had failed in his task, Gressette said, he would resign.

When he had finished, the legislature rose and gave him an ovation. And Senator Long took the floor again, this time to propose that the members remain on their feet for a standing vote of confidence for Gressette.

Before the day was over Byrnes issued a statement. "Gantt has succeeded in forcing himself into Clemson," Byrnes said, but he would not be welcomed at the college "by independent men and women of the student body. . . . Thank goodness," said the former Supreme Court Justice, "not even the Supreme Court has ordered that be done—as yet!"

The Clemson board of trustees met with Governor Russell and the Gressette Committee during the morning to set the strategy for making the formal announcement. At noon word went out to reporters that press conferences would be held separately by Russell, by Gressette and by President Edwards—in quick successive order, at two P.M., at two-thirty and at three.

Promptly at two Russell came through a door into a paint-fresh new executive conference room, handed out a few copies of his statement and read quickly: "We shall meet and solve this problem peaceably, without violence."

The reporters scampered across the street to the capitol and heard Gressette read: "Peace and good order must be maintained both on and off the college campus."

Bethea was there, hunched deep down in an upholstered chair, an incongruous figure in the light bark-cloth-papered room. Reporters did not have time to stop and ask him for a comment.

It was a short walk from the capitol to the studios of WIS-TV where Edwards was to read his statement before the cameras. A few seconds after the press corps arrived, Edwards emerged, took his position before a microphone and began to talk: The Trustees approved "complete and good-faith" compliance with the court order, and Gantt was to be admitted "exactly as any other transfer student."

When Edwards finished, someone passed out copies of Cauthen's statement—the endorsement of law and order by the manufacturers, bankers, businessmen and broadcasters. It almost got passed by in the rush.

I had made the rounds with the rest of the newsmen, and, as I started to leave, I saw Brown and Cauthen sitting against a far wall. I went over and Senator Brown offered me a ride back to my hotel. The three of us walked out into the street again.

"Well, John," said Brown, pulling himself erect, cocking his head on one side and then giving Cauthen a smile, "it's been a long day, hasn't it?"

"Yes, it has, senator," said Cauthen, returning the smile, "but I think everything's going to be all right now."

And it was all right.

By 1965 Negro suffrage was commonplace in South Carolina, racial desegregation was proceeding peacefully in public schools and colleges, the state's economy was progressing rapidly, and the one-party tradition appeared to be shattered beyond repair. The national Democratic Party's liberal program, especially on civil rights, had finally prompted Senator Thurmond and several other conservative Democratic leaders to join the Republicans—after a flirtation of several years. With the aid of Thurmond and the other bolters, the Republican presidential nominee of 1964 carried South Carolina, a feat no Republican had accomplished since Reconstruction.

Among the stalwarts remaining loyal to the Democratic Party was state Senator Edgar A. Brown of Barnwell. For forty years a prominent political figure, Brown was sometimes called "Prime Minister" of South Carolina and head of the "Barnwell Ring." Without denying Brown's great prestige and considerable power, veteran journalist W. D. Workman, Jr., disputes these claims as extravagant. In his biography of Brown he discusses the question under the chapter heading "The Ring That Isn't." Workman has also included some of the senator's own comments, appearing in italics.

38

"THE RING THAT ISN'T" *

W. D. Workman, Jr.

There was a time when I was chairman of the Senate Finance Committee and President Pro Tem of the Senate, and down the street in Barnwell from me was my neighbor, J. Emile Harley, who was Governor. And, all at the same time, around the corner from him was Sol Blatt, who was Speaker of the House, and over at Williston was Win [Winchester] Smith, another member of our delegation and he was chairman of the House Ways and Means Committee. At that time we had all the state government located in Barnwell County, but there was no "ring" and we didn't work together. There was no unanimity of action, even back in those times. We often split off on state issues, on state personalities, and that sort of stuff.

The Barnwell Ring, as such, crystallized when Strom Thurmond thought it up as a medium to use somebody as a whipping post over the state, and he picked this "ring," although principally it was me, because I was known better since I had had two statewide races and I was well known. I had been down-graded by drys, do-gooders, and people who weren't too scrupulous about their political tactics. Actually, the core of what he designated as "the Barnwell Ring" had been functioning fifteen years before Strom Thurmond ever came up with the "Barnwell Ring" as a designation, which we got a lot of fun out of.

The Barnwell Ring is the natural successor to that leadership in the Senate which started back there in '28 when Senator [R. M.] Jefferies and myself and others, largely low-country, small-county leaders who could be re-elected and re-elected, worked together for conservative fiscal government. . . .

* Excerpts from *The Bishop from Barnwell: The Political Life and Times of Senator Edgar A. Brown* (Columbia: W. D. Workman, Jr., 1963), pp. 99–100, 104–8, 115–20, 122–28; Copyright © 1963 by W. D. Workman, Jr. Reprinted bv permission of W. D. Workman, Jr.

Before the Barnwell Ring became a popular—if somewhat synthetic—issue in the governors' race of 1946, it had gained some currency in South Carolina political circles as far back as 1937. It was in that year that Blatt tangled with Representative L. Caston Wannamaker of Chesterfield County in a nip-and-tuck race for Speaker of the House. At the time, Blatt was beginning his third term in the House, having been first elected in 1932. He had been reelected in 1934 and, as the House convened in January of 1935, he had been chosen by his colleagues, without opposition, to be Speaker *Pro Tempore*.

The speakership had opened up in 1937, when Speaker Claude A. Taylor of Spartanburg decided to run for Congress, and did not seek reelection to the Legislature. Blatt threw his hat into the ring, but Governor Olin D. Johnston, then serving his first term as chief executive, opposed Blatt's election and instead favored Wannamaker with whatever influence he could bring to bear. However, Blatt had some powerful support as well, stemming from the State Highway Department (with which Johnston was warring), and from three well-placed colleagues from Barnwell county—Lieutenant Governor J. Emile Harley, who was presiding over the Senate; Representative Winchester Smith of Williston, who was second vice-chairman of the Ways and Means Committee; and Senator Brown, who had himself been speaker of the House in 1925-26, and who had been in the Senate since 1929 and had achieved prominence there.

It was only natural that Blatt's opposition should seize on the term "Barnwell Ring" and link it with the "highway ring" which was being fought by the Johnston forces. The upshot of the contest for speaker was Blatt's narrow election, and the initial establishment of the Barnwell Ring as a factor of political potency extending far beyond the confines of Barnwell County.

As the years went by, only Brown and Blatt remained in the public eye as the twin links of the so-called Barnwell Ring. Smith dropped out of the legislature when Barnwell County lost its second representative as a result of the 1940 census. And Emile Harley died on February 27, 1942, while serving as governor.

The Barnwell Ring was trotted out into the political spotlight again in 1946, when an eleven-man race for governor got under way.

That 1946 campaign was a typical, although somewhat intensified, example of South Carolina's traditional "county-to-county" Democratic campaigning. The schedule of stump speakings, worked out by the State Democratic Executive Committee, brought all candidates together successively at the same time and place at every county seat in the state. Frequently two stump speakings were held each day, with occasional "side meetings" arranged individually by the candidates during evening or other "off" hours. The regular speakings, as in the case of the 1946 campaign with its numerous candidates, sometimes would last for three hours or more—providing spectacle for the citizens and ordeal for the candidates.

At the very first campaign meeting of that race, attended by a small crowd of Fairfield county citizens in the Mount Zion high school auditorium, "ring rule" was denounced by several aspirants for governor.

Almost without exception, the candidates declared their own independence of any "ring," and proceeded to slap directly or indirectly at "liquor rings" or "political rings" which allegedly were wielding undue influence in state affairs.

The first candidate to put names to a "ring" was Dr. Carl B. Epps of Sumter. He singled out "Sol Blatt, lawyer from Barnwell; Edgar A. Brown, another lawyer from Barnwell; and Dick Jefferies, of the Santee-Cooper" as members of "the political ring now controlling South Carolina. . . . South Carolina is in the hands of a political ring seeking to perpetuate itself."

J. Strom Thurmond, who had recently returned from World War II service, and who even more recently had resigned (on May 15) as circuit judge, also used the opening campaign meeting as a starter for his own attacks on the "ring rule," but called no names at this stage of the game.

At Winnsboro, Thurmond contented himself with a show of indignation over "the common knowledge that the government of South Carolina is under the control of a small group of cunning and conniving people." Warming to his subject, he said, "We must break up this government of the ring, by the ring, and for the ring." That continued to be the Thurmond theme throughout the campaign, frequently capturing public attention and newspaper headlines at the expense of his other more mundane platform planks—industrial and agricultural development, improved school facilities, stricter control over liquor, etc.

The Barnwell Ring also came under attack from Roger W. Scott, a leathery Dillon farmer who exaggerated his natural "countrified" language and demeanor in his stump appearances. Always blunt and colorful in his speech, Scott impartially whacked away at the Barnwell Ring, at Thurmond, and at various other candidates in the race. The county-to-county campaign was no more than two days old when Scott

told Democrats at Lancaster that they had better elect representatives
to the General Assembly who would not "bow down to Baal—the old
beast from Barnwell." Scott also lit into Sol Blatt, and charged both
Brown and Blatt with manipulating committee assignments so as to
insure compliance with their will.

"I don't know what would happen," he added in his bucolic twang,
"if Edgar happened to die and they'd have to change gods real quick."

Scott realistically pointed out that "there is no such thing as a 'Barnwell ring' within itself." The influence exerted by the Barnwell legislators, he said, stemmed from the support given them "from every
nook and cranny in South Carolina." Then, with serpent-tooth analogy
and attitude, he added: "The Ring has its fangs in every county of
the state."

It was at Lancaster that Ransome Williams injected the weirdest
note of all in slapping at the Barnwell Ring. He had moved from the
lieutenant governor's office into the governor's chair on Jan. 2, 1945,
with the resignation of Governor Olin D. Johnston.

"If I had not accepted the governorship," he said, with some sort
of strange inference that a lieutenant governor might not accept that
office, "Edgar Brown was there ready to take it."

By the time the campaign caravan reached Barnwell on the morning
of a hot and muggy June 25, interest in the "ring" aspect of the
gubernatorial race was at a high peak. The two hundred persons
who crowded into the small Barnwell County courtroom included
state officials from Columbia and local officials, not only from Barnwell, but from adjoining counties as well. They all had been drawn
to attend by broad hints that the Barnwell speaking would be a
"stomp-down good meeting."

They were not disappointed, for not only did the campaign pitches
pick up steam, but the objects of the anti-Ring speeches—Brown and
Blatt—were on hand for the meeting.

Brown himself presided, as county Democratic chairman, and invited all candidates to speak freely within the bounds of respectability.
The nearest approach he made to answering Thurmond's charges
was the comment that South Carolina had a friendly spirit and good
government, despite newspaper reports which would indicate
otherwise.

As soon as he got the floor, Thurmond launched into his most
vigorous denunciation of the Barnwell Ring, to an audience reaction
which mingled applause with heckling. With his customary energy
and deadly serious manner, Thurmond declared:

"I am the candidate who has attacked the Barnwell Ring on the stump and I will attack it today. . . . So long as this ring and its henchmen dominate South Carolina, you won't get the reforms the people want. When I get through telling what I know about the ring, the eyes of the people of South Carolina will be opened."

Later in the meeting, Dr. Epps argued plaintively that he was the man who first had started the attacks on the Barnwell Ring.

"Remember," he said, futilely, "I am the original ring-killer."

But Barnwell was not without its defenders, even among the candidates.

A. J. Beattie, the dignified former state comptroller general who was seeking election as governor, said that the people of the county were the best judges of their own representatives, and that they had sent able men to represent them in Columbia.

And Marcus A. (for Aurelius) Stone, the slow-moving, slow-talking lumber man from Florence and Dillon, scoffed at the whole line of attack on Brown and Blatt. A week earlier, when the caravan had hit Conway, Stone had declared in his dry, deliberate way, "From all that we're hearing, Edgar Brown must be *some* senator. I say that any man who is able to have the respect, confidence, and solid support of his home county folks and a wide following throughout the state merits some credit and not all condemnation. This man must surely possess some tactful leadership, some knowledge of the matters of his fellow citizens. He must have vision and a bit of good horse sense, and perhaps does not deserve all the rotten, sarcastic, and tainted ridicule that is being campaigned upon him. His accusers might remember to read, 'Render unto Caesar the things that are Caesar's and unto Edgar Brown the things that are Edgar Brown's.'" . . .

While the main onslaught against the Barnwell Ring was being conducted along with the race for governor, there were occasional sniping shots fired from the political fringes. Up in Greenville county, for example, some of the candidates for the House of Representatives devoted a part of their time at a mid-July Traveler's Rest rally to take pot-shots at the Barnwell legislators.

Former Representative P. Bradley Morrah, Jr., back on the hustings after a five-years' absence on active Army duty in World War II, called attention to the fact that he had been an author of the reapportionment act, which, on the basis of 1940 census figures, had eliminated one of Barnwell County's two seats in the House—and thus removed Winchester Smith from the General Assembly.

And at the same meeting, John Bolt Culbertson, an avowed labor-liberal spokesman, attacked both Brown and Blatt, and reminded his listeners that he had sought (unsuccessfully) several years earlier to remove both men from their posts as trustees of state institutions. That suit, brought on grounds that the state constitution prohibited dual office-holding, had been dismissed by the state Supreme Court, partially on grounds that Culbertson, as a private citizen, was not properly a party to such an action. In any event, it had served no purpose except momentarily to draw attention to the fact that many members of the General Assembly, including those from Barnwell County, were simultaneously serving as trustees of the University of South Carolina or other state institutions. (That same issue was to arise again with the advent of the Thurmond administration.)

After the July exchange of volleys between Thurmond on the one hand and Messrs. Brown and Blatt on the other, the Barnwell Ring issue languished a bit. It had been a diverting campaign issue and had captured its share of news coverage. But it was difficult then, as it is now, to determine precisely what impact it made upon the electorate in terms of votes swayed one way or the other.

Thurmond had many things working in his favor: a war record which lent itself to political exploitation, broad associations with political acquaintances and lawyers throughout the state as a result of service both in the senate and on the bench, and—perhaps even more important than any of these—a driving determination, boundless energy, and a complete willingness to apply the necessary time and effort to the task of being elected.

Whatever the proximate cause, if one could be determined, the first primary saw Thurmond pull ahead of the pack with an appreciable lead over the next highest man. The August 13 total for Thurmond was 96,691, which give him a 13,000 lead over the runner-up, Dr. James C. McLeod, a Florence physician. Two weeks later, Thurmond won the nomination with a vote of 144,420 to McLeod's 109,169. He carried Barnwell County in the first primary, with 933 votes out of a total of 3,285. (Lieutenant Governor Williams was second in Barnwell with 893.) But the anti-Thurmond vote consolidated for the run-off, and he lost Barnwell County to Dr. McLeod—1,211 to 830, dropping more than a hundred votes from his first primary showing.

At the same time, Blatt was re-elected on the first primary with a vote of 1,713 to 1,443 over his chief opponent, a local insurance agent named Sim W. Folk. Hugh W. Quattlebaum of Blackville was the third candidate in the house race but polled a light vote.

Senator Brown was not up for re-election that year, being then in the middle of his fifth four-year term in the Senate.

In near-by Colleton county, an "auxiliary" member of the Barnwell Ring, Senator R. M. Jefferies, was re-elected to a sixth term in the Senate. There was nothing to link Jefferies with Blatt, but there were professional and personal as well as political ties between Jefferies and Brown.

Jefferies had entered the Senate in 1927, two years before Brown's entry, and through the years the two had joined hands in many a legislative endeavor, notably those affecting state finances. They likewise shared a consuming interest in public power. Jefferies was chief legislative guardian of the Santee-Cooper development, of which he was general manager, and Brown was chairman of the Clark's Hill Authority. The personal connection, with legal professional overtones, grew out of the fact that Jefferies' son, R. M. ("Little Dick") Jefferies, Jr., married Brown's only child, Emily, and was a member of Brown's law firm at Barnwell.

The net result of the 1946 primaries, insofar as the Barnwell Ring was concerned, was the re-election of all members of the supposed Ring, along with the election—as governor—of their chief political adversary. The stage was thus set for a continuation, in the State House, of the battle which had commenced on the campaign stump during the governor's race.

What could have been a very spirited engagement on the legislative front was averted, however, when Blatt announced, in mid-August (and before the final settlement of the governor's race), that he would not seek re-election as Speaker of the House.

Acting "in the interest of peace and harmony in the state, and at the earnest solicitation of my family," Blatt stepped aside and watched a two-way fight for the office develop between Representatives Thomas H. Pope, Jr., of Newberry, and C. Bruce Littlejohn, of Spartanburg. Governor Thurmond threw his weight behind Littlejohn, and saw him elected Speaker on January 14, 1947, by a vote of 67 to 50.

Another Thurmond supporter, Representative Charles N. Plowden of Clarendon County, earlier had announced for Speaker but did not run. Instead, he emerged as chairman of the powerful Ways and Means Committee of the House as the Thurmond administration took over.

The Senate, meanwhile, continued on the even tenor of its ways, although with a new presiding officer in the person of Lieutenant Governor George Bell Timmerman, Jr. Senator Brown was firmly in the saddle as chairman of the Finance Committee and as President *Pro Tempore.* The presence of a new governor downstairs, on the ground floor of the State House, left the old timers of the Senate unshaken, even though the chief executive had campaigned on the promise of wrecking the Barnwell Ring.

Governor Thurmond found himself immediately faced with the necessity of working with Brown in matters of state fiscal policy, if for no other reason than that the veteran senator was a member, like the governor, of the State Budget Commission. Furthermore, Brown, as chairman of the Senate Finance Committee, had been a member of the three-man Budget Commission since 1942, and already had served in that capacity with two earlier governors—Olin Johnston and Ransome Williams.

Looking back in later years from the vantage point of United States Senator, Thurmond recalls no particular unpleasantness or difficulty in working with Brown on the Budget Commission. Brown, however, was suspicious of Thurmond's motives in many instances, and was somewhat resentful of the influence the vigorous new governor obviously was trying to exert upon all phases of state government.

I had some close associations with him as a member of the three-man Budget Commission. I never had a meeting of the Budget Commission that I didn't have trouble with him—trying to get me to do something that he wanted done. I never had a pleasant meeting of the Budget Commission with him in my life.

Jim Smith, who I think is one of the finest characters this state has ever produced in state government in my time—he's been my righthand man—used to say: "Mr. Brown, do you think we can live it out?"

Here is one of the first things Strom did, with that fine character Jim Smith, and Jim never has gotten over it. Every new administration, we'd re-elect the director of the budget [state auditor], and that was Jim. Strom broke the rule that we elected him for a period of four years by insisting that any time that Jim wasn't satisfactory to any one member—that was either Thurmond, Charlie Plowden or me—that we had his resignation.

That crushed Jim very much. He never did get over it and isn't over it yet.

Again, in 1958, the Barnwell Ring was injected into a statewide race which actually had little or nothing to do either with Barnwell County or with the principals of the so-called "Ring." This was the race for governor in 1958, as the term of Governor George Bell Timmerman, Jr., expired.

It was a three-way race for governor in the first primary for the Democratic nomination. Lieutenant Governor Ernest F. (Fritz) Hollings lived up to everyone's expectations by announcing his candidacy, and basing it largely on the experience gained in three terms as a member of the House of Representatives and in one term as lieutenant governor.

Hollings' chief rival in the primary was Donald S. Russell, who had stepped down from the presidency of the University of South Carolina to make the race. Russell, a successful lawyer and an even more successful businessman, had been a legal associate of James F. Byrnes at Spartanburg, and later, when Byrnes was Secretary of State, had served as Assistant Secretary of State for Administration.

The third man in the race—and the first man out of it—was William C. Johnston, brother of United States Senator Olin D. Johnston, and himself a former mayor of the city of Anderson. . . .

Hollings came out on top in the June 10 first primary, but with nowhere near the majority needed to insure his nomination. He polled 158,159 votes, carrying 29 counties; Russell netted 132,099 votes and carried 13 counties; but Johnston was far behind, with 86,981 votes and four counties. The results pitted Hollings and Russell in a run-off, with Johnston out in the cold.

But no sooner had the dust settled from the first primary than Russell was off on a completely new and surprising line of attack. In sharp distinction to his relatively high level of campaigning of the first primary, Russell launched into a series of bitter tirades which charged Hollings with being "the trusted lieutenant" of "the Barnwell Ring." Russell's almost frenzied two-weeks' campaign between the first and second primaries also sought to make Hollings out as the candidate of the liquor interests.

But the note which surprised most South Carolinians was the "ring rule" charge, which was sounded so frequently and so stridently by Russell between June 10 and June 24. Newsmen and politicians alike lifted eyebrows high in the realization that the Russell attack against the Barnwell Ring was not only a blast at Senator Brown and Representative Blatt, but was, by implication, an attack against the entire General Assembly. If that line of political attack had had any validity at all, it should have been used throughout the campaigning which led up to the first primary. For during that period all candidates for the legislature had been busy with their own races, and could not have afforded either the time or the political risk to become involved in the governor's race.

Bringing the charge up after the first primary, however, was a major tactical blunder on Russell's part. With the exception of a few run-off races for the legislature here and there about the state, most of the General Assembly's membership had been settled by the first primary. The successful candidates then had ample opportunity—and appreciable incentive—to support Hollings against the frantic charges made by Russell against "bossism" in South Carolina.

Hollings showed the good sense to keep on the even tenor of his earlier campaigning, and to maintain (at least outwardly) an even temper and a sense of humor. . . .

Russell's pleas, however, fell far short of persuading the voters to rally around his candidacy. It was obvious that his frenetic warnings about "ring rule" and "liquor interests" did not take hold, either because they were not valid issues, or because the people wondered why Russell had waited until after the first primary to make his allegations.

Hollings picked up 32,532 additional votes in the second primary, giving him a winning total of 190,691. Russell, on the other hand, was able to boost his first primary showing by only 13,063 votes, for a total of 145,162. Hollings carried all but seven counties in sweeping to victory. In Barnwell, where he had won 2,374 to Russell's 483 in the first primary, his margin grew to 3,590 over Russell's 504 in the run-off.

If Russell's attack on the Barnwell Ring had proved to be an exercise in futility so far as the voters of South Carolina were concerned, it nevertheless came as a distinct shock to Brown.

I was amazed at Don Russell's attack in 1958. I never had the slightest difference with Russell because of my association with Fritz Hollings. Since he was lieutenant governor [and presiding officer of the Senate] I was committed to support him. But Russell and I were great friends, and our relations, business and personal and social, were all right then and are all right now. Russell never had any dispute or argument with me, but he and my colleague, Sol Blatt,

*and Sol Junior, who is on the Board of Trustees of the University
of South Carolina, had fallen out over university affairs.*

*Russell was interested in enterprise after enterprise in which he
and my cousin and business associate, Dewey Johnson, were together.
I was always invited in on that—the State Bank and Trust Company,
the Auto Finance company, the North Augusta Bank. We'd had a
lot of successful enterprises. He didn't have anything against me. He
was just so shocked at Hollings' leading him so far. I always thought
that he got some bad advice from his campaign strategists and has
always regretted his attack on the so-called "Barnwell Ring," certainly
as to myself.*

*Cecil Wyche had called me up on Sunday before the first primary
and said: "You haven't been helping us any. You've been helping
Fritz Hollings, but Donald Russell's going to lead that ticket way
yonder. He may beat him in the first race and I want you to come
up and celebrate with us Tuesday night." I said: "I wish you well."*

*Well, he didn't beat him in the first race, and they were bitterly
disappointed. I always thought that Walter Brown from Spartanburg
and his advisers (I'm not so sure that Jimmy Byrnes wasn't in on it,
but he disavows it) thought they had to get him a quick issue, a flash
issue, to let him bounce back in the race. And somebody suggested
that he jump on the Barnwell Ring. And they put out those scurrilous
caricatures, pictures of Fritz with a ring around him, with Fritz's
head up as a bottle of liquor and a ring around it—the damnedest
things you ever saw in your life—and circulated them in the Up-
country.*

There may never be a full disclosure of the motives and methods
behind the 1958 attack on the Barnwell Ring, but there was nothing
of the sort repeated in 1962, when Russell once more made a bid for
the governorship, with Lieutenant Governor Burnet R. Maybank as
his principal opponent.

The 1962 campaign was not even officially under way before Sol
Blatt openly acknowledged that he was supporting Russell in the
governor's race. This may have come as a surprise to persons who
had remembered the intensity of Russell's attacks on the Barnwell
Ring four years earlier, but those on the inside of state politics knew
that there had been no love lost between Blatt and young Burnet
Maybank in the years Maybank had served in the House of Representatives.

Brown's role in the 1962 gubernatorial contest was less clear. He
was known to have been associated with Russell in a number of

business ventures of some proportions, and to have maintained good relations with him even through the 1958 campaign, when Brown was supporting Hollings.

Four years later, Brown again found himself with a lieutenant governor on his hands as a candidate for governor, and was virtually obliged to support the man who had been presiding officer of the Senate. This fact was acknowledged by Brown and accepted by the public, but there was little on the surface to show that Brown did much of anything in the 1962 governor's race.

Russell came to talk with me before this last [1962] race and I said: "I don't see you in that race." Maybank and Bob McNair were both definitely in the governor's race then. [McNair, the state representative from Allendale county, never got officially in the race for governor. Instead, he ran for lieutenant governor, against Senator Marshall J. Parker of Oconee, and was elected.]

He sat right there in my office. Dewey Johnson sat by him. Dewey was always for him, but never against me at any time—blood's thicker than water you know. They had just come by to have lunch with us and I was teasing him [Russell] about having heard that he was going to Florida to represent the Du Pont company, and Dewey chimed in and said: "No, I think he is still thinking about politics."

Donald said: "I am."

I asked: "You going to run for governor again?"

And he said: "I'm thinking very seriously about it. I can't get it out of my blood. I don't want to leave South Carolina. There's no reason why I should. I'm getting along all right. I've got all the business I want. I don't need the Du Pont money, I can make all the living I want here. I'm going to build me a summer place and I'm going to stay in Spartanburg. What do you think about it?"

I said: "It will take a lot of shoe leather, and you'll have to get off of your high horse and quit going to see the bankers, and get with the raggedies and get some working people's votes."

He went on and ran anyway, without my support. Tacitly I was helping Burnet, but Burnet couldn't make the grade. He didn't make the showing.

But my personal relations with Donald never cooled off at any time. I'll bet I talked with him a dozen times about business matters and investments. He called me the Sunday before the election and said: "You know, I'm going to be elected on the first ballot in this race. The tide is sweeping better than I thought it was, and I want you to know that I want to join hands with you and continue good government in South Carolina, and we can go on hand in hand."

We aren't going to have any trouble. I think he's going to make a good governor. I don't say that Fritz hasn't—I think Fritz has made a fine governor. He's done a lot.

Public reaction against the Barnwell Ring has been more of a state of mind than any case of documented charges. In fact, seldom has there been anything approaching a bill of particulars against either the Ring or its individual members. There have been, still are, and will continue to be detractors of Brown and Blatt as persons, and of their collective political power—but little has been advanced in the way of specific allegations of misdeeds. In general, the complaints have simply grown from the vague feeling that here are men with more than ordinary political power, stemming from extraordinary political capacity, and that something is necessarily and inherently wrong when so much influence is concentrated in so few hands. Then, too, those who have crossed swords with the master politicians from Barnwell have found cause to complain while licking their wounds.

Perhaps the most often overlooked aspect of the Barnwell Ring situation is the obvious fact that neither Brown nor Blatt could exercise any influence beyond that of a single individual, if their fellow legislators ever rejected their leadership. Neither man holds office by a natural right to office. Each man does hold office by right of election —and both of them are constantly subject to rejection by members of the House or Senate. What power they wield stems from the backing given to them by their associates. The truth of the matter is that criticism of the Barnwell Ring is, in fact, criticism of the total legislative establishment of South Carolina. At any given time over the long span of years during which Brown and Blatt have been in the General Assembly, they could have been lowered to the status of the lowliest member—whenever their fellows lost confidence in their leadership.

South Carolinians, after having lived through the tribulations of the Reconstruction Period, when Radical rule wrecked the state's economy and pillaged the state treasury, have been since then ultrasensitive to anything smacking of graft and corruption in state or local government.

This is probably why the South Carolina Constitution of 1895 is full (too full, for really efficient fiscal operation) of financial safeguards, such as those which limit the amounts of bonded indebtedness to be incurred by political subdivisions. The powers of the governor and of the other constitutional officers are limited, and made subject to legislative surveillance. Thus, in South Carolina there has been a minimum of scandal in high public office.

True, the state has had its strong men who have swept into office on a surge of raw political power, and who have used that power for political advantage. Such men frequently have been charged, with varying degrees of accuracy, of using their gubernatorial or other authority for political advantage—including playing fast and loose with appointive or pardoning powers to further their own interests.

Yet, withal, South Carolina has been remarkably free of unscrupulous efforts on the part of its top officials to dip into the public till, whether at the state or local level.

Since South Carolinians have thus been spared much of the political corruption which has flourished in other and generally more metropolitan areas, they lack a full understanding of what "ring rule" can mean. Their concept of a "ring" would hardly coincide with that found in the *Dictionary of American Politics:* "The inner circle of a party machine; a group of spoilsmen who loot the public treasury for their own personal or political gain."

The so-called "Barnwell Ring" simply does not measure up to the status of a "ring" under either of those definitions.

There has been no party "machine" in Barnwell, for the reason that Brown and Blatt simply do not "mesh" mechanically or politically. Under South Carolina's one-party political system, which lasted from the days of Wade Hampton up to the 1960's, politicking on the local level as well as statewide has been a matter of individual personality and appeal, and seldom have two men of admitted political ability and acumen reflected more different personalities than have Brown and Blatt.

Both of them do have in common that political and governmental awareness which has made them successful and effective in their varied political endeavors. And, quite obviously, they both come from the same small town. But there the similarities end, and the distinctions begin.

Edgar Brown is an easy-going, amiable sort of a fellow, whose geniality partially conceals a remarkable political insight developed through a half-century of active participation in and observation of the political world. He has been a devout follower and leader within the Democratic Party, all the way from the Barnwell precinct to the National Executive Committee. He has unsuccessfully sought statewide office (the United States Senate) on three separate occasions—but he has won every high party office within the grant of South Carolina Democrats.

Solomon Blatt, on the other hand, has never dabbled in statewide politics, except insofar as might have been necessary to shore up his own interests within the House of Representatives. He has been, from start to finish, a state legislator whose consuming concern has been service and influence within the South Carolina House of Representatives. He has not sought high place within the Democratic Party, although his counsel often has been sought by those who do hold high position. He has never run for any office outside of Barnwell County except for Speaker of the House, and he has served longer in that capacity than any other South Carolinian.

Blatt is affable enough, but always with an inner intensity which contrasts with the air of almost complete relaxation which characterizes Brown. Of the two, Blatt is by far the more sensitive to criticism, and the more prompt to reply to it.

Through the long years of their politcal association in Barnwell, the two men have been friends, but never really bosom companions. They have seldom visited one another except in line of business—and for the most part, political business at that. They have worked with remarkable harmony in handling the affairs of Barnwell County, and have jointly insisted on a degree of fiscal well-being in county affairs which well could be emulated by other counties.

At the level of state government, however, they have differed frequently and sometimes spiritedly. For one thing, Brown has been a constant advocate of public power, whereas Blatt has just as consistently championed privately-owned utilities and the free enterprise system in the area of power generation.

On major matters affecting the state's economic or governmental structure, Brown and Blatt have conferred often, and from time to time they have planned courses of action in their respective legislative houses aimed at furthering, or hindering, a given piece of legislation. On lesser matters, though, they have made up their minds individually, and have not sought to bend one another's will if—as has been the occasion frequently—they have happened to be on opposite sides.

When Governor Robert E. McNair addressed the General Assembly on January 13, 1970, he remarked about the forthcoming Tricentennial celebration and added: "In a sense we are concluding one period of development, and we are beginning another. We have seen unprecedented growth lift South Carolina to new levels of economic achievement; now we face the challenge of consolidating those gains, and preparing for a new and greater period of progress ahead."

The governor noted 160,000 new jobs and a rise in total personal income of 102 percent during the 1960s. A record $706 million was invested in new and expanded industry in 1969 alone. And he expected tourism to reach $500 million in 1975. To this optimistic outlook we might add that the state's agriculture is more mechanized and diversified than ever before, and sharecropping is rapidly disappearing—a drop from 100,000 tenant families in 1930 to 4,000 in 1969. Yet, by most statistical measures South Carolina still ranks near the bottom of the fifty states with regard to income, wealth, and literacy. Moreover, there was a continuing exodus of South Carolina Negroes to other states during the past decade. Almost 200,000 departed not to return.

On January 19, 1971, John Carl West was inaugurated governor of South Carolina. In his inaugural speech he also took note of the state's great progress, for which he gave much credit to outgoing Governor McNair. He then pledged himself to a far-reaching program to improve health, housing, and education, to accelerate industrial and agricultural development, to strengthen law enforcement, and to eliminate "any vestige of discrimination because of race, creed, sex, religion or any other barrier to fairness for all citizens." Governor West's strong proposal to eliminate discrimination of minorities marked a new day in political pronouncements within South Carolina. The following selection is Governor West's inaugural address.

39

SOUTH CAROLINA
LOOKS TO THE FUTURE *

John C. West

Nineteen Hundred-seventy was the year that the citizens of South Carolina marked the 300th anniversary of the founding of this state, and we now move with confidence and optimism into the Fourth Century of our stewardship of this land. Our Tricentennial years [*sic*] was a time of reawakening to our history and heritage; it was a time of new awareness of the essential character and strength of the people of this state.

It was also a time to gain new understanding of our particular moment in history, and to view the past and the future with a new degree of sensitivity and perspective.

It was a time to realize that no state has produced more greatness in the character of its individual leaders; no state has given more freely of itself in the building of this great nation. But it was also a time to understand that ours is a history of people—of people who have known struggle and survival, disappointment and endurance, frustration and despair. We have emerged as a state in the twentieth century still limited in material attainment. But out of the trials and tests of the past, we have built a wealth of human and spiritual resources with which we can now look to our Fourth Century—a new Century of Progress for People.

As never before, we can look forward with confidence to a new era of achievement, to new milestones of accomplishment for our people, to a reawakened spirit of unity which should project our state to new heights of greatness, unparalleled in this state, or in any state at any time in history.

I make these statements not in the sense of the politician reaching for the easy superlative on a most memorable day. Instead, I speak with the assurance of one who senses an elevation of the spirits and

* *Journal of the House of Representatives of the First Session of the 99th General Assembly of the State of South Carolina . . . ,* 3 vols. (Columbia: State Budget and Control Board, 1971) , I, 155-60.

renewed confidence of the people in themselves. I speak as one who has observed and experienced the resurgence of our state in recent years, and has detected the new energy and new determination present within the fiber of our people.

In the last decade, South Carolina has made more progress in every meaningful way than at any comparable period in her 300-year history. In fact, I challenge historians of today or tomorrow to match the progress that South Carolinians have made in the last ten years with that made by any state—including our own—in any hundred-year period of the past.

If there has been a single factor which has influenced this phenomenal growth and progress more than any other, it has been the quality of leadership our state has had in the Office of Governor.

I should like to say especially to our retiring Governor, Robert E. McNair, that yours has been a period of unusual service and unprecedented accomplishment. You have served more consecutive years as Chief Executive than any Governor in the history of our state, but your place in the history books will be for reasons other than length of term. Yours will be recorded as a period in which this state experienced its greatest human advancement. By reason of your distinguished service, you will unquestionably be accorded a well-deserved place as one of the greatest governors who has ever served the State of South Carolina.

I would be remiss if I did not mention also the one who has not only been your helpmate, but one whose years as First Lady have brought new dimension to that position, and a new and lasting sense of pride for the people of South Carolina. Through such accomplishments as the restoration and furnishing of the Governor's Mansion, you have not only won national acclaim, but with your charm, grace and dignity, Mrs. McNair . . . Josephine . . . a lasting place has been won for you and your family in the hearts of all South Carolinians.

Thanks to the caliber of leadership South Carolina has experienced, the decade of the sixties was one of unparalleled progress for our people. But more importantly, it was a period in which the foundation was laid for the seventies—a foundation giving us the capacity to reach for and attain any goals to which we as a people may aspire.

Therefore, it is appropriate on this occasion marking the beginning of the New Century in South Carolina that we set for ourselves certain goals, goals whose urgency and priority at this moment in our history cannot be questioned. The time has arrived when South

Carolina for all time must break loose and break free of the vicious cycle of ignorance, illiteracy and poverty which has retarded us throughout our history.

If to some these goals seem too lofty, impossible of achievement, or unrealistic, I submit that nothing is impossible if we unite together with energy, determination, and dedication toward a common cause.

We can, and we shall, in the next four years eliminate hunger and malnutrition, and their attendant suffering from our state.

We can, and we shall, in the next four years, initiate new and innovative programs which will in our time provide adequate housing for all our citizens.

We can, and we shall, this year initiate far-reaching programs to provide more doctors, nurses and health personnel as well as better systems for delivery of health care to each citizen. Our goal shall be that each citizen may live with proper protection from disease and proper treatment of illness for his full life expectancy.

We can, and we shall, in the next four years, eliminate from our government, any vestige of discrimination because of race, creed, sex, religion or any other barrier to fairness for all citizens.

We pledge to minority groups no special status other than full-fledged responsibility in a government that is totally color-blind.

We can, and we shall, accelerate programs of industrial and agricultural development until every citizen who is underemployed has the opportunity for full and rewarding employment, and every young person, has a job opportunity that is productive, meaningful and challenging.

We can, and we shall, strengthen our law enforcement system by providing better training, better pay and better equipment for our officers; by strengthening our laws and court procedures dealing with criminals; and by working for the removal of the root causes of crime.

We can, and we shall, seek and channel the energy, dedication and social consciousness of our young people into solving the problems of our times.

We do not need—and we cannot afford—an alienation of the generations, and I pledge that this will be an administration which actively seeks the involvement of the young and old alike.

We can, and we shall, in the next four years, take whatever action is necessary to assure the preservation of our living environment, and to provide the type of resource management which will make it possible for all interests in our society to live in harmony with each other. There need not be—and there shall not be—economic or ecological sacrifice in the progress of South Carolina in the next four years.

Finally, and perhaps most important of all, we can, and we shall, provide a better educational opportunity for all citizens of whatever age or status, from a comprehensive pre-school program for the very young to a continuing educational program for adults ranging from basic literacy to sophisticated, advanced research-oriented graduate programs.

These goals, admittedly ambitious, are no more impossible of achievement than those articulated by the brave young President, John F. Kennedy, who stated so eloquently in 1961 that we could perform the seemingly impossible task of placing a man safely on the moon and returning within the decade of the sixties—a dream of man for untold centuries.

It has been just as much a dream that man one day could conquer the plague of human hunger and privation, and could live in peace and dignity with his fellow man. The fact that these conditions have been a part of man's recorded lot since Biblical times should make us no less determined to attack them with all our energy and capabilities in this decade.

The setting of these goals is in itself an important first step toward their ultimate accomplishment, and—in all candor—this first step is perhaps the easiest. Certainly it is the simplest. But if these words can launch our state into positive action, if they can unleash the energies of our people and their government toward solutions, then they will have proved to be a valuable first step.

More important than action and good intentions at this point must be the establishment of guiding principles to direct and channel our efforts in this undertaking. Basically, I see three principles to be of immediate and primary importance.

First, the goals, as stated, must be accorded priority status. In today's complex society with constantly increasing demands and expectations of people, there is a tendency to overlook fundamental problems, and to scattergun society's thrust on less essential, but more glamourous functions. In a state with limited financial resources, we must concentrate with laser beam accuracy on the basic human problems, using the constant criterion of Progress for People toward stated goals.

Second, the achievement of these goals can become a reality only if the people of this state unite and work together, putting aside differences of race, politics, generation, or other. Two thousand years ago, the greatest philosopher and teacher who ever lived said, "And if a Kingdom be divided against itself, that Kingdom cannot stand, and if a house be divided against itself, that house cannot stand." The politics of race and divisiveness have been soundly repudiated in South Carolina.

We are all one—God's people, and our differences—whether they be age, sex, religion or race—should be considered as blessings and strengths. As we work toward the elimination of discrimination, as we build toward a better life for all, as all the people of our state join together in this most noble of undertakings, perhaps we shall begin to realize the truths as expressed in the words of the hymn:

> God moves in a mysterious way
> His wonders to perform.
> Ye fearful saints, fresh courage take;
> The clouds you so much dread
> Are big with mercy and shall break
> In blessing on your head.

Third, in directing our efforts toward achievements which have eluded man throughout his time on this earth, we must have the active involvement of all citizens. Government is but the instrument of the will of the people—having no power in and of itself; deriving not just its power, but its will and its effectiveness from its citizens. It is not our purpose to change that relationship; it is our goal to strengthen it. What we outline today in terms of human progress are not simply governmental projects. If we are to eliminate hunger, provide better housing, improve the delivery of health care for all, we must have the deep involvement and commitment of the private sector working in close cooperation with the public sector and providing necessary support from our whole free enterprise system.

If we are to bring the generations together, if we are to eliminate discrimination, it requires more than a law or mandate from government. Basic to all our hopes and aspirations is the willingness of our people to accept change, and to gain a new respect for the opinions and the rights of all people.

Providing a better education for all, especially within our present limited tax sources, requires new and innovative concepts, the most important aspect of which will be the voluntary involvement of citizens in the educational program.

As we address ourselves to Progress for People, it is implicit that I am also talking about Progress by People. It is most important that each citizen recognize his responsibility and his opportunity to participate in Progress for People, and to make the years ahead rewarding and fulfilling, and . . .

I pledge to each of you, my fellow South Carolinians, on this the most important day of my life, every ounce of strength, every talent which I possess, to move with you toward these goals for a better life for all South Carolinians and a new and brighter era in the history of our state.

INDEX

Abney, B. L., attorney, 318
Abolition movement, 98, 134
Adams, John, 77, 79–83
Adams, John Quincy, 109–12
Agents (of the colony), 37–38, 40. *See also* Yonge, Francis *and* Sharpe, John
Agriculture, experimental. *See* Farm, experimental
Aguinaldo, General Emilio, 359
Alabama, secessionist overtures of, 144
Albemarle (ship), 15, 17
Albemarle, first account of, 4
Albemarle Point, 18
Allen, J. M., member of Constitutional Convention of 1868, 208; scalawag, 220
Allston, Governor Robert F. W., 142
American Revolution, 74
Anderson, Major Robert, commands U.S. Army force at Fort Sumter, 148; surprised by Confederate floating battery, 152; orders defenders into casemates, 152–53; refuses to evacuate Fort Sumter, 154; receives Confederate emissaries, 156; plays for time, 157; prepares for Confederate attack, 157–58; mentioned, 148–57 *passim*
Anderson, Robert B., Negro delegate to Constitutional Convention of 1895, 289, 291–92
Anderson *Daily Mail,* 320
Anderson *Intelligencer,* 345
Andrews, Sidney, describes desolate Charleston, 189–90
Anglican church, 34, 61. *See also* Church of England
Ansel, Governor Martin F., 319
Architecture, 58
Aristocracy, attacked by Wade Hampton, 237; decay of, 248
Aristocracy, local; landgraves and cassiques, 8–10. *See also* Gentry

Arnim, Frank, carpetbagger, 220
Artillery Company, Gadsden's 64–65, 70
Asbury, Francis, 75
Ashley, Lord. *See* Cooper, Anthony Ashley
Assembly (Carolina lower house), 36, 40. *See also* Commons House of Assembly *and* Parliament, Carolina
Assumption of debts, 77
Attorney-General and Solicitor-General, opinions of, 38–39, 42
Attucks, Crispus, 290
Ayer, Lewis M., anti-Davis Confederate congressman, 167; victor over Rhett in congressional race, 170

Back country, complaints of, 68–69
Baker and Lord (agents), 87–88
"Balance of Government," 7, 9–10
Ball, W. W., student, 277
Bampfield, S. J., Negro editor, 286
Bandholtz, Col. H. H., 334–35
Bank of the United States (first), 77
Bank of the United States (second), 108
Baptist, 119–21
Barbadians (settlers), 18
Barbados, 14, 16; influence of, 58
Barnett, Governor Ross, 385
Barnwell, Robert W., cooperationist, 137; Confederate senator, strong supporter of Davis, 165; doubts Davis's ability, 166; stands by Davis, 167–68, 172
"Barnwell Ring," 392–407. *See also* Brown, Edgar A. *and* Blatt, Solomon
Barony. *See* Land system
Barrett, John G., author of *Sherman's March Through the Carolinas,* 174–75
Beattie, A. J., 397
Beauregard, General Pierre G. T., commands Confederate forces at Charleston, 149; prepares to reduce

415

Beauregard, General Pierre G. T.
(*continued*)
  Fort Sumter, 149–52; seeks Fort
  Sumter undamaged, 155; in command
  at Columbia, 175; mentioned, 156–57
Bell, J. O., carpetbagger, 220
Bennett, Governor, 102
Benton, Lemuel, Republican congress-
  man elected in 1792, 77
Bermuda, 17
Bethea, A. W. Red, opponent of desegre-
  gation at Clemson, 388–91
Bethel (Presbyterian) Church, 122
Bethesda Church (Camden), 130
Bible Society of Greenville, The, 123
Birth of a Nation, The, Hollywood's
  first significant movie, 336; in
  Spartanburg, 337; in York, 338;
  produced by Griffith, 342–43; seen
  by Wilson, opens in New York, 343;
  in Charlotte and Columbia, 344; in
  Charleston and elsewhere, 345;
  in Chester and Rock Hill, 345–46;
  returns to S.C., 346; its impact, 347
Bitzer, Billy cameraman, 342
Blackbeard (Edward Teach or
  Thatch), 28
Blatt, Solomon, legislative member of
  "Barnwell Ring," 393; elected House
  speaker, 394; attacked as "Ring"
  member, 395–96, 398; re-elected, 398;
  falls out with Russell, 402–3; supports
  Russell, 403; political influence
  of, 405–7; relations with Brown,
  406–7; personality, 407
Blatt, Solomon, Jr., 403
Blease, Coleman L. ("Coley"), elected
  governor, 304, 319; summary of
  political career, 316; analysis of his
  support, 316–19; early life, 319;
  inaugural, 319–20; feud over judicial
  appointments, 320; condones gambling
  and blind tigers, 320–21; tempestuous
  relations with legislature, 321;
  hostile to press, 322; inconsistent on
  reform, 322–23; in temporary eclipse,
  326; defeated by Byrnes, 351
Bleaseism, nature of, 316–19. *See also*
  Blease, Coleman L.
Blue Laws, 127
Blue Ridge Railroad Scrip, 228, 230–31
Board of Trade, 28, 32, 35–36, 37–38
Boatwright, Alice, property of, destroyed,
  181

Bonham, Milledge L., congressman,
  142; governor, 151, 170
Bonnet, Stede, pirate, 29–30, 32
"Bourbons," 234, 240, 246–54 *passim;*
  268, 278, 284, 288, 294
Bowen family, role in Civil War,
  356–58
Boyce, William W., Confederate congressman; mildly critical of Davis,
  167; joins anti-Davis forces, 171
Bratton, John, 272, 274, 276; candidate
  for governor, 279
Brawley, William H., 277–78
Brayne, Captain Henry, 15
Brayton, Ellery M., Republican Party
  chairman, 285
Britton, Captain, Freedmen's Bureau
  officer, 198
Broad River. *See* Electric power
Brooks, Preston S., 138
Brown, Edgar A., political leader,
  383–84; role in Harvey Gantt case,
  386–87, 391; heads "Barnwell Ring,"
  392–93; and origin of "Ring," 394;
  and attack on "Ring" in 1946, 395–98;
  and "Ring" survival, 398–99; friction
  with Thurmond, 400; and Russell
  attack, 401–2; personal account of
  Russell attack, 402–3; personal
  account of 1962 election, 404–5;
  "Ring" strength and cooperation,
  405–6; personality of, 406; relations
  with Blatt, 406–7
Brown, John, 132, 142–43
Brown, Thomas W., murdered taxi-
  driver, 360, 365–67
Brown, Walter, 403
Brown family of Rhode Island, 91–92
Bryan, Hugh, planter, 60–61
Bryan, John P. K., 289
Bryce, Mrs. Campbell, 177
Buchanan, James, 141
Buist, G. L., state senator, 278
Bull, Stephen, 18
Bull, Lieutenant Governor William,
  Sr., 58
Bull, William (II), 65, 69–70
Burke, Aedanus, 75, 90
Burr, Aaron, 77, 82
Butler, Andrew P., 137
Butler, General Mathew C., 175–76,
  defeats Gary for U.S. Senate, 237;
  opponent of Tillman, 276
Butler, Pierce, senator, 79

Byers, Samuel H. M., author of "Sherman's March to the Sea" (song), 177

Byrnes, James F., campaigns for re-election, 348–53; summary of career, 370; author of *All in One Lifetime*, 370–71; elected governor, 371; battles Klan, 371–72; supports sales tax, 371–72; educational program of, 373–74; improves mental health care, 374–75; uses convicts in governor's mansion, 375–76; and Clarendon school case, 376–77; opposes Supreme Court decision, 377–78; retires again, 378–79; and sales tax, 380; secretary of state, 384; and the Harvey Gantt case, 387, 390; legal associate of Russell, 401; denies opposition to "Barnwell Ring," 403

Cabot, John, explorations of, 2

Cain, Richard H., Negro congressman, 223, 230

Calhoun, Floride (wife of John C.), 89, 107. *See also* Colhoun, Floride Bonneau

Calhoun, John C., 84, 89, 104–17, 132–33, 135, 189, 348, 350–51

Calhoun, Patrick (father of John C.), 106

Calvary Baptist Church, meeting in, 286

Camden *Confederate*, 165

Cameron, Flora, in *Birth of a Nation*, 337, 343

Cameron, Simon, U.S. secretary of war, sends instructions to Major Anderson, 156–57

Campaign of 1800, 80–83

Campbell, Lawton, author of *Swat the Spies*, 333

Camp meetings, 129

Camp Wadsworth, arrival of Twenty-Seventh Division, 327; camp life, 327–28; the Vanderbilts, 328–29; housing, 328–29; soldiers' newsletters, 329–30; organization and training, 330; artillery range, 330–31; Spartan-burg hospitality, 331–32; camp social affairs, 330, 332–33; Christmas at camp, 333–34; military and civilian hardships, 334–35; departure of Twenty-Seventh Division, 335

Canby, General E. R. S., 209

Cannon, Daniel, carpenter, 70

Capital, removal of, 76

Cardozo, Francis L., Negro member of Constitutional Convention of 1868, 204; education of, 222; state treasurer, 223, 28

Cardozo, J. N., commentator on Charleston's commercial life, 92

Carolina (ship), 15, 17–18

Carteret, Lord, 39, 42

Cassiques. *See* Aristocracy, local

Cattle, 24–25, 56

Cauthen, Charles Edward, author of *South Carolina Goes to War, 1860–1865*, 132–33, 160–61

Cauthen, John K., textile executive, 383; marshals support for admission of Gantt, 384, 386–88, 391

Chamberlain, Governor Daniel H., member of Constitutional Convention of 1868, 208; carpetbagger, 220–21

Chambliss, Major N. R., 175

Charles I, 4

Charles II, 4

Charleston (Charles Town), S.C., founding of, 18–19; site of, 22; pirates and the harbor of, 27–29; convention meeting in, in 1719 that proclaimed the end of proprietary rule, 37; rice introduced by Woodward of, 46; as center of rice trade, 48; as a city-state, 54–55; trade of, 57; society of, 59; intellectual life of, 61; opposition in, to the Stamp Act, 67; effect of removal of capital from, to Columbia, 76; celebration in, over fall of the Bastille, 78; effect of Napoleon's embargo on trade of, 92; cotton prices in, from 1814 to 1819, 98; decline in trade of, 101; and the Nullifiers, 116; blue laws of, 127; criticism of National Democrats' choice of, as next convention city, 141; Civil War destruction in, 188–90, 355; vice in, 320–21; appearance of *The Clansman* in, 340; appearance of *Birth of a Nation* in, 345

Charleston Baptist Association, 120

Charleston *Courier*, establishment of, 84; debates right of secession, 142; defends Davis's administration, 165, 167–69, 171–72

Charleston Daily Courier, reports of, 191–93, 209. *See also* Charleston *Courier*; Charleston *News and Courier*

Charleston Daily News, reports of, 193, 209

Charleston *Evening News,* debate over right of secession, 142

Charleston *Evening Post,* 340

Charleston Mercury, 139–40, 209. *See also* Rhett, Robert B.

Charleston *News and Courier,* accounts of Tillman's campaign, 279; claims election frauds, 284; reports vice, 321; and Blease's attack on press, 322; and Reverend Dixon, 337–38, 340; and *Birth of a Nation,* 337, 345

Charleston *Post,* 320

Charlotte, N.C., and *Birth of a Nation,* 338, 344

Charter (1665), 5; the surrender of, 34–42

Chesapeake and *Leopard* Affair, 91, 93

Chesnut, Colonel James, Confederate emissary, delivers ultimatum to Major Anderson, 153–54; announces Confederate attack, 156–57; returns to Confederate lines, 158; defends Davis's administration, 168

Chesnut, General James, 222

Chesnut, James, Jr., 142

Chesnut, John, ex-slave member of Constitutional Convention of 1868, 222; member of House, 229

Chesnut, Mrs. Mary Boykin, diarist, complains of Anderson's moving into Fort Sumter, 151; attends dinner party, 156; prays when she hears cannon fire, 159; comments on S.C. criticism of Davis, 166

Chester, 345–46

Chester *Reporter,* 223

Chester *Semi-Weekly News,* 346

Cheves, Langdon, congressman, 84, 89, 137

Chisolm, Col. A. R., Confederate emissary, 153–58 *passim. See also* Chesnut, Colonel James

Christ Church, 122

Church buildings, 119–20

Church of England, 12. *See also* Anglican church

Citadel, The, and controversy between Tillman and University of S.C., 268, 274–75, 280–81

Citizens Councils, and the Harvey Gantt case, 385, 387–88

City Gazette, 81

Clansman, The, written by Dixon, 336–38; its critics, 339; plays in the South, 339–41; in New York City, 341; made into movie, 342–43; original setting, 346

Clarendon County school case, 376–77, 380, 387

Clark, E. P., Mass. editor, praises Hampton, 239–40

Class structure in colonial South Carolina, 57–58

Clay, Henry, 107–10, 116, 136

Clemson, Thomas G., death of, 268, 275; visited by Tillman, 270; rewrites will, 271; bequest of, accepted by S.C., 277–78; attacked by McMaster, 278

Clemson College, established, 278; supported by Tillman, 270–71, 277–78, 280–81; racially integrated, 380–91. *See also* Tillman, Benjamin R.

Clemson University. *See* Clemson College

Clergy, 120–22

Clubs (in Charleston), 59

Cochran, John R., scalawag, 220

Coghlan, T. J., member of Constitutional Convention of 1868, 205

Colhoun, Floride Bonneau (maiden name of John C.'s wife), 89

Colleton, Sir Peter, 20

Colleton, Thomas, 16, 18

Columbia, S.C., Sherman's occupation of, 174; question of burning cotton, 175–176; the burning of, 178–82; amount of destruction, 182; Sherman's efforts to arrest destruction of, 181; ordnance explosion kills 16 Union soldiers, 184; Union supplies for destitute people of, 185; departure of Union troop from, 185; destruction of, 188, 355; appearance of *The Clansman* in, 339; appearance of *Birth of a Nation* in, 344; Chamber of Commerce of, and Gantt case, 388. *See also* Sherman, General William T.

Columbia *Daily Register,* 279

Columbia *State,* claims fraud, 284; critic of Blease, 319; feud with Dixon, 337–41; and Harvey Gantt, 384

Commerce, age of, 91

Committee of correspondence, 66

Commons House of Assembly, 54–55, 59, 63, 66. *See also* Assembly

Compromise of 1850, 136–38

Compromise Tariff (1833), 116

Concessions and agreements, 6
Confederate government, S.C. criticism of. *See* Davis, Jefferson *and* Rhett, Robert Barnwell
Congo Party, 142
Congregationalists, 119
Congress, Stamp Act, 64, 66, 70
Conservatives. *See* "Bourbons"
Constitutional Convention of 1868, personnel of, 202, 221–22; regulation of suffrage and office-holding, 203–4; steps toward social and economic equality, 205–6; education and rights of women, 206–7; reform of local and judicial administration, 207–8; finance, 208; serious work and discipline, 209
Constitutional Convention of 1895, sponsored by Tillman, 283; referendum for, 284; claims of fraud, 284–85; Republican and Negro opposition to suffrage discrimination, 285–87; election of delegates and Tillmanite victory, 288–89; proposed suffrage provisions, 289; Negro delegates' objections, 290–92; Irby and Tillman speak, 292–93; Negroes deny fraud, 293; Tillmanite victory, 284–95; Negro vote reduced, 294
Constitution of 1868, 202
Constitution of 1895, 202, 294–95, 304, 405
Constitution of the United States, 76, 106, 133, 137
Constitutions, Fundamental (1669), 6–14, 23
Convention, National Democratic (1856), 140
Convention, state (1852), 137–38
Cooper, Anthony Ashley (later Earl of Shaftesbury), 5–7, 12, 19–20, 90
Cooper, Dr. Thomas, 134
Cooperationists, 136–39
Corbin, D. T., 209; carpetbagger, 220, 224, 242
Corley, Simeon, scalawag, 220
Cotton, 24, 44, 86–88, 91, 94–97, 100, 110–11, 123; Sea Island, 96–97; manufacturing of, 97; prices of, 98–99, 101
Cotton gin, 86–87, 96–97
Council, colonial, 23, 32, 54, 69. *See also* Grand Council
Counties, establishment of, 23
Courts, administrative, 8

Courts, local, 9
Craven, Wesley Frank, author of *The Southern Colonies in the Seventeenth Century, 1607–1689,* 14–15
Crawford, Samuel, U.S. Army surgeon and diarist, 152–54, 156
Crawford, William H., secretary of the treasury, 109
Crews, Joseph, scalawag legislator, 220, 225
Crittenden, Charles Christopher, author of "The Surrender of the Charter of Carolina," 34–35
Croushore, James H., co-editor with David M. Potter of *A Union Officer in the Reconstruction,* 194
Culbertson, John Bolt, 398
Cummings Point, 156, 159
Current, Richard N., author of *Great American Thinkers: John C. Calhoun,* 104–5
Cuthbert, Captain G. B., commander of Palmetto Guards, 156

Daniel, Charles, and Harvey Gantt case, 383–84
Dargan, Colonel John J., defends Negro political rights, 287
Darlington Flag, 141
David, Mrs. Hattie D., 351
David, J. M., 199
Davis, Jefferson, lieutenant in the U.S. Army, 153
Davis, Jefferson, president of the Confederacy, mentioned 149, 151; criticism of, 161–73 *passim;* visits Charleston, 171
Davis, John W., 376
Dayton, Colonel Lewis M., 181
"Debt of the Law to the Lawless, The" *Collier's,* 338–39
Declaratory Act, 70–71
Defense of the province, 35–36
De Forest, John W., Freedman's Bureau agent, 194; author of "Drawing Bureau Rations," 195; distributes clothing, 195–97; reports on race relations, 197–98; mediates disputes, 198–99; distributes food supplies, 199–201; seeks local guidance, 201
DeLarge, R. C., Negro member of Constitutional Convention of 1868, 208; member of Congress, 223; member of S.C. House, 224–25

Democratic National Convention at Philadelphia, 350, 352

Democratic Party, 132, 138–43. *See also* Jeffersonian Democracy *and* Republicans of South Carolina (Democrats)

DeSaussure, Henry William, Federalist, 81–82, 89

Dill, Solomon G. W., assassination of, 212; scalawag, 219–20

Disallowance of laws, 37

Dixiecrat Party, 370

Dixon, Reverend Thomas, novelist and playwright, 336; author of *The Clansman* and *The Leopard's Spots*, 337–38; attacks Ogden, 338; southern tour of his play, 339–41; feud with S.C. press, 338–41; meets Griffith, 342; flair for publicity, 343; mentioned, 344–46

Drayton, William Henry, 64

Dred Scott decision, 142

Duke, James B., furnishes money, 296; has sore foot, 297; takes interest in electric power, 298–99; builds textile mills, 299–300; builds steam plants, 300; organizes Duke Power Company, 301. *See also* Electric power

Duncan, Blanton, home of, Sherman's headquarters, 177

Dunovant, General R. G. M., 150–51

Duties (export and import), 36. *See also* Tariffs

Dwight, Timothy, president of Yale, 106–7

Earle, Baylis, 331

Earle, Joseph H., candidate for governor, 279

Earle, Willie, victim of lynching, 360–69

Easely (Easley), W. K., 199

Eaton, Peggy O'Neal Timberlake, 113–14

Education, colonial, 61

"Educational Revolution," 373

Edwards, B. W., state senator, 271

Edwards, Robert C., president of Clemson, 383; and Harvey Gantt case, 383–84, 386, 388–89, 391

"Eight Box Law," 282

Electoral Commission of 1877, 241

Electric power, role of Duke, Lee, and Wylie, 296–301; evolution of dual hydro and steam system, 300–301; Wateree-Catawba development, 298–

Electric power (*continued*) 99; Broad River development, 299–302; Saluda River development, 302–3. *See also* Duke, James B.

Elizabeth I, 3

Elliott, Robert B., Negro member of Constitutional Convention of 1868, 204, 206; member of Congress, 223, 227

Elliott, Major Stephen D., Confederate commander of Fort Sumter, 171

Embargo, by Napoleon in 1808, 91–92, 111

Emigration, 89, 100–101, 103

England, colonial efforts of, 2

Episcopal, 119–21

Epping, J. P. M., carpetbagger, 220

Epps, Dr. Carl B., attacks "Barnwell Ring," 395, 397

Evans, Governor John G., 287; delegate to Constitutional Convention of 1895, 288

Evans, Josiah J., 138–39

Excommunication, 124–26

Fairfield *Herald*, 165

"Farewell Letter." *See* Tillman, Benjamin R.

Farm, experimental, 16, 18–19, 24, 44

Farmers, small, 57, 100

Faubus, Governor Orville, 385

Featherstone, C. C., 319

Federalism, 77, 80, 82–86, 88–90

Federalist Club, 80

Figg, Robert McC., Jr., 376

Finley, David E., member of S.C. House, 280

First Cavalry, 328

Folk, Sim W., lost to Blatt in election, 399

Force Bill (1833), 115–16

Ford, Timothy, 88–90

Fort Hill Letter, 114

Fort Johnson, 158–59

Fort Moultrie, 148, 158, 177

Fort Sumter, Confederate need for capture of, 149; Confederate preparations for reduction of, 150–53; Confederate demand for evacuation of, 154; Union fortification of, 152, 155; scarcity of Union rations within, 152–57; Confederate attack upon, 158–59. *See also* Anderson, Major Robert

Forty-Second Regiment, 327

Foster, Captain John G., prepares defenses of Fort Sumter, 152, 155
France, colonial efforts of, 2
Freedmen's Bureau. *See* De Forest, John W.
Freeman, Wayne, 383–84
Fremont, John C., 141
French Patriotic Society, 78
French Revolution, 74, 78, 79

Gadsden, Captain Christopher, 62–71, 83
Gadsden, Thomas, 70
Gaillard, S. E., Negro state senator, 230
Gantt, Harvey, arrives at Clemson, 381–82; applies for admission, 383–84; reapplies for admission, 384–85; legal maneuvers of, 386; opposition to admission of, 386–87; court orders admission of, 390
Garden, Alexander, Anglican Commissary, 60–61
Garth, Charles, colonial agent, 63–64, 66–67
Gary, General Martin W., opposes Hampton's conciliatory program, 234–37; defeated for U.S. Senate, 237; forerunner of Tillman, 238; calls Hayes a "usurper," 240; defended by Sheppard, 241; death of, 246
Genêt, Citizen Edmund, 78
Gentry (as a class), 58
Gervais, John Lewis, 68
Gibbes, James G., 176
Gibbes, Dr. Robert W., home of, burned, 180
Gilbert, Sir Humphrey, 3
Gilman, Caroline, 126
Gilmore, J. T., Negro member of S.C. House, 227
Gilstrap, Ed, jailor, 360
Gish, Lillian, 342
Gist, Governor William H., 143
Gleaves, R. H., Negro presiding officer of S.C. Senate, 221, 223, 238
Glen, Governor James, 57
Glenn, John, 347
Gonzales, N. G., reports for *News and Courier*, 271, 274; mentioned, 288, murdered, 322
Gonzales, W. E., 338, 340–41
Goodwyn, Mayor T. J., walks over Columbia with Sherman, 177; reassured by Sherman, 177–78; criticized by Sherman, 183

Governor, office of, 23, 54–55
Grady, Henry W., 252
Grand Council, 8, 10, 12. *See also* Council
Graniteville, S.C., textile village, housing, 255–56; social distinctions, 256–57; wages: three-dollar-a-day men, 256–58; operatives' diet, 258–59; hours of work, 259–60; religious meetings, 260, 263–64; Negro workers, 260; whiskey drinking, 260–61; isolation of, 261; photographer's shop, 261; music and dancing, 262; labor supply, 264–65; women's fashions, 265–66; use of tobacco, 266–67
Grant, Joseph J., Negro member of S.C. House, 227
Grant, President Ulysses S., 217
Grant (1663) by Charles II to Lords Proprietors, 4–5
Grayson, William J., Unionist, 136
Great Awakening, 60
Green, Reverend Roger, 4
Greenville, S.C., cold winter of 1867, 195; poverty of its citizens, 195–97; description of, 361; trial of taxi-drivers in, 360–69; First Baptist Church of, 361; Court House of, 361–64
Greenville *Enterprise*, 169
Grenville, George, 63
Gressette, Marion, state senator and head of Gressette Committee, 377, 383; and Harvey Gantt case, 383, 385, 387–91; opposes violence, 390–91
Gressette Committee. *See* Gressette
Griffith, David W., early career, 342; meets Dixon, 342; produces *Birth of a Nation*, 342–43; mentioned, 344, 346
Guerry, Bishop William A., 320
Gus, in *Birth of a Nation*, 343
Guy, William, 27

Hagood, Johnson, 291
Hamilton, Alexander, 81
Hammond, James H., 138, 142; criticizes Davis's administration, 164, 166
Hampton, Wade, I, 88–90
Hampton, General Wade, III, in 1865 receives blame for burning of Columbia, 175, 183; denies charge, 175; home of, destroyed, 176–77; takes control of S.C., 234; prestige of, as governor, 235; calls special session of

Hampton, Gen. Wade (*continued*)
legislature, 235; opposed by Gary,
236–37; supported by Woodward,
238–39; efforts of, at conciliation,
239–40; cordial relations with President Hayes, 240–45; and charges
against Republicans, 242–45; elected
to U.S. Senate, 246, 288; defeated for
re-election, 280; does not fear Negro
domination, 288; mentioned, 268, 276,
281, 291, 339, 351, 406
Hand, Professor William H., report of,
304–15
Harley, Governor J. Emile, member of
"Barnwell Ring," 393–94
Harllee, Colonel William C., political
opponent of Byrnes, 350–53, 354
Harper, Robert Goodloe, Federalist, 80
Harrington, James, political philosopher,
7–8
Hartstene, Captain H. J., 151
Haskell, Alexander C., opponent of
Tillman, 276
Haskell, John C., 272, 274; and opponent
of Tillman, 276–77
Haskellites, 282
Hatch Act of 1887, dispute over funds,
272–78 *passim*
Hayes, President Rutherford B., with-
draws troops, 234; cooperates with
Hampton, 240–45
Hayne, H. E., Negro officeholder, 223
Hayne, Robert Y., 114
Hazen, Major General William B.,
U.S.A., believes Union soldiers burned
Columbia, 176, 179; fights fire, 181
Headrights, 6, 12–14, 21. *See also* Land
system
Heath, Sir Robert, 4–5
Hemphill, Robert, planter, 215
Hemphill, R. R., legislator from
Abbeville, 269, 274
Henderson, William, opponent of "any
fair elections," 293–94
Hogan, Frank, lawyer, 352
Hollander, L. P., 333
Hollings, Governor Ernest F. ("Fritz"),
moderate leader, 383–84; refuses to
support Barnett, 385; advises caution
in Gantt case, 389; elected governor,
401–3; praised by Brown, 405
Hollis, Daniel W., 89; author of
College to University (*University of
South Carolina*, Vol. II), 268–69

Holmes, Reuben, carpetbagger, 220, 225
Hoover, President Herbert, 334
Hopkins, Harry, 352
Horsey, Samuel, 39
Howard, General Oliver O., fights fire
in Columbia, 181; destroys railroad
property, 184
Huguenots, 23
Hurd, Roosevelt C., Jr., 362–63, 366,
367–69
Hurd, Roosevelt C., Sr., 362–63, 369
Hurley, Timothy, carpetbagger, 221, 227,
230
Hurricane destruction (to rice crops),
49–51

Indians, removal of, 115
Indian trade, 25, 56, 109
Indigo, 24, 56, 87
Intellect, colonial, 61
Internal improvements, 102–3, 108–9,
111, 133
Irby, John L. M., Tillman leader in
Constitutional Convention of 1895,
288–89, 290, 292
Izard, Ralph, 78

Jackson, Andrew, 109–10, 112–15
Jacobites, 67
James, Captain George S., signals
attack on Fort Sumter, 158
James Town, 19
Jarrell, Hampton M., author of *Wade
Hampton and the Negro: The Road
Not Taken*, 234–35
Jay Treaty, 79
"Jazz Age," 336
Jefferies, Mrs. Emily Brown, 399
Jefferies, Richard M. ("Dick"), member
of "Barnwell Ring," 393, 395; and
close connection with Brown, 399
Jefferies, R. M., Jr. ("Little Dick"), 399
Jefferson, Thomas, 74–75, 78–83
Jeffersonian Democracy, 74–86, 88, 90.
See also Democratic Party *and*
Republicans of South Carolina (Demo-
crats)
Jenkins, James (Methodist minister),
121
Jessen, Senator H. H., 390
Jews, 119
Jillson, Justus K., carpetbagger, 221
"Jimmie's tax," 373. *See also* Byrnes,
James F.

John Adams (sloop-of-war), 80
Johnson, President Andrew, 202
Johnson, Dewey, 403–4
Johnson, Governor Robert, 26, 29–33, 37, 54
Johnson, William S., 67, 70
Johnston, Dr. George Milligen-, 58
Johnston, Governor Olin D., U.S. senator, 384, 401; opponent of Blatt, 394; resignation as governor, 396; mentioned, 348
Johnston, William C., 401
Jones, A. O., Negro officeholder, 226
Jones, Harmon, ex-slave member of Constitutional Convention of 1868, 222
Joy, Fat, 362, 368
"Judge Lynch." *See* Lynching
Judicial system, 9

Kansas-Nebraska Act, 140
Keith, L. J., Negro member of S.C. House, 231
Keitt, Lawrence M., 142, 164
Kennedy, Fronde, supervisor of WPA's *History of Spartanburg County*, 327
Kennedy, President John F., 412
Kennedy, Robert, 389
Kiawahs (Indians), 17
Kimpton, H. H., 227–28
Know-Nothing Party, 139–40
Ku Klux Klan, assassinations attributed to, 212; riots of 1870–71, 213–14; loose organization of, 214–15; white criticism of, 215–17; Negro retaliation against, 216–17; Laurens riot, 225; troubles, 229; Ku Klux trials, 242–43; Klansmen can return to S.C., 244; and *The Clansman* and *The Birth of a Nation*, 336–47 *passim;* revived Klan opposed by Byrnes, 371–72

Landgraves, *See* Aristocracy, local
Land system, 8–9, 12–13, 18, 20–21. *See also* Headrights
Latin American revolutions, 74
Laurens, Henry, 58–59, 65–66, 68, 290
Laurens County, Klan riot, 214–15; weak high schools of, 313–14
Law, Agnes, home of, burned, 181
LeConte, Emma describes burning of Columbia, 179; describes the plight of the homeless, 182; exults in death of 16 Union soldiers, 184

Lee, Floride, 277
Lee, Samuel J., Negro Speaker of S.C. House, 223; spoilman, 227
Lee, Captain Stephen D., Confederate emissary, 153–58 *passim; mentioned,* 270. *See also* Chestnut, Colonel James
Lee, William States, engineer, 298
Leetmen, 11
Legare, Mary, 80
Leopard Spots, The (Dixon), 338
Lesesne, H. D., disapproves *Mercury's* course, 165
Lexington Water Power Company, 302
Liberty Tree, 71
Library Society, Charles Town, 61
Lincoln, President Abraham, 132, 148, 151, 169
Littlejohn, C. Bruce, 399
Little Rock, Arkansas, 378, 380
Lloyd, Caleb, 66
Logan, General John A., fights fire in Columbia, 181; occupies Preston home, 185
Long, Senator John D., 390
"Lost Cause," 354–59
Lowndes, Rawlins, 69, 76, 93
Lucas, Eliza, 58–59. *See also* Pinckney, Eliza Lucas
Lutheran, 119
Lynch, Thomas, 64
Lynching, 360–69 *passim*
Lyon, Attorney-General J. F., 320

McArthur, Henry Clay, 175
McBryde, John M., president of University of S.C., 268; considers position at University of Tenn., 269, 272; urges compromise with denominationalists, 270; lobbies, 271; yields on free tuition, 272; resigns, but withdraws resignation, 272–73; appointed director of state agricultural experiment station, 273; sees establishment of second University of S.C., 274–75; criticized by Tillman, 277, 279
McCrady, General Edward, 6, 288
McGowan, General Samuel, 236
McIver, Judge Henry, 271
McKenzie, James, alderman, 176
Mackey, Dr. Albert G., chairman of the Constitutional Convention of 1868, 202–3, 209; scalawag, 220

Mackey, E. W. M., 209; scalawag member of S.C. House, 225
Mackey, T. J., 293
McLees, Reverend John, 127
McLeod, Dr. James C., 398
McMaster, Fitz W., opponent of Clemson College, 278, 281
McMillan, George, author of "Integration with Dignity," 380–81
McNair, Mrs. Josephine, 410
McNair, Governor Robert E., 404, 408, 410
McQueen, Congressman John, 142; defends Davis, 167; becomes anti-Davis, 173
Madagascar, 46
Madison, James, 78, 84, 108
Madison, village near Graniteville, 260, 266
Malaria, 52
Malet, W. W., 120–21, 129
Maltravers, Henry Lord, 4
Manigault, Gabriel, merchant, 57–58, 168
Manigault, Peter, Speaker of the House, 70
Manning, Governor John L., 138
Manning, Governor Richard I., 317, 326, 335
Manor, 10–11
Manufacturing, beginning of, 91
Marshall, Chief Justice John, 115
Marshall, Thurgood, 377
Martin, Everett Dean, 123
Martin, James, assassination of, 212
Maybank, Lieutenant Governor Burnet, Jr., runs for governor, 403–4
Means, Governor John H., 137–38
Meeker, Leonard, 378
Melton, C. D., 209; scalawag, 220
Melton, S. W., scalawag, 220
Memminger, Christopher G., 136–37, 144; mission to Virginia of, 144
Mercantile business, 100
Merchant, colonial, 57
Mercury (Charleston), 139–40, 209
Meredith, James, 382
Methodist, 119–21, 129
Mexican War, 135
Miles, Congressman William Porcher, secessionist, 144; mildly anti-Davis, 167; openly attacks Davis, 172–73
Milledgeville, Ga., spared by Sherman, 184

Miller, Thomas E., Negro delegate to Constitutional Convention of 1895, 289–90, 293–94
Milligen, Dr. George, 58
Minority rights, 105
Mispah Church, 125
Mississippi, secessionist overtures of, 144
Mississippi Plan, 283
Mississippi State College (Agricultural and Mechanical College, 270, 275, 277
Missouri Controversy (of 1819–21), 109
Mittag, J. F. G., scalawag, 220
Monroe, James, 109
Montagu, Lord Charles, 70
Moody, Christopher, pirate, 30
Moore, James, 37
Moore, John H., author of "South Carolina's Reaction to the Photoplay, *The Birth of a Nation*," 336–37
Moore, Paul V., 331
Morrah, P. Bradley, Jr., 397
Morrill funds, dispute over, 270–78 *passim*
Morris Island, 150
Morse, S. F. B., 220
Moses, Governor Franklin J., Jr., advocates land for freedmen, 206; member of financial commission, 208; scalawag, 208, 227–28; Speaker of House, 225
Moses, Judge Franklin J., Sr., death of, 236
Moultrie, Governor William, 78
Mountaineer, 128
Mullins, W. S., representative, 171
Murray, E. B., state senator, 272
Murray, George W., Negro congressman, 287
Murray, John Scott, scalawag, 220
Murrell, William, planter, 87
Music in the colony, 59

NAACP (National Association for the Advancement of Colored People), 338, 343, 372, 376–77, 385
Nance, Lee, assassination of, 212
Nash, Beverly, ex-slave member of Constitutional Convention of 1868, 222
Nashville Convention (1850), 136
National Grange. *See* Patrons of Husbandry
Navigation Acts, 62
Negro militia, early activities, 211; organized and armed by Governor

Negro militia (*continued*)
Scott, 212–13; confrontations with whites, 214; arms recalled, 216; retaliate against Klan, 216–17. *See also* Ku Klux Klan
New York Herald, reports Civil War destruction in S.C., 188
New York *World*, 329
Nichols, Major George W., 178
Nicholson, General Francis (provisional governor), 38–40, 322
Niles, Hezekiah, editor of *Niles Register*, 99
Niles Register, 99
Non-intercourse acts, 92
Nullification, 104–17, 133–34

Ogden, Robert, 338, 342
Olmsted, Frederick Law, 120–21
O'Neall, Judge John Belton, 122, 131; fears country is ruined, 166
105th Regiment Infantry, 333
Orangeburg, 341
Orangeburg *Times-Democrat*, 345
Orr, Governor James L., as cooperationist, 137–38, 140, 142; elected to Confederate Senate, 165; censured Davis, 166; clearly unfriendly to Davis, 167, 172; aids in relief of up country, 199; reconciled to defeat, 202; addresses convention, 209; scalawag, 220
O'Ryan, General John F., 332, 335
Over There Club, 333
Owen, William, 19
Oxford, Miss., racial disturbances in, 380–82, 385
Oyster Point, 19–20

Palatine, office of, 8, 10, 12
Palmetto Club, 388
Panic of 1819, 109
Panic of 1857, 142
Pardee, H. L., 223
Parker, Marshall J., 404
Parker, Niles G., state treasurer, 227–28
Parliament, British, 63–64, 66, 70
Parliament, Carolina, 10, 12, 23. *See also* Assembly
Parris, Henry, Negro member of S.C. House, 224
Parsons, James 68
Patrons of Husbandry, growth and decline in S.C., 250–51

Patterson, John J. ("Honest John"), carpetbag U.S. senator, 220–21, 227, 230–31
Patterson, Governor John M., 385
Payment (for Charter), 41–42
Pelzer, its founding, 302
Perry, Benjamin F., Unionist, 136–38, 142–43, 145; fears despotism, 164; mentioned, 166
Pettigrew, J. J., 164
Petigru, James L., Unionist, 89, 134–35; fears despotism, 164
Physicians, colonial, 61
Pickens, Francis W., governor and secessionist, 134, 138, 140, 142, 145; wartime executive, 151; critic of Davis, 164, 166
Pickens County Jail, 366
Pickens District, Freedmen's Bureau, relief for, 199–201
Pickering, Timothy, Federalist, 79
Pierce, President Franklin, 138
Pike, James S., 224
Pinckney, Governor Charles, 58, 76, 79–83, 93, 290
Pinckney, Charles Cotesworth, 80–82, 89
Pinckney, Eliza Lucas, 60. *See also* Lucas, Eliza
Pinckney, Thomas, minister to England, 79–80
Pineland School, 375
Pirates, 26–33; pardon for, 28
Plantation life, 56–57, 59, 90, 95
Plattsburg Officers' Training School, 327
Plowden, Representative Charles N., 399–400
Poe, Col. Orlando M., levels public buildings, 184
Poinsett, Joel R., Unionist, 134, 136
Pope, Samson, 284
Pope, Representative Thomas H., Jr., 399
Population trends, 98, 102
Pork, 24–25
Porter, Reverend A. Toomer, 191
Port Royal (settlement), 15–17; captured by Federal forces, 187
Port Royal (ship), 15, 17–18
Potter, David M., co-editor with James H. Croushore of *A Union Officer in the Reconstruction*, 194
Powell, William S., author of *The Proprietors of Carolina*, 2–3

Poyas family, friends of Sherman, 177, 184
Presbyterian, 119–21
Preston, William C., 188
Prioleau, Charles K., gives Blakely gun to Confederacy, 150
Privateers, 26
Privy Council, 36, 38–42
Proprietors, Lords, 4–7, 10, 14, 16, 25, 31–32, 34–38, 41–42, 44, 48
Prosperity, colonial, 55–57
Provisional government, 38, 41
Provisions, recommended to be brought, 25
Pryor, Roger, Virginia secessionist, arrives in Charleston and gives fiery speech, 151–52; aide to General Beauregard, 156; refuses to fire first gun, 158

Quakers, 90
Quattlebaum, Hugh W., 399
Quincy, Josiah, Jr., 58, 60
Quitrents, 9, 13, 41–42, 48

Race problem, 44, 52–53
Racing in colonial Charleston, 59
Rainey, Joseph H., Negro congressman, 223, 226
Raleigh, Walter, 3
Ramsay, David, 64
Randolph, B. F., assassination of, 212
Randolph, Secretary of State Edmund, 78
Randolph, John, on the Tariff of 1828, 111
Ransier, A. J., Negro member of Constitutional Convention of 1868, 204; member of Congress, 223; spoilsman, 230
Ravenel, Henry W., defends Davis's Administration against Mercury's criticism, 165; expresses doubts about Davis, 166
Read, Senator Jacob, 79, 83
Redeemers. See "Bourbons"
Reed, Isaiah R., Negro delegate to Constitutional Convention of 1895, 289, 291
Reeve, Judge Tapping, 107
Reid, Whitelaw, criticizes burning of Columbia, 182
Religion: colonial, 60; antebellum, 118–131

Religious conversion, 122–23
Religious faith, 126
Religious music, 120
Religious service, 120
Republican Party, 132
Republican Party corruption; Solomon claims' bribes, 227, 230; Blue Ridge railroad scrip, 228, 230–31; Bond ring, 227, 229; Republican Printing Company, 228; plush living in Columbia, 228; meager returns for blacks, 228–29; in the 1920s, 349
Republican Party leadership; scalawags, 219–20; carpetbaggers, 220–21; northern Negroes, 221; S.C. Negroes, 221–23; executives, 223–24; outsiders' view of, 224; native whites' objection to, 224–26; capacity and incompetence of, 225–27; corruption, 227–31
Republican Printing Company, 228
Republicans of South Carolina (Democrats), 76–80, 83–85, 88. See also Jeffersonian Democracy and Democratic Party
Republican, The (Greenville), 130
Revolution of 1719, 37–38
Revolution of 1800, 83, 88
Rhett, Colonel Alfred, Confederate defender of Fort Sumter, 171
Rhett, Robert Barnwell, senator and secessionist, 135–36, 138, 141–42; editor of the Charleston Mercury, disappointed over failure to receive important Confederate post, 160; begins castigating Confederate government, 160; fears reunion, 161; Fort Sumter episode calms Rhett's fears temporarily, 162; opposes Davis's military policy, 162–63; opposes close commercial ties with North, 162; demands tariff revision, 163; offers general criticism of several Confederate departments, 163; criticizes Davis's use of patronage and secret sessions of Congress, 164; introduces anti-administration resolutions in state convention, 168; softens criticism in early 1863, 168–69; renews attacks on Davis, 169; defeated by L. M. Ayer for Congress, 170–71; general support of his criticism, 172–73
Rhett, Colonel William, 29–32
Rice, 24, 44–53; cultivation of, 47–53, 56, 87–88

Rice, J. H., 272
Richardson, Governor John P., opponent of Tillman, 276–79
Richmond *Enquirer*, defends Davis's administration, 166–67, 169
Rion, James H., 271
Rivers, Prince, on bribe-taking, 230–31
Roanoke Island, settlement at, 3
Robertson, Ben, author of *Red Hills and Cotton*, 354–55; death of, 354; relatives of, 356–59; defender of southern cause, 359
Robertson, Thomas J., member of Constitutional Convention of 1868, 202–3, 208; scalawag U.S. senator, 219–20
Robertson family, role in Civil War, 356–58
Rock Hill, 337, 346–47
Rogers, E. S., attorney, 376
Rogers, George C., Jr., author of *Evolution of a Federalist*, 86–87
Roman Catholic, 119–20
Roosevelt, President Franklin D., mentioned, 348–51
Ross, Duke, three-dollar man, 258
Ruff, Dr. P. B., 126
Ruffin, Edmund, Virginia secessionist, arrives on Morris Island, 150; honorary member of Palmetto Guards, 156; fires cannon at Fort Sumter, 159; mentioned, 151
Russell, Governor Donald, 384, 390–91; enters governor's race, 401; attacks "Barnwell Ring," 401–3; defeated, 402; elected governor, 403–4
Russell, Donald, Jr., 389
Rutledge, Andrew, 58
Rutledge, Governor Edward, 80
Rutledge, John, 64, 79, 92
Rutledge, John, Jr., Federalist, 78, 80, 84

Sabbath, observance of, 126–27
St. Andrews Parish, Civil War destruction in, 190
Sales for non-payment of debts, 100–102
Saluda Baptist Association, 123
Saluda River. *See* Electric power
Santee River, 44–53
Sasportas, T. K., Negro member of Constitutional Convention of 1868, 222; member of S.C. House, 224
Savage, Henry, Jr., author of *River of the Carolinas: The Santee*, 44–45, 296–97

Sawyer, F. A. carpetbagger, 221
Saxby, George, 65
Sayle, Governor William, 14, 17
Scalawags. *See* Republican Party leadership
Schaper, William A., 89
Schofield, Martha, 224
Schurz, General Carl, visits S.C. in 1865, 188–89
Scire facias (proceedings), 39
Scott, Governor Robert K., revitalizes and arms Negro militia, 212–13; promises to recall arms, 216; spoilsman, 227; mentioned, 216
Scott, Roger W., attacks "Barnwell Ring," 395–96
Secession, 115, 132–45
Secretary of war (John C. Calhoun), 109, 114
Sectionalism, 76–77
Seddon, James A., Confederate secretary of war, 169
Seignory. *See* Land system
Sermons, 120
Seventh Regiment, 327
Shaftesbury, Lord. *See* Cooper, Anthony Ashley
Shand, Reverend Peter J., 176
Sharpe, John, 40. *See also* Agents
Sheldon plantation, 58
Shell, G. W., president, Farmer's Association of S.C., 279
Shell Manifesto, 278
Sheppard, John C., lieutenant governor of S.C., 269; opponent of free tuition, 271
Sheppard, W. A., defender of Gary, 241
Sherman, Richard P., author of *Robert Johnson: Proprietary and Royal Governor of South Carolina*, 26–27
Sherman, General William T., occupies Columbia, 174; walks over Columbia and greets old acquaintances, 177; reassures Mayor Goodwyn, 177–78; awakened by fires, 178; joins in efforts to control fires, 181; denies giving any orders to burn city, 183; blames Hampton for Columbia's destruction, 183; sheds no tears over Columbia's burning, 184; leaves supplies for destitute citizens, 185; departs from Columbia, 185; destruction in South Carolina, 188, 355–56, 358
Shirley, Thomas, British merchant, 92

Shrewsbury, Henry, Negro member of Constitutional Convention of 1868, 222

Silk, 24

"Silk Stocking Regiment," 327

Siloam Church, 124–25

Simkins, Francis B., co-author with Robert H. Woody of *South Carolina During Reconstruction*, 186, 202, 210, 218; author of *Pitchfork Ben Tillman, South Carolinian*, 246

Simms, William Gilmore, reports cotton fire in Columbia, 175; admits Union soldiers tried to arrest fire, 181–82

Simons, Charles H., Negro member of S.C. House, 227

Simons, Harris, family of, befriended by Sherman, 177, 184–85

Simons, James, Sherman's friend, 177

Simpson, R. W., 271

Sinkler family, pillaged estate of, 190

Sirmans, M. Eugene, author of *Colonial South Carolina: A Political History, 1663–1763*, 6–7, 54–55

Skinner, Chief Justice, 66, 69

Slater, Samuel, cotton manufacturing, 91

Slavery, Indian, 25

Slavery, Negro, 11, 103, 106, 120; religion of, 124–26, 128–29, 134–35, 144; rice planters' employment of, 46–49, 56–57, 89

S.L.E.D. (South Carolina Law Enforcement Division), 385, 389

Sligh, James A., state senator, 272

Smalls, Robert, ex-slave member of Constitutional Convention of 1868, 222; member of Congress, 223; delegate to Constitutional Convention of 1895, defends Negro suffrage, 291; denies fraud charges, 293; mentioned, 286

Smith, Alfred Glaze, Jr., author of *Economic Readjustment of an Old Cotton State*, 94–95

Smith, Senator Ellison D. ("Cotton Ed"), 326, 348; walks out of convention, 352; mentioned, 326, 348, 354

Smith, Farley, 385

Smith, Jim, state auditor, 400

Smith, Captain John, 3

Smith, Representative Thomas Rhett, 89

Smith, William Loughton, Federalist, 77, 79–80, 90, 93

Smith, Winchester, member of "Barnwell Ring," 393–94, 397

Smith v. *Allwright*, 370

Social life (colonial), 58–59

Social revolution, 74–75

Society for the Propagation of the Gospel, 27

Society Hill, 121

Society of Cincinnati, 84

Solomon, Hardy, bribes legislators, 227–30

Sons of Liberty, 65, 69–70

Sons of Temperance, 130

South Carolina, effect of Fundamental Constitutions on development of, 6; role of, in suppression of piracy, 26–33; reason for lack of industrial development in, 52–53; prosperity of, during colonial period, 55–60; religious indifference of, 60–61; culturally divided into two sections, 75–77; population trends of, from 1790 to 1810, 89–90; cotton replaces rice as leading export crop in, 95–99; decline in economic preeminence of, 99–103; deterioration of soil of, 103, 192; religious scene in, 119–31; Civil War destruction in, 187–91; loss of foreign trade by, 191; plight of transportation system in, 191–92; Civil War battle casualties of, 192; collapse of financial resources of, 192–93; lost wars, 355; character of people of, 356–57; lynchings in, 360; and racial crisis over desegregation, 381–90; progress by, in the 1960s, 408–10; goals of Governor West for, 411–14

South Carolina, University of, 85, 89; and free tuition dispute, 268, 269–72; improved prospects, 273; establishment of second University, 274–75; Tillman opposition to, 270–78 *passim;* defeat of second University, 280–81. *See also* McBryde, John M. *and* Tillman, Benjamin R.

South Carolina College. *See* South Carolina, University of *and* University of South Carolina

"South Carolina Exposition, The," 113

South Carolina high schools in 1910, inexperienced principals of, 305; change of principals, 306; teachers of, 306–7; teacher certification, 307; improvements of, 307–8; weaknesses of: one- and two-teacher schools, 308–9; brief recitation periods, 310; need for

South Car. high schools (*continued*)
efficiency, 311–12; meager appropriations, 311-12; need and cost of standard high schools, 312–13; weak Laurens County high schools, 313–14
South Carolina Secession Convention, 132
South Carolina State Gazette, 81
Southern Patriot (Greenville), 136
Southern Power Company, 298
Southwest (old), settlement of, 94–95, 100, 112
Spain, colonial efforts of, 2
Spartanburg and Camp Wadsworth, 326–35 *passim;* and *Birth of a Nation,* 337
Spartanburg County, Klan disturbances in, 214; and Camp Wadsworth, 326–35 *passim*
Spartanburg *Express,* 165
Spartanburg *Herald,* 288, 331, 333; and *Birth of a Nation,* 344
"Squaw Camp," 329
Stamp Act (1765), 62
State Budget Commission, 400
State-rights, 106–7, 114–15, 117, 134–35
State Rights Party, 139–41
State Temperance Society, 131
Steinmetz, Charles, 302
Stone, Colonel George A., U.S. Army, 175
Stone, Marcus A., defends Brown, 397
Stoney, Thomas P., political opponent of Byrnes, 350–53
Strom, Pete, 385
Sugar Act (1764), 62
Sullivan's Island, 150–52, 155
Sumter, Thomas, 1792 Republican, 77, 80
Sunday school, 127–28
Swails, Stephen A., presiding officer of state senate, 223; spoilsman, 227
Swanberg, W. A., author of *First Blood: The Story of Fort Sumter,* 148–49
Swat the Spies, 333
Sweatt v. *Painter,* 380

Tariffs, 77, 94, 102–3, 108, 110–14, 116, 133–34, 141–42. *See also* Duties
Tarlton, R. S., Negro member of S.C. House, 227
Taxation (by mother country), 62
Taylor, Claude A., Speaker of the House, 394
Taylor, Rosser Howard, author of *Ante-*

Taylor, Rosser Howard (*continued*)
bellum South Carolina, 118–19
Tebaut, Tunis, blacksmith, 70
Temperance Advocate, 131
Temperance movement, 130–31
Temple, O. P., seeks to lure McBryde to University of Tenn., 269, 272
Tesla, Nikola, 298
Textiles, growth of, 254; villages, conditions of, 255; organized by Duke, 299–300; Pelzer established, 302. *See also* Graniteville
Theater (colonial), 59
Thompson, Governor Hugh S., 269
Thornwell, Dr. James H., 139
Thurber, Captain John, 46
Thurmond, Governor J. Strom, prosecutes accused lynchers, 360; presidential nominee, 370; joins Republican Party, 392; attacks "Barnwell Ring," 393, 395–96, 398; elected governor, 398; relations with Brown, 399–400
Tillinghast, J. A., 345
Tillman, Benjamin R. ("Pitchfork Ben"), inheritor of populist discontent, 238, 268; seeks agricultural college, 270–71; frustrated by McBryde, 273–74; quits politics, then re-emerges, 275–76; advocates direct primary, 276; outclasses opponents, 276–77; Clemson bequest approved, 277–78; enters governor's race, 278–79; elected governor, 279; promotes Clemson at expense of second University of S.C., 280–81; governor, 282; proposes constitutional convention, 283–84; mentioned, 285, 287, 291; delegate to and chairman of Convention, 288–89; makes pleas for suffrage provisions, 289–90, 292–93; sees reduced Negro vote, 294; suffers stroke, 316; breaks with Blease, 316; analysis of his support, 317–19; death of, 326; mentioned, 341, 346, 348–49, 351. *See also* Tillmanism
Tillman, George D., Reconstruction convention delegate, 289
Tillman, James H., 294; murderer of Gonzales, 322
Tillman Hall, 381–82
Tillmanism, background of: emergence of new classes, 247–48; opposition of white masses to black suffrage, 249;

Tillmanism, background of (continued) economic reverses and failure of Patrons of Husbandry, 250–51; dissatisfaction with merchant-creditors, 251; dissatisfaction with Bourbon government, 251–53; nature of 317–19. See also Tillman, Benjamin R.

Timber, 56

Timmerman, Governor George B., Jr., 400–401

Timothy, Peter, "Secretary of the Post Office," 68

Tindall, George B., author of South Carolina Negroes, 1877–1900, 282–83

Tobacco, 24

Tolbert, Joseph A., 349

Tolbert, Joseph W. ("Tieless Joe"), 349

Toleration, religious, 11

Tomlinson, Reuben, carpetbagger, 221; member of S.C. House, 224

Toombs, Robert, Confederate secretary of state, 149

Township settlements, 13, 22

Trade, foreign, 101

Treaty of Paris (1763), 62

Treaty of Paris (1783), 74

Trenholm, George A., residence of, burned by Sherman's Army, 176

Trescot, William H., criticizes Davis's foreign policy, 166

Truman, President Harry S., 376

Tuition, free, controversy over, 270–72

Turnbull, Robert J., wrote "Crisis" articles, 134

Turpin, Reverend Mr., 128

Twenty-Second Engineers, 327, 330–31

Twenty-Seventh Division. See Camp Wadsworth

Tycoons, northern, 51–52

UDC (United Daughters of the Confederacy), 340

Union League clubs, activities of, 211–12

University of South Carolina. See South Carolina, University of and South Carolina College

Ursuline Convent, burned, 180; gets new home, 185

Van Buren, Martin, 113

Vanderbilt, Colonel Cornelius, 328

Vanderbilt, Mrs. Cornelius, 328

Vanderbilt, Cornelius, Jr., 328, 333

Vanderbilt, Grace, 328–29

Verplanck Bill, 116

Virginia, 15

Virginia Company, 3–4

Vishinski, Andrei Y., 378

Waddell, Moses, brother-in-law of John C. Calhoun, 106

Wadsworth, Senator James, 335

Walker, Harry, legal counsel to Governor Hollings, 385

Walker, Leroy P., Confederate secretary of war, orders Beauregard to "reduce" Fort Sumter, 149; mentioned, 155

Wallace, Professor David D., 134, author of The History of South Carolina, 316–17; and Birth of a Nation, 344

Wallace, Henry, Negro preacher, 129

Wallace, Dr. John, residence of, burned by Sherman's army, 176

Wannamaker, Representative L. Caston, 394

War Hawks, 107–8

War of 1812, 92, 94, 108, 111

War of the Spanish Succession (Queen Anne's War), 26

Warrants, land, 20–21

Washington, Booker T., 338

Washington, George, 77–78, 81

Washington Street Methodist Church, destruction of, 180

Wateree-Catawba. See Electric power

Waterways, grants adjacent to, 20

Watson, E. J., commissioner of agriculture, 321–22

Watt, Sam, assistant prosecuting attorney in Greenville, 368

WCTU (Women's Christian Temperance Union), 341

Webster, Daniel, 111–12, 115–16

Wells, Private Edward L., 176

West, Governor John C., inaugural address 1971, 408–14; goals for S.C., 411–14

West, Joseph, experimental farming in colony, 14, 16, 18, 44

West, Rebecca, author of "Opera in Greenville," 360–61

Westinghouse, George, 298, 302

Weyman, Edward, 70

Wheeler, General Joseph, Confederate troops of, destroy property, 190–91

Whipper, W. J., Negro Speaker of S.C. House, 221, 223, 225, 229; delegate

Whipper, W. J. (*continued*)
to Constitutional Convention of
1895, 289, 291
Whitaker, Chief Justice Benjamin, 59
Whitefield, George, rector, 60
Whiting, Major William, Confederate
commander on Morris Island, 150
Whitney, Eli, 86, 97
Wigfall, Senator Louis T., 150
Wigg, James, Negro delegate to Con-
stitutional Convention of 1895, 289–91
Wiggins, A. L. M., 386
Wightman, Reverend William, 128
Willard, Judge A. J., supported by
Hampton, 236
Williams, A. B., 288
Williams, Governor Ransome, 396, 398
Williamson, Joel, author of *After
Slavery: The Negro in South Carolina
During Reconstruction, 1861–1877*,
210-11, 218–19
Wilmot Proviso, 135–36
Wilson, Samuel, 24–25
Wilson, President Woodrow, 326; and
Birth of a Nation, 343
Wine, 24
Wise, Governor Henry A., 141
Wofford, Thomas, attorney, 367
Wolfe, John Harold, author of "The
Roots of Jeffersonian Democracy,"
74–75
Women in churches, 124
Woodmason, Charles, clergyman, 68
Woods, General W. B., commands
drunken Yankee brigade, 181
Woodward, Dr. Henry, 46
Woodward, Major Tom, supports
Hampton, 238–39

Woodward, William E., author of *The
Way Our People Lived*, 254–55
Woody, Robert Hilliard, author of
"Christopher Gadsden and the Stamp
Act," 63–64; co-author with Francis
B. Simkins of *South Carolina During
Reconstruction*, 186–87, 202–3, 210, 218
Woolens Bill, 111
Workman, W. D., Jr., author of *The
Bishop from Barnwell*, 392–93
Worley, Richard, pirate, 31
Wragg, Joseph, Charleston merchant,
57
Wragg, William, in S.C. Assembly, 66
Wright, Jonathan J., member of Con-
stitutional Convention of 1868, 208
Wyche, Judge C. C., 390, 403
Wylie, Dr. Walker G., furnishes idea for
hydroelectric power, 296–98

"X.Y.Z." affair, 79–81

Yale, 106–7
Yamassee Indian War, 35
Yeadon, Richard, edits Charleston
Courier, 165–66. *See also* Charleston
Courier
Yeamans, Sir John, 16–17
Yonge, Francis, 37–38, 40. *See also* Agents
York, 338, 344, 346–47
Yorkville, 337. *See also* York
Yorkville *Enquirer*, 340
Youmans, Leroy F., state attorney gen-
eral, 243; and opponent of Tillman,
276
Young, James, Negro member of S.C.
House, 227